# Indian Placenames
## in America

ALSO BY SANDY NESTOR
AND FROM McFARLAND

*Indian Placenames in America*
*Volume 1: Cities, Towns and Villages* (2003)

# INDIAN PLACENAMES IN AMERICA

## VOLUME 2: MOUNTAINS, CANYONS, RIVERS, LAKES, CREEKS, FORESTS AND OTHER NATURAL FEATURES

### Sandy Nestor

McFarland & Company, Inc., Publishers

*Jefferson, North Carolina, and London*

LIBRARY OF CONGRESS CATALOGUING-IN-PUBLICATION DATA

Nestor, Sandy.
Indian placenames in America, volume 2 : mountains,
canyons, rivers, lakes, creeks, forests
and other natural features / Sandy Nestor.
p.     cm.
Includes bibliographical references and index.

ISBN 0-7864-1983-0 (illustrated case binding : 50# alkaline paper) ∞

1. Names, Indian — United States.   2. Names, Geographical —
United States.   3. United States — History, Local.   I. Title.
E98.N2N47   2005          917.3'001'4 — dc21          2003011417

British Library cataloguing data are available

Cover illustration: ©2004 Clipart.com.

Manufactured in the United States of America

*McFarland & Company, Inc., Publishers
Box 611, Jefferson, North Carolina 28640
www.mcfarlandpub.com*

To the Indians of America — may their
names forever grace this great land

# Contents

*Preface* . . . . . . . . . . . . . . . . . . . . . . 1

ALABAMA . . . . . . . . . 3
ALASKA . . . . . . . . . . 9
ARIZONA . . . . . . . . 20
ARKANSAS . . . . . . . 30
CALIFORNIA . . . . . 30
COLORADO . . . . . . 39
CONNECTICUT . . . . 43
DELAWARE . . . . . . . 47
FLORIDA . . . . . . . . 48
GEORGIA . . . . . . . . 52
IDAHO . . . . . . . . . 58
ILLINOIS . . . . . . . . 60
INDIANA . . . . . . . . 62
IOWA . . . . . . . . . . . 64
KANSAS . . . . . . . . . 65
KENTUCKY . . . . . . 68
LOUISIANA . . . . . . . 68
MAINE . . . . . . . . . 72
MARYLAND . . . . . . . 80
MASSACHUSETTS . . . 84
MICHIGAN . . . . . . . 89

MINNESOTA . . . . . . . 93
MISSISSIPPI . . . . . . . . 98
MISSOURI . . . . . . . . 101
MONTANA . . . . . . . 102
NEBRASKA . . . . . . . 103
NEVADA . . . . . . . . . 104
NEW HAMPSHIRE . . 107
NEW JERSEY . . . . . . 111
NEW MEXICO . . . . . 115
NEW YORK . . . . . . . 119
NORTH CAROLINA . . 126
NORTH DAKOTA . . . 132
OHIO . . . . . . . . . . . 133
OKLAHOMA . . . . . . 136
OREGON . . . . . . . . . 137
PENNSYLVANIA . . . . 145
RHODE ISLAND . . . . 152
SOUTH CAROLINA . . 153
SOUTH DAKOTA . . . . 155
TENNESSEE . . . . . . 157
TEXAS . . . . . . . . . . 158

Contents viii

UTAH ......... 159

VERMONT ....... 163

VIRGINIA ....... 165

WASHINGTON ... 169

WEST VIRGINIA .... 177

WISCONSIN ....... 179

WYOMING ....... 183

*Notes* ................. 185

*Bibliography* ........... 187

*Index* ................ 205

# *Preface*

> *To Native Americans the European concept of "discovery of the New World" is both ludicrous and insulting.... What many refer to grandly as the Age of Discovery was in fact the Age of Collision — an era of confrontation between cultures and continents from which neither the Old nor the New World ever recovered.*
>
> William Graves, *National Geographic* editor, 1991

John W. Van Cott wrote in his book *Utah Place Names*: "Sadly, the origin of many ... are scattered in hundreds of isolated books and journals, in the dim memories of third and fourth generations, and in the legends and stories." John Huden, who wrote about Indian placenames in the eastern states, paraphrased Nils Homer (author of *Indian Place Names in North America*), "Probably there is only one effective way of determining meanings.... That is to try to fit them into surviving patterns found among tribes that have not yet lost their language.... It is in most cases a hazardous task."

As a companion to Volume I of *Indian Placenames in America*, which covers cities, towns, and villages, this book covers rivers, lakes, mountains, and other natural features in the United States with Indian names. It includes coves, harbors, mesas, buttes, washes, canyons, national forests and monuments. Mesas are similar to mountains, but with flat tops; buttes are similar to mesas, but they are usually solitary entities. Washes, which are predominant in the Southwest, are intermittent streams that usually flow through canyons.

Homer's statement that interpreting Indian names was hazardous was certainly correct. Since their name origins have been so corrupted over the ages, how can we ever hope to discover their true meanings? Unable to pronounce the Indian names, white settlers corrupted them. During the 1800s, Indian children in schools were forced to speak the European tongues and told to forget their own. Many of those who

1

retained their native language died long ago. Writer William Yardley noted, "Every time one of our elders dies, it's like a library burning down." With their deaths, we lose more of the Indian language. Many of today's young Indians left their tribal homes, lost interest in their heritage, and therefore did not carry on their language.

Some names differed because of the way they were interpreted by various authorities, but essentially they meant the same thing. As an example, Canyon de Chelly was understood from one source to be derived from a Navajo expression meaning "where the water comes out of the rock." Another authority defined it as "the place where it flows from the canyon." Another example is "river that runs upside down," or "water that is hidden," both indicating water that flows beneath the sand, then reappears at some point. Conversely, the Kiowa Indians' name was thought by one authority to mean "principal people," yet defined as "going out," by another. The Chochilla River in California was interpreted from three authorities, each with completely different meanings: "dry river," "hot dish," and "horse thief." These examples of differing opinions leave a multitude of place-name origins open to conjecture.

The text is formatted by state, with the features in alphabetical order. In most cases the place name is followed by the name of the county in which the feature is located. If the feature stretches over many counties, the counties are not listed, although in some cases, individual entries show multiple counties where a feature's length was known. Rivers are listed in the state in which they rise, regardless of where they principally flow. For example, the majority of the Niobrara River flows through Nebraska, but since it rises in Wyoming, it is listed in Wyoming's entries. Little information was available for the very small creeks, so only the county in which they rise is noted. The height of mountains and length of streams is indicated where the data were available.

In works such as this, there are always opportunities for errors, especially with conflicting evidence and different dialects. Much time was spent in trying to determine the name origins and locations; the latter proved especially frustrating when sources showed a particular stream rising in two different counties. Maps were checked for verification, and the U.S. Board on Geographic Names databases were consulted.

# ALABAMA

**AFFONEE CREEK** (Bibb)   This small steam flows into the Cahaba River. Affonee was derived from the Choctaw word nofoni, meaning "bones." Another interpretation was from afana, for "staked," which may have referred to some type of fence. Located along the creek was once a small village of the same name with a post office about 1859. Analisses L. Elam was one of the postmasters.

**ALABAMA RIVER** (Elmore/Montgomery)   The Alabama River is about 312 miles long and begins at the junction of the Coosa and Tallapoosa rivers, then joins the Tombigbee River. French cartographers called it Riviere des Alibamons, their name for the Alabama Indians, a Choctaw word meaning "thicket clearers," "or those who clear the land." Settlement in the region began when British sympathizers relocated from Georgia after the American Revolution. During the 1800s, numerous trading posts were established and sternwheelers plied the river transporting their goods. Located near the river was a place called the Holy Ground, said to contain "wizard circles," consecrated land, so none of the Indian prophets' enemies could approach the area.

**AUTAUGA CREEK** (Chilton)   Autauga was named for a Creek Indian village situated along its banks, derived from atigi, meaning "border." The community of Prattville was founded in 1839 along the stream, and later became known as the "Birthplace of Industry" in Alabama after New Jersey industrialist Daniel Pratt started one of the first factories there. Known as McNeil's Mill, the establishment produced more than 200 gins a year. Autauga Creek flows into the Alabama River.

**BASHI CREEK** (Clarke)   Bashi Creek flows into the Alabama River. Its name was derived from the Choctaw word backaya, meaning "line," "row," or "course." This was a descriptive name because the Bashi was considered a boundary line between Indian communities. Another interpretation was from hashuk basi laua, Choctaw for "sedge grass abundant."

**BOGUE CHITTO CREEK** (Perry)   Bogue Chitto Creek flows into the Alabama River. The name was taken from the Choctaw words bok and chito, meaning "big creek." In 1821, a lottery was established in order to acquire funds to build a turnpike that would extend from Mobile to Bogue Chitto Creek.

**BOGUELOOSA CREEK** (Choctaw) This creek enters Okatuppa Creek. Bogueloosa was derived from bok and lusa, Choctaw for "black creek." The little town of Hinton was established along the creek and grew as a farming and lumbering community.

**BUTTAHATCHEE CREEK** (Winston) Buttahatchee comes from the Choctaw words bati and hacha, for "sumac river." It flows through the state and enters the Tombigbee River in Mississippi. Wandering Chickasaw Indians used the region as their hunting grounds, and their burial grounds and mounds are still present along the stream. Sanford Prison was built along the Buttahatchee to house Confederate captives during the Civil War.

**CAHABA RIVER** (St. Clair)   Flowing approximately 200 miles, the Cahaba joins the Alabama River. It supplies much of Birmingham's fresh water. The name is derived from the Choctaw words oka and aba, meaning "water above." Setting out to drive the Indians from this region, Colonel Russell and his men marched to the Cahaba River in 1814. Some of his men were captured by the Choctaw Indians and later killed. Because of conflict with the Indians, it wasn't until the 1820s that settlement occurred in this region.

**CALEBEE CREEK** (Macon)   At the mouth of this stream was a Creek Indian village, which Brigadier General John Floyd attacked during the Creek War, known as the Battle of Calebee Creek. The name may come from the Creek word kalapi, meaning "overcup oak." The Calebee flows into the Tallapoosa River.

**CHEAHA MOUNTAIN** (Cleburne) Cheaha is the tallest mountain in the state at 2,407 feet above sea level. The Choctaw Indians called it chaha, defined as "high

place." One of Andrew Jackson's battle engagements occurred along the slope of Cheaha Mountain during the Creek Indian War of 1813. Cheaha State Park is comprised of 2,719 acres and occupies the upper slopes of the mountain.

**CHIKASANOXEE CREEK** (Chambers) Early settlement near this creek occurred in 1840 when a settler established a sawmill and tannery. The Chikasanoxee flows into the Tallapoosa River. Its name may be derived from the Creek expression, koha and chanaksi, meaning "cane ridge."

**CHILATCHEE CREEK** (Perry)   This stream merges with the Alabama River. It bears the Choctaw expression chida and hacha, meaning "fox stream."

**CHIPOLA RIVER** (Houston)   This river is about 125 miles long and flows into the state of Florida to join the Apalachicola River. During the Civil War a group of soldiers fought in a skirmish against the Union Army, but unable to beat them, their leader fled to the Chipola River. Chipola was derived from the Choctaw word champuli, for "sweet." Another interpretation was a Creek expression meaning "on the other side of the stream."

**CHOCCOLOCCO CREEK** (Calhoun) Terminating at Logan Martin Lake, Choccolocco Creek is the largest stream in Alabama designated as a creek. It means "shoal big," derived from the Creek words chahki and lako. It was also interpreted as "Big Horse," another name for Chief Choccolocco.

**CHOCTAWHATCHEE RIVER** (Dale) The Choctawhatchee River was home to numerous Creek villages until the Indians were displaced during the Second Seminole War of 1835–1842. It is about 175 miles long and flows into Choctawhatchee

Bay in the state of Florida. This name may have been taken from the Chatot tribe, who were associated with the Choctaw Indians. The name means "river of the Choctaws"(Choctaw signifies "red").

**COATOPA CREEK** (Sumter)  This name was taken from the Choctaw words koi and hotupa, meaning "panther wounded." J.R. Larkins founded a small community that served as a stop on the Tennessee, Virginia and Georgia Railroad and named it after the creek. The Coatopa is tributary to Sucarnochee Creek.

**COHABADIAH CREEK** (Cleburne) Cohabadiah Creek joins the Little Tallapoosa River. Its name is derived from the Creek expression koha "cane" and apata-i, translated as "covering," and referred to the canebrakes along the stream.

**CONECUH RIVER** (Bullock)  Ponce de Leon came through the area while searching for the Fountain of Youth. DeSoto later founded a small settlement on the river and named it Montezuma. The Conecuh empties into Pensacola Bay in Florida. Its name was derived from the Creek words koha and anaka, meaning "canebrakes near." Another suggestion was from the Creek expression kono and ika, for "polecat's head." Others believe it is a Muscohegan word for "swamp mound ghost." Folklore says there was buried treasure on a mound in the river, with a chain that was visible on the mound. Any attempt to pull up the chain caused moaning sounds to emanate, thus reference to a ghost. At one time the prosperous town of Old Sparta was located along the Conecuh, but its life was shortened by Union Army raids and yellow fever.

**COTACO CREEK** (Marshall)  Cotaco may be derived from the Cherokee words ikati and kunahita, interpreted as "swamp (or thicket) long." It joins the Tennessee River. An early settler named Elisha engaged in farming, and also operated a saw mill and grist mill along the creek during the 1850s.

**COTAHAGA CREEK** (Sumter)  This waterway flows into the Tombigbee River. Cotahaga was derived from the Choctaw words kati-a and hikia, meaning "locust tree there standing."

**COWIKEE CREEK** (Bullock)  The Walter F. George Reservoir of the Chattahoochee River receives Cowikee Creek. It was interpreted as a Hitchiti expression for "water carrying place," or "water carrier," derived from oki and awaiki, or Creek for "creek that runs upon itself." Near the Cowikee a skirmish occurred between the Creek Indians and the Alabama Militia in 1837.

**CUBAHATCHEE CREEK** (Bullock) The Cubahatchee empties into the Tallapoosa River. It bears a Creek expression meaning "creek where lye was made," or "mulberry tree creek," derived from ki-api and hachi.

**EMUCKFA CREEK** (Clay)  This creek flows into the Tallapoosa River. Emuckfa was thought to be from the Hitchiti word immookfau (or imukfas), descriptive of an ornament the Indians made from shells, such as a necklace. On the way to the Battle of Horseshoe in 1814, Andrew Jackson and his army camped along the Emuckfa.

**ENITACHOPCO CREEK** (Clay)  First called Candutchkee (Creek for "boundary creek"), the name was changed to Enitachopco for an ancient Hilibi village, interpreted from the Creek words anati and chapko, meaning "thicket long." The Enitachopco joins Hillabee Creek. Andrew Jackson's army, led by William Weatherford, crossed the creek on their way to a confrontation with the Red Stick Creek Indians in 1814.

**ESCAMBIA CREEK** (Monroe) Little Escambia Creek ultimately forms the Escambia River, which flows into Florida, then terminates at Escambia Bay. It was thought to be a Choctaw expression uski and amo ("cane to gather"). Another definition was from the Creek word shambia, meaning "clear water."

**ESCATAWPA RIVER** (Washington) The 90-mile-long Escatawpa terminates at Pascagoula Bay in the state of Mississippi. It was also known as Dog River. Sawmills established during the 1830s were heavily dependent upon the river for their supply of logs. Escatawpa was derived from the Choctaw words uski, a, and tapa, meaning "cane there cut."

**HALAWAKEE CREEK** (Chambers) Saw mills and grist mills were supported by the creek during the 1830s, which continued operating until the late 1890s. Halawakee is derived from the Creek word holwaki, meaning "bad." The Creek terminates at Lake Harding.

**HATCHECHUBBEE CREEK** (Russell) James Glenn established the first settlement in the county along this creek during the 1830s, and leased some land from the Indians for his farming endeavors. But about 1835 he and his family were forced to flee when the Indians declared war on the white intruders. Hatchechubbe joins the Chattahoochee River. Its name comes from the Creek words hachi and chaba, meaning "creek halfway."

**HAYSOP CREEK** (Bibb) This creek enters the Cahaba River. Haysop may have been derived from the Choctaw expression, hushi and apa, "birds eat," or ahe and osapa, meaning "potato field." Another

interpretation described the black gum tree.

**HILLABEE CREEK** (Tallapoosa) Gold-bearing deposits were discovered here during the 1800s, and as a result a 20-stamp mill and cyanide plant were built to serve the miners. The creek begins at the confluence of Little Hillabee and Enitachopco creeks and enters the Tallapoosa River. The Hillabee took its name from the ancient Creek town, Hilibi, meaning "quick."

**IHAGEE CREEK** (Russell) The Ihagee flows into the Chattahoochee River. It may be a corruption of the Creek expression ihagi or haihagi, meaning "the groaners," or from haihkita ("to groan").

**KINTERBISH CREEK** (Sumter) This stream flows into the Tombigbee River. The name is derived from the Choctaw words kinta and ibish, meaning "beaver lodge."

**KOWALIGI CREEK** (Elmore) A Muskogee Indian tribe living along the Coosa River moved to Kowaligi Creek in 1738 until they were removed to Oklahoma about 1836. Country music singer Hank Williams wrote about the creek in 1952 with his song, *Kawliga*. The stream received its name from the Creek words ika and ilaidshas, meaning "his head I kill."

**LETOHATCHEE CREEK** (Lowndes) A settlement with a post office was named for the nearby creek, derived from the Creek words li, ito and hachi, meaning "wood arrow creek." The Letohatchee is tributary to the Alabama River.

**LUBBUB CREEK** (Fayette) The Lubbub joins the Tombigbee River. It may be a Choctaw word meaning "warm water," taken from oka lahba. Early settlers established a ferry on the creek during the 1820s and founded a small community, which thrived on the rich timber industry.

**LUXAPALLILA CREEK** (Marion) The Luxapallila flows into the state of Mississippi where it joins the Tombigbee River. Its name was derived from the Choctaw expression lusi and balali, interpreted as "turtle there crawls." In 1818 an act of the Territorial Council created election precincts, one of which was located at a settler's home on Luxapallila Creek.

**NAHEOLA BLUFF** (Choctaw) This name is derived from the Choctaw word naholla, meaning "white man." Others ascribed it to a supernatural entity, perhaps in reference to one of the Indians' mythical beings. Founded about 1878, the small community of Naheola took its name from the bluff.

**NANNA HUBBA BLUFF** (Washington) The bluff bears the name of the Naniaba Indians who may have been part of the Choctaw tribe. It was derived from nani and apa, meaning "fish eaters," or "fish killers," in reference to fishermen. It was also translated from nanih aba, Choctaw for "hill above." Thomas Mims, who built Fort Mims on Nanna Hubba, was murdered along with other settlers by the Red Stick Creek Indians in 1813. During the Civil war Union General Granger ordered General Benton and his men, who were stationed on the bluff, to attack the town of Citronelle. This same year the Confederate ships *Baltic* and *Nashville* were surrendered to Federal officers near the bluff.

**OAKMULGEE CREEK** (Bibb) One of the earliest settlers along this stream in 1819 was a Baptist minister named Crow who purchased land and established a church. The creek flows into the Cahaba River. Oakmulgee was taken from the

Hitchiti words oki and mulgi, meaning "bubbling (or "boiling") water."

**OMUSEE CREEK** (Houston) The Omusee flows to the Chattahoochee River. The name was derived from the Creek word yamasi, meaning "gentle" or "quiet," or it may have been a shortened form of the Yamassee tribe.

**OPINTLOCCO CREEK** (Lee) Opintlocco is taken from the Creek word opillako, signifying "big swamp." The stream joins Chewacla Creek.

**OSANIPPA CREEK** (Chambers) Osanippa was corrupted from the Creek word asunapi, meaning "moss stems." The stream flows into Lake Harding. After the Creek Treaty was signed in 1832, nervous settlers built Fort Cusseta near the Osanippa for their protection in case of any future Indian uprisings.

**OSELIGEE CREEK** (Chambers) Nimrod Doyle was the first white settler in the region to established a trading post along the creek about 1816. Oseligee may be a Creek word meaning "lower leaf."

**PATSALIGA RIVER** (Montgomery) This 60-mile-long river enters the Flint River. Patsaliga comes from the Creek expression pachi and laiki, interpreted as "pigeon roost," or "sitting pigeon," and may have referred to the extinct passenger pigeon.

**PINTLALA CREEK** (Montgomery) Originally called Manack's Creek, the name was changed to Pintlala, from the Creek word pithlo, interpreted as "canoe," referring to pulling or seizing of the craft. It was also translated as "swamp-big." A depot was established along the stream for General Jackson's provisions during the Creek War of 1813–14.

**PUSS CUSS CREEK** (Choctaw) This stream enters Okatuppa Creek, which may bear a Choctaw expression meaning "child crying," derived from puskus and paya.

**SAUGAHATCHEE CREEK** (Chambers) The Saugahatchee joins the Tallapoosa River. There was once a granite quarry near the creek, and some of the material was used in the 1890s to build the Atlanta Terminal Station. Saugahatchee is from the Creek words sauga and hachi, meaning "rattle creek," indicating a gourd.

**SEPULGA RIVER** (Conecuh) George Leonard was a moving force in development of this region after the establishment of a ferry during the 1820s. Death of many settlers from malaria or typhoid because of the swampy conditions caused the land and ferry to be sold. The Sepulga later became a highway for the transportation of cotton. The name may be from the Creek expression asi, ap and algi, meaning "yaupon tree grove," or Choctaw for "smoky."

**SIPSEY RIVER** (Fayette) The river flows about 100 miles to join the Tombigbee River. Sipsey was derived from a Chickasaw-Choctaw word sipsi, meaning "poplar" or "cottonwood," descriptive of the trees that grew along the river's banks.

**TALLADEGA CREEK** (Clay) Settlement along the river began after the Indians were forcibly removed in 1836. The Riddle brothers moved into the area and built the first forge, producing iron for plows and horseshoes. In the 1840s, gold was discovered and one of the mines operated until World War II. Talladega Creek flows into the Coosa River, and bears a Creek word meaning "border town."

**TALLAHATTA CREEK** (Clarke) The Tallahatta flows to merge with Bashi Creek. Early settlement along this creek began when Baptists built the Liberty Baptist Church which formed the nucleus of a community. They constructed a road that was later used to transport timber. Tallahatta is from the Choctaw words tali and hata, meaning "rock white."

**TALLASEEHATCHEE CREEK** (Clay) Mention of an Indian village called Talimuchusa was recorded by a member of DeSoto's Expedition in 1540. This creek enters the Coosa River. Tallaseehatchee was interpreted from the Creek words tallasi and hatchi, as "old town creek." During the early 1800s the first mill was built along the stream using slave labor. A quarry was later established and the granite was used to build a dam on the creek for a mill pond.

**TALLAWAMPA CREEK** (Choctaw) This creek flows into the Tombigbee River. Tallawampa may have been taken from the Choctaw words toloa and ampa (or ambi), which were interpreted as "to sing," "to eat," or "to kill."

**TATTILABA CREEK** (Clarke) Tattilaba was derived from the Choctaw words iti hata, meaning "white wood," or from illi and aba, defined as "dead above," descriptive of a dead tree. The Tattilaba is a tributary to Jackson Creek.

**THOLOCCO, LAKE** (Dale) Fanny Hutchinson of Enterprise was awarded $10 in 1930 for selecting the name for this artificial lake. Tradition says Tholocco was a word of respect for someone. It may have referred to Samuel Dale who was given the name during the Creek War by his Indian opponents. But others believed it was a Choctaw expression meaning "whitewood dead above," derived from iti hata, ili, and aba.

**TUCKABUM CREEK** (Choctaw) Also known as Tickabum and Buckaburne, this creek enters the Tombigbee River. Tuckabum was interpreted from various Choctaw words: tukafa, meaning "to fire," iti and hakbona, for "moldy," tikpi buna, meaning "double bend in a stream," or hatakabi, for "murderer" or "man killer."

**TUMKEEHATCHEE CREEK** (Elmore) Tumkeehatchee was derived from the Creek wi tamka hachi, meaning "sounding water creek." The stream flows into the Tallapoosa River.

**UCHEE CREEK** (Lee)   Uchee Creek joins the Chattahoochee River. A band of Yuchi Indians (members of the Creeks) migrated from Georgia to this stream during 1729–1740. Uchee may be derived from yu and chi, meaning "at a distance sitting down," or "seeing far away." It was also interpreted from the Hitchiti word ochesee, meaning "people of a different speech."

**UPHAPEE CREEK** (Macon)   Creek villages were located along the banks of this creek, notably including Yufalo, the home of Osceola, famous warrior during the Seminole War of 1835. Uphapee was thought to come from the Hitchiti word nofapi, meaning "beech tree."

**WEDHADKEE CREEK** (Randolph) The Wedhadkee flows into the state of Georgia to join the Chattahoochee River.

It is a Creek expression, wi and hatki, meaning "water white." In the 1850s, the Rock Mills was established along the creek. In later years, the mill became famous for its high quality yarn. Wehadkee Yarn Mills was an offshoot of the first mill and continues in business to this day.

**WEOGUFKA MOUNTAIN/CREEK** (Clay)   Weogufka is taken from the Creek words wi and ogufki, meaning "water muddy." The stream enters the Coosa River. At one time a small settlement with a post office was established along the creek. Weogufka is the tallest mountain in the state, and was used as a transmission station during the Civil War. Prospectors arrived in the 1830s to search for copper, but instead discovered placer gold on the mountain.

**WEOKA CREEK** (Elmore)   This stream flows into Coosa County and then back into Elmore County where it terminates at Jordan Lake. The name was interpreted as a Creek expression for "barking water." During the early 1840s, a water saw and grist mill were established along the creek.

**YANTLEY CREEK** (Choctaw)   Yantley is from the Choctaw word oka yanalli, meaning "running water." It enters Tuckabum Creek.

# ALASKA

**ADAK ISLAND**   Adak is one of Andreanof Islands in the Aleutian Chain. It bears an Aleut name derived from adaq, meaning "father." Historically occupied by Aleuts, the Russians began trade with them during the 1700s. The island was restricted during World War II when the U.S. military took over and used the island for defense.

**ADUGAK ISLAND**   Located at the tip of Umnak Island in the Aleutian Chain, this island is about one and one-half-miles wide. Father Veniaminov may have named it about 1840. Adugak is derived from the Aleut word adukak, interpreted as "somewhat long."

**AGHIYUK ISLAND**   One of the Semidi Islands, Aghiyuk is situated in the Aleutian Chain. The name was derived from achaiai, an Aleut word meaning "cormorant." With numerous bird colonies that contain more than a million of the sea birds in this south central coast of the state, it is an appropriate name.

**AGULOWAK RIVER**   This Eskimo expression is derived from ahbuhlerok, meaning "many rapids." The stream flows into Lake Aleknaqik, northwest of Dillingham. Natives used the river as a camping site while hunting and fishing for their winter stores.

**AIKTAK ISLAND**   Part of the Fox Islands in the Aleutian Chain, Aiktak is a little over a mile long. It is from the Aleut word, aikhaq, meaning "to travel," or an expression descriptive of someone taking a voyage. The island is home to more than 100,000 puffins.

**AKULIK CREEK**   Located in the Arctic Slope, the creek enters the Chukchi Sea. It is taken from the Eskimo word ahkoolik, interpreted as "fancy trimming," but what it described is obscure. Akulik was also thought to mean "middle part," derived from akuniq.

**AKUN ISLAND**   This Aleut name (hakun) designates "that over there."

About 1770, the Russians caused clashes between the Aleuts and Alutiiq natives of the Alaska peninsula, ending with the capture of the Aleuts, who were tortured and slain. During the early 1900s, sulfur was commercially mined on the island, but inclement weather caused too much damage to the equipment and the enterprise shut down after about a year.

**AKUTAN BAY/ISLAND**   The bay is about 10 miles wide and 18 miles long, located between Akutan and Akun Islands in the Aleutian Chain. The name is an Aleut expression meaning "I made a mistake," or "behind the salmonberry bushes." Although there are very few trees on the Island, it has an abundance of berry bushes. The island was home to the Alaska Whaling Company that later became a U.S. Navy refueling station.

**ALAGNAK RIVER**   Originating from Lake Kukaklek in Katmai National Park, the river bears an Eskimo name for "raspberry." It travels about 80 miles and enters the Kvichak River. The Alagnak is one of the largest producers of red salmon in the world. Part of the river was designated Wild and Scenic by the National Park Service.

**ALAID ISLAND**   This three-mile-long island is part of the Semichi Islands in the Aleutian Chain. Alaid was named by the Russians and may be an Eskimo word for "heart rock." Vitus Bering discovered the island in 1741.

**ALAPAH CREEK/MOUNTAIN**   Alapah is an Eskimo word for "cold." The creek begins in the Alapah Mountains and flows into the Kanayut River. The U.S. Geological Survey named the creek for the mountain, which is about 7,000 feet high.

**ALASKA RANGE**   Extending 650 miles from Iliamna Lake to the White River in

Canada, the mountain range's highest point is Mount McKinley at 20,320 feet. It may have been named in 1869 by explorer William Dall, although Harder noted the name may have been suggested by Senator Charles Sukner in 1867. Alaska is Aleut for "mainland."

**ALEKNAGIK, LAKE**  Aleknagik was interpreted as "wrong way home." Returning home in their canoes from fishing, natives would often encounter fog and lose their way. The lake is about 20 miles long. When the flu epidemic hit in 1918, those who survived fled the village of Aleknagik which is located along the lake.

**ALYESKA, MOUNT**  Alyeska is located on the southwest part of the Chugach Mountains and rises about 3,939 feet. The U.S. Forest Service named the mountain in 1959 for the Alyeska Ski Area, which may be Aleut from either alashka or alaesksu, meaning "great land." This was another derivation of Alaska.

**AMAK ISLAND**  President Herbert Hoover designated this island as part of the Aleutian Islands Reservation in 1930. Located in the Bering Sea, Amak is about three miles wide. It is an Aleut word meaning "blood," derived from amaq.

**AMAKNAK ISLAND**  During World War II, Fort Schwatka was built as a defense post on Amaknak for the protection of Dutch Harbor. Located in Unalaska Bay and part of the Fox Islands, Amaknak stretches four miles. Natives who lived here were supplied food by Reverend Sheldon Jackson when he introduced reindeer from Siberia. Named for an old burial cave on the island, Amaknak is derived from the Aleut word amaiknaq, meaning "place of impurity."

**AMALIK BAY**  The bay is located in the Katmai National Monument off the coast of the Alaska Peninsula. Amalik is an Eskimo word of obscure origin. Tradition holds that for more than 15 years fishermen would often spot a horse in the region. It got there after a barge hauling horses began to take on water, and the animals were offloaded at the bay. Out of more than a dozen, only one survived.

**AMATIGNAK ISLAND**  This southernmost island of the Aleutian Chain is about six miles long and part of the Delarof group of islands. Amatignak is an Aleut word meaning "wood chips."

**AMAWK CREEK/MOUNTAIN**  The creek rises at Amawk Mountain and joins the Koyukuk River. It is an Eskimo expression meaning "wolf creek." The mountain rises about 5,700 feet in the Brooks Range, and was named by Robert Marshall in 1930.

**ANAKTUVUK RIVER**  Rising in the Endicott Mountains, the stream joins the Colville River. Anaktuvuk is derived from an Eskimo expression meaning "the place of caribou droppings." The river valley is a traditional hunting ground of the nomadic Nunamiut people.

**ANIAK RIVER**  Aniak is a Yup'ik word for "place where it comes out," designating the mouth of the river. It was once called Yellow River because of the water's color caused by silting. During 1900 a gold rush began along the river and miners from Nome rushed to the site. In 1914, the village of Aniak was established along the river after a trading post was built.

**ANIAKCHAK RIVER**  Located on the Alaska Peninsula, the river rises at Surprise Lake in Aniakchak Crater and terminates at Aniakchak Bay. It is the only national river that flows from an active volcano. W.R. Smith and A.A. Baker, members of the U.S. Geological Survey, reported the name in 1924.

**ANIYUYAKTUVIK CREEK** This creek flows between the Angmakrok and Kayaksak Mountains and enters the Kukpuk River near the Arctic Slope. Named Ahneeyouhayktuvik in 1962, it was translated as an Eskimo word for "place where wind has hardened snow so that a snow house can be built."

**ANVIK RIVER** The Anvik enters the Yukon River near the village of Anvik. Lt. Zagoskin of the Imperial Russian Navy first called it Reka Anvig. Local natives guarded the river because it was the place where trade was conducted with other tribes. During spring and fall of each year the Eskimos would arrive. The first native there would stand up his tribal pole, then go back to camp. He would return each day to check the status. If trading was to be conducted, another trader would put his pole next to the first. If it was not, one of the traders would break the other's pole and leave. The natives called the site gitr'ingithchagg, meaning "at the mouth of the long, skinny river." Anvik could be a Siberian Yup'ik word for "that place where we come out."

**AROLIK LAKE/RIVER** The lake is situated in the Togiak National Wildlife Refuge and took its name from the river, which rises at the junction of its east and south forks. It was first called Kwiyadik in 1898. The U.S. Coast and Geodetic Survey renamed it Arolik in 1913, an Eskimo word defined as "moon."

**ARRIGETCH CREEK/PEAKS** Rising between 6,000–7,200 feet, these peaks are the highest in the region. The creek originates from the peaks and joins the Altana River. Arrigetch is an Eskimo word meaning "fingers extended," or "fingers of hand

outstretched," descriptive of the granite pinnacles.

**AUKE BAY/CREEK** The bay is just off the coast of Mendenhall Peninsula near Juneau. Auke is a Tlingit word derived from aklu, which means "little lake." Auke Creek empties into the bay. It was originally named Aylward Creek by a miner named Edward Aylward, but changed to Auke about 1902. The Bureau of Commercial Fisheries ran a biological laboratory at the bay during the 1960s.

**CHIGNIK BAY/ISLAND** After the Fisherman's Packing Company of Oregon checked the site out for prospective salmon and initially caught more than 2,000 barrels of the fish, it established a cannery along the bay in 1888. As a result, the community of Chignik was established on the south shore of the Alaska Peninsula. Chignik is an Eskimo (Sugpiaq) word meaning "wind" or "big wind." The island, about a mile and a half wide, was named after the bay.

**CHILKAT ISLANDS/RIVER** These islands are located south of Skagway and were named by Captain L.A. Beardslee in 1880. The Chilkats were a band of the Tlingit Indians, and their name was interpreted as "salmon storehouse." The river has its origins at Chilkat Glacier and enters Chilkat Inlet.

**CHISANA RIVER** There was once a mining camp situated along the banks of the Chisana, which rises at Chisana Glacier and enters the Nabesna River. The name was interpreted from the Tanana word ches-tna, meaning "red river."

**CHISTOCHINA RIVER** Located in the Alaska Range, this river has its origins on Chistochina Glacier and joins the Copper River. The community of Chistochina was established as a trading center for trappers and prospectors; it also functioned as a fish camp for the Ahtna natives. The name may be derived from the Ahtna word che-les'-chi-tna, interpreted as "marmot creek."

**CHUGINADAK ISLAND**  Chuginadak is the largest of the Islands of Four Mountains in the Aleutian Chain, and stretches about 14 miles. It is an Aleut word that means, in part, "to roast." Cleveland Volcano is situated on the island. On February 19, 2001, it erupted for over three hours, spewing volcanic ash more than 25,000 feet into the air, covering the village of Nikolski. This very active volcano continues to erupt frequently.

**DISTIK, MOUNT**  Mount Distik is located on Admiralty Island and rises about 3,801 feet. Distik is a Tlingit word, but its origin is obscure. The name was reported in 1926 by H.J. Coolidge. Local natives believed the mountain was a place where a squaw and her son took refuge at the time of the great floods. Only by going to the top of the mountain were they able to survive the water which drowned all other people and flooded the earth.

**DOOLTH MOUNTAIN**  This mountain is situated on the west coast of Chichagof Island and is about 2,159 feet high. The name was derived from the Tlingit word dulth, meaning "everything good and plenty," descriptive of the abundant game and fish in the region. It was named in 1907 by the U.S. Coast and Geodetic Survey.

**DOONERAK, MOUNT**  Doonerak rises to 7,610 feet and is one of highest mountains in the Brooks Range. Robert Marshall called it the Matterhorn of the Koyukuk, and named it Doonerak in 1929, an Eskimo word meaning "spirit," or

"devil." The mountain was first climbed by G.W. Beadle, Gunnar Bergman and Alfred Tissieres on June 30, 1952. Beadle, a well-known geneticist and Nobel Prize winner, was in his 50s when he climbed Doonerak.

**DULBI RIVER**  The Dulbi River region is a major goose nesting site. The river bears the appropriate name, derived from the Koyukuk word dalbatna, meaning "river of young geese." It flows into the Koyukuk River.

**EEK   LAKE/RIVER/MOUNTAINS** Located on the coast of Prince of Wales Island, the lake is less than a mile long. Eek Mountain rises about 4,000 feet high, and its name was taken from the river, which is a tributary of the Kuskokwim River. During the early 1900s gold lured miners here who conducted placer mining. Eek is derived from the Eskimo word, eet, which means "two eyes."

**EGEGIK RIVER**  The Egegik River rises in Becharof Lake and terminates at Egegik Bay. It name was derived from the Yup'ik word, igagik, meaning "neck," in reference to the location of Egegik Village along the river. Another interpretation was "swift river," designating the water flowing into Bristol Bay.

**EKLUTNA, MOUNT**  This mountain is located in the Chugach Mountain Range and rises about 4,000 feet. Eklutna is derived from eydlytnu, and may be a Tanaina word for "by several objects river." T.G. Gerdine of the U.S. Geological Survey reported the name as Eklootna in 1906.

**ESHAMY BAY/CREEK/LAKE**  Eshamy Bay and Lake are located on the Kenai Peninsula. The creek rises at Eshamy Lake and flows into Eshamy Lagoon. The name may be from an Eskimo expression meaning "good fishing grounds."

**GULKANA RIVER**   First called Tonkina River by Lt. H.T. Allen in 1885, the name was changed in 1899 and spelled Kulkana, from a Tanaina expression (origin unknown). At one time an ice pier was built to test the force of the ice on the river during its breakup. The experiment allowed engineers to come up with a design for a permanent bridge that would withstand the stress. The Gulkana flows to the Copper River near the town of Glennallen.

**HOLOKUK    MOUNTAIN/RIVER** The mountain is about 3,400 feet high and located in the Kuskokwim Mountain Range. Originally spelled Wloyukuk, it is an Eskimo word derived from olo, or ulu, interpreted as "stone knife." The river flows into the Kuskokwim River.

**HOHOLITNA RIVER**   In 1898, a trader named A. Lind noted the name of this river was derived from haliknuk, an Eskimo word meaning "sudden," referring to something that came up unexpectedly. The river begins at Whitefish Lake and joins the Kuskokwim River near the village of Sleetmute.

**IDITAROD RIVER**   Iditarod is a well-known name associated with the famous dog-sled races. The river is more than 300 miles long and empties into the Innoko River. It was originally called haidilatna, but corrupted to Iditarod, a Shageluk word meaning "clear water." Another translation was from hidedhod, for "distant place." Gold was discovered near the settlement of Iditarod in 1908, and one of the mines (Discovery Claim) become an extremely well-paying claim.

**IGIKPAK, MOUNT**   Part of the Schwatka Mountains, Igikpak is about 8,510 feet high. It is an Eskimo phrase that means "two big peaks," and may indicate two rock columns that form the top of the mountain, its peaks carved by moving ice. Known as the "crown jewel of the Arctic," Igikpak is the highest peak in the western Brooks Range and Arctic National Park.

**IKPIKPUK RIVER**   This river is formed by the confluence of the Kigalik River and Maybe Creek, and flows to empty into Smith Bay on the Arctic Plain. Ikpikpuk is an Eskimo word meaning "big cliff" or "big bank." A portion of the river is a nesting area of the peregrine falcons.

**ILIAMNA, LAKE**   Lake Iliamna is about 75 miles long and 20 miles wide. Iliamna is said to be the name of a mythical great blackfish that lived in the lake and bit holes in the natives' bidarkas. In 1898, prospectors converged on the lake with the discovery of copper. Lake Iliamna was one of the most significant places for salmon spawning in the world, and the largest contributor to the Bristol Bay fisheries.

**ILUILIUK BAY**   Iluiliuk is an Eskimo word derived from ilulaq, meaning "dwelling together," or "harmonious." It was also the name of a village on Unalaska Island. Overlooking the bay on the island is the oldest Russian Orthodox Church in the state. The bay is about one and a half miles wide.

**INMACHUK RIVER**   Rich placer mines were discovered along this river, which flows into Kotzebue Sound at the town of Deering. Inmachuk is an Eskimo word derived from ipnichuk, interpreted as "big cliff," or "new salt water."

**IPNEK CREEK/MOUNTAIN**   Originating in the Ipnek Mountain, the creek joins the Koyukuk River. In 1932 Robert Marshall gave the creek an Eskimo name meaning "sheep." Located in the Gates of the Arctic National Park, the mountain is 5,875 feet high.

**ITKILLIK RIVER**   This river rises near Ulo Pass in the Endicott Mountains and enters the Colville River near Harrison Bay. In 1855, the river was named it'kaling kok, meaning "Indian river." It was also interpreted from the Eskimo word itqiliq, meaning simply "Indian."

**IVISHAK RIVER**   Part of the river is designated Wild where it flows through the Arctic National Wildlife Refuge. Fed by glaciers, the stream originates in the Brooks Range and empties into the Sagavanirktok ("swift") River. Ivishak was interpreted as an Eskimo expression for "red river" or "red paint."

**KACHEMAK BAY**   Russians gave this bay its name about 1847 and spelled it Chugachik and Kochekmak. It is located on the southwest coast of the Kenai Peninsula. William Dall translated it from kacheckmak, meaning "high water cliff," or "high cliff bay." It was also thought to be an Aleut word meaning "smoky bay," in reference to the coal seams found there. The 'smoky' referred to the smoldering coal in the clay banks.

**KAGATI LAKE**   J.E. Spurr conducted the first geological exploration of this region in 1898. The lake is about four miles long, situated in the Kilbuck-Kuskokwim Mountain area. Kagati is an Eskimo word meaning "source," because the lake is a source of the Kanektuk River.

**KAHILTNA RIVER**   Kahiltna is an Athabascan word defined as "from the source," indicating the river's origin at Denali Mountain. Gold placers have been worked for decades along the river. At one time an entrepreneur had a camping spot along the Kahiltna he promoted as a tourist mining lodge. The Kahiltna flows from Kahiltna Glacier, and is home to the Tule Geese who have their nests along certain areas of the river.

**KASAAN ISLAND**   Kasaan Island is located in the bay along the east coast of Prince of Wales Island. First known as Long Island, the name was changed to Kasaan in 1931 by the U.S. Coast and Geodetic Survey. It is a Tlingit word that means "pretty town," or "town on the point."

**KATMAI, MOUNT**   This mountain is more than 7,000 feet high, and was the site of a large volcanic eruption that occurred on June 5, 1912. Katmai collapsed into itself and left a crater lake about 3 miles in diameter and 3,700 feet deep. At the same time of the eruption, Novarupta Volcano also exploded which created what is called the "Valley of Ten Thousand Smokes." Ten times more forceful than the Mount St. Helens eruption in 1980, it took more than 60 hours for the dust to settle enough so the sun could shine through. Since the lake has risen in the last 20 years, scientists surmise that if the water ever spills out of the crater, it could potentially cause a horrendous flood. Katmai's name origin is unknown.

**KAYAK ISLAND**   Kayak was thought to be the place Vitus Bering named Saint Elias in 1741. Captain Cook visited the island in 1778 and renamed it Kaye's Island for Dr. Kay who was the chaplain to King George III. In addition, he put pieces of silver Dr. Kay had given him into a bottle and buried it on the island. Kayak is located in the Gulf of Alaska, and bears an Eskimo word for "canoe."

**KHANTAAK ISLAND**   Khantaak is a Tlingit word meaning "wooden food dish."

Located in Yakutat Bay, the island is about six miles long. In 1958, a tremendous earthquake occurred on the island which killed three people. President of the Bellingham Canning Company and the Yakutat postmaster were on the island at the time. They managed to escape by boat before the tsunami hit the island. The tremor was measured at a magnitude 7.9.

**KISKA ISLAND**   This 24-mile-long island is one of the Rat Islands group. The former village of Kiska was established on the island, and bears an Aleut word that was corrupted by the Russians from angig, meaning "gut." During World War II, the Japanese occupied Kiska until August of 1943.

**KLUTINA RIVER/LAKE**   In 1898, prospectors who camped at the lake named it Klutina. Taking its name from the lake, the stream originates at Klutina Glacier and empties into the Copper River. Klutina is derived from the Ahtna word khlutitna meaning "glacier river." It was also interpreted as "river with big head."

**KOBUK RIVER**   More then 350 miles long, this river's name was derived from an Eskimo word meaning "big river." In 1886, explorer Lt. G. Stoney noted the name Kobuck, but suggested the river be called Putnam for Charles Putnam, an officer in the U.S. Navy who was lost at sea in 1880, but residents later renamed it Kobuk.

**KONGAKUT RIVER**   The Kongakut rises in the Davidson Mountains and empties into Sitka Lagoon. Kongakut is an Eskimo word interpreted as "deer pond." It is also known as River of Caribou, because the Porcupine River caribou herd follows the Kongakut River during its migration. The herd's number is estimated at more than 150,000 head.

**KUPARUK RIVER**   Whalers plied this river to trade with the Eskimos in the early 1800s, and a trading post was established at the mouth of the river. Kuparuk is an Eskimo word derived from kuqauraq, meaning "big river."

**KUSHTAKA LAKE**   Located near Kushtaka Glacier in the Chugach Mountains, natives believed the lake contained an evil spirit that caused the water to boil, breaking up the winter ice. This phenomenon actually occurs because of coal gas build-up at the bottom of the lake. Kushtaka may be Aleut for "demon" or "ghost."

**KUSKOKWIM RIVER/MOUNTAIN**   The river empties into Kuskokwim Bay. It is an Eskimo word, with the last syllable meaning "river," but the root word is not known. Kuskokwim Mountain was inhabited by prospectors when a gold rush occurred in 1910, but was very short-lived, lasting less than a year.

**LITUYA BAY/MOUNTAIN**   Located in Glacier Bay National Monument, the bay is known for its gigantic waves. Lituya is a Tlingit word meaning "lake within the point." The entrance to the bay was so dangerous the Tlingits left in 1853. One of the largest waves was recorded in 1958 after a 7.8 earthquake struck. The mountain was described by John Muir during his explorations: "Lituya, as seen from here, is an immense tower, severely plain and massive. It makes a fine and terrible and lonely impression."[1]

**NAKNEK RIVER**   One of the largest salmon runs in the world is along this river. The Naknek originates in Naknek Lake and empties into Kvichak Bay on the Alaska Peninsula. The name was corrupted by the Russians from the Eskimo word naugeik, meaning "muddy."

**NATOA ISLAND**   Since numerous places along the island contain very sheer cliffs, Natoa was given an appropriate Eskimo word that means "summit." Located in the Gulf of Alaska, the island is a little more than a mile long.

**NENANA RIVER**   Lt. Allen named the river Cantwell for John Cantwell, an explorer during 1884. It was changed to Nenana, derived from nenashna, an Athabascan word meaning "a good place to camp between the rivers." The Nenana rises at Nenana Glacier in the Alaska Range and joins the Tanana River at the community of Nenana.

**NEWHALEN RIVER**   The community of Newhalen is located on the north shore of Iliamna Lake at the mouth of Newhalen River, which rises at Sixmile Lake and empties into Lake Iliamna. It is derived from the Yup'ik word noghelingamuit, meaning "people of Noghelin." In turn, Noghelin translates to "land of prosperity" (or "abundance"), descriptive of the numerous caribou and fish in the region.

**NIGU RIVER**   Rising at Imakturok Pass in the Gates of the Arctic National Park, the Nigu River joins the Etivluk River in the Brooks Range. The region was once a trading route for the coastal Eskimos and Inland Athabascan Indians. Nigu is an Eskimo word for "rainbow."

**NUKA BAY/ISLAND**   Nuka Bay is located on the east coast of Kenai Peninsula. During the early 1800s natives living there were urged by Russian priests to relocate to Fort Alexandrovsky (today's English Bay). After the discovery of gold, the Nuka Bay Mines and Nukalask Mining Company were established. The island was the site of a prosperous fox farm in the 1920s until the price of fur fell and the business was discontinued. Nuka is an Eskimo word derived from nukaq, meaning "young bull caribou."

**NUNIVAK ISLAND**   This island is in the Bering Sea and was discovered by Capt. Lt. Vasiliev in 1821. The island has been inhabited for more than 2,000 years by the Nuniwarmiut people (Cup'ik Eskimos). Nunivak is derived from the Eskimo word Nounivak, meaning "big land." The Evangelical Covenant Church was established on the island in the 1930s by Eskimo missionary Jacob Kenick, followed by a Bureau of Indian Affair's school.

**OGLODAK ISLAND**   Oglodak is situated in the Aleutian chain between Atka and Tagalak Islands. It is a little more than a mile across. The name was derived from the Aleut word agligak, translated as "albatross." On March 9, 1957, the third largest earthquake to hit the region in the 20th century occurred just south of this island, at a magnitude of 9.1.

**OGOTORUK CREEK**   Ogotoruk Creek originates at Sigrikpak Ridge and empties into the Chukchi Sea. It is an Eskimo word for "poke" (a type of bag). During the 1950s, plans were made to detonate thermonuclear bombs at a remote site near the creek. Personnel at Lawrence Livermore National Laboratory in California called it "Project Chariot," a program to use the bombs for peaceful purposes, such as creating harbors.

**SADLEROCHIT      MOUNTAINS/ RIVER**   Located in the Brooks Range, these mountains are about 4,000 feet high and stretch more than 40 miles. Thousands of head of Central Arctic caribou winter near the mountains. Sadlerochit is an Eskimo word for "area outside of the mountain." The Sadlerochit River has its origins in the Franklin Mountains and empties into Camden Bay.

**SAGAVANIRKTOK RIVER** Sagavanirk is an Eskimo word derived from sawunukto, which means "strong current." It rises between the Endicott and Philip Smith Mountains and empties into the Beaufort Sea.

**SEDANKA ISLAND** Part of the Fox Islands in the Aleutian Chain, Sedanka is an Aleut name corrupted from siginaq, meaning "braided" or "curled." During his explorations in 1777, Captain Cook anchored off the island.

**SHEENJEK RIVER** Rising at glaciers on the Continental Divide, the Sheenjek flows through the Arctic National Wildlife Refuge and enters the Porcupine River. Part of the stream is classified as Wild and Scenic. It is an Athabascan word that means "salmon."

**SINUK RIVER** After gold was reported on the river by a government reindeer hunter, a number of prospectors headed there but came out empty handed. The Sinuk River rises near Tigaraha Mountain and empties into Norton Sound. It is an Eskimo word for "stream mouth."

**STIKINE RIVER** Originating in British Columbia, the Stikine flows to the Alaskan Panhandle and empties into the Pacific Ocean. During the 1830s, Russians built a fort named Dionysian near the mouth of the river. Hudson's Bay Company later took over the fort, which was subsequently destroyed by the Stikine natives. During the gold rush days the river was a primary means of transportation for miners on their way to the gold fields. In addition to gold, garnet was discovered on a ledge near the mouth of the river, as was copper. Stikine is a Tlingit word meaning "great river."

**SUKAKPAK MOUNTAIN** The mountain is a 4,200 foot high limestone formation in the Brooks Range, and was a traditional boundary between the Athabascan Indian and Nunamiut Eskimo territories. Sukakpak is an Eskimo word for "deadfall," descriptive of a trapping method used by the Eskimos, entailing a heavy stone supported by a stick. Animals would dislodge the stick while attempting to get the bait and the rock would fall, trapping the animal.

**SUSITNA RIVER** It was believed the first exploration to this region was in 1834 by a Creole named Malakov. Russians arrived in 1847 and named the river Susitna, from the Tanaina word sushitna, meaning "sandy river." The stream rises at Susitna Glacier in the Alaska Range and empties into Cook Inlet.

**TAKU RIVER** This river begins in British Columbia and empties into Taku Inlet near Juneau. The Taku Indians had control of the river, acting as middle men for natives because they would not allow other natives to trade directly with the whites. The river was named for the Taku natives, which was interpreted as "ocean people."

**TINAYGUK RIVER** The abundance of moose in the region caused this river to be given the Eskimo name for "moose." Located entirely within the Gates of the Arctic National Park and Preserve, the river flows into the Koyukuk River. The entire length of the Tinayguk is designated as Wild and Scenic, and because of is remoteness is seldom visited.

**TONGASS ISLAND** Situated in Nakat Bay, the island is about eight miles long. Tongass is derived from the Tlingit expression tangas nit quou, meaning "sea lion pillar people," descriptive of carvings on the natives' community house. In 1907, President Theodore Roosevelt signed a bill which created the Tongass National Forest.

**TOTEM BAY**   Located off Kupreanof Island, the bay was named by the U.S. Coast and Geodetic Survey in 1886 because the rocks resembled totem poles. Totem is derived from the Chippewa word ototeman, which means "brother-sister kin." This may be one of the few places in the state named for other than the indigenous tribes of Alaska.

**TUKUTO CREEK**   This creek originates in Howard Hills and joins the Etivluk River. It may have been derived from the Eskimo word taktuktoq, meaning "fog," or taqtu for "kidney." Another interpretation was a corruption of nioqtun, meaning "drill" or "bit."

**UGAK BAY**   Located in the Gulf of Alaska near Kodiak Island, the bay is part of the Gray Whales' migration route from Baja, California, to the Bering Sea. Ugak is from the Aleut word qugaq, which means "evil spirit."

**UGAMAK ISLAND**   Part of the Krenitzin Islands in the Fox Island group, Ugamak is Aleut for "ceremony island." This five-mile-long island is a natal rookery for sea lions.

**UMNAK ISLAND**   Umnak Island is one of the Fox Islands in the Aleutian Chain. During the 1750s, Russian explorers claimed the territory. The name was derived from the Aleut word umnaqs, meaning "fish line." Early natives called the area Agunalaksh ("the shores where the sea breaks its neck"). During World War II U.S. forces established a tactical air base that would be deployed to protect Dutch Harbor. An Aleut legend says this was the only island with trees when they arrived. One of the trees reached up to the clouds and looked like a piece of seaweed the natives used for fish lines. They believed if the tree was destroyed the people would disappear from the earth.

It was cut down by the Russians, and soon thereafter all the Russians died. The Aleuts constructed a house around what was left of the stump, which may still be standing.

**UNALAKLEET RIVER**   The Unalakleet rises in the Kaltag Mountains and enters Norton Sound. The name was first reported as Reka Unalaklik by the Russians in 1842. Unalakleet means "place where the east wind blows," or "south side," derived from the Eskimo word, ungalaklik.

**UNIMAK ISLAND**   Part of the Fox Island group, Unimak is the largest Island in the region (22 miles wide and 65 miles long). It is derived from the Aleut word unimga, interpreted as "big one of them." Located on the island is Mount Shishaldin (known as "Smoking Moses"), an active volcano, which last erupted in 1999. The Aleuts call the volcano sisquk, meaning "mountain which points the way when I am lost." About 910,000 acres of the island were designated as the Unimak Island Wilderness in 1980.

**UNGA ISLAND**   Unga is part of the Shumagin Islands and bears an Aleut word meaning "south." It was also defined as "spout" because of the shape of a geographic feature on the island. During the early 1900s, gold was discovered and the Apollo Mine opened, bringing out more than $2 million until the vein ran out in 1912. In the 1830s, the village of Unga was a Russian sea otter station known as Delarov until it was changed to Unga.

**UTUKOK RIVER**   Utukok is an Eskimo word that means "ancient" or "old." The river rises in the De Long Mountains and enters Kasegaluk Lagoon on the Arctic Plain. Flint located along the river banks was used by the Nunamiut Eskimos to make knives, arrowheads and scrapers, which they traded with other Eskimos.

**WALAKPA BAY**   This is the site where Will Rogers and Wiley Post were killed in a plane crash on August 15, 1935. The bay is located near Barrow on the Arctic Plain. Walakpa is an Eskimo word that means "big village."

**YUKON RIVER**   More than 2,000 miles long, the great Yukon is third longest and one of the most important rivers in the world. It rises in Canada in the Yukon and empties into the Bering Sea. Hudson's Bay Company explored the river in the 1840s and built Fort Yukon. The company also named the river, from the Athabascan word yukonna or youcon, meaning "great river." Arthur Harper and Leroy McQuesten initially came to Alaska in search of gold, but their wealth ultimately lay in the trading posts they established along the river, serving the miners of the region.

# ARIZONA

**AGATHLA PEAK** (Navajo)   A remnant of an old volcano, this peak stands like a lone sentinel that rises about 6,825 feet. It is also called Agathla Needle. The name is derived from the Navajo word aghala (or agaa's) meaning "much wool," in reference to wild deer and sheep that rubbed against the rocks during the shedding seasons. It was also interpreted as "place of animal hides" because the Navajo Indians scraped deer hides on the rocks to clean them. Tradition also says a snake made its home at the base of this peak and sated himself with the abundant animals, then spit out the fur, thus "much wool." Navajo legend considers this peak the center of their world. Agathla was put here by the Holy People because the sky and sun were too low and their people suffered from the heat, thus the peak put great distance between the land and the sky.

**APACHE MAID MOUNTAIN** (Coconino)   The mountain may have received its name after U.S. Army troops in a fight with Indians at this point in 1873 killed an Apache woman Another theory is the mountain was named for a young Apache girl who got lost and nearly starved until she was found. Apache may be derived from a Zuni word, apachu, meaning "enemy," or Yuman for "fighting men." The Apaches call themselves Tinde ("the people").

**ARAVAIPA CREEK (GRAHAM)/ CANYON** (Pinal)   The 34-mile-long creek is a main tributary to the San Pedro River and rises near Eureka Spring. It may be a Pima word for "girls," or Papago for "small spring." The Apache Indians called the creek and region their home until they were driven out by the whites. In 1871, an Aravaipa chief received permission for his people to grow crops along the creek. Citizens from Tucson resented the intrusion, and on April 30 they killed more than 140 of the Indians in Aravaipa canyon (called the Camp Grant Massacre).

**AZANSOSI MESA** (Navajo)   Louise Wetherill and her husband established the first trading post in the area. To honor Louise, the mesa was named for her. Derived from the Navajo word asdzaatsosi, Azansosi means "slim woman."

**BABOCOMARI RIVER** (Cochise)   The region became a center of cattle raising during the 1870s after the McLaury brothers claimed property rich in grazing land along the river. In 1874, Camp Wallen was built in order to protect the cattlemen from Apache raids. It was moved to Fort Huachuca after a malaria epidemic broke out. Bobocomari is a Papago expression descriptive of caliche that hang over the banks in cell-like formations (calcium carbonate that forms a crust in very dry regions).

**BABOQUIVARI MOUNTAIN** (Pima) Rising about 7,750 feet above sea level, this mountain is located on the Tohono O'odham Reservation. It is considered by the Papago Indians the center of their universe. I'itoi lived on the mountain and left it to help his people survive in the desert. He created the people and animals. It is believed that a cave in the mountain was I'itoi's home, and the Indians still place eagle feathers, rattles and other items as tribute to him. They also believe I'itoi still looks down on them and protects them. Baboquivari is a Papago word translated as "with its bill in the air," descriptive of the mountain's shape. It was also defined as "water on the mountain," and "mountain narrow in the middle."

**BALUKAI MESA** (Apache)   Located southeast of Black Mesa, Balukai is about 20 miles long. It bears a Navajo word for "white rock" or "reeds under the rim." The mesa was linked with the Navajo Blessingway ceremonies, entailing rites for people who had to leave their families for different reasons, women who were expecting babies, etc. Ceremonies are conducted today

for good luck and health of the people. The Blessingway story says that Balukai Mesa is part of a female body. Navajo Mountain represents the female figure, Black Mountain its body, and Balukai contains the feet and legs.

**BATAMOTE MOUNTAIN** (Pima) Batamote is a Papago word for "arrow weed." Bighorn sheep roamed this region when the white settlers arrived in the 1800s. As more people moved in, the bighorn grazing lands began to disappear and their numbers dwindled. The Bighorn Sheep Society was later established and was a driving force for increasing the bighorn population.

**BEGASHIBITO CANYON** (Navajo) Begashibito is a Navajo word for "cattle water," a descriptive phrase since it was a watering place for cattle. Local Navajo legend says a good spirit resides in the canyon and helps people who are in great need.

**BEKIHATSO LAKE** (Apache)   This lake is located on the Navajo Indian Reservation and means "big lake," or "big water place." It was also defined as "groaning lake," because of a water monster called Teehooltsodfi. The Indians were afraid of the lake because of the sounds that emanated from it.

**BIDAHOCHI        BUTTE/SPRING** (Navajo)   The spring was used by the Navajos who made their camp here while traveling to Keams Canyon. The butte was named Bidahochi, Navajo for "many red streaks up its slope," in reference to a red rock slide scar. During the 1880s, Julius Wetzler operated a trading post in the region.

**BODAWAY MESA** (Coconino)   Bodaway Mesa is located on the Navajo Reservation, but bears a Paiute name. It may have come from Ba Adowe or Bayoodzin, the name of a Paiute chief, whose name means "gap." During the 1840s, he and his tribe lived in the territory, which was later inhabited by the Navajo Indians.

**CANYON DE CHELLY** (Apache) Chelly is defined as "where the water comes out of the rock," "the place where it flows from the canyon," or "rock canyon." The Navajo Indians came to the canyon in the 1750s after they were forced to leave their homes in northern New Mexico by the Ute and Comanche Indians. They were permitted to return home in 1868. Spider Rock is located in the canyon. According to Navajo legend there were only two beings in the beginning: that of Spider Woman, the earth goddess, and Tawa, god of the skies. Parents taught their children that Spider Woman would throw them off the rock if they misbehaved. She was also an important figure in Hopi mythology, who believed Spider Woman weaved the clouds to make rain.

**CHAISTLA BUTTE** (Navajo) Also known as Turkey Butte, Chaistla Butte is located just north of the community of Kayenta. It was interpreted as a Navajo expression for "beaver pocket," and Hopi for "elk."

**CHAOL CANYON** (Coconino) The canyon is about 1,000 feet long and a tributary to Navajo Canyon. It was suggested the canyon be named for a man named Dortch, but the U.S. Geographic Board refused the request and selected Chaol, a Navajo word for "pinyon." Numerous petroglyphs are located on some of the walls of the canyon.

**CHEDISKI MOUNTAIN** (Navajo) Chediski is an Apache word meaning "long white rock," descriptive of white sandstone on part of the mountain. Other in-

terpretations were "solid object that juts out," and "white mountain that sits back alone." In June of 2000, a lost hiker started a fire near the mountain. It merged with the "Rodeo" fire, another man-made blaze, which destroyed at least 467 homes and scorched nearly 469,000 acres. It was later learned that a White Mountain Apache set the fire so he could earn money as a firefighter. The historic town of Show Low barely missed being totally destroyed.

**CHIKAPANAGI MESA** (Coconino) Located between Matkatamiba and Olo Canyons, Chikapanagi Mesa was named for a Havasupai Indian child. His name was interpreted as "bat," because the boy's face looked like a bat to his people.

**CHILCHINBITO SPRING** (Navajo) Chilchinbito Spring is located on the Hopi Indian Reservation under Black Mesa, and bears a Navajo word for "sumac spring." Navajo women used the sumac plant for basket weaving. It was near this spring that a group of Paiute Indians chased a Navajo man and were subsequently killed by the Navajos. The Paiute bones were later used in the Navajo Enemy Chant and war dances. Located near the spring today is a trading post and school.

**CHINDE MESA** (Apache) While U.S. Geological Survey members were exploring the region, they stayed at a hogan one evening. Coming out of the structure, they startled the Navajo Indians who thought the men were spirits. Chinde Mesa bears an apt name which means "spirit" (also "haunted"). The mesa is located north of the Petrified Forest.

**CHIRICAHUA MOUNTAINS** (Cochise) These mountains are part of the Coronado National Forest. They were home to the Chiricahua Indians, most notably Cochise and his band. The name was translated as an Apache expression for "people of the rising sun." It was also thought to come from the Opata word chicuicagui, which meant "mount of wild turkeys." The Opata Indians were originally from Mexico near Sonora. During peace talks with Cochise in 1871, the U.S. Government gave the Apache Indians land that included the Chiricahua Mountains.

**CHUSKA MOUNTAINS** (Apache) The Chuska Mountains extend into New Mexico and are legendary to the Navajo Indians. They form part of their sacred figure, Yoo-tzill, of which Chuska is the head, the Lukachukai Mountains form his body, and the Carrizo Mountains are his legs. White spruce are prevalent in the Chuskas and Navajo tradition says the spruce is a sacred tree that attracts rain. Chuska was derived from ch'ooshgaii, meaning "white spruce."

**CIBEQUE CREEK** (Navajo) Flowing about two miles, the Cibeque bears an Apache word meaning "reddish bottom land," descriptive of the creek bed. It lies entirely within the White Mountain Apache Reservation. During 1881, Colonel Eugene Carr came to this site to arrest Noch-ay-del-klinne, an Apache medicine man who taught a religion predicting the white man would be thrown out of Indian land. Army troops from Fort Apache captured the medicine man, but an in an attempt to escape, Noch-ay-del-klinne was killed.

**COCONINO PLATEAU** (Coconino) Located on the south side of the Grand Canyon, this region once belonged to the Havasupai Indians until the Navajos moved to the plateau during the 1850s. Coconino is a Havasupai word meaning "little water," and was named in 1892 by C. Hart Merriam.

**COMA'A SPRING** (Navajo) During the 1880s, an Indian agent convinced the Hopi Indians to settle here in order that the Navajo would not be able to take over their reservation. But the Navajo Indians attacked the Hopi, burned their village, and drove them off. Coma'a is a Ute word derived from goma'a, interpreted as "rabbit."

**COMOBABI MOUNTAIN** (Pima) This mountain is located on Papago Indian Reservation and bears a Papago word that means "where the kom trees grows." Kom is the Papago expression descriptive of the trees that grow red berries.

**DEL SHAY CREEK** (Gila) Tonto Apache Chief Del-che lived in this region with his tribe, and was regarded an enemy of the whites. After a price was put on his head in 1874, the Apaches killed their chief and brought his scalp to Col. W.H. Corbusier of the Army to prove Del-che was dead. The creek bears the chief's name, which means "red ant."

**DINNEBITO WASH** (Navajo) Dinnebito is a Navajo name meaning "his spring." During 1823 Colonel Jose Vizcarra explored Dinnebito Wash, which is a tributary of the Little Colorado River.

**HARCUVAR MOUNTAIN** (Yuma) Located in the Harcuvar Wilderness, the mountain rises from 2,400 feet to more than 5,100 feet high. In the 1920s, the Hargus Ranch was established in a canyon at the foot of the mountain and operated as a sheepherding station until about 1940. Gold was discovered in the mountain in 1869 and the Harquahala Mine brought out more than $1 million before it shut down. Once known as Penhatchapet, the mountain bears a Mohave expression meaning "a little water," or "sweet water."

**HARQUA HALA MOUNTAIN** (Yuma) Rising about 5,690 feet high, the mountain contains a natural spring where rare cacti survive. Harqua Hala is derived from ahhaquahla, a Mohave word for "running water," or "running water high up," descriptive of a local spring. In 1869, Apache Indians stole some Durham cows belonging to King Woolsey and were pursued into the mountains. Unable to reach the springs for water and losing strength, many of the Indians were killed during the foray. The same year gold was discovered and the Harquahala Mine opened. It was later sold for more than $1 million. The Smithsonian Institute built an observatory on the mountain in the 1920s.

**HASHBIDITO CREEK** (Apache) Spanish explorers first called the creek Arroyo del Carrizo. It was later given the Navajo name derived from hasbidito, or hashbito, interpreted as "turtle dove spring," or "mourning dove." The name is also spelled Hasbidito. The creek originates near Gigante Butte on the Navajo Indian Reservation and joins Agua Sal Creek.

**HASSAYAMPA RIVER** (Maricopa) The waters of the Hassayampa flow beneath a sandy stream bed through part of its course, and intermittently disappear under the sand. It bears a descriptive Apache word meaning "river that runs upside down," or "water that is hidden." The name was also thought to be Mojave for "water place of big rocks." Indian legend that says if you drink the water from this river above the trail you will always tell the truth, but if you drink below it you will never know the truth. During the mid–1800s, gold was discovered along the river, and resulted in establishment of the Vulture Mine by Henry Wickenburg.

**HOPI BUTTES** (Navajo) Located in the northeastern part of the state, the Spaniards called these buttes Moqui, which means "dead." The Hopi Indians were insulted with that name, and petitioned the U.S. Government to change it, which was granted. Hopi means "peaceful people," or "people who live in the proper way." These volcanic buttes are filled with springs and water wells.

**HOSKININNI MESA** (Navajo) In 1823, Colonel Jose Vizcarra visited the mesa, which straddles the states of Arizona and Utah. During 1864, when Kit Carson was removing the Navajo Indians to the Bosque Redondo Reservation, headman Hoskininni led his people in resistance to their removal. Hoskininni is Navajo for "angry one," or "angry warrior." This may have referred to the fact that Hoskinini was very harsh to his people in an effort to keep them alive while they fought the whites.

**HUACHUCA MOUNTAINS** (Cochise) Fort Huachuca was established in 1877 at the foot of the Huachuca Mountains by Captain Whitside and his army. Its excellent observation of the Santa Cruz and San Pedro valleys made it an ideal location to protect the settlers. The mountains are located in the Coronado National Forest. Huachuca is an Apache word meaning "thunder," referring to the monsoon seasons. The Chiricahua Apaches claimed this region as their ancestral lands.

**HUALPAI MOUNTAIN** (Mohave) Situated about 12 miles southwest of Kingman and rising 8,417 feet, these mountains were once home to the Hualpai Indians, whose name means "people of the tall pines." They were removed in 1870 by the U.S. military to the Peach Springs Reservation.

**HUETHAWALI MOUNTAIN** (Coconino) This is a fairly isolated site in the Grand Canyon. The mountain is about 6,200 feet high, and bears a Havasupai word derived from huegawoola, meaning "observation point," or "bear mountain." It was also thought to come from huethwali, meaning "white rock mountain."

**JADITO MESA/SPRING/WASH** (Navajo)   The Coronado Expedition explored this region in 1540. Jadito Mesa was named for the spring, which is Navajo for "antelope springs," indicative of the herds of antelope prevalent in the region. The wash travels from Black Mesa and empties into the Little Colorado River.

**KAIBAB PLATEAU** (Coconino)   First called Buckskin Mountain by the Mormons because of the abundant mule deer, the plateau was later renamed by John Wesley Powell. Kaibab is a Paiute word for "mountain lying down." It may also come from the Navajo word nat'oh dzil, meaning "tobacco mountain." Located north of the Grand Canyon, the plateau covers an area of more than 800,000 acres. It is the only place in the world inhabited by the unique, tassel-eared, white-tailed Kaibab squirrel.

**KAIBITO PLATEAU** (Coconino)   This plateau is south of Lake Powell, between the Colorado and San Juan Rivers, and takes its name from a Navajo word meaning "willow spring." The Navajo Indians moved to this region some time after the 1680 Pueblo Revolt. During the 1880s, Thomas Keam discovered copper, but since the mineral was on the Western Navajo Indian Reservation, he was not allowed to develop its resources.

**KEET SEEL CANYON** (Navajo)   Numerous ancient pueblo ruins are situated in this canyon. Keet Seel is a tributary of Dowozhiebito Canyon, and cuts into the west rim of Skeleton Mesa. It was thought to be derived from the Navajo word kits'i-ili, meaning "shattered (or 'empty') house."

**KO-OP-KE MOUNTAIN** (Pinal)   Also spelled Copeka, the mountain is situated on the Papago Indian Reservation and rises about 1,450 feet. After the Indians constructed a dam, the site was given the descriptive name kup, meaning "place of the dam." The proper name for the mountain is Shopishk.

**LOKASAKAL SPRING** (Navajo)   This spring is located on the Navajo Indian Reservation. It is derived from the Navajo word lu-ka, meaning "place where reeds grow," or "clump of reeds."

**LUKACHUKAI MOUNTAINS** (Apache)   Rising more than 9,000 feet above sea level and about 60 miles long, the mountains are situated on the Navajo Indian Reservation. Lukachukai Village was situated in the foothills. The name was interpreted from the Navajo words luk'a and eh'ogui, meaning "white spruce," "covered with white spruce," or from loka cogai, meaning "place of slender reeds." During World War II, the Vanadium Corporation of America conducted the first uranium mining in the mountain region.

**MAZATZAL MOUNTAINS** (Gila, Maricopa)   Although Mazatzal is an Apache word meaning "bleak" or "barren," the mountains are actually covered with pine trees. Another interpretation was from mazatzark, meaning "space between." The name was recorded on Army records in 1867 during a conflict with the Indians. The mountains rise about 7,000 feet and contain remnants of 700-year-old cliff dwellings.

**MOENKOPI WASH** (Coconino)   Flowing about 90 miles, the wash originates at

Black Mesa and terminates at the Little Colorado River. Part of the wash is located on the Navajo Indian Reservation. It is a Navajo word meaning "the place of running water." The Hopi farming community of Moenkopi also located near the mesa, and uses the Moenkopi to irrigate its crops.

**NAAHTEE CANYON** (Navajo) Located near the Hopi Indian Reservation, this name comes from the Navajo word naa a diih, interpreted as "without eyes," or "eyes become none," and may describe the loco weed and its effects. A post office was established in the canyon about 1916 (closed in the 1920s), followed by a trading post operated by Lorenzo Hubbell.

**NANKOWEAP CANYON** (Coconino) Copper was discovered in the canyon during the 1890s, but there was not enough of the mineral to make it profitable. Miners followed the Nankoweap Trail, developed by John Wesley Powell about 1882, in their search for gold near the canyon. The Anazasi Granaries, more than 900 years old, are situated just above the creek. The canyon, which is located in Grand Canyon National Park, bears is a Paiute word interpreted as "echo," or "singing," a descriptive name. It was also interpreted from the Paiute expression meaning "place where Indians had fight," in reference to a skirmish between a Paiute named Johnny and other Paiute tribes.

**NAVAJO MOUNTAIN** (Coconino) During John Wesley Powell's second expedition in 1872, he named this 10,416-foot mountain Mount Seneca Howland. It was later changed to Navajo, a word steeped in mystery with many interpretations: "a place of large plantings," "a somewhat worthless field," or a Tewa word, nanahu, designating an Apache Indian band. Some think it is a Tewa word, na-ba-hu-u for "arroyo of cultivated fields." The name may also signify "great planted fields." The Navajo Indians call it Naatsis' ("it sits there protecting them from the enemy," or "head of earth"). The summit was home of Monster Slayer and Child Born of Water (the Hero Twins) who used lightning bolts to slay their enemies. The Creation Story says that the first human originated from Navajo Mountain.

**NAZLINI CANYON/ CREEK** (Apache) In 1886, Lorenzo Hubbell established a trading post near the creek, which operated until the 1970s. Situated within the Navajo Indian Reservation, the canyon is just east of the community of Nazlini. A boarding school in addition to the community school run by the Bureau of Indian Affairs is located in the canyon. Nazlini is a Navajo word meaning "running (or 'crooked') river." It was also defined as "makes a turn flowing," descriptive of a bend in the creek.

**NITZIN CANYON** (Coconino) Nitzin Canyon is situated on the Navajo Reservation within the Navajo National Monument and known for its ruin, Inscription House, which contained about 75 rooms and granaries. In 1909, Byron Cummings and John Wetherill found an inscription on one of the walls that read C H O S 1661 A d n, thus the name Inscription House. Because of its instability the ruins are not open to the public. Nitzin is a derived from the Navajo word niidzi, meaning "we stand in a row."

**NOKAI CANYON** (Navajo) This canyon flows into the state of Utah and drains into the San Juan River. It bears a Navajo word meaning "Mexican waters."

**ORAIBI WASH** (Navajo) Oraibi is a Hopi expression for "eagle traps." The wash is an intermittent stream which originates at Black Mesa and flows about 85 miles into Tolapi Lakes.

**PAPAGO CREEK** (Coconino) This creek runs through Grand Canyon National Park. It was thought to come from the Papago word papah, meaning "beans" and ootam meaning "people," designating bean eaters. Actually part of the Papago word for bean is mawi, and its full expression was interpreted as "it is a bean."

**PARISSAWAMPITTS CANYON** (Coconino) Situated on the Kaibab Plateau above Crazy Jug Point, the waters of Parissawampitts flow into Tapeats Creek. Parissawampitts is a Paiute word meaning "boiling water," indicative of a spring in a canyon that bubbles (or boils) up from the ground.

**PINAL MOUNTAINS/CREEK** (Gila) First settled by the Yavapai Indians, the Apaches later took over the land near the stream. Pinal is an Apache word for "deer." The Yavapais called the mountain walkama, meaning "pine mountains." Silver was discovered in the mountains, but because of the Apache Indians no mining took place until about 1870. One of the richest lodes was the Silver King Mine. A group of miners later discovered the Globe Claim, and by 1876 the town of Globe had been established along Pinal Creek. The mountains rise about 7,800 feet.

**SANENECHECK PEAK** (Navajo) This isolated peak is about 6,680 feet high and located on the Navajo Indian Reservation. It was interpreted as a Navajo word for "thief rock."

**SEGI MESAS** (Navajo) Situated on the Navajo Indian Reservation, these mesas bear the Navajo expression "rocky places," derived from tseye or tsegi. The name was also interpreted as "canyon" or "mesas trenched by canyons." Cliff dwellers once lived on the mesas and some of their ruins can still be seen.

**SEZHINI BUTTE** (Apache) This butte is also situated on the Navajo Indian Reservation, and is derived from the Navajo word, tzezhini, translated as "black rock."

**SHATO PLATEAU** (Navajo) Shato is part of the Navajo Indian Reservation. It is a Navajo word meaning "sunny side to water," descriptive of water that runs down the side of a rock wall that faces the rising sun. John Wetherill established a trading post in the area about 1915.

**SHINUMO ALTAR/CREEK** (Coconino) Photographer Frederick Dellenbaugh named this peak during the 1800s because it reminded him of an altar. Located in the Grand Canyon on the Navajo Indian Reservation, the name was translated from a Hopi word for "peace." Another interpretation was from a Paiute word for "old people cliff dwellers," their name for the Shinumu Indians who may have been a branch of the Hopi Indians. During the 1880s, William W. Bass came to the Grand Canyon searching for gold presumably hidden by a member of the Mountain Meadows Massacre. Unable to find the cache, Bass made his fortune by leading tours to the bottom of the Grand Canyon. He also built a trail from Havasu Point to the bottom of the Grand Canyon along Shinumo Creek.

**SHIVWITS PLATEAU** (Mohave) Located on the western part of Grand Canyon, the plateau was named by John Wesley Powell for a Paiute tribe called the Shivwits, meaning "people of the springs." It was also thought to be a Paiute word for "coyote spring," or "little people." Some copper mining was conducted on the plateau during the 1870s.

**SONOITA CREEK** (Santa Cruz) Bordered by cottonwood trees, the creek bears a Papago word for "corn place." The Sonoita is about eight miles long. When the Santa Fe Railroad built its branch line in the 1880s, it laid its tracks from Benson to Nogales along the full length of the creek.

**SONSELA BUTTE** (Apache)   Considered sacred to the Navajo Indians, Sonsela means "stars lying down," derived from the Navajo word sosila. This referred to legend of eight round stones which became iridescent at night. The name was also defined as "twin (or two) stars."

**TODOKOZH SPRING** (Apache)   Water in this spring is sulfurous, and so bears a descriptive Navajo word translated as "saline (or "bitter") water." The spring is situated on the Navajo Indian Reservation northeast of Salahkai Mesa.

**TOLANI LAKES** (Coconino)   Located on the Navajo Indian Reservation, this group of lakes bears a Navajo expression for "many waters." At one time a trading post was located along the lake shores.

**TSAILE CREEK/BUTTE**  (Apache) This creek originates in the Chuska Mountains and joins Canyon del Muerto and Canyon de Chelly. The butte, located near the community of Tsaile, is considered sacred by the Navajo Indians. Only the medicine men are allowed on the butte, who climb it to gather herbs for various ceremonies. Tsaile has a number of interpretations from the Navajo language: "standing black rock;" tseehili for "where water enters a box canyon;" tzezhin tsiits'iini, meaning "lava head" (the butte was a lava formation); and tlish bitsoo meaning "tongue of the snake."

**TSEDAA   HWIIDEZOHI   PEAK** (Navajo)   This is another feature considered sacred by the Navajo Indians, where

only the medicine men were allowed to venture. The Indians believed the peak was actually the home of the mythological being, Bide', who raised the deer. They also believed when a cloud settled over the cone-shaped peak, rain would come. The name is derived form the Navajo word tsedaa hwiidzohi, meaning "line on the canyon's edge," or "line carved into the rock."

**TSIN LANE CREEK** (Apache)   Flowing about 10 miles, the creek rises on the side of Mexican Cry Mesa, and is a tributary of Lukachukai Wash. Tsin Lane is derived from the Navajo word tsin lani, meaning "many trees."

**TUNICHA MOUNTAINS** (Apache) Located just west of the Chuska Mountains, these mountains are about 6,200 feet high and bear the Navajo name tontsaa, meaning "big water," descriptive of the many lakes in the mountains. They were first called Sierra de Tunecha by Lt. James Simpson in 1849. The Navajo Indians call the southeastern part of the mountain ch'oshgai, meaning "white spruce," and the northern part lok'a'ch'egai, meaning "reeds extending out white." The mountains stretch into New Mexico.

**TUZIGOOT NATIONAL MONUMENT** (Yavaipa)   Don Antonio de Espejo may have been the first white man to this area in 1583. Comprising about 42 acres, the monument is a remnant of one of the largest pueblos built by the ancient Sinagua Indians about 1100 A.D. They were gone by 1400 A.D. In July of 1939, the site was set up as a preserve for the pueblo of Pre-Columbian times. The pueblo contained more than 100 rooms. Tuzigoot may Apache for "crooked water."

**TYENDE CREEK** (Apache, Navajo) Rising from Black Mesa, this creek joins

Chinle Wash. Tyende may come from the Navajo word teendeeh, meaning "things fall into deeper water," or "where the animals fall in (or bog down)." This was in reference to pits that were dug to capture the animals, or natural muddy bogs along the creek that trapped them.

**UINKARETS PLATEAU** (Mohave) John Wesley Powell named the plateau and gave it a Paiute name interpreted as "pine mountain," or "where the pines grow." The plateau was created by molten lava that poured over the rim of the Grand Canyon millions of years ago.

**VEKOL MOUNTAIN** (Pinal) The mountain is located on the Papago Reservation. It is believed to be a Papago or Pima word for "grandmother," and was named after the Vekol Mine. In 1880, the Pima Indians told John Walker about an old silver mine and led him to its location. Walker was later offered more than $100,000 for the claim, but he refused to sell. The mine operated until it was abandoned in 1912.

**WEPO SPRINGS/WASH** (Navajo) Situated on the Hopi Indian Reservation, the springs are near the community of Walpi. Wepo is a Hopi word meaning "onion." It was also translated as "upper spring." During 1692, the Tewa Indians chased Ute Indians along Wepo Wash who had attacked the village of Oraibi during the Spanish Reconquest. In 1823, Colonel Jose Vizcarr and his men explored the region near this wash.

**WUPATKI NATIONAL MONUMENT** (Coconino)   The monument is north of Flagstaff and west of the Little Colorado River. Wuptaki is a Hopi word that means "great rain cloud ruins," and was given this name by J.S. Clark of Flagstaff. It was also interpreted as Hopi for "tall house," and "house of enemy ancestors." In prehistoric times the region was occupied by the Anasazi and Sinagua Indians. Hopi legend tells the story of ruins here that were once occupied by the Snake Clan people during their migration from the Grand Canyon where they came up from the Underground world. Navajo legend says the ancient ruins were destroyed by the elements because of the Anasazi's greed. The monument was created in 1924.

**YON DOT MOUNTAINS** (Coconino) The mountains are about 6,235 feet high and located near Bodaway Mesa. They bear the Navajo name derived from yaa ndee'nil meaning "series of hills going down."

# ARKANSAS

**BODKAU CREEK** (Hempstead)   The Bodkau is about 125 miles long and flows to the Red River in the state of Louisiana, where it becomes Bayou Bodcau in Bossier Parish. The name may have been derived from Botka, a Muskogean word meaning "wide," but its origin is suspect.

**DORCHEAT BAYOU** (Nevada)   This 115-mile-long bayou flows into Louisiana and enters Lake Bistineau. International Paper established its company along the bayou because of the wealth of timber it could use in its manufacture of paper. During the early 1800s, the bayou was the only means of transportation in certain regions. Dorcheat may come from a Caddo word meaning "people" or "clan." Or it may have meant "gap," from datche, supposedly after a bear ate a "gap" in a piece of timber.

**OUACHITA MOUNTAINS/RIVER/ LAKE** (Perry, Yell, Scott)   Ouachita was derived from the Choctaw word washita, meaning "good hunting grounds," or "hunting trip." It was also translated as "sparkling silver water." Running east and west, the mountains stretch from Little Rock to the state of Oklahoma, where the Quapaw Indians lived. During the 1700-1800s, the Cherokee Indians moved to the mountains after they were forced from their homes. The river rises in the Ouachita Mountains, is about 70 miles long and travels through the states of Arkansas and Louisiana. Confederate soldiers used the river as a means of transportation during the Civil War. Lake Ouachita in within the Ouachita National Forest and was formed when the Army Corps of Engineers built a dam in 1953 for flood control. The lake comprises about 48,000 acres, and contains one of the largest crystal veins in the world.

# CALIFORNIA

**ANACAPA    ISLAND    (Ventura)** Anacapa is located about 14 miles off the coast of the city of Ventura. The first explorer to sight the island was Juan Rodriguez Cabrillo in 1852. Gaspar de Portola visited the island in 1770, followed by Juan Perez in 1774 who named it Isletas de Santa Tomas. When explorer George Vancouver arrived at the island in the late 1700s, he renamed it eneeapah, taken from the Chumash word, eneepah, meaning "island of deception," "mirage," or "ever changing." It was spelled Anacapa by the U.S. Coast Survey in 1852. In the late 1700s and on into the 1800s, Russian, British and American fur traders searched the island's coves and shorelines for sea otter. Because its fur was highly valued, the otter was hunted almost to extinction. For a period of time, George Nidever used the island to raise sheep. During prohibition, it was a haven for bootleggers who stored their liquor there. Today, the island is owned by the U.S. Government.

**AVAWATZ MOUNTAINS** (San Bernardino)   Tradition says the Spanish were mining for gold in this region long before the arrival of white prospectors. Miners discovered silver and gold in the mountains and worked the diggings off and on during the 1850s. The mountains are south of Death Valley and were named ivawatch by the Paiute Indians, which means "mountain sheep." The spelling was later changed to Avawatz.

**BOLAM CREEK/GLACIER** (Siskiyou) This name was derived from a Wintu word, part of which means "peak." The creek is located on the north slope of Mount Shasta, as is Bolam Glacier. Its meltwater drains into Bolam Creek, which flows into Whitney and Graham Creeks.

**BOLLIBOKKA MOUNTAINS** (Shasta) Bollibokka is a combination of two Wintu words, bolla and boka, translated as "black bush," and may refer to the black-berried manzanita prevalent in the region. Others believe it comes from buli and phaqa for "mountain manzanita."

**BULLY CHOOP PEAK** (Trinity)   This peak, located near the Whiskeytown National Recreation Area, is home to a fire lookout station that was built in the 1930s. Bully Choop was derived from the Wintu phrase boli chuip, interpreted as "high sharp peak" or "sharp point." During 1849, gold was discovered in the mountains.

**CAHTO CREEK** (Humboldt)   This region was home to the Cahto (or Kato) Indians. A lake once covered the valley and created swamp-like conditions, so the creek bears an appropriate name "water mush." It was derived from the Pomo Indian words cah and to.

**CAPAY VALLEY** (Yolo)   Part of this valley is now covered by Lake Berryessa. It was home to the Pomo Indians until white settlement. Nasario Antonio purchased land in the valley during the 1830s and established a ranch, using the range for grazing more than 25,000 head of cattle and horses. Capay is a Wintu word for "stream."

**CHEMEHUEVI MOUNTAINS** (San Bernardino)   In 1853, Lt. A.W. Whipple led a government survey to this region to see if a transcontinental railroad would be viable. Located near the Colorado River, the mountains were named for the Chemehuevi Indians who were part of a Shoshonean tribe. Their name origin is obscure, but they called themselves Nuwu ("people"). The Pima Indians called them aha-lakat, meaning "small bows," while the Yuma's name for the Chemehuevis was mat-hatevach ("northerners").

**CHOWCHILLA RIVER** (Madera)   One of the first recorded references to the Chowchilla Indians was in the memoirs of John C. Fremont. This war-like tribe (a band of the Yokut Indians) made its home along the Chowchilla River. Their name was interpreted as "killers," because they were an aggressive tribe. Other translations were "dry river," "hot dish," and "horse thief."

**CLIKAPUDI CREEK** (Shasta)   A Wintu village was located along this stream until attacked by the Yana Indians because they believed the Wintus were infringing on their traditional hunting ground. Clika-pudi has been interpreted as "battle ground," in reference to the attack, or "kill," after traders supposedly poisoned the Indians near the creek.

**CONCOW VALLEY** (Butte)   The valley was once home to the peaceful Maidu Indians, notably the Concow band. They were eventually removed to the Round Valley Reservation. Concow is a Maidu word derived from ko-young-kau, which means "plain earth" (or "place"). During the 1850s, there was some quartz mining conducted in the region.

**COSO HOT SPRINGS** (Inyo)   Of uncertain origin, Coso may mean "broken coal," or "charcoal" in the Shoshone language. It was also interpreted as "fire." A miner named M.H. Farley made the first written record of the springs in 1860. Frank Adams established a resort at the springs about 1912, which brought people who took advantage of the waters believing they had curative powers.

**COSUMNES RIVER** (El Dorado, Sacramento)   The Cosumnes rises in the Sierra Nevada Mountains and enters the Mokelumne River. It was thought to be a Miwok word meaning "salmon people." Others interpreted it as "fish" or "salmon." Extensive gold mining was conducted along the river in the 1800s.

**CUYAMA RIVER/VALLEY** (Ventura)   The valley and river were once inhabited by the Chumash Indians until the 1800s when the land was taken over by cattle ranchers. Cuyama River rises in North Ventura County and flows about 85 miles to the Santa Maria River. It is a Chumash word derived from kuyam, translated as "clams."

**CUYAMACA PEAK** (San Diego)   The region was home to the Kumeyaay Indians who called the peak ah-ha-kwe-ah-mac, meaning "the place where it rains." Another interpretation was from ekwiamak, meaning "rain above." Located in the Cuyamaca Rancho State Park, the peak is about 6,512 feet high.

**DEKKAS CREEK** (Shasta)   Dekkas is a Wintu word derived from da-kas, interpreted as "climb up." The creek joins the McCloud River.

**DIDALLAS CREEK** (Shasta)   This name was derived from a Wintu word meaning "daybreak." The creek enters Squaw Creek.

**ELTERPOM CREEK** (Trinity)   Elterpom was thought to be a Wintu word, part of which means "ground" or "land." It is a tributary of the South Fork of the Trinity River.

**GUALALA RIVER** (Sonoma, Mendocino)   Gualala may be a Spanish rendering of the Pomo word walali, meaning "water coming down place," which described the river flowing through the woods and down to the sea. The name was applied to the river by Ernest Rufus, captain of Sutter's Indian Company. The community of Gualala, originally a land grant given to General Rafael Gracie, was founded after his grant was made invalid by the court.

**GUATAY MOUNTAIN** (San Diego)   Guatay was interpreted from the Diegueno word kwaitai, meaning "large," descriptive of the mountain's size. It was also thought to mean "big house," from waa-tay, referring to a large tepee, or kwa'tay, meaning "the big one." At one time a rare cypress grew on the side of the mountain, which the Indians called eel-shhar ("grows only here").

**HETCH HETCHY VALLEY** (Tuolumne)   Situated in Yosemite National Park, the valley was discovered in 1850 by Joseph Screech. Hetch Hetchy is a Central Miwok word that described a type of grass or plant with seeds the Indians gathered for food. Another definition was "trees," or "valley of the two trees," indicative of two yellow pine trees at the end of the valley. The Northern Paiutes traveled to the valley to gather acorns for their winter stores. John Muir tried to get the U.S. Government to preserve the valley, but in order to bring power and water to San Francisco, the O'Shaughnessy Dam was built in 1923, and the valley was innundated.

**IAQUA BUTTES** (Humboldt)   An exploration party came upon the resident Whilkut Indians in 1851 and were greeted with ay-a-qui-ya, interpreted as "hello" or "good day" (from where Iaqua was derived). The buttes are contained in the Old Growth Reserve and preserved by the Bureau of Land Management.

**IVANPAH MOUNTAINS** (San Bernardino)   Ivanpah is Southern Paiute for "good (or "clear") water." Local legend says the name means "dove spring," but the evidence is not supported. The Ivanpah Mountains contain the only known dinosaur tracks in California, and also the world's largest Joshua tree forest. The mountains were exploited for its silver in the 1800s.

**JOLON CREEK** (Monterey)   Once home to the Salinan Indians, the village of Jolon was established in 1860 along this creek as a gold camp. Not much gold was found, and Jolon soon became a ghost town. Jolon may be a Salinan word for "place of meeting," or "place of dead oaks," which referred to the Spaniards' method of girdling the trees, then later using the dead wood for various purposes.

**KAWEAH RIVER** (Tulare)   First called

Four Creeks, the name was changed in 1853 to Kaweeyah, a Yokut word meaning "I sit down," or from kah-wah, defined as "I squat here," or "here I rest." It was also interpreted as "crow water," indicative of the buzzards and crows by the thousands that inhabited the site. The river rises in the Sierra Nevada and empties into the Tulare Lake Basin. There was some gold mining along the river, but not much was taken out and the miners left for more productive gold fields. The river was discovered by the Gabriel Moraga Expedition in 1806.

**KEKAWAKA CREEK** (Trinity)   This creek bears the Wintu word wailaki, meaning "north language," in reference to Wintu tribes who lived north of the stream. Another interpretation was from keka waka meaning "creek frog."

**KIBESILLAH MOUNTAIN** (Mendocino)   Coast Survey member John Rockwell made mention of this name in 1878. The former village of Kibesillah was founded in 1867 by H. Chadbourne, with logging providing its main source of industry. Kibesillah was derived from the Pomo word kabe sila meaning "rock flat." It was also interpreted as "head of the valley," descriptive of the mountain's topography.

**KOIP PEAK** (Tuolumne)   Koip Peak is located in Yosemite National Park. Willard Johnson, who was a member of the U.S. Geologic Survey, named this peak about 1883. It is about 12,979 feet tall, and bears the Paiute name, koipa, meaning "mountain sheep," or koi-kill, interpreted as "that which is killed."

**KOKOWEEP PEAK** (San Bernardino) Kokoweep was thought to be a Paiute word for "canyon of winds." This was in reference to the wind that blows through a canyon that winds through Mineral Springs to Ivanpah and into a valley where the peak is located.

**KONOCTI, MOUNT** (Lake) This mountain, which is also a dormant volcano, is about 4,300 feet high and was first named Mount McKee for an explorer in 1851. It was later renamed Uncle Sam Mountain. The U.S. Geographic Board changed it to Konocti, derived from kno'ktai, a Pomo Indian word interpreted as "mountain woman" or "thrown horse." The latter is indicative of the mountain's shape. Mount Konocti was once the site of a mercury mine.

**KUNA PEAK** (Tuolumne) Willard Johnson with the U.S. Geologic Survey named this peak in 1883, which may be Mono Indian word for "fire wood," or Shoshone for simply "fire." Conversely, the town of Kuna, Idaho, bears the Shoshone expression interpreted as "the end," descriptive of the end of the railroad line at that point.

**LOSPE MOUNTAIN** (Santa Barbara) Lospe is a Chumash word, ospe, meaning "flower field." The mountain is located near the town of Guadalupe.

**MATILIJA CREEK/SPRINGS** (Ventura) The region was once home to the Chumash Indians. J.W. Wilcox discovered the springs in 1873. After bathing in them for several weeks, he noticed his injuries from the Mexican War were healing. In 1875, R.M. Brown built the Arroya Matilija resort along the creek, and people flocked here to use the healing water. The county built a dam across the creek to prevent flooding on the Ventura River, and later sold the resort to a private party, so the springs are no longer open. Matilija is a Chumash word meaning "poppy."

**MATTOLE RIVER** (Humboldt) The Mattole (or Medol) Indians were resident here until the white man entered the region. Rising in the Coast Range, the river terminates at the Pacific Ocean near Cape Mendocino. It has been defined as a Mattole word for "clear water."

**METTAH CREEK** (Humboldt) Home to the Yurok Indians, this name means simply "creek." During 1872, Camp Mettah was built to protect settlers from the Yuroks.

**MONACHE MOUNTAIN** (Tulare) The mountain is located in the Sequoia National Forest near the community of Olancha. It is derived from the Yokut word mo'nekh, which means "fly."

**MONO LAKE** (Mono) Mark Twain once said of this 700,000 year-old lake that it was a "sullen, silent, sail-less sea."[2] The lake is three times saltier than the ocean and may be the oldest lake in North America. Resident Mono Indians traded brine fly grubs they harvested from the lake to the Yokuts in exchange for acorns. Mono is derived from the Yokut word monachi which means "flies." First record of the name was by Lt. Tredwell Moore's party in July of 1852.

**MUGU, POINT** (Ventura) Juan Cabrillo was mapping these coastal waters during 1542 and made landfall near the point. He named it Point Mugu, which is derived from the Chumash word muwu (or mu'wa) meaning "seashore" or "beach." President Truman approved a new missile center there in 1946, which was built three years later. The Naval Air Missile Center was created for the purpose of supporting its Test Center. The site had earlier been used as a training site for the Seabees during World War II.

**NAWTAWAKET CREEK** (Shasta) This creek bears the Wintu Indian expression naw and waket, meaning "south creek." It is a tributary of the McCloud River.

**NEGIT ISLAND** (Mono)   In 1882, member of the U.S. Geological Survey, L.C. Russell, gave this small island in Mono Lake its name. It is a Mono Indian word interpreted as "blue-winged goose," and may have referred to the seagulls that nest on the island. It is the habitat of more than 40,000 California gulls that breed there in the spring.

**NOPAH RANGE** (Inyo)   Members of the U.S. Geological Survey named this range in the early 1900s. Nopah is a Paiute word translated as "water" or "no water range." Nopa Peak rises about 6,395 feet. During 1875, silver was discovered in the mountain range.

**OLANCHA   PEAK/PASS**   (Inyo) Olancha was taken from the Yokuts Tribe who called themselves Yaudanchi. The name was interpreted as "sleeping beauty," possibly in reference to a feature on the peak that resembles a reclining woman. About 1862, Minnard Farley explored the region and named the pass.

**OTAY MOUNTAIN** (San Diego)   Located in the Otay Mountain Wilderness, the mountain bears a Diegueno Indian word that means "brushy" and may be descriptive of the region. The mountain contains the world's largest stand of Tecate cypress trees.

**PALA MOUNTAIN** (San Diego)   Rising about 1,900 feet above sea level, Pala is a Temecula (or Pala) word meaning "water," and was named by Chief Nahachish when he went to the mountain to get water. The Tourmaline King is an active mining claim located on Pala Indian Reservation near the mountain.

**PAOHA ISLAND/LAKE** (Mono)   In 1882, L.C. Russell of the U.S. Geologic Sur-

vey named this island (as he did Negit Island). It is derived from a Mono Indian word pauha, interpreted as "water babies." Indian legend says the island was haunted by spirit children who held celebrations in the moonlight, their hair resembling vapor wreaths that rose from the hot springs. The lake was named by Elden H. Vestal in 1951, but he interpreted the name from a Paiute word for "white" or "daylight."

**PATTYMOCUS MOUNTAIN** (Siskiyou)   Pattymocus is a Wintu word meaning "basket upside down," descriptive of the mountain's shape.

**PETALUMA CREEK** (Sonoma)   This name is taken from the Miwok words, pe'ta and lu-ma, meaning "flatback," descriptive of the Indian village situated on a low hill. This region was visited by Captain Fernando Quiros in 1776, when he followed the creek's course in search of Bodega Bay. The town of Petaluma was established along the creek, and became one of the busiest ports in the state transporting supplies on schooners and steamboats.

**PIRU CREEK** (Ventura)   The Piru Indians were part of the Haminot Tribe, whose name may be derived from pi-id-huky, or pi'idhuku, meaning "plant," "sedge," or "grass." This plant was used by the Indian women to make baskets. About 1842, a small amount of gold was discovered, but the region became better known for its fruit ranchos.

**POKYWAKET CREEK** (Shasta)   This tributary of McCloud River takes its name from the Wintu expression po-kee and waket, meaning "raw creek." The Wintu Indians gathered raw acorns and brought them to the creek to be cured.

**PUTAH CREEK** (Lake)   William Wolfskill named the creek in 1841, which may be a Patwin word that means, in part, "east." The stream empties into the Yolo Basin. A small mining camp was established during the late 1800s when a fair amount of gold was discovered there.

**SANEL MOUNTAIN** (Mendocino) The mountain was named for a Pomo Indian village, derived from Se-nel or Shanel, meaning "sweathouse" or "ceremonial house."

**SCHONCHIN BUTTE** (Siskiyou)   Located in Lava Beds National Monument, Schonchin was the name of a Modoc chief, but the origin is unknown. He was one of the chiefs who signed a peace treaty in 1864. Local tradition says that during the signing, he pointed to this butte and said the butte would fall before his people would ever go to war with the whites. He kept his word, but his brother was a participant in the Modoc War in 1872. A fire lookout was built on the butte in 1939 by the Civilian Conservation Corpsmen.

**SEIAD CREEK** (Siskiyou)   A member of the Whitney Survey named this creek in 1863, which was once home to the Shasta Indians. Seiad was interpreted as a Yurok word for "far away land." Gold was exploited along the creek during the 1890s, mainly drift and hydraulic mining.

**SESPE CREEK** (Ventura)   Sespe is a Chumash word meaning "knee cap." The junction of this creek with the Santa Clara River was the site where the Southern Pacific Railroad came through in 1886.

**SHASTA, MOUNT** (Siskiyou)   The Shastas called themselves weohaw, meaning "stone house," which designated a cave in the region. Located in the Cascade Range, Mount Shasta is one of the range's highest and biggest volcanoes. Peter Skene Ogden may have given Shasta its name in

1827, but some authorities disagree, believing Ogden was actually near Mt. McLoughlin. Indian legend says the great spirit made this mountain because the rest of the land was so flat. So he made a hole in the sky and forced ice and snow down the hole to form the mountain.

**SISKIYOU MOUNTAINS** (Siskiyou) In 1827, Peter Skene Ogden with the Hudson's Bay Company was the first white man across these mountains. Siskiyou may be a Chinook word meaning "bobtailed horse." Tradition says the mountains were named in 1828 by Alexander McLeod of the Hudson's Bay Company after he lost a horse in one of the mountain passes. Part of the Siskiyou Mountains stretch over into Oregon.

**SISQUOC RIVER** (Santa Barbara) There was once a Chumash Indian camp along this river called Asuskwa, from where Sisquoc was derived, meaning "quail," an abundant bird in the area. The Sisquoc flows through the San Rafael Wilderness near of the town Santa Barbara and winds down to the valleys of Santa Maria and Arroyo Grande.

**TAHOE LAKE** (Placer/El Dorado) When Mark Twain visited this region and saw the lake, he thought it was one of the most beautiful places in the world. The lake was used by the Washoe Indians as their summer camp. First called Lake Bigler, it was later changed to Tahoe, from the Washoe word, da-a-wa-ga, which means "edge of lake." Others derived it from Da-o, meaning "deep" and "blue," or tah-oo-ee, for "a great deal of water." The lake is about 22 miles long and 12 miles wide.

**TAHQUITZ PEAK** (Riverside)   Located in the San Jacinto Mountain Range, this peak was believed to be the home of an evil spirit according to Cahuilla legend. The spirit made its present known to the Indians by swooping down in the form of a meteor with a long tail. Tahguitz bears the Cahuilla word for this spirit, derived from tahkoosh or talwish. The name was recorded in 1897.

**TAJIGUAS CREEK** (Santa Barbara) The creek takes its name from a Chumash village once located along the stream. It may be derived from tayiyas, descriptive of the holly-leaved cherry that grew in the region.

**TALLAC, MOUNT/LAKE** (El Dorado) When the Whitney Survey came this way, they wrote in their field notes the name Crystal Peak. It was changed to Tallac in 1877 by the Wheeler Survey, a Washoe word derived from dala'ak, meaning "large mountain," or tahlac, for "great mountain." In 1878 E.J. Baldwin purchased about 1,000 acres of land along the lake and built Tallac House, a resort hotel that operated until about 1920.

**TAMALPAIS, MOUNT** (Marin) Rising about 2,570 feet high, Tamalpais overlooks San Francisco Bay. It was interpreted from the Miwok word tamal pawi, for "western mountain" or "bay mountain." It was also attributed to a Tamal word for "mountain." In 1896, a standard broad gauge railroad was built to the mountain, and was considered the most crooked railway on earth. It consisted of over 280 curves, one of which was in the shape of a bow knot, and ascended more than 2,500 feet. The engine wheels were designed to clamp the rails as they progressed up the mountain.

**TECTAH CREEK** (Humboldt) This little creek may be derived from te'kta wroi, a Yurok word defined as "log creek."

**TECUYA CREEK** (Kern) An inland group of Chumash Indians known as the Emigdian once lived along the creek. They differed in that they avoided all contact with the white man, unlike their coastal relatives. Tecuya is from the Chumash word takuy, which means "holding."

**TEHACHAPI MOUNTAINS/PASS** (Kern) The pass was traveled by settlers working their way further west. Members of the Pacific Railroad named the pass Taheechaypah in 1853, but the spelling was later changed. Tehachapi may have been derived in part from ti'aci, meaning "to freeze" in Southern Paiute. Another interpretation was from a Shoshonean word, tahichipi, for "crow's nest," or "land of plenty of acorns and good water." The mountains were home to the Great Basin people called the Kawaiisu, who foraged for the rich food supply in the Tehachapis.

**TEHIPITE VALLEY** (Fresno) In 1869, Frank Dusy discovered this valley, and took the first photos of it ten years later. Dusy was the founder of Fresno and Tulare Counties and also named some features in the Sierra Nevada Mountains. Tehipite may be a Mono Indian word meaning "high rock," descriptive of a massive granite tower.

**TENAYA LAKE** (Mariposa) Lafayette Bunnell, who was part of Boling's Mariposa Battalion, named the lake in 1851. He wrote: "Looking back to the lovely lake, where we had been encamped during the night, and watching Ten-ei-ya as he ascended to our group, I suggested to the captain that we name the lake after the old chief…"[3] Chief Tenaya, a Yosemite Indian, was later hunted by Boling and managed to elude him, but he was later killed by the Mono Indians. The chief's name origin is not known.

**TINEMAHA, MOUNT/CREEK** (Inyo) The mountain took its name from the creek, which was named by Chester Versteeg about 1935. The name honors a Paiute chief named Tinemaha (or Tinemaker; origin unknown).

**TISH-TANG-A-TANG CREEK** (Humboldt)   The Hoopa Indians established a village along this creek. Somehow the white settlers corrupted the Hoopa word, djictanadin, thought to mean "neck of land projecting into the water."

**TOPA TOPA MOUNTAINS** (Ventura) Located near the town of Ojai, these mountains were named for a rancheria inhabited by the Chumash Indians. It was derived from topotopow, meaning "many gophers."

**TRANQUILLON MOUNTAIN** (Santa Barbara)   The mountain, which is a plug of an ancient volcano, is part of the Santa Ynez Mountain Range. The Coast Survey named it Arguello, which was changed by William Eimbeck in 1873 to Tranquillon, a Chumash word that describes a type of grain.

**TRUCKEE RIVER** (Placer)   The river was named in 1884 for Paiute Chief Truckee. Explorers met the chief while scouting for water, and thought his name was tro-kay ("all right"). The Truckee flows 100 miles and joins the Little Truckee River. During the late 1800s, the Truckee River was a major highway for the transportation of logs from the mountains to the lumber mills.

**TUCKI MOUNTAIN** (Inyo)   Located in Death Valley National Monument, the mountain is part of the Panamint Range. Tucki may be a Shoshone word meaning "sheep." During the 1800s, the mountains were found to have a wealth of silver.

**TUJUNGA CREEK** (Los Angeles)   Located in the Los Angeles basin, Tujunga is derived from the Southern Paiute word ti'anga, which means "mountain ridge."

**TUNE CREEK** (Shasta)   Tune comes from a Wintu word meaning "the end." The creek is a tributary of McCloud River.

**TUOLUMNE RIVER** (Tuolumne) When explorer Alferez Morago visited in 1806, he called the river Rio de Dolores (Spanish for "river of sorrows"). It was later changed to Tuolumne, thought to be from the Miwok word talmalamne, for "stone wigwams." Of course, there were no stone wigwams, but the expression probably referred to the Indians who sometimes lived in caves. The river rises in the Sierra Nevada Mountains and enters the San Joaquin River.

**UMUNHUM, MOUNT** (Santa Clara) Rising 3,486 feet, Mount Umunhum is the second largest peak in the Santa Cruz Mountain Range. Almaden Air Force Station was established there and operated from 1956 to 1980. Umunhum is a Costanoan word meaning "hummingbird," representative of their mythology that the hummingbird was one of the creators of the earth.

**WAUCOBA MOUNTAIN** (Inyo) This feature rises about 11,123 feet. It is a Paiute word for the bull pine. Its seeds were harvested by the Indian for their winter stores.

**WEICHPEC SPRING** (Humboldt) Weichpec Spring is located on the Hoopa Indian Reservation at the junction of the Trinity and Klamath rivers. The Indians established their village along the stream and named it Weitspus, a Yurok word meaning "at the forks." Weichpec is a corruption of weitspus. During the early 1800s a white settlement was located near the village.

**WITTAWAKET CREEK** (Shasta) Wittawaket is a tributary of the McCloud River. The name originates from the Wintu word, wittawaket, meaning "the creek that turns around," descriptive of the creek's shape.

**YCATAPOM PEAK** (Shasta) This peak is about 7,596 high and located in the Trinity Alps. It bears a Wintu word meaning "leaning mountain." Others defined it as "where the big chief lives."

**YOLLA BOLLY MOUNTAINS** (Trinity, Tehama) This mountain bears a Wintu name that means "snow mountain," or "high snow covered peak."

**YOSEMITE VALLEY/NATIONAL PARK** (Mariposa) Joseph Walker and his expedition were the first white men to see the valley in 1833. Lafayette Bunnell, who was with the Mariposa Battalion (in pursuit of the Yosemite Indians), sug-gested the name Yosemite in 1851. He chose the Yosemite word that means "grizzly bear." In 1864, an Act of Congress gave the valley to the state, which in 1906 became part of Yosemite National Park.

**ZACA LAKE** (Santa Barbara) The Chumash Indians who lived here believed the lake was formed when Thunder made a big hole in the ground. After one of the braves saw Thunder and scorned it, the other Indians fled in fear. When they returned they discovered the Indian was gone, and in his place was the lake. Zaca may be the Chumash word for "peace" or "quiet place."

**ZAYANTE CREEK** (Santa Cruz) A German named Major Graham settled here about 1841 and built what may have been the first power sawmill in the state. Zayante may be a Indian proper name, but its origin is not known.

# COLORADO

**ACHONEE MOUNTAIN** (Grand) Situated in the Indian Peaks Wilderness, Achonee is about 12,649 feet high. It was named for Ochinee, a Cheyenne or Arapaho chief, whose name means "one eye." In 1864, he and his band were camped at Sand Creek when the Army, led by Colonel Chivington, attacked and slaughtered the Indians, including Ochinee. During 1864, Mary Hudnal, granddaughter of Ochinee, wrote: "Grandfather Ochinee (One-Eye) escaped from the camp, but seeing that all his people were to be slaugh-tered, he deliberately chose to go back into the one-sided battle and die with them rather than survive along…" When Mary's mother was asked if she knew Chivington, she said "Know Colonel Chivington? I should. He was my father's murderer!"[4]

**ANTERO, MOUNT** (Chaffee) Antero is located in the Sawatch Range and rises about 14,269 feet. The Hayden Survey may have named the peak in 1870, honoring Ute Chief Antero (origin unknown) who worked to promote peace with the whites during the 1860s. He was also one of the signatories to the Washington Treaty of 1880. At one time miners thought the mountain contained silver, but none was ever found. However, in 1884 Nathaniel Wanemaker discovered blue aquamarine in the mountain, which is still the only viable gem source for this stone.

**APIATAN MOUNTAIN** (Grand)   This mountain is about 10,319 feet high, and named for a Kiowa Indian chief, a singer of songs, whose works were published in *The Indian Book*, by Natalie Curtis. His name was interpreted as "wooden lance," and referred to a feathered ceremonial lance. Apiatan was a delegate to Washington, D.C. and a protester of the government's plan to open up reservation land.

**APISHAPA RIVER** (Las Animas) Apishapa River is 117-miles long and originates in the Sangre de Crisco Mountains, flowing into the Arkansas River. It may be a Kiowa word meaning "stagnant (or "stinking") water," because at certain times of the year the water became quite sluggish. During the 1840s there was a stage station and mail route operating along the river.

**ARIKAREE RIVER** (Yuma)   This river was named for the Arikaree Indians, and means "horn," in reference to bones they fastened in their hair for adornment. The river is about 130 miles long and is a tributary of the Republican River in the state of Nebraska.

**COCHETOPA PASS** (Saguache)   In the Ute language, Cochetopa means "buffalo gate," or "pass of the buffalo," descriptive of the Indians and buffalo who used the pass to travel between the Gunnison region and San Luis Valley. During the 1850s, the U.S. Congress authorized a survey for potential rail routes between the

Mississippi River and the Pacific Ocean. The route through the pass was later used by Union Pacific Railroad for its transcontinental railroad.

**CURENCANTI PASS** (Gunnison)   Rising 10,450 feet, Curencanti was the name of a Ute Chief named Curicata, who used the region as his hunting grounds. His name origin is unknown.

**ENENTAH, MOUNT** (Grand)   Mount Enentah is situated in Rocky Mountain National Park. The name was derived from the Arapaho expression enetah-notaiyah, meaning "man mountain." This descriptive name referred to a stand of pine trees near the mountain's summit that resembled a man's head.

**HIAMOVI MOUNTAIN** (Grand)   Hiamovi is about 12,395 feet high. It was thought to have been named for a Cheyenne Indian chief who contributed songs and legends to *The Indian Book*, written by Natalie Curtis in 1908. His name was interpreted as "god," "spirit," or "high chief."

**KANNAH CREEK** (Mesa)   Early settlers were James Ponsford and his family about 1884. An immigrant from England where he was a hotel porter, Ponsford built the Melrose House Hotel along the creek in 1908. Most of the guests were sheep and cattle ranchers. Kannah was derived from the Ute word, kanav meaning "willow," or from kanawiya, for "a valley with willows." Another interpretation was from the Ute expression meaning "tipi pole."

**KAWUNEECHEE VALLEY** (Grand) Arapaho Indians named the valley through which the Colorado River flows. Kawuneechee was derived from the Arapaho expression koo'oh neechee (or cawoonache), meaning "wolf" or "coyote chief."

**KENOSHA PASS** (Park)    A stagecoach driver from Kenosha, Wisconsin, is credited with naming the pass. Kenosha is a Chippewa word meaning "pike fish." Probably the only thing significant that occurred over this pass was a stagecoach robbery in 1864. The Reynold gang from Texas took about $40,000 in currency and gold dust valued at $23,000.

**KIOWA CREEK** (Elbert)    This creek is often dry. An exception was in 1878 when a horrendous cloudburst occurred on the South Platte-Arkansas divide and inundated Kiowa Creek at its headwaters. The stream bears the name of the Kiowa Indians, and means "principal people." Another interpretation was from kwuda, meaning "going out." The community of Elbert was settled about 1860 in the Kiowa Creek area.

**NAKAI PEAK** (Grand)    The peak bears a Navajo word meaning "Spanish people," or "white stranger." It was the name of a Navajo council member Raymond Nakai, and also a clan of the Navajo Indians, called Nakai Denih. The peak is about 12,216 feet high.

**NANITA LAKE** (Grand)    Nanita has been interpreted as a Navajo word, which designated the Plains Indians. It was also thought to be a Comanche word descriptive of a tribe of Indians from Texas. The lake is located in Rocky Mountain National Park.

**NARRAGUINEEP CANYON** (Dolores)    In 1885, Fort Narraguineep was built at the head of Narraguineep Canyon to protect local cattle ranchers from the Indians. Its name was derived from the Ute word naragwinap, meaning "battleground," an interesting name because the Indians never attacked the fort.

**NEOTO, MOUNT** (Larimer/Grand)

Located on the Continental Divide, the mountain is about 11,734 feet high. Neoto may be derived from the Arapaho expression hoho'eniinote'hitte, interpreted as "mountain sheep's heart."

**NOKONI LAKE** (Grand)    Nokoni was thought to be the name of a band of Comanche Indians, whos name was translated as "traveling in a circle. The lake is located in Rocky Mountain National Park.

**ONAHU CREEK** (Grand)    The creek flows through Rocky Mountain National Park. It may be an Arapaho word meaning "warms himself" referring to an Indian's horse that warmed himself by the campfire on cold nights.

**O-WI-YU-KUTS PLATEAU** (Moffat)    The plateau bears the name of an Indian Chief, whose name was also spelled Awaiukut. It was also interpreted from the Ute word uwaayakach, meaning "they're not coming," or uwayakach, for "it's not raining."

**PAHLONE PEAK** (Chaffee)    Rising 12,667 feet, this peak was named for Ute Chief Ouray's son, Pahlone. His name was also interpreted as "short hair," and "thunder."

**PICEANCE CREEK** (Rio Blanco)    Originally spelled Pic Ance, the name was changed to Piceance, an unidentified Indian expression meaning "tall grass." This creek contained the only known source of natural sodium bicarbonate that was used to make household products.

**PONCHA SPRINGS** (Chaffee)    Before white settlement, the Ute Indians used these springs. When the town of Poncha Springs was established, it took its name from the springs. An early settler named Joe Hartwick attempted to grow tobacco here using the water from the springs and became quite successful. Poncha means "tobacco," but the tribal designation is obscure.

**RAWAH PEAKS** (Larimer)    There are two peaks with the same name: North Rawah at 12,473 feet high, and South Rawah which rises 12,644 feet. The name was derived from the Ute word ura'wa, which means "crest of a mountain ridge."

**SAWATCH RANGE** (Gunnison, Chaffee, Saguache)    Nicknamed the "backbone of the continent," the range is about 100 miles long and overlooks the Arkansas Valley. An expedition from Harvard University came to the region in 1869 and named the peaks in the Sawatch Range Princeton, Harvard and Yale. Prospectors rushed to the mountains when gold and silver were discovered in the 1860s. Sawatch is derived from the Ute word sa-qua-qua-chi-pa, meaning "blue earth" or "water at the blue earth."

**SHAVANO MOUNTAIN** (Chaffee) This mountain was named for Tabeguache Ute Chief Shavano, whose name means "blue flowers." Another interpretation was from the Shawnee word for "southerner." The Angel of Shavano is a distinctive feature on the eastern face of this peak and resembles an angel. The mountain is about 14,229 feet tall and was first climbed by Charles Fay in 1888.

**TABEGUACHE MOUNTAIN/CREEK** (Chaffee)    These features were named for the Tabeguache Ute Indian band. The name was reported as meaning "place where the snow melts first." It may have been derived from mogwataviingwantsingwii, meaning "cedar bark sun-slope people." The mountain is 14,155 feet high. Found only on the Uncompahgre Plateau area are the Desert Bighorns, with the main populations along Tabeguache Creek.

**TAHOSA VALLEY** (Larimer, Boulder) The valley is situated between Rocky Mountain National Park, privately held land, and Roosevelt National Forest. In 1885, Enos Mills built his cabin, which later became the Long's Peak Inn. Today it is a conference center run by the Salvation Army. Mills was partly responsible for Estes Park being established in 1915. Tahosa may be a Kiowa word meaning "dwellers of the mountain tops."

**TANIMA PEAK** (Boulder)    First known as Kirkwood, Tanima was derived from the Comanche expression tanumutuhka, meaning "liver eaters." Tanima was also the name of an Indian tribe. The peak is located in Rocky Mountain National Park and rises about 12,420 feet.

**TIMPAS CREEK** (Otero)    Timpas Creek flows 54 miles to the Arkansas River near the town of Swink. During 1866, a stagecoach station was established along the creek, which was an important source of water for those traveling the Santa Fe Trail. The town of Timpas took its name from the creek, but it was short-lived because the water was saline and sporadic, so irrigation attempts failed. Timpas was derived from a Southern Paiute word, tump, for "stone," or "iron."

**TOMICHI CREEK** (Gunnison)    Rising in the Sawatch Range, Tomichi Creek joins Cochetopa Creek. During the 1880s, placer mining camps dotted the stream's banks. The community of Tomichi was established along the creek, but an avalanche in 1898 destroyed it. Tomichi may be a Ute word meaning "dome-shaped rock," or "boiling," descriptive of local hot springs.

**TONAHUTU CREEK** (Grand)    This tributary of Grand Lake flows through Big Meadows. Tonahatue is an Arapaho word derived from toonoxteeni, meaning "meadows." It was also thought to mean, in part, "black."

**UNAWEEP CANYON** (Mesa)  The canyon was home to the Ute Indians until they were removed by treaty in 1881. Copper was discovered in 1875 by the Hayden Survey which started a minor rush. The Pyramid Mining Company built the first roads into the canyon, and the mining towns of Pearl and Copper City were established in the 1890s. Unaweep may be a Ute expression meaning "canyon with two mouths," or from kund-wiiyap, meaning "fire canyon," indicative of the canyon's color.

**UNCOMPAHGRE PEAK** (Hinsdale)/ **RIVER** (Montrose, Ouray)  The peak is 14,309 feet tall and was first climbed in 1874 by members of the Hayden Survey. It is the tallest peak in the San Juan Mountain Range. Uncompahgre is derived from the Ute words unca-pah-gre, meaning "hot water spring," and refers to the hot springs near the town of Ouray. It was also translated as "where water makes rock red." The river is about 75 miles long and joins Gunnison River. A section of the river was one of the last strongholds of the Ute Indians until they signed a peace treaty in 1863. Chief Ouray and his wife, Chipeta, built their home along the river.

**UTE MOUNTAINS** (Montezuma) Home to the Ute Indians before white settlement, the mountains were named for them. Ute may have originally come from Yutah, interpreted as "dwellers on the tops of mountains." The Ute Indians call themselves Nunt'z ("the people"). The Navajo word for the mountains is "black mountain sloping down." They believed these mountains hung from the sky, held by a string of rain, and storms were created when the mountains got angry with its people.

**YAMPA RIVER** (Moffat, Routt)  In 1776, Franciscan priests Dominguez and Escalante met up with a band of Comanche Indians known as Yamparica ("yampa eaters"). There was also a village named Yampa, originally called Egeria (a Roman water spirit), which was a center of commerce for timber, cattle, grains and coal. Yampa may be a Ute word that describes a root akin to the sweet potato.

# CONNECTICUT

**ASPETUCK RIVER** (Fairfield)  Aspetuck is a Paugusset word meaning "height" or "high place," perhaps in reference to the local hills. It was also thought to mean "fish net place." During the early 1800s, factories and foundries were built using the water power of the river.

**BANTAM LAKE** (Litchfield)  Covering about 1,200 acres, Bantam is the largest natural lake in the state. It is a Mahican word meaning "he prays." Once a favorite camping spot for the Pootatuck Indians, the lake later became a summer resort, and in 1859 the town of Morris was established along its shores.

**CHIMON ISLAND** (Fairfield) Chimon is one of the Norwalk Islands and part of the Connecticut Coastal National Wildlife Refuge. It may be a Paugusset word for "he paddles a canoe," or derived from mamichimins, meaning "little island." The island comprises the largest nesting colony of herons and egrets in the entire state.

**COCKENOE ISLAND** (Fairfield) Cockenoe is part of the Norwalk Islands and was home to the Pequot Indians. The island bears a Montauk word meaning "he interprets and sets things down." During the 1960s, plans were made to build a nuclear power plant here, but it never occurred; instead, a bird sanctuary was created.

**HAMMONASSET RIVER** (Middlesex) Once inhabited by the Hammonasset Indians (Eastern Woodland Indians), settlement along the river occurred during the 1660s when the towns of Clinton and Killingworth were founded. Hammonasset was translated as "at the place of small islands" (or "sand bars"), or "where we dig holes in the ground," indicative of farmlands along the river.

**HOCKANUM RIVER** (Tolland) During the Industrial Revolution, the river was important for the numerous mills established along its banks. The Hockanum enters the Connecticut River. Its name may come from the Podunk Indian word for "a hook," descriptive of the river's course.

**MANITOOK LAKE** (Hartford) This man-made lake was built in order to supply water for a millpond about 1836. Manitook is a Wangunk expression for "observation place," or "cornfields, we guard them."

**MOOSUP RIVER** (Windham) The community of Moosup was founded along the river about 1700, and its economy was tied to wool carding mills using the Moosup's water power. David Aldrich and Edwin Milner came to the region in the 1870s and built one of the early textile mills along the river. Moosup was derived from Narragansett Chief Mausup (origin unknown).

**MYSTIC RIVER** (New London) The Mystic River flows about 10 miles and terminates at Long Island Sound. Dutch explorer Captain Adraien Block was the first European to see this river and recorded the name as Sickenames (or Siccanemos) for a Pequot sachem. Mystic is a corruption of missi-tuk, which means "great tidal river." The town of Mystic was founded near the river, with shipbuilding its major industry until the War of 1812. Sealing and whaling later came into prominence.

**NATCHAUG RIVER** (Windham) General Nathaniel Lyon, credited with saving Missouri for the Union and first Union General killed in the Civil War, made his home along the river. The first settler may have been one Benjamin Chaplin who made his living manufacturing baskets and trays. The Natchaug empties into the Shetucket River and bears a Nipmuc word for "between rivers."

**NAUGATUCK RIVER** (Litchfield) Naugatuck was interpreted from a Quinnipiac word meaning "one large tree," "lone tree by the fishing place," or "far distant." The community of Naugatuck was founded near the river, and its economy was based on the manufacture of notions (needles, buttons, etc.). In 1843 Charles and Henry Goodyear established Goodyear's Metallic Rubber Shoe Company along the stream. During the Civil War the factory made raincoats and blankets for the Union Army.

**NEPAUG RIVER** (Hartford) Nepaug may be a Wangunk word for "fresh (or "good") pond," in reference to the water's clarity. During the 1850s the river was a hive of activity with more than 90 industries taking advantage of its water power.

**NONNEWANG RIVER** (Litchfield) Nonnewang is a Mahican expression for "dry land," indicative of the river's habit of going dry in the summertime. An historical 18th century Mill House is located along the stream.

**PEQUABUCK RIVER** (Hartford) Pequabuck is a Wangunk name for "clear, open pond." During the 1890s, the Immanuel Lutheran Church was built along the banks of the river to serve German immigrants. The region was mainly agricultural until industries were established using the water power of the river.

**POCOTOPAUG LAKE** (Middlesex) Settlement near the lake occurred in 1739 when colonists moved there from Massachussets. Pocotopaug is a Wangunk word for "divided (or "two") ponds." Indian legend tells the story about the Indians who lived in the area and were afraid of the lake because so many of their people drowned. They prayed to their spirit, who said in order to stop the drowning the Chief's daughter had to be sacrificed. Overhearing the conversation, the daughter sacrificed herself and jumped into the water. Folklore says that no one else drowned in the lake until this century.

**POMERAUG RIVER** (New Haven) The water power of this river brought in industry and the establishment of the town of Southbury along its banks. Pomeraug may be a Paugusset word for "place to walk (or "play")." It was also interpreted as "rocky place."

**QUASSAPAUG LAKE** (New Haven) Summer homes dot the lake shore, where at one time satinet mills and the well-known Diamond Match Company were located. Quassapaug may be a Quinnipiac word for "stones in the pond," or "gravelly pond." It was also thought to be derived from kehtequasset, meaning "the largest."

**QUINEBAUG RIVER** (Windham) Richard Dresser purchased land near the river about 1707, which would later be established as the village of West Thompson. The American Optical Company was built along the river, followed by the Quinebaug Mills in 1851. Quinebaug is an Algonquian word meaning "long pond."

**QUINNIPIAC RIVER** (New Haven) Wallingford village was established under the directive of the Connecticut General Assembly in 1667. Other villages were founded including Quinnipiac, with their main source of income from the harvesting of oysters. Quinnipiac may be a corruption of the Quinnipiac word quinnipe-auke, meaning "long-water land," or quinnuppin-uk, defined as "where we change our route." Other interpretations were "on great trail," and "turning point."

**SCANTIC RIVER** (Hartford) Once home to the Podunk Indians, settlers founded the village of Somers originally as an agricultural community. Industries later followed that were established along the river, which included a gunpowder business and a satinet mill. Scantic is a Nipmuc word meaning "branch of the river."

**SHENIPSIT LAKE** (Tolland) Boundary lines were determined at this lake between the Nipmuc, Podunk and Mohegan Indian tribes. It was a favorite spot for the Indians because of the abundance of fish. Shenipsit may be a Mohegan for "at the great pool," or "big pond at."

**SHEPAUG RIVER** (Litchfield) The Tunxis Indians named this river, which means "great pond," or "rocky waters," descriptive of the rocky outcroppings and boulders along the banks of the river.

**SHETUCKET RIVER** (New London) Sprague's Mill and the town of Sprague were established near the stream in 1861. The mill continued in operation until the 1960s. A dam was completed on the river in 1833, spearheaded by William Green who purchased land on both sides of the stream in 1826. Shetucket may be a Mohegan word for "great river," or "land between river."

**TITICUS MOUNTAIN/RIVER** (Fairfield) Harry Anderson built a hunting and fishing resort in the mountain in 1908 which was called the Port of Missing Men. He initially purchased the property to build mansions for the wealthy, but the deal fell through. The river originates at the foothills of West Mountain. First called Buffalo Creek, the name was changed to Titicus, derived from the Mahican word mutighticoos, meaning "place without trees."

**TOTOKET MOUNTAIN** (New Haven) Totoket is a Niantic word for "great (tidal) stream." During the 1890s, numerous quarries were in operation, principally harvesting a stone called trap rock. It broke into pieces that looked like blocks and was used for paving and building foundations.

**TUNXIS ISLAND** (New Haven) Local folklore says this island was created when someone stepped into mud, and after pulling out his foot some of the mud stock to his shoe. The man's wife refused him entry to his home until he got rid of the dirt, so he rinsed his shoes off in Long Island Sound, and created the island. Tunxis

may be a Paugusset word for "at the place of the small stream."

**UNCOWAY RIVER** (Fairfield) Pequannock Indians, along with their sachem, Queriheag, lived along the banks of the river. When the white man came to the region, they met a group of Indians called the Cupheags (meaning "harbor" or "place shut in"). In 1648, Queriheag built a grist mill at the town of Fairfield after making an agreement with the town leaders. Uncoway is a Paugusset word for "beyond the fishing place," "the furthermost," or "at the end of the rapid stream."

**WEPAWAUG RIVER** (New Haven) Colonists purchased land in 1639 and founded a town along the Wepawaug River, on which they depended for their supply of fish, clams and oysters, and transportation of their goods. Wepawaug is a Paugusset expression for "crossing place," or "narrows."

**WILLIMANTIC RIVER** (Tolland) The Willimantic is about 35 miles long and originates near Stafford Springs. It joins the Shetucket River at the town of Willimantic. The Nipmuc Indians used this region as their fishing and hunting grounds. Willimantic means "land of the swift running waters," descriptive of a portion of the river that drops more than 95 feet through a series of falls. It was also interpreted as a Mohegan word meaning "good cedar swamp."

**WONONSKOPOMUC LAKE** (Litchfield) The lake is located in Salisbury Township. In 1746, a blockhouse was constructed near the lake for the settlers' protection. Wononskopomuc is a Mahican word for "rocks at the bend of lake."

**WYASSUP LAKE** (New London) This natural lake is located in the town of North

Stonington. Wyassup may be a Mohegan word for "wild flax," or "rushes."

**YANTIC RIVER** (New London/Tolland) The Yantic originates on the two county boundary lines and enters the Quinebaug River. Yantic may be a Mohegan expression for "extended river," "as far as the tidal stream" or "on this side of the stream." During the late 1600s, Christopher Leffingwell was provisionary to George Washington during the Revolution. He built the first paper mill in the state, and later established a chocolate processing mill along the river.

# DELAWARE

**APPOQUINIMINK RIVER** (New Castle) The river was a route used by traders to reach the Susquehanna River for bartering with the Susquehannock Indians. The Appoquinimink is about 15 miles long and joins the Delaware River. It was thought to be an Algonquian word meaning "wounded duck," or "large wild duck," but some authorities disagree. During the height of the beaver trade, the Dutch and English tried to gain control of the river.

**MISPILLION RIVER** (Sussex)  First mention of this name was in 1664 when it was spelled mispening, a Lenape word for "big tuber at." The river flows into Delaware Bay. Early settlers to the river region were the Swedes and Finns in the 1600s. The Mispillion runs through the heart of Milford, which was founded in 1787 and supported by shipbuilding.

**NANTICOKE RIVER** (Sussex)  The Nanticoke flows about 63 miles from its confluence of the St. Johns and Gravelly Rivers into the state of Maryland, and terminates at Nanticoke Sound. The Lenape Indians favored the river for its abundant fish and game. The river later supported a thriving shipbuilding industry in addition to being a transportation route for the shipment of coal. Nanticoke is a Lenape word derived from nentego, defined as "tidewater people."

**POCOMOKE RIVER** (Sussex)  The Pocomoke originates in the Great Cypress Swamp on the Delaware-Maryland Border and flows about 75 miles to Pocomoke Sound at Chesapeake Bay. Pocomoke City was established along the river in 1878, and its economy was tied to shipping tobacco and agricultural products. The river bears an Algonquian word meaning "it is pierced," or "broken ground."

**TOCKWOGH RIVER** (New Castle) While exploring this river, Captain John Smith learned of the warring Tockwoghe Indians from the Massawomeks (part of the Mohawk tribe). The name was interpreted from the a Mohegan word tiawco, meaning "bridge makers." It was also thought to describe a root the Indians used as food.

# FLORIDA

**ALAQUA CREEK** (Walton)  During the Creek War a dozen Indians were captured along this creek, many of them women and children. The Militia later mutilated and killed most of the people, but some of the Indians managed to escape to the Apalachicola River. For the settlers' protection during the war, a small fort was built near the mouth of the stream. Alaqua is derived from the Seminole word hilukwa, meaning "sweet gum."

**ASTATULA LAKE** (Lake)  Local folklore says Astatula means "lake of sunbeams," or "lake of sparkling moonbeams." But it comes from the Seminole expression isti and italwa, meaning "people of different tribes."

**CALOOSAHATCHEE RIVER** (Lee, Hendry, Glades)  This river was named for the Colusa Indians, interpreted as "a fierce people." First named Calusa, the name was changed to Caloosahatchee. The 75-mile-long river originates at Lake Hicpochee and empties into the Gulf of Mexico. Settlement along the river began shortly after the Civil War. During the 1930s, the river was dredged and straightened as part of a flood control project.

**CHASSAHOWITZKA RIVER** (Citrus)  The Chassahowitzka National Wildlife Refuge, which borders the river, was established in 1943 as a winter preserve for migratory water birds. The river is about four miles long and originates from Chassahowitzka Springs. Its name was derived from chasi and houwitchka, Seminole for "pumpkin opening place."

**CHOKOLOSKEE ISLAND** (Collier)  Chokoloskee is part of the 10,000 Islands situated in the Everglades National Park. The island was once home to the Colusa Indians, and later became a trade center for homesteaders. The Smallwood Trading Post was established in 1903 and is still in operation. Chokoloskee comes from the Seminole words, chukka and liski, for "old house," descriptive of the Indian houses built on stilts.

**ECOFINA RIVER** (Bay, Washington)  DeSoto's army came through the region and camped at the river, which they called Many Waters. Ecofina may be a Creek word derived from ekana and feno, meaning "natural bridge."

**ECONLOCKHATCHEE RIVER** (Orange, Seminole)  The Little Big Econlockhatchee State Forest borders part of this river. The waterway empties into the St. Johns River. Econlockhatchee is a Creek word derived from ekana, laiki and hatchee, meaning "earth mound river," or simply "mound river."

**FAKAHATCHEE RIVER** (Collier)  Settlement occurred at a place called Daniel's Point during the early 1900s. A logging company was established near the river in the 1940s which harvested bald cypress known as the Fakahatchee Strand (strands are narrow sloughs that developed in the mangrove swamps). The river terminates at Fakahatchee Bay. It is a Creek word derived from fakka and hatchee, thought to mean "clay (or "mud") creek." The Fakahatchee is the largest of the strands in the Big Cypress Swamp. It is also home to many rare species of orchids, notably the "ghost orchid," which was common until 1977 when poachers greatly reduced their numbers.

**FENHOLLOWAY RIVER** (Taylor) This river was first named Slippery Log Creek by a member of Jackson's army when the troops passed through the region in 1818. It was later changed to Fenholloway, from a Creek expression meaning "high foot log." In 1838, Zachary Taylor and his army build a fort along the river for the settlers' protection during the Seminole War of 1835-1842.

**HATCHINEHA, LAKE** (Polk) The lake is part of the Kissimmee River system. Hatchineha may come from the Creek word achenaho, which means "cypress."

**HOMOSASSA RIVER** (Citrus) Homosassa is derived from homo and sasi, Seminole for "pepper is there," or "place where wild peppers grow." The town of Homosassa was supported by sugar manufacturing when David Yulee built a sugar mill in the early 1800s. During the Civil War, Yulee's home was destroyed and the sugar mill ceased to operate. The 9-mile long river later became a transportation route for steamships. In 1886, the river was promoted by financiers for the benefit of sportsmen.

**HYPOLUXO ISLAND** (Palm Beach) The island was named by Mrs. H.D. Pierce in 1873 after she asked the Seminole Indians what the name meant. They told her Hypoluxo signified "water all around," describing land-locked Lake Worth on which the island is located. It was also defined as "round mound" for the Indian shell mounds. About 300 families live on the island.

**ICHETUCKNEE RIVER** (Suwannee) This region was once inhabited by the Utina Indians. The Ichetucknee is the shortest river in Florida, fed entirely by springs. Its name comes from the Creek expression wa, echas and toka, interpreted as "a beaver pond."

**ISTOKPOGA LAKE** (Highlands) Once known as Drowned Man's Lake, the name was changed to Istokpoga, from the Creek expression iste and paga, meaning "a dead man," or "lake where a person was killed in the water." It was also thought to signify "people live at end of it," in the Seminole language. Istokpoga is the fifth largest lake in the state, and may have the largest concentration of Ospreys in the world.

**KANAPAHA LAKE** (Alachua) This region was home of the Timucua ("my enemy") Indians who built their homes with poles and palmetto leaves. Kanapaha was derived from cani and paha, meaning "palmetto house."

**KISSIMMEE RIVER** (Osceola) Rising at Lake Tohopekaliga in central Florida, the Kissimmee is about 140 miles long and empties into Lake Okeechobee. Kissimmee is a Caloosa word for "heaven's place." Others have interpreted the name as Seminole for "mulberry yonder." Hamilton Disston purchased four million acres of swampland, then had the Kissimmee River dredged to make it deeper, which connected the town of Kissimmee to the outside world of commerce

**LOCHLOOSA LAKE** (Alachua) Marjorie Rawlings, who wrote the well-known book *The Yearling*, lived near this lake. Lochloosa is a Choctaw word meaning "black terrapin," derived from luski and lusa.

**LOXAHATCHEE RIVER** (Palm Beach, Martin) One of the few subtropical rivers classified as Wild and Scenic, Loxahatchee was derived from the Seminole word locha hatchee, which means "turtle creek." Another interpretation was "false river." The Loxahatchee River–Lake Worth Creek Aquatic Preserve was established in 1970.

**OCKLAHAWA RIVER** (Marion)   With a length of about 79 miles, the Ocklahawa River is a tributary of the St. Johns River. It is derived from the Creek expression ak lowahe, meaning "muddy." There was such a wealth of shellfish for the Indians to eat that shell mounds have created small islands in the river. During 1832, James Gadsden took part in a treaty negotiation along the river at a place called Payne's Landing. The treaty was an effort to induce the Seminole Indians to move farther west. This river region contains one of the largest concentrations of southern bald eagles.

**OKAHUMPKA LAKE** (Sumter)   This region was home to Chief Micanopy and his people until the town of Okahumpka was founded in 1885 by Rev. Edmund Snyder. Okahumpka may be a Creek word meaning "single lake," or derived from okeehumpkee, for "deep water," indicative of a deep spring in the area.

**OKEECHOBEE, LAKE** (Okeechobee, Martin, Palm Beach, Hendry, Glades) The great Okeechobee is the second largest freshwater lake totally within one state (750 acres). It is also the second largest freshwater lake entirely in the United States. The name may come from the Hitchiti expression oki and chubi, meaning "water big." In 1837 the Battle of Okeechobee was fought between the U.S. Army and the Seminole Indians, a battle the Indians won. During the 1880s Hamilton Disston dredged a canal from Fort Thompson to the lake.

**OLUSTEE CREEK** (Columbia, Union)

Providence Baptist Church was established along this creek in 1834, and may be one of the oldest Baptist churches in the state. The village of Providence, the second oldest community in Florida, was a stopping place for explorers. At one time there was a trading post on the river that dealt with the Seminoles. Olustee Creek forms the boundary line between Columbia and Union counties. It is derived from the Seminole word oklasti, meaning "blackfish." Olustee was also interpreted as a Creek word meaning "water black."

**PALATLAKAHA   CREEK**   (Lake) Archibald Gano came to the region in 1889 and built a sawmill along the Palatlakaha, followed by establishment of a crate mill. He also invented the tomato crate. Palatlakaha is a Seminole word meaning "swamp big."

**PANASOFFKEE LAKE** (Sumter)   The town of Panosoffkee was founded near the lake in 1882. The region was once rich in timber and brought in numerous lumber mills until about 1904 when the trees were depleted. Panasoffkee is derived from Pvne Sufke (pronounced Pummy Soofe), a Creek word meaning "deep ravine" (or "valley"). Seminole Chief Halleck-Tustenugee used the region as a hiding place. One of the most feared Seminole chiefs, he agreed to surrender to the U.S. Army numerous times, but continually reneged on his promises, and continued raiding towns and killing the whites. He finally gave himself up at Warm Springs located near the lake.

**PITHLACHASCOTEE RIVER** (Pasco) This blackwater river rises in the Crews Lake region and empties into the Gulf of Mexico. Pithlachascotee is locally known as the Cootee, and bears a Creek name derived from pithlo and chiskita, meaning "canoe to chop out." It is also a Seminole expression for "river where canoes are made."

**SOPCHOPPY RIVER** (Wakulla)   An old map of 1683 shows the name as Rio Chachave, which may be a Spanish corruption of sokhe and chapke, Creek for "twisted long," descriptive of the river's course. It was also interpreted from the Seminole-Creek, lokchapi, meaning "red oak acorn stem." The town of Sopchoppy was established along the river in the 1850s.

**STEINHATCHEE RIVER** (Taylor, Dixie)   The village of Steinhatchee is located along what was once known as Deadman's Bay. The region was a strategic spot during the Second Seminole War in the 1830s. Steinhatchee is a Creek word that means "dead man's creek," and the mouth of the river is still named Deadman's Bay. The Steinhatchee empties into Apalachee Bay at the Gulf of Mexico. Used as a haven for pirates, local tradition says buried treasure is hidden somewhere along the river banks, but it has never been found.

**THONOTOSASSA LAKE** (Hillsborough)   Lake Thonotosassa was a camping place for the Seminole Indians, who called it Tenotosassa, meaning "lake flints," or "flint is here," a material they quarried to make their tools and arrowheads. The Indians also held their annual Green Corn Dance here during the full moon in June, where ceremonies were performed and disputes were settled. The region became known for its orange orchards.

**TOHOPEKALIGA LAKE** (Osceola)   Tohopekaliga bears the Creek words tohopke and alaiki, meaning "fort site," and probably referred to the stockades the Indians built on the islands located within the lake. The town of Kissimmee is located along the lake, which is the sixth largest natural lake in the state and part of the Kissimmee Chain of Lakes. In 1882, a canal was constructed between Tohopekaliga and Lake Cypress as part of a drainage project. Cypress Island is situated in the middle of the lake and comprises about 132 acres. In 1999, the Florida Fish and Wildlife Commission purchased it and designated it an environmentally sensitive land.

**TOMOKA RIVER** (Volusia)   This region was home to the Timucua Indians during the days of Spanish exploration. The river was the Indians' last stand from attacks by the Creek Indians (instigated by the British in the 18th century). Tomoka was thought mean "lord" or "ruler." The name may be a corruption of Timucua, meaning "my enemy." In 1825, a sugar mill plantation was established by Colonel Thomas Dummett, and in 1881 a ferry was built for transportation across the river. Horses brought over by the Spaniards left descendents, known as marshtackies, which ran free here until the late 1900s.

**TOTOSAHATCHEE CREEK** (Orange)   Totosahatchee is a derived from the Seminole or Creek expression totlosi and hatchie, meaning "chicken creek." It joins the St. Johns River south of the village of Christmas.

**TSALA APOPKA, LAKE** (Citrus)   This lake lies close to the Withlacoochee River. It was the site of the Seminoles' last defense led by Chief Osceola who had his headquarters at the head of the lake. Tsala Apopka is a Creek expression meaning "trout eating place."

**WEEKIWACHEE RIVER** (Hernando)   During the War Between the States, this river became an important transportation route after the Florida coast and major ports were closed by the Union Army. The river originates at Weeki Wachee Spring and terminates in the Atlantic Ocean. It is a Seminole word for "little spring," or "winding river."

**WEKIVA RIVER** (Seminole, Lake) The Wekiva is a tributary of the St. Johns River and bears a Creek expression meaning "spring of water," or "bubbling water." The region was the hunting ground of the Timucua Indians, whose mounds can still be seen at Wekiwa Springs State Park.

**WETAPPO CREEK** (Gulf) Wetappo Creek was dredged in the early 1900s to make way for a new canal, which opened in 1915 and became part of the Intracoastal Waterway. Wetappo is a Creek word meaning "broad water."

**WITHLACOOCHEE RIVER** (Polk) The Withlacoochee is a south-to-north running stream that crosses into the state of Georgia, then back into Florida where it terminates in the Gulf of Mexico. Withlacoochee comes from the Creek expression we, thlako and chee, meaning "little big water." It was also interpreted as "crooked river," because the river twists and turns. Clashes occurred along the river between the Seminole Indians and the U.S. Army when the Indians refused to leave after a treaty was signed in 1823.

# GEORGIA

**ALAPAHA RIVER** (Pierce) Taken from the Creek word apala, this name was translated as "on the other side." Others believe it is from arapaha, a Timucua expression meaning "bear house." During the Indian War of 1836 the river was the site of the Seminole Indians' last stand (close to the hamlet of Willacoochee), where many were massacred. The Alapaha meanders into Florida where tobacco farms were established along its banks.

**ALCOVY RIVER** (Gwinnett) Rising in the county, the 80-mile river empties into Lake Jackson. Alcovy may be derived from the Muskogean word ulcofauhatchie, defined as "river among pawpaw trees," or "place of pawpaw."

**ALECKS CREEK** (Wayne) Lower Creek Chief Alleck lived along this river, which bears his name. It is derived from aleckcha or alikcha, which means "doctor."

**ALTAMAHA RIVER** (Tattnall) The Altamaha is the largest river on the state's coast. It rises at the junction of the Ocmulgee and Oconee rivers and travels about 137 miles to Altamaha Sound, an inlet of the Atlantic Ocean. The river region is home to the endangered wood stork. Named by Hernando DeSoto in 1540, Altamaha may a combination of Spanish al and ha, along with the Creek word, tama, meaning "chief lodge."

**AMICALOLA RIVER/MOUNTAIN** (Dawson) Originating in the Amicalola Mountains, the stream joins the Etowah River. Amicalola is derived from the Cherokee expression amo and kalola, meaning "tumbling waters," descriptive of the highest waterfalls in the state (959 feet). In 1864, Colonel James Findlay and his Georgia State Cavalry Home Guards pursued the Union Army over the mountain and captured them. The mountain rises from 1,700 to about 3,325 feet and is part of the Blue Ridge Mountain Range.

**ANEEWAKEE RIVER** (Douglas)  A Cherokee family by the name of Anakwanki lived in the region and the river was named in their honor. It was also interpreted from ani and waca, Cherokee for "cow people." The river enters the Chattahoochee River.

**APALACHEE RIVER** (Morgan)  The Apalachee flows about 65 miles to merge with the Oconee River. First known as Chulapocca, the name was changed to Apalachee, a Hitchiti word interpreted as "those on the other side." Apalachee may be the oldest recorded name in the state.

**APALACHICOLA RIVER** (Decatur) Rising at the junction of the Chattahoochee and Flint Rivers, the Apalachicola flows into Florida to terminate at Apalachicola Bay. Its rich floodplains brought in settlers during the early 1800s and the founding of the town of Apalachicola. It may be a Hichiti word for "land beyond," or "those people residing on the other side." The name was also defined from the Choctaw word, apelachi, for "ally," or apelichi, meaning "ruling place."

**ARMUCHEE CREEK** (Chattooga) This region was home to the Cherokee Indians until the Trail of Tears to Arkansas and Oklahoma in 1838. The community of Armuchee was established near the creek and used the water power for its grist mills, cotton gins, and sawmills. Armuchee is a Cherokee word that means "land of beautiful flowers," "much water," or "much fish." It has also been translated from the

Choctaw word alamushi, meaning "hiding place."

**CANOOCHEE RIVER** (Emanuel) The Canoochee River is about 100 miles long and flows into the Ogeechee River. Canoochee may be derived from the Creek word ikandshi, meaning "graves are there," or from kanooche, for "little ground."

**CEMOCHECHOBEE CREEK** (Randolph)  In 1814, a fort was built along the creek by Union troops for the settlers' protection against the Indians, until a treaty was signed in 1825 by the Lower Creek Indians. The first thread mill was established there just before the Civil War. Cemochechobee is derived from the Hitchiti expression sarnochi and chobi, defined as "big sandy creek."

**CHATTAHOOCHEE RIVER** (White) Flowing through Georgia, Alabama and Florida, the river is more than 435 miles long and joins the Flint River to empty into Lake Seminole in Florida. The Chattahoochee was considered a border line between the Creek and Cherokee Indian tribes. It was one of the most important waterways because it connected the Gulf of Mexico to the interior. Chattahoochee was derived from the Creek expression chatu-huchi, meaning "marked rock" or "picture rocks."

**CHATTOOGA RIVER** (Walker)  Designated a Wild and Scenic river, the Chattooga merges with the Coosa River in Alabama. Chattooga was derived from Tsatu-gi (or Cha tu'gi), the name of an old Cherokee village. It was interpreted as "he drank by sips" or "he has crossed the stream and come out on the other side." Others believe it is derived from chatauga, meaning "chicken."

**CHESTATEE RIVER** (Lumpkin)  Settlement along the river occurred during the early 1800s when gold was found in the region. This discovery forced the Cherokee Indians to be removed along the Trail of Tears. A tributary of the Chattahoochee River, the stream empties into Lake Lanier. Chestatee may be a Cherokee word meaning "pine torch place" or "place of the lights," because deer hunters used torches at night. It was also translated as "fire light place."

**CHICKASAWHATCHEE CREEK** (Terrell)  In 1836, the Battle of Chickasawhatchee was fought here when the Creek Indians attacked and killed a number of people before the Federal Army took them into custody. The stream flows into the Flint River. It may be derived from Chickasyhatchy, a Hichiti expression translated as "council house creek."

**CONASAUGA RIVER** (Fannin)/**LAKE** (Murray)  The lake is the highest body of water in the state of Georgia at about 3,200 feet. The river flows into Tennessee and returns to Georgia, where it joins the Coosawattee River. Conasauga was derived from the Cherokee word kahnasagah, interpreted as "grass."

**COOSA RIVER** (Floyd)  Once known as the Arbacoochee (Creek for "unhealthy place" or "pile of scalps at the foot of a war pole"), Coosa is a corruption of the Choctaw word kusha, meaning "cane" or "canebrake." The 286-mile-long river rises at the junction of the Oostanaula and Etowah Rivers and joins the Tallapoosa River. After the Cherokee were removed in 1835, settlers moved in and took advantage of the transportation the Coosa afforded them.

**COOSAWATTEE RIVER** (Gilmer) This river is about 50 miles long and joins the Conasauga River. The region was once home to the Cherokee Indians and in 1825 made the community of Newtown their

nation's capital. They changed the town's name to New Echota. Coosawattee is derived from the Cherokee word ku-sa-weti-ye, meaning "old creek place."

**CURRAHEE MOUNTAIN** (Stephens) The mountain is about 1,740 feet high and situated near the town of Toccoa. It was derived from a Cherokee word meaning "it stands alone," or from gurahiyi, meaning "water cress place," a plant the Cherokee Indians used for food.

**EASTONALEE CREEK** (Stephens/ Franklin)  Eastonalee is derived from the Cherokee word ustanali, which referred to a natural barrier of rocks that lay across the stream. It was also interpreted as "rocky bridge across the waters." The Indians established a village along the creek with the same name. Eastonalle may be a derivative of Oostanaula (see Oostanaula entry).

**ECHECONNEE CREEK** (Crawford) The creek's steep banks enabled the Indians to trap deer that came here drink. They named the creek Ichoconnaugh, which signified "deer trap creek." It was later spelled Echeconnee. The creek joins the Ocmulgee River.

**ETOWAH RIVER** (Lumpkin)  This river was named for the Cherokee Etowah Mounds, historical capital of their nation. Etowah was derived from etawaha, for "dead wood," or the Creek word italwa, meaning "town." The river rises in the mountains of the county and empties into the Oostanaula River. During the 1950s, the Etowah Mounds were discovered near the river. Some anthropologists believe they were earth islands, symbols of the ancient Indians' beliefs.

**ICHABUCKLER CREEK** (Stewart) The Ichabuckler merges with the Chattahoochee River. It may be derived from a Muskohegan expression meaning "tobacco pipe creek."

## ICHAWAYNOCHAWAY CREEK
(Randolph/Terrell)   Locally known as the Notchaway, this creek is a county boundary line which terminates at the Flint River. Ichawaynochaway was derived from a Muskogean word meaning "buck sheep creek" or "where deer sleep."

## IFCONJO CREEK (Monroe)   Ifconjo
may be deried from the Creek word ifkancho, interpreted as "tick," descriptive of ticks on cattle. This creek is a tributary of the Ocmulgee River.

## KIOKEE CREEK (McDuffie)   Baptist
preacher Daniel Marshall and his people settled along this creek and built the Kiokee Meeting House. The stream, which joins the Savannah River, was originally named Okiokee ("falls creek"). The name was changed to Kiokee, a Creek word meaning "mulberry water."

## NACOOCHEE RIVER (White)   This
river flows through the Nacoochee Valley and may be the site of the ancient Cherokee town, Guaxul ("evening star"). Nacoochee was interpreted as a Choctaw expression for "little arrow." Legend says Nacoochee was an Indian princess who jumped to her death from Yonah Mountain because of a disenchanted love affair. In the 1820s, gold was found on the river, bringing in a slew of miners and the onset of a small gold rush.

## OCHLOCKONEE RIVER (Worth)
The Ochlockonee is a blackwater river that flows about 150 miles and empties into Ochlockonee Bay in the state of Florida. It may be a Hitchiti expression oki and lagana (or lakni), meaning "water yellow." The town of Ochlocknee was established

as a protective enclave against Indian uprisings. It was surveyed and platted about 1911.

## OCMULGEE RIVER (Gwinnett)   Hernando DeSoto came through this region in 1540 during his explorations. The Ocmulgee is about 255 miles long, originates at the confluence of the Yellow, South and Alcovy rivers, then enters the Altamaha River. The Georgia Legislature granted Josia Hardy a charter to operate a ferry on the river, which became a major transportation route for the shipment of cotton. Ocmulgee was derived from the Hitchiti words oki and mulgis, meaning "water it is boiling (or "bubbling").

## OCONEE RIVER (Hall)   This river
flows for 250 miles and enters the Ocmulgee River. It bears a Creek word meaning "the place of springs," or "the water eyes of the hills." A fort was built at the head of navigation of the river, and the region opened for settlement after the Creek Indians ceded their land about 1783.

## OGEECHEE RIVER (Greene)   Ogeechee is a blackwater river about 250 miles long, and may be a corruption of the Yuchi Indians, who bear a Muskogean word meaning "seeing far away." The river empties into Ossabaw Sound in the Atlantic Ocean. In 1864, Major General Osterhaus crossed the Ogeechee and drove Confederate soldiers toward the city of Savannah.

## OOSTANAULA RIVER (Gordon)
The community of Resaca was established along this river and experienced the first major battle of the Atlanta Campaign in 1864. The river rises at the junction of the Coosawattee and Conasauga Rivers, then flows into the Etowah River. Oostanaula may be a Cherokee word meaning "rock ledge across a stream," or "shoally river."

**OOTHKALOOGA CREEK** (Bartow/ Gordon)   Oothkalooga is derived from the Cherokee word tsutygilagi, translated as "beaver," or "where there are beaver dams." The creek flows into the Oostanaula River. Major Ridge, a Cherokee leader who was a representative to the Cherokee Council, built his home along the creek in the early 1800s.

**OSSABAW ISLAND** (Chatham)   Located about 20 miles south of Savannah, Ossabaw is one of the largest of the state's islands. During the 16th century, sailors encountered Indians they called Guale. John Morel purchased the land in the 1760s and went on to become a successful planter, along with other plantation owners who raised sea island cotton. Ossabaw may be from the Creek word asiape (or asapo), meaning "holly bush place." The island was purchased by the state in 1978, and today is a wildlife preserve. Descendants of Spanish pigs brought over during the early 1600s still roam the island.

**PACHITLA CREEK** (Calhoun)   This is one of the regions DeSoto and his party stopped during their explorations, and was once home to tribes of the Creek nation. The Pachitla flows into Ichawaynochaway Creek. It may be a Muskogean word for "dead pigeon" or "pigeon town." It was also thought to be Choctaw for "opossum."

**TALLAPOOSA RIVER** (Paulding)   The Tallapoosa is 268 miles long and merges with the Coosa River at the town of Selma in Alabama. It is a Creek word meaning "golden water," "stranger," or "swift current." Others believed the name was derived from the Choctaw words tali and pushi, meaning "rock pulverized." In 1814 the Battle of Horseshoe Bend occurred, where General Jackson fought more than 1,000 Creek Indians, destroying the Creek Confederation.

**TALLY MOUNTAIN** (Haralson)   Rising about 1,520 feet high, this mountain is located near the town of Tallapoosa. The name was thought to be a family surname, or derived from the Cherokee word tali, meaning "mountain."

**TOBESOFKEE CREEK** (Lamar)   Surveyors once called the stream Hunger and Hardship Creek because they were worn out at this point. The Tobesofkee joins the Ocmulgee River. Its name was derived from the Creek words meaning "stirrer," designating a ladle, or "corn gruel." It was also defined in part as "deep."

**TOWALIGA RIVER** (Henry)   The Towaliga joins the Ocmulgee River. The name was derived from the Creek words tawa and laigi, meaning "sumac place." Another theory was a Muskogean word meaning "roasted scalps," because scalps were dried at a site near the river.

**TUGALOO RIVER** (Stephens)   After the American Revolution, settlers moved to the river region and took up farmlands that were once inhabited by the Cherokee and Creek Indians. The Tugaloo rises at the confluence of the Chattooga and Tallulah rivers and flows about 45 miles into South Carolina where it joins the Seneca River. Tugaloo was derived from Cherokee word ama-tu-gwaluny, defined as "water rolling over rocks there," or "rough flowing water." It was also translated as "forks of stream."

**TUSSAHAW CREEK** (Henry)   This creek empties into Jackson Lake. In 1826, a mill was established along the creek, only to be destroyed by Sherman's army in 1829. Tussahaw was taken from a Muskogean expression meaning "stream of life," "to inflict pain on you" (referring to an insect sting), or "warrior shooting at you."

**TYBEE ISLAND** (Chatham)   The 1500s brought the Spaniards who claimed the island and called it Los Bajos. John Wesley, founder of the Methodist Church, settled on Tybee and was the first person to say a prayer on American soil. After the Civil War the island became a summer resort. Tybee is a Euchee word which means "salt," or may be for Choctaw Chief Itu Ubi, meaning "wood killer."

**UCHEE CREEK** (Columbia)   Uchee is a Muskogean word meaning "seeing far away," and named for the Yuchi Indians, members of the Creek Confederation, who lived along the creek until they were removed during the early 1800s. The creek joins the Savannah River.

**UPATOI CREEK** (Talbot)   The small village of Upatoi is located near this creek, which may be a Muskogean word meaning "sheet-like covering" or "bullfrog." It was also interpreted as "furthest out" or "on the fringe." The Upatoi joins the Chattahoochee River.

**WAHATCHEE CREEK** (Elbert)   Wahatchee Creek merges with the Broad River. It was home to Nancy Hart, a freedom fighter during the Revolution. Wahatchee may be derived from the Muskogean word waya-chi, which means "mighty wolf."

**WASSAW ISLAND** (Chatham)   Wassaw is a barrier island that was designated a National Wildlife Refuge in 1969. Loggerhead turtles have used the island as their nesting ground for thousands of years. Today, these turtles are monitored by staff who work for the Caretta Project. Wassaw is from the Creek word wiso, interpreted as "sassafras," a plant that is abundant on the island.

**YAHULA CREEK** (Lumpkin)   This creek is a tributary of the Chestatee River. During the 1940s a 10-stamp mill was built after some gold was found along the stream. Legend says Yahula (a mythical figure of the Cherokee Indians) lived along this creek. Yahula may have been a Cherokee trader who was captured by the spirit people. Other derivations were from yahulu, which means "hickory," and the Creek word yoho'lo, descriptive of a song.

**YONAH MOUNTAIN** (White)   Rising 3,167 feet high, the mountain is situated in the Chattahoochee National Forest, and was once the hunting ground of the Cherokee Indians. Yonah is Cherokee meaning "bear." A Cherokee chief had a daughter named Nacoochee, who fell in love with Sautee, son of a Chickasaw chief. They had to meet secretly because the tribes were at war. When Nacoochee's father discovered them, he had Sautee thrown off the mountain. The girl then flung herself over the mountain, preferring to be united with him in death.

# IDAHO

**BANNOCK CREEK** (Power) The Bannock and Shoshone Indians were resident along the creek until they were removed to the Fort Hall Reservation in the 1860s. Bannock may have been derived from penointikara, meaning "honey eaters."

**CALIPEEN RIVER** (Shoshone) Calipeen is a Chinook word for "pistol," because of a pistol thought to have been lost by someone near the river. W.H. Dauges, U.S. Forest Ranger, selected the name.

**DAHLONEGA RIVER** (Lemhi) Dahlonega is a transfer name from the state of Georgia, where miners from that state came here and discovered gold, naming their claim the Dahlonega Belle, which was located along the creek. During the 1820s, the Cherokee Indians dominated the region in Georgia they called ta-lo-ne-ga, their word for the color of gold, "yellow." The river has its origin at the base of Morgan Mountain.

**EENA CREEK** (Benewah) U.S. Forest Service employee W.H. Daugs named the creek, which is a Chinnook word meaning "beaver." The creek originates at Nakarna Mountain and joins the east fork of Charlie Creek.

**HYAAK CREEK** (Latah) This creek was also named by W.H. Daugs of the Forest Service in 1927. Hyaak is a Chinook word that was interpreted as "swift." It joins the Palouse River.

**KALISPELL BAY** (Bonner) This area was once home to the Blackfoot and Blood Indians who called the bay Kalispel, meaning "prairie above the lake." Jesuit missionaries arrived during the 1840s and built their missions in the region. With timber readily available, lumber companies were established and a narrow gauge railroad was constructed in the Kalispell Bay area, which provided access to the timber markets.

**KAMIAH BUTTES** (Lincoln/Minidoka) These buttes are a series of three hills at about 1,000 feet above the Columbia Plateau. Kamiah is the birthplace of the Nez Perce Indians who call themselves Nee-mee-poo ("the chosen ones"). During the winter they stayed in long houses and braided ropes from the Cannabis hemp and made baskets. Kamiah could mean "tattered ends of hemp," or "the place of many rope litters." Indian legend says Coyote once met a monster who was eating all the animals. Coyote tricked the monster into inhaling him, but Coyote had a knife and fire frill, which he used to allow the animals to escape. Coyote then cut out the monster's heart and created the Nee-mee-poo from the blood of the heart. The heart to this day lies buried under the mound protruding from the earth in the center of the Nez Perce National Historical Park.

**KANIKSU MOUNTAIN/NATIONAL FOREST** (Boundary) These features bear a Coeur d'Alene word meaning "black robe," and was indicative of the Jesuit missionaries. The mountain is located in Kaniksu National Forest, just below the Canadian border. The national forest was originally called the Priest River Forest Reserve which was established in 1891.

In 1967, Kaniksu Mountain (along with three other nearby areas) was the scene of a catastrophic fire that burned more than 73,000 acres.

**KIWA CREEK** (Latah)   First known as Little Shuswap, the creek was renamed sometime after 1915 to Kiwa, a Chinook word meaning "crooked," descriptive of the creek's course. This stream is only a little over a mile long and empties into Strychnine Creek.

**LAPWAI CREEK** (Nez Perce)   Presbyterian missionary Henry Spalding moved here in 1836 and built a mission he named Lapwai. It is a Nez Perce word that means "butterfly," for the butterflies that gathered at a nearby millpond. Spalding also grew Idaho's first potato here. In November of 1876, settler Emily Fitzgerald observed a meeting between a Nez Perce (Wallowa band) Indian named Thunder Rising and a group of white commissioners on the creek. They met to discuss land rights of the Indians. She wrote: "When we got there, Joseph's band had arrived… On the other side of the building were a lot of Treaty Indians who came in to hear how their wild brothers were treated… I wish you could have seen them…"[5]

**LOCHSA RIVER** (Idaho)   Lewis and Clark passed a trail near this river that was used by the Flathead Indians for their fishing parties. The expedition planned to use the river to make their way further westward, but the trail ended where a canyon narrowed, and they had to find another route. The Lochsa rises in the Bitterroot Mountains and joins the Selway River. Lochsa is a Salish word meaning, "rough water," descriptive of the river's many miles of churning water and the fact it plunges down from its origin into a deep canyon.

**NAHNEKE MOUNTAIN** (Elmore)   The mountain, located in the Sawtooth Wilderness, takes its name from a Shoshone expression meaning "sway backed," and is descriptive of the feature's topography. It rises about 9,578 feet high.

**NAPIAS CREEK** (Lemhi)   Gold played an important part in this creek's history. Frank Sharkey and a number of miners made their way from Montana to the Napias where they discovered gold. As a result, the mining town of Leesburg was established about 1866, which drew more than 3,000 people. By 1874 all the gold had played out. Napias is an Indian word that means "money" or "gold."

**PAHSIMEROI RIVER** (Custer)   Originating in the Lost River Range, the Pahsimeroi joins the Salmon River. It is from the Shoshoni phrase, pah, sima and roi, meaning "water one grove," designating a lone grove of pine trees near the riverbank. The Lemhi Indians fished this river for salmon during the spring. Idaho Power Company established a fish hatchery on the river for the purpose of trapping and rearing summer Chinook salmon.

**POTLATCH CREEK** (Clearwater/ Latah)   This creek flows into the Clearwater River. First named Yaka ("black bear"), it was renamed Colter by the Lewis and Clark Expedition when they camped here in May of 1806. General Howard had the resident Indians removed to reservations in 1877. Potlatch is a Nez Perce word similar to "convention."

**SELWAY RIVER** (Idaho)   The Nez Perce made their home in the region, which was later settled by the white men migrating west. The Selway is about 100 miles long, originates in the Bitterroot Mountains, and joins the Lochsa River. It bears a Nez Perce word that means "smooth water," or "good canoeing."

**SPOKANE RIVER** (Kootenai)   Flowing about 100 miles, the Spokane River has its origins at Coeur de'Alene Lake and flows into the Columbia River. The Spokane Indians called themselves "children of the sun," or "sun people." The chief called himself Illim-Spokane, "Chief of the sun people." Settlement near Spokane Falls started in 1871. The Spokane Indians have a legend about a monster that lived in their midst. While an Indian girl was picking berries she saw the monster asleep and ran back to her village to tell the chief. The warriors tied him up, but when the monster awoke he broke the cords like they were string. The monster fled through the land, tearing a deep channel until he reached Lake Couer d'Alene. The waters of lake ran into the channel and created the Spokane River.

**TOLO LAKE** (Idaho)   Tolo was a Nez Perce woman who made friends with the whites during the Nez Perce war of 1877. Her real name was Alablernot, but the whites called her Tolo (name origin unknown). The lake was a gathering place for the Nez Perce people for their potlatches, in addition to preparing for their winter food supply. While the Idaho Department of Fish and Game was deepening the lake in 1994, crew members discovered a field of ancient mammoth fossils. It was later determined that the bones belonged to the largest known mammoth in North America (14 feet tall at the shoulders and weighing 5-6 tons).

# ILLINOIS

**CAHOKIA CREEK** (Macoupin)   The Cahokia is about 55 miles long and enters the Mississippi River. The stream's course was changed twice: in 1861 when it was diverted for railroad improvements for the Pittsburgh Railroad and Coal Company; then in the late 19th century when the railroad diverted it further west. In 1792, James Piggot settled in the region and established a ferry on the creek, which became a central point for travelers. Cahokia is an Illinois word meaning "wild goose."

**CHICAGO RIVER** (Cook)   Formed at the city of Chicago, the river's name is Algonquin for "place of the skunk," or "wild onion." Some historians believe it means

something "strong" or "great." The river is more than 150 miles long, and was considered by settlers a muddy pond. The river was later dredged and straightened, allowing for better navigation and shipping. The city of Chicago once depended on this river for its water supply.

**ILLINOIS RIVER** (Grundy/Will)   The Illinois became an important commercial waterway when the city of Peoria was established along its banks, bringing industry to the region. Joliet explored the river area in 1673. The Illinois is about 273 miles long, rises at the confluence of the Des Plaines and Kankakee rivers, and enters the Mississippi River. It was named after the Illinois Indians who called themselves Illiniweek, meaning "human being."

**KASKASKIA ISLAND/RIVER** (Randolph) When the Mississippi River flooded in 1881, it claimed the land and left Kaskaskia Island, which can only be reached by land via St. Marys, Missouri, or by boat. About 1700 Jesuit Sebastian Rasle was responsible for settling a band of Indians near the mouth of this river, which became their principal home until they were removed. Kaskaskia may have indicated "hide scraper." During the Civil War George Rogers Clark and his Kentucky Long Knives launched an attack on the island and stopped the British from taking control. The Kaskaskia River is about 320 miles long, rises near the town of Urbana, and empties into the Mississippi River.

**KICKAPOO CREEK** (Peoria) This river is about 25 miles long, originating near Peoria and joining the Illinois River. In 1836, a steam flour mill was established using the water power of the creek. The name comes from the Kickapoo Indians, interpreted as "red bud," descriptive of a shrub that grew prolifically along its banks; the plant is also known as the Judas tree. Another translation was "he moves about."

**KISHWAUKEE RIVER** (McHenry) Founded in 1895, Northern Illinois State Teachers College was established along the river, occupying about 67 acres. The 60-mile long river originates in Woodstock and enters the Rock River. The banks of the Kishwaukee are dotted with trees, which have created a safe habitat for the river otters that live there. Kishwaukee is a Potawatomi word meaning "big tree," or "sycamore." It was also interpreted as "river of clear waters."

**MACOUPIN CREEK** (Montgomery) Peoria and Cahokia Indians used this re-

gion as their major hunting ground. By the time of white settlement, most of the Indians had left the area. A few came back to hunt occasionally, but after an extremely bad winter in 1830 that wiped out the wild turkeys, they never returned. The Macoupin joins the Illinois River. It is an Algonquian word that means "water lilies," descriptive of the tubers along the creek the Indians used for food.

**MUSCOOTEN BAY** (Cass) The Muscootens were one of the principal tribes of the Illinois Indians who had their village along the river's banks, which the French called Mound Village. Their name means "meadow."

**PISTAKEE LAKE** (Lake) Part of the Chain of Lakes, Pistakee is an Illinois word taken from pestekouy, meaning "buffalo," for the scores of the animals that roamed the region. LaSalle and his party explored the region during the 1600s.

**SANGAMON RIVER** (Champaign) The Kickapoo Indians had their villages along this river during the early 1800s until the Battle of Tippecanoe, when they moved to Lake Peoria. The Sangamon flows 250 miles to join the Illinois River. Abraham Lincoln's family lived near the river. After Lincoln encountered sandbars and snags on a journey down the Sangamon, he invented a device that could lift boats over shoals (it was never manufactured). Sangamon is an Algonquian word, part of which means "outlet."

**SOMONAUK CREEK** (LaSalle) Early settler Reuben Root claimed land here in 1835, which later became the home of the Somonauk United Presbyterian Church. The abundance of timber brought others to settler in the mid-1800s. Somanuak may be a Potawatomi word meaning "paw paw grove."

# INDIANA

**BAUGO CREEK** (Elkhart)   Once the site of an old Potawatomi village, the community of Jamestown was founded along the creek in 1835. The Indians occasionally visited and conducted trade soon after the first general store was established. This creek is about 20 miles long and flows into the St. Joseph River. Its Potawatomi name, bau-baugo, was interpreted as "devil river," or similar phrase, descriptive of the extremely swift currents during freshets.

**CHIPPEWANUCK CREEK** (Kosciusko)   In 1836, a treaty with the Potawatomi Indians was signed along the banks of the Chippewanuck, which resulted in removal of the tribe. About 14 miles long, this creek joins the Tippecanoe River. Chippewanuck is derived from the Potawatomi words che-pyuk and wah-nuk, meaning "spirit (or "ghost") hole."

**GRAND CALUMET RIVER** (Lake)   This river flows about 16 miles to join the Illinois River in the state of Illinois. During the 1870s, a harbor was built at the confluence of the Illinois and Grand Calumet. When the Gary Works company was established in the early 1900s, the river's course was changed to accommodate the plant. Calumet was thought to be a French word, but may actually be a French corruption of an Algonquian word killamick or kennomick, meaning "a long body of deep, still water."

**IROQUOIS RIVER** (Jasper)   The Iroquois is about 85 miles long and flows to the Kankakee River in the state of Illinois. The river was named for the Iroquois Indians, whose name has been interpreted as

"real adders," and "people of the long house." The Indians call themselves "we who are of the extended lodge." The American Fur Company established a post along the river in 1822 to conduct trade with the Indians.

**KANKAKEE RIVER** (St. Joseph)   The Kankakee river region was inhabited by the Potawatomi Indians and fur traders, and was explored by Father Marquette in 1679. Once known as the Great Kankakee Swamp because of its enormous marsh basin, the named was changed. Kankakee is derived from the Potawatomi word tian-kakeek, translated as "low land" or "swampy country." The river flows into the Illinois River.

**MANITOU LAKE** (Fulton)   Manitou is derived from the Potawatomi word man-ne-to, meaning "spirit." Legend says a serpent named Meshekanabek once lived in the lake. He and his allies wreaked havoc on the Indians, frightening all their game away, and dragging those unfortunate Indians beneath the waters. A young Indian brave named Messou killed Meshekanabek after it slew one of his relatives. The serpent's henchmen he tied up and sent to caverns located at the bottom of the lake. Manitou comprises about 715 acres.

**MAUMEE RIVER** (Allen)   In 1680, French-Canadians established a trading post at the foot of the rapids. General William H. Harrison had a fort built along the river during the War of 1812 to serve as a supply depot for invasion into Canada. The Maumee River forms at the confluence of the St. Joseph and St. Marys rivers, then flows about 100 miles into Lake Erie. Maumee may a corruption of Miami, which was interpreted as a Lenape word for "all friends," or" a Chippewa expression meaning "people who live on a point." Other derivations were a French corruption of wemiamik, meaning "all beavers."

**MAXINKUCKEE LAKE** (Marshall) Potawatomi Indians occupied this site when white settlers arrived about 1832. Six years later the Indians were removed to Kansas. The lake then became a resort, with cottages and summer homes dotting the lakeside. In 1883, the Terre Haute and Logansport Railroad laid its tracks to the lake, which brought in more settlers. Maxinkuckee Lake is comprised of about 1,800 acres. Its name was derived from the Potawatomi word mog-sin-kee-ki, which means "big stone country," in reference to the numerous rock bars situated in the lake.

**MUSCATATUCK RIVER** (Jefferson) The town of Vernon is almost entirely surrounded by the river, which is about 53 miles long and joins the East Fork White River. Muscatatuck is derived from the Lenape word mosch-ach-hit-tuk, interpreted as "clear river" or "pond river," indicative of the numerous ponds along its course. It was called Scattertuck by settlers because they could not pronounce the word correctly. The river is part of a wildlife refuge for migratory birds and waterfowl.

**MUSKELONGE LAKE** (Kosciusko) Bearing a Chippewa word meaning "the great pike," this lake comprises about 32 acres and is located near the town of Warsaw.

**PATOKA RIVER** (Orange)    The Patoka is about 138 miles long and flows into the Wabash River. The region was once a major hunting ground for the Indians until settled about 1835 when land claims were entered. Patoka may be a Miami word meaning "Comanche," since the Comanches were taken as slaves by the Miami and Illinois Indians. Other interpretations were an Illinois word meaning "wild goose," or "logs on the bottom." The town of Patoka was established along the river which supported sawmills, distilleries and cooper shops. It later became a shipping center for grains and fruits.

**SALAMONIE RIVER** (Jay)    This river joins the Wabash River, and may bear the Miami word on-sah-la-mo-nee, meaning "bloodroot." It was also thought to mean "yellow paint," because the Indians made a yellow dye from the bloodroot. During the 1930s, the 850-acre Salamonie River State Forest was established after residents aided in purchasing land along the Salamonie. The forest was created in order to reclaim eroded land.

**SHAKAMAK LAKE** (Greene)    Shakamak is the first man-made lake in the state, created during the 1920s. It is located at Shakamak State Park and comprises about 56 acres. The name may be from a Lenape word meaning "slippery fish," taken from shack-a-mak. It was also defined as a Kickapoo word meaning "river of the long fish."

**SHIPSHEWANA LAKE** (Lagrange) This lake was a favorite camping site for the Potawatomi Indians, and is their expression for "vision of a lion." The 200-acre lake is situated near the town of Shipshewana. George Lotterer claimed land on the lakeshore and founded the village of Georgetown about 1837, but it did not survive.

**TIPPECANOE RIVER/LAKE** (Kosciusko)    Tippecanoe is a Miami word, derived from ketapkown, meaning "place of buffalo fish." At one time Chief Musquabuck and his tribe lived along the lake which was a former Indian reservation. The river is about 180 miles long and joins the Wabash River. During 1811, a major battle occurred along the river between Chief Tecumseh and the U.S. Army. The name gave rise to William Henry Harrison's famous presidential slogan, "Tippecanoe and Tyler Too."

**WAWASEE LAKE** (Koscuisko)   Originally called Turtle Lake, this feature comprises about 2,618 acres, and is the largest natural lake in the state. It bears the name of Potawatomi Chief Wah-we-as-see, which means "full moon," or "round one." He was known locally as Old Flat Belly. One of the state's oldest fish hatcheries was established on the southeastern corner of Wawasee Lake.

**WEASEL CREEK** (Miami)   First known as Wesaw Creek, the name was changed to Weasel, a corruption of wesaw. It is a Miami word descriptive of an animal's bladder. The creek is tributary to Eel River.

# IOWA

**KEOKUK LAKE** (Muscatine)   Although the Illinois Indians were original inhabitants of the region, the lake bears a Fox or Sac name, taken from Chief Keokuk, interpreted as "the watchful fox." It was also known as Cooper Lake. Part of the town of Keokuk is located on a bluff overlooking the lake and was once an embarkation point for soldiers during the Civil War. The lake, which comprises about 100 square miles, was created when a dam and hydroelectric plant were constructed in 1913.

**MAQUOKETA RIVER** (Jackson)   Because of the numerous bears in the region, the river was given the name Maquoketa, an Algonquian word meaning "bear river." Others translated it as "high bank." The Maquoketa is about 130 miles long. Winnebago, Sac, Fox and Sioux Indians considered this region their fishing and hunting ground until settlement in 1833. The river was also a haven for desperadoes, horse thieves, and counterfeiters. During 1840, more than a dozen outlaws were taken by a posse during what was called the Bellevue War.

**MUSCATINE ISLAND** (Muscatine)   Muscatine was derived from the Mascoutin Indians, a war-like tribe who were driven across the Mississippi River and settled on the island. Their name may have signified "fire people." Another theory was from the Mascoutin word for "burning island," referring to the overgrown brush that would result in prairie fires. Excellent soil on the island supported a large market of watermelon, canteloupe and sweet potatoes in the 1870s. The Big Sand Mound Nature Preserve is located on the island, created from deposits left over from an ancient river during the Wisconsin Ice age.

**NISHNABOTNA RIVER** (Carroll)   This river was formed by the East and West

Nishnabotna and flows about 100 miles long into the Missouri River. The Nishnabotna was a major transportation route during the time Samuel Tefft operated a ferry. The river later became an important source of hydroelectric power. Nishnabotna may be a Sioux word, but only part of the word is known: ni signifying "river."

**NODAWAY RIVER** (Montgomery) The Nodaway rises at the confluence of the Middle and West Nodaway rivers, and flows about 188 miles to the Mississippi River. Nodaway bears a Potawatomi word that means "placid." It was also defined as "deep channel," or "rattlesnakes."

**OKOBOJI LAKE** (Dickinson) The French were thought to have visited the lake in the early 1700s, since at one time it was known as Lac d'Esprit. In 1883, the Burlington, Cedar Rapids Railroad had a hotel constructed near the lake. J.A. Beck purchased land and built another hotel in the 1890s, which was the beginning of the lake's life as a resort. Okoboji may be derived from the Algonquian word okoboozhy, which means "place of rest," "reeds," "to the south" or "spreading out." At one time there was an island in the lake (Spirit Lake) the Indians never dared to set foot on. They believed if they landed their canoes on the island, they would be seized by a demon and never seen again.

**WYACONDA RIVER** (Davis) This 60-mile-long river empties into the Mississippi River near the town of La Grange. It may be a Sioux word meaning "spirit." Legend says two Sioux Indians were found dead here, without any indication of fighting. The Indians believed it was because some deity that inhabited the river killed them.

# KANSAS

**CHEYENNE BOTTOMS** (Barton) Originally a marshy lowland (hence, Bottoms), the Kansas Fish and Game Commission diverted Arkansas River water to the site, which created the 19,000-acre lake. It was later designated a wildlife refuge for migratory birds. The lake took the name of the Cheyenne Indians because it was there the Cheyennes fought with the Pawnee Indians in 1849 over control of their hunting ground. Cheyenne means "southerners."

**CHIKASKIA RIVER** (Kingman) Flowing about 145 miles, the Chikaskia termi-nates in the state of Oklahoma where it empties into the Salt Fork of the Arkansas River near the town of Tonkawa. Chikaskia is derived from an Algonquian word shah'ga'skah, which means "white finger nails." It was also interpreted as an Osage word for "white salt river," or "white spotted deer," all designating something white. The most popular definition is reference to "salt." The short-lived village of Chikaskia was located along the river, founded by a Mr. Parker.

**CHINGAWASSA SPRINGS** (Marion) Known as Carter's Mineral Springs, the name was changed in 1888 to Chingawassa in 1888, for an Osage chief, whose name was interpreted as "handsome bird." Members of the Kansas State Unviersity visited the springs the same year and made scientific tests of its waters. The results showed a high sulfur content, and it was thought the springs would be attractive to those seeking healing waters. Eventually, the hotels that were built closed down from lack of interest.

**GEUDA SPRINGS** (Sumner,Cowley) The springs bear a Ponca or Sioux word meaning "healing waters." In 1867, a German of the Dunkard faith came to the region as a missionary to the Indians. He called the springs Gude, which also has the same meaning. Before the springs became a health resort, the Indian women would travel many miles to have their babies there.

**KAHOLA CREEK** (Chase) Kahola is a tributary to the Neosho River. The name was probably a corruption of Cahola, which is a Kansa expression for "living by the river." In 1847, the Kansa (or Kaw) Indians ceded their land on the lower Kaw River, and were given a reservation along the creek. Kahola was also the name of a village on the reservation, but when a smallpox epidemic hit in 1853, it was burned down.

**KANSAS RIVER** (Geary) Derived from the Kanza (or Kaw) Indians, Kansas has been interpreted as "south wind people." This tribe lived along the river for as long as anyone can remember. The river is about 170 miles long and joins the Missouri River near Kansas City. Captain C. K. Baker was the first person to navigate the river using a steamboat in 1854. Because of massive flooding near Kansas City, dams and reservoirs were constructed along the river's tributaries to prevent further inundation.

**NEOSHO RIVER** (Morris) Settlers called this stream the Grand River, and the Indians named it Six Bulls River. The Neosho is 460 miles long and flows into Oklahoma. The name may be derived from an Osage word for "clear water." A more accurate definition may be derived from necoitsahha, meaning "dead man's creek," a name the Indians gave the area because of a battle between the Kansas and Plains Indians at one time.

**NINNESCAH RIVER** (Stafford) Flowing about 170 miles, this river rises at the confluence of the North Fork River and South Fork River, then empties into the Arkansas River. Ninnescah is an Osage word translated as "abundant water," "white spring," "salt water,' or "running white water." The original form of the word is Ninneskua (skua means "salt").

**OSAGE RIVER** (Wabaunsee) The Osage River rises at the junction of the Marais des Cygnes and Little Osage rivers, then joins the Missouri River in the state of Missouri. The river was named for the Osage Indians, taken from their own name, wazhazhe, the meaning of which is obscure. They occupied the land until white settlement in the early 1800s. Although the river served as a transportation route, it was sporadic because of the rise and fall of the water level.

**PAWNEE RIVER** (Finney/Gray) The river was named for the Pawnee Indians, their name meaning "horn people," because of their distinctive hair style from the grease and paint they applied to their scalp locks. The Pawnee Indians were part of the Caddo family, and the name was probably a corruption of pariki. The stream empties into the Arkansas River at the town of Larned.

**POTTAWATOMIE RIVER** (Franklin) The Potawatomi flows from east Kansas and joins the Osage River near the town of Osawatomie. It has been defined as "fire maker" or "people of the fire nation."

**SAPPA CREEK** (Decatur)   Sappa is a Sioux word meaning "black." The last Indian raid occurred along the creek in 1878 after the Northern Cheyenne escaped from a reservation in Oklahoma. Led by Dull Knife, the Indians made their way to Kansas, looting along the way. They were later captured at the creek and sent to prison. Sappa Creek is about 100 miles long and joins Beaver Creek.

**SHUNGANUNGA CREEK** (Shawnee) Potawatomi Chief Abraham Burnett had a farm along this creek. Educated at a Baptist missionary school, he became an important mediator among his tribe. Cyrus Holliday was partly responsible for selecting a site along the creek that would become the city of Topeka. Shunganunga Creek was formed from an ancient ice sheet, and may be an Osage word for "little house." Most authorities believe it means "race course." The creek joins the Kaw River.

**WACONDA SPRINGS** (Mitchell)   Because the waters contained numerous mineral deposits, the springs were touted to have curative properties. As a result, bath houses and a sanitarium were established. The sanitarium later housed a bottling plant that shipped *Waconda Water* to all parts of the United States. The springs were situated on a mound that was more than 60 feet across. Waconda is a Kaw (or Kanza) word that means "great spirit." When the Solomon River was dammed up, it caused the springs to be turned into a lake.

**WAKARUSA RIVER** (Wabaunsee)   In 1841, Rufus Sage wrote about the treacherous river while settlers were trying to cross: "...its banks being so precipitous we were compelled to lower our wagons by means of ropes..."[6] Apparently an Indian who lived nearby did quite well monetarily pulling some of the wagons out of the river. James Findlay was principal in getting a bridge built across the river. Wakarusa may be a Kaw word meaning "knee deep in mud," or "hip deep," and refers to the legend of a young Indian girl who rode her horse into the river. As the horse went further across the stream, the girl became immersed in the water, and cried "Waykarusa." It was also interpreted as "river of big weeds." This river joins the Kansas River.

**WEA CREEK** (Miami)   This small stream joins Bull Creek. During the early days, the oil that seeped from the nearby Wea Tar Pits were used to grease wagon axles. George Brown discovered the oil in 1860, which precipitated the petroleum industry that began in the late 1800s. Wea is taken from the Wea Indians, who were a sub-tribe of the Miami Indians. Their name was interpreted as "eddy people," derived from wayah-tomuki. The majority of Weas died from smallpox.

# KENTUCKY

**KENTUCKY LAKE/RIVER** (Marshall) The lake was created in 1938 when a dam was built by the Tennessee Valley Authority with a workforce of more than 5,000 men. It comprises more than 160,000 acres. The purpose of the dam was to control floods on the Lower Ohio and Mississippi rivers. The Kentucky River begins at the confluence of the North Fork and Middle Fork rivers in the central part of the state, and flows 259 miles to join the Ohio River. A series of locks were built, enabling navigation along the entire length of the river. Kentucky was derived from a Wyandot word ken-tah-the, meaning "land of tomorrow," or the Iroquois word kentahe, meaning "meadow land."

**KINNICONICK RIVER** (Lewis) The village of Kinniconick is located along the river, which is a Shawnee word for "willow bark," descriptive of the willows prevalent in the region. It may also be a name that meant a substitute for tobacco, or the plant that produced it. The tobacco was a rolled wood mixed with scrapings from other woods, including sumac, cornel, red osier and the bearberry plant to form the mixture. Thomas Harrison built the Kinniconick Hotel in the early 1800s, which is still in existence. The stream is about 90 miles long.

# LOUISIANA

**ABITA SPRINGS** (St. Tammany) The springs may have been found by Choctaw Indians during the 1850s. Folklore says the springs were the fountain of youth for which Ponce de Leon was searching. During the 1880s, the region became known as the "ozone belt," after numerous spas were established. The springs no longer exist because they were covered over with cement. Abita may be a corruption of Abicka, a Creek word signifying "pile at the base," or "heap at the root," in reference to the Indians' custom of covering the bottom of a war pole with enemy scalps.

**ATCHAFALAYA RIVER** (St. Martin) The river originates at the confluence of the Red and Mississippi rivers and flows about 225 miles into the Gulf of Mexico. Atchafalaya was derived from the Choctaw words hacha and falaia, meaning "long river." During the early 1700s, the Chitamacha Indians, considered one of the most powerful tribes in the region, established their villages along the river.

**BASTINEAU, LAKE** (Webster) With its French sounding name, Bastineau Lake is a corruption of the Caddo word, bestino, meaning "big broth lake," indicative of its foaming waters. Spanish explorers came to the region where they traded guns and ammunition for salt and horses with the Indians. A Frenchman named Francious Grappe purchased the land and lake in 1787.

**BAYOU GOULA** (Iberville)   Situated near the stream, Bayou Goula village is the oldest settlement in Iberville Parish and home to the Bayougoula Indians (a Muskhogean tribe) who were discovered by Frenchman Iberville about 1699. The name is derived from the Choctaw words, bayuk and okla, interpreted as "river people."

**BAYOU LOUIS** (Catahoula)   Bayou Louis is derived from the Choctaw expression bauk and lusa, meaning "black bayou." The community of Sicily was established along the bayou by a colony of Russian Jews. During the Civil War, Union forces came up the bayou on the ship *Lexington*, and captured Confederate artillery and cotton.

**BAYOU MANCHAC** (East Baton Rouge) The bayou was once a major trade route between the Mississippi River and the Gulf of Mexico. It enabled the British to trade with the north while avoiding Spanish-controlled New Orleans. But in 1814, Andrew Jackson had the bayou filled in to keep the British from cutting him off. Manchac originates at Baton Rouge and merges with the Amite River. In early days it was called Ascantia (Choctaw for "cane-brake is there") and then Iberville by the French until it was officially named Manchac, a Choctaw word for "rear entrance."

**BAYOU PLAQUEMINE** (Iberville) The Plaquemine was an important route to the interior of the state during the 1790s. The town of Plaquemine was settled along the bayou and named for the persimmon trees dominant in the area. It is derived

from the Illinois word plakimin, meaning "persimmon," the fruit of which the Indians used for making bread. The Opelousas Steamboat Company was given permission by the Louisiana Legislature in 1826 to establish a steamboat and ferry on the bayou.

**BOGUE FALAYA RIVER** (St. Tammany)   This river bears the Choctaw expression bok and falaia, meaning "bayou long." It enters the Little Bogue Falaya near the town of Covington and then joins the Tchefuncta River. The town of Covington was founded along the river in 1813 with the arrival of John Wharton Collins, a merchant from New Orleans.

**BONFOUCA BAYOU** (St. Tammany) This stream was named for Chief Bonfouca, a Choctaw Indian, whose name means "river residence." The region was settled in the 1700s because of easy access to the city of New Orleans by way of the bayou. Francois Rillieux and his wife, Marie, were a prominent family who settled on the bayou in 1720. After the death of her husband, Marie purchased from the Biloxi Indians all of St. Tammany Parish that was between the bayou and the Pearl River. In 1826, a Mr. Gusman established a brick factory, which became a base of the Parish's economy for many years.

**CALCASIEU RIVER** (Vernon, Rapides) When this territory was designated a neutral area in 1806, it brought numerous bandits and pirates; one of the most notable was Jean Lafitte and his buccaneers, who were said to have hidden a wealth of treasure along the river. Calcasieu is from the Attakapas expression katkosh and yok, meaning "eagle to cry," or "crying eagle." It was also the name of an Attakapas chief. The river flows for 200 miles and empties into the Gulf of Mexico.

**CASTINE BAYOU** (St. Tammany)

There is disagreement as to the origin of Castine. Some believe it to be from the Choctaw words kashti and bayak, meaning "flea bayou," because of the flea infestation in this region. The Creole people said it came from Castagne, the name of an early French settler, but the name was already in use long before the French entered the region.

**CATAHOULA LAKE** (LaSalle) Because traces of gas and oil were found near the lake, some believe it was once part of the Mississippi River. The Attakapa Indians called the lake etac-oulow, meaning "river of the great spirit." They held sacrificial ceremonies there, and legend says the lake is still haunted by the unfortunate maidens. Chacahoula (also spelled Chuckahoola) was translated from Choctaw as "beloved home," derived from chuka ("home") and hullo ("beloved").

**CHINCHUBA CREEK** (St. Tammany) The creek contains the remnants of shells, pottery and a mound, which led authorities to believe the region was once a Choctaw settlement. Chinchuba was derived from the Choctaw word hachunchuba, meaning "alligator." The creek empties into Lake Pontchartrain.

**CHOUPIQUE BAYOU** (Calcasieu) Choupique Bayou empties into the Calcasieu River. An early settler of 1850 built a corn mill along the bayou to serve parish residents. Choupique may be a Choctaw word meaning "bowfin," or "mudfish." Others have interpreted it as a Choctaw word for "filthy," or "stench."

**FORDOCHE BAYOU** (St. Landry) The bayou bears a Caddo expression meaning "wild animal lair." In 1863, Spaight's Battalion, also known as the Swamp Angels, fought in a number of

skirmishes with the Union Army, including the Battle of Fordoche Bayou.

**KISATCHIE NATIONAL FOREST** (Natchitoches) This is the only national forest in the state, and consists of about 600,000 acres. Kisatchie is a Caddo word interpreted as "long cane," or Choctaw for "reed river." Caddo and Natchez Indians were resident here, followed in later years by the French and Spanish. Timber men later moved in to cut down the wealth of virgin longleaf pine. Since reforestation wasn't conducted in the early days, the forest was depleted. In 1930, the national forest was established due to the efforts of naturalist Caroline Dorman, and the forest was replanted.

**MONGOULOIS LAKE** (St. Martin) This lake bears a Mobile name that was interpreted as "people of the opposite clan." Oil was discovered in the vicinity during the 1920s, and in 1930 Texaco developed an oil field near the lake.

**NATALBANY RIVER** (St. Helena) The Natalbany is about 45 miles long and has its origins in the Parish near the Mississippi state line. Schooners plied the river during the early 1800s and gave residents of the town of Ponchatoula access to the markets of New Orleans. Natalbany is from the Choctaw words nita and bano, thought to mean "bear camp," "lone bear," or may have designated a person who cooked bear meat. At one time there was a dense bear population in the region.

**TCHEFUNCTA RIVER** (St. Tammany) The Tchefuncta joins the Bogue Falaya, then empties into Lake Pontchartrain. During the Civil War, the *Grey Cloud*, a Federal Navy ship, sailed into the river where it engaged in a confrontation with the Confederates. Tchefuncta is derived from the Choctaw word hachofakti, which means "chinquapin," a type of chestnut.

**TECHE BAYOU** (Beauregard)   Acadians from Nova Scotia moved to the bayou in 1790 and established farms, taking advantage of the rich soil. The bayou flows 125 miles to the Atchafalaya River. Teche may be a corruption an Attakapas word for "snake." According to Indian legend, the Chitimacha Indians believed a snake of huge proportions that lived in the region was killed by one of the warriors, its death throes cutting the bed of the bayou. One section of the bayou was called the Sugar Bowl because it was inhabited by wealthy planters who grew canefields, and processed the product with their own sugar mills. The bayou was the setting for Henry Wadsworth Longfellow's famous work, *Evangeline.*

**TICKFAW RIVER** (Livingston)   When Livingston Parish was organized, its seat of government was located along the Tickfaw at the town of Van Buren. Many of the settlers were engaged in the timber industry, a mainstay of their economy. In 1870, strawberries were introduced along the river when it was found the soil and climate were well-suited for growing the fruit. Tickfaw is derived from the Choctaw words, tiak and foha, which mean "pine rest," an apt name since Tickfaw was a lumber town. Another theory was "wild beasts shed their hair," from poa and tikafa, also Choctaw. The river is about 105 miles long and flows into the Natalbany River.

**TUNICA BAYOU** (West Feliciana) Tunica Indians settled near this bayou and their name was given to the stream, which means "people." Others translated it as a Choctaw word for "post" or "pillar," designating some type of boundary marker. First named Willing's Bayou, it was changed to Tunica about 1816. The bayou rises in the Tunica Hills and joins the Mississippi River.

**WHISKEY CHITTO CREEK** (Vernon) Whiskey Chito joins Six Mile Creek in Allen Parish. In 1846 explorer LaTourette wrote on his map B. Shiwkey Chitto. This odd name was corrupted from the Choctaw words uski (or oski) and chito for "large canebrake." The creek is within the migratory path of the Arctic Peregrine Falcon.

# MAINE

**ABAGADASSET RIVER** (Somerset)
Early settlers arrived at the mouth of the Abagadasset and Cathance rivers about 1730, where the town of Bowdoinham was established. A land title dispute occurred between the Bowdoin family and Kennebec Proprietors until a survey was conducted, along with a quit claim deed from Chief Abagadasset. The Bowdoins won the suit in 1763. Elihu Getchell built the first sawmill in 1760, using the water power of the river. Abagadasset is an Abnaki word defined as "stream opening out from between mountains," or "following a shore curved."

**AGAMENTICUS MOUNTAIN** (York)
A Pawtucket Indian named Aspinquid, considered an Indian saint, is buried on this mountain. He died in 1692 at the age of 94. Tradition says thousands of animals were sacrificed at his funeral. During the 1800s, the mountain was used as a point of navigation for clipper ships, and served as a radar base by the U.S. Army in the 1940s. The base was destroyed by fire in 1945. Agamenticus may be Abnaki for "other side of the river."

**ALAMOOSOOK LAKE** (Hancock)
Alamoosook is located near the Orland River, and was home to the ancient Red Paint People. Its name was corrupted from the Malaseet word adlemetit, translated as "spawning bed." During the early 1900s, Charles Adkins built a hatchery to rebuild the Atlantic salmon, which was the first such hatchery in the country for the species.

**ALLAGASH RIVER** (Aroostook/Piscataquis)    Allagash is an Abnaki word for "bark cabin." During the logging era, a dam was built to divert the Allagash for floating logs to the Penobscot River. In 1842, water flow from Telos and Chamberlain lakes were diverted by timbermen in order to serve the lumber mills. Then a canal was built to siphon water from the Allagash into the Penobscot, and severely altered the streams' directions. Supreme Court Justice William Douglas wrote, "Precious water, sorely needed if the Allagash is to be restored as the most wondrous canoe stream in the nation, runs needlessly into the East Fork.... We must move fast, if the whole chain of lakes and streams that make up the Allagash is to be preserved. Relics of old dams must be removed."[7] His words fell on deaf ears. The river is about 92 miles long and was established as the Allagash Wilderness Waterway by the Maine Legislature in 1966.

**AMBAJEJUS LAKE** (Piscataquis)    For more than 70 years the Great Northern Paper Company mills processed spruce and fir trees that were driven down the Penobscot River and into Ambajejus Lake, then loaded onto a log boom for transport to its mills. Ambajejus is an Abnaki word for "two currents, one on either side."

**ANASAGUNTICOOK, LAKE** (Oxford)
This lake was once known as Whitney Pond, where the town of Canton was established. In 1814, Gustavus Hayford built the first mill and dam along the lake. It was named for the Androscoggin tribe who were also called the Anasaguntacook, interpreted as "at the river with a sandy bottom."

**AROOSTOOK RIVER** (Aroostook)
The Aroostook is 140 miles long and joins

the St. John River in New Brunswick. It may be Micmac for "beautiful," "shining river," or "river with silver bottom." It was also thought to come from waloostook ("dark swift river"). Most of the settlers along the river migrated from New Brunswick. Warren and Evert Drake operated the first ferry across the Aroostook river until the advent of steamboats. Eventually, railroads took over and the river was no longer used for transportation.

**BAGADUCE RIVER** (Hancock)    The town of Penobscot was established along the river in 1760. Bagaduce may have been derived from the Micmac word, majabigwaduce, variously interpreted as "big bay," "bad bay," and "tideway." It was also spelled Baggadoose and Maja-bagaduce. Some believe Bagaduce was named for a French office, Major Bigavduce. Another interpretation was a derivation of marchebagaduce, meaning "no good cove. " Folklore says Bagaduce meant a place of sorrow because at some point in time an incident occurred causing the Indians great distress.

**BASKAHEGAN RIVER** (Washington) The river rises in a remote corner of eastern Maine, near New Brunswick, and because of its remoteness only a few towns have been established along the stream. Baskahegan was known for its log drives and as a hunting ground of the Penobscot and Passamaquoddy Indians. The river bears an Abnaki expression for "branch downstream," or "like a branch," descriptive of one being able to choose which branch of the river to follow.

**CARRABASSETT RIVER** (Franklin) In 1646, Jesuit missionary Father Druillettes traversed the river and built a mission at the town of Norridgewock. Father Sebastian Rasle arrived later and stayed to learn the Abnaki language. The English tried to get the Indians to sell their land, but Father Rasle convinced them not to do so. The English later attacked, killing Rasle and an Indian named Carrabasset, for whom the river was named, Abnaki for "small moose place," or "sturgeon place."

**CASCO BAY** (Cumberland)    Casco Bay has so many islands in it, tradition says there are as many islands as there are days in the year; consequently, they are called the Calendar Islands. During the 1850s, the bay and port were one of the largest shipbuilding centers in the United States, with more than 95 wharves located along the bay. During World War II, the bay served as a naval base. The Upper Goose Island Preserve in the bay harbors the largest great blue heron colony in New England. Casco may be a corruption of ancocisco, an Abnaki word for "great blue heron," or a Micmac word for "mud" or "muddy."

**CATHANCE RIVER** (Washington) Bowdoinham Village (see Abagadasset), once called Cathance Landing, was one of the leading shipbuilding towns in the state. Ships were constructed and taken to river, where they were destined for various ports on the Atlantic seaboard. Cathance is a tributary to Merrymeeting Bay, and bears a Maliseet word for "principal fork."

**CAUCOMGOMOC LAKE** (Piscatiquis) Caucomgomoc is the third largest lake in Maine. In 1894, Gregg Clarke opened up the first recreational activity offering canoe trips. Caucomgomoc is Abnaki for "lake abounding with gulls."

**CHEBEAGUE ISLAND** (Cumberland) The island was once a summer retreat for the Maine Indians who gave Chebeague its name, an Abnaki word meaning "island of many springs," or "almost separated." George Cleeves held the original grant and gave the island to Walter Merry in 1650. Chebeague depended, for the most part, on the rock slooping industry, which was used to build lighthouses and breakwaters. In the mid-1800s, Chebeague's economy turned to the tourist industry

**CHESUNCOOK LAKE** (Piscataquis) Located in the mountains of western Maine, Chesuncook bears an Abnaki expression for "at the place of the principal outlet." It was also thought to be derived from chesunk, meaning "goose place," signifying the sound a goose makes while flying.

**CHIPUTNETICOOK LAKES** (Aroostook/Washington)   Once called the Schoodic Lakes, this group of lakes bears the Abnaki expression for "at the place of the big hill stream." The former town of Forest City was established as a lumber camp along the lake shore.

**COBBOSSEECONTEE LAKE** (Kennebec)   This nine-mile lake is located in the town of Manchester. Before settlement, the lake was the fishing site for the Abnaki Indians, and later a base for the State Forestry and privately owned seaplanes. It bears an Abnaki word meaning "place of abundant sturgeon." Located in the lake is a small island called Ladies Delight, upon which a lighthouse was built in 1908 to warn launches of a reef in the water.

**COBSCOOK BAY** (Washington)   This bay is an inlet of Passamaquoddy Bay. Cobscook may be derived from the Malacite word opscook, defined as "rock under water," or kapsook, for "water falls," indicative of the water that boils over unseen rocks in the bottom of the bay.

**HARRASEEKET RIVER** (Cumberland) The indented peninsula of Casco Bay forms the Harraseeket River, which is an Abnaki word for "full of obstacles," "small islands," or "river of many fish." During the 1800s, numerous landings were built

and logging companies shipped out the lumber from the head of tide of the river. Other industries that benefited from the river were gristmills and fulling mills. Another product was salt that was harvested from the marsh water.

**KATAHDIN, MOUNT** (Piscatiquis) Thoreau was one of the first to write about the mountain and described them as "a vast aggregation of loose rocks, as if at some time it had rained rocks..."[8] Katahdin may come from the Abnaki word katahdu, defined as "highest land," "big mountain," or "chief mountain." It is the highest point in Maine (5,267 feet high) and dominates the remote wilderness of Baxter State Park. Surveyor Charles Potter was the first white man to scale the mountain in 1804. Legend says Katahdin was ruled by the Mountain King and his daughter, Lightning. An Indian brave named Kinaldo fell in love with Lightning who gave him a magic potion so he would forget his former life, but his memory returned and he wished to go home. The Mountain King let him go but said those who tasted the wind could no longer live among men. When a storm arose, the lightning struck Kinaldo, who died at the foot of the mountain.

**KENDUSKEAG RIVER** (Penobscot) Samuel de Champlain came up the Kenduskeag River in 1605 and found an Indian village he called Kadesquit. This was the place where the French and Indian river trade was conducted. The village of Kenduskeag was created when the towns of Glenburn and Levant were "cut" and Kenduskeag formed in 1852. The name was taken from the stream, which comes from a Quoddy (or Maliseet) word meaning "eel-weir place."

**KENNEBEC RIVER** (Piscataquis)   The river is more than 150 miles long and originates at Moosehead Lake. It flows to the Androscoggin River and then empties into the Atlantic Ocean. Kennebec is an Abnaki word for "long, quiet water," It was also translated as "long reach." Shipbuilding was prevalent along the river, as were the logging and ice harvesting industries.

**KENNEBUNK RIVER** (York)   Kennebunk was established near the river about 1650, and because of the town's proximity along the river, shipbuilding and trade with the West Indies were important industries. Kennebunk is an Abnaki word meaning "the long cut bank," or "long sandbar," designating an Indian landmark.

**KINEO MOUNTAINS** (Piscataquis) Indians traveled from remote areas to these mountains to collect the flint called hornstone, and used the material to make tools and arrowheads. Kineo is Abnaki for "sharp peak." The Indians called the mountain Moose Rock, a sacred place to them, because they believed it was the petrified body of a moose their wonder worker, Glooskap, had killed. The Maine Department of Inland Fisheries and Wildlife began a Peregrine Falcon reintroduction program in the mountains, and in 1989 the first breeding pair had their young.

**MACHIAS   RIVER**   (Aroostook) Machias means "bad little falls," or "a bad run of water," an Abnaki word signifying a section of the Machias River that drops down into deep gorge. The river has its origins in Big Machias Lake and travels 35 miles into Machias Bay. The British charted the region in 1527. During the early days of the timber industry, the river provided the means for transporting logs.

**MADAWASKA LAKE** (Aroostook) Madawaska was founded near this lake by the Acadians in 1785, who came from St. Anne Des Pays-Bas, New Brunswick. They refused to take the oath of allegiance and escaped from the English in 1755, moving temporarily to the St. John River until they settled at Madawaska. The name was derived from madoueskak, which may be a Micmac word for "porcupine place." Other definitions were "grass lands extending to the river banks," and "a junction of rivers."

**MANANA ISLAND** (Lincoln)   Vikings may have been the first people to visit this island about 1,000 A.D., since rune-like carvings were found in the rocks, but some authorities believe the carvings are a natural phenomenon. The island was later inhabited by cod fisherman. Manana may be derived from the Abnaki word monanis, meaning "the small island."

**MARANACOOK LAKE** (Kennebec) One of the first settlers to the lake region was James Craid in 1740, who later sold parcels of land along the lake shore. He also established a gristmill and sawmill. Maranacook is Abnaki for "plugged up lake," "deep lake," or "black bass here."

**MATINICUS ISLAND** (Knox)   Located about 20 miles south of Rockland, this little island is only two and a half miles long and a mile wide. Matinicus was derived from manasquesicook, an Abnaki word for "a collection of grassy islands," or "far out island." Another interpretation was "place of many turkeys." Cod fishing was an important industry, in addition to ship building and outfitting ships for the West Indies trade during the 1840s.

**MATTAWAMKEAG RIVER** (Aroostook)   Mattawamkeag is an Abnaki word that means "the river that runs through it," or "a river with many rocks at its mouth." The latter refers to a large gravel bar at the entrance of the Mattawamkeag River. It was also interpreted as a Micmac word for "on a sand bar," and "fishing place beyond gravel bar." The river is about 70 miles long and joins the Penobscot River near the town of Mattawamkeag.

**MEDOMAK RIVER** (Lincoln)   The community of Waldoboro was established along the river, living its early life as a shipbuilding town, and became the second busiest shipping center on the Eastern Seaboard. Medomak is a Penobscot word for "place of many alewives." The ship *Medomak* has the distinction of being the first five-masted schooner to be launched in the state of Maine (1888).

**MEGUNTICOOK RIVER** (Knox) Megunticook was derived from a Micmac expression meaning "big mountain harbor," or from the Penobscot word amehkay-ihtekok, meaning "at a stream below a height" (or "mountain"). The town of Camden is situated near the river and in its early days thrived on coastal trade, shipbuilding, and fishing.

**MESSALONSKEE LAKE** (Kennebec) With an area of 5.5 square miles, this lake is one of the Belgrade Chain of Lakes. It is an Abnaki expression for "white clay here." The lake once contained a village established by the Taconnet Tribe. During the 1850s, four dams were constructed along the stream below the lake, and settlers used its water power for their gristmills, sawmills and other industrial factories.

**METINIC ISLAND** (Knox)   Metinic is located a little more than 10 miles from the town of Rockland. During the 1740s, the Post family purchased the island from resident Indians. Folklore says that while carpenters were putting a roof on a home during the War of 1812, they witnessed a battle between the USS *Enterprise* and British warships. The island has traditionally been occupied by fisherman and used as a cod

station. Metinic may be Abnaki for "far out island."

**MONHEGAN ISLAND** (Lincoln) Monhegan is a rocky island about ten miles off the coast of Maine, and stretches about 2.5 miles long and a mile wide. Named by the local Indians (who may have been Micmacs), Monhegan means "island of the sea," or "out to sea island." The island was a landmark for sailors, headquarters for exploring expeditions, and a place for men to trade furs with the Indians. It was first settled in 1720 by George Weymouth. Early residents made their living fishing for lobsters, and today the small population is still engaged in the industry.

**MOOSELOOKMEGUNTIC LAKE** (Oxford)   The lake comprises about 25 square miles. It is an Abnaki word thought to mean "portage to the moose feeding place," or "moose feeding among trees." The town of Oquossoc is surrounded by the lake.

**MOUSAM RIVER** (York)   This river is about 23 miles long and originates at Mousam Lake, then flows into the Atlantic Ocean. During the 1730s a fortification was built along the river by Sergeant Larrabee and used for protection against the Indians. It was torn down about 30 years later. In 1825 the Kennebunk Manufacturing Company built dams on the river for its cotton mill. Mousam was thought to be an Abnaki word for "grandfather."

**NAHUMKEAG ISLAND** (Kennebec) Nahumkeag is a Maliseet word for "eels run out." The island comprises a mere 3-4 acres. A blockhouse was built during 1716 for settlers' protection, but it was destroyed by the Indians in 1726.

**NARRAGUAGUS RIVER** (Hancock) This river rises at Eagle Lake and empties into Narraguagus Bay. It is an Abnaki word for "above the boggy place," in reference to a tidal marsh bordering the river. Logging was conducted during the mid-1800s and the timber floated down the river to the town of Millbridge, where the product was shipped out. In 1853, President Franklin Pierce ordered a lighthouse to be constructed on the river, which operated until 1934.

**NEQUASSET LAKE** (Sagadahoc) Nequasset village was settled along the lake in 1638, but it was destroyed by Indians. It would be 1734 before the village was resettled. The lake provided water for the mills that were established. Boatbuilding was an important industry as was ice harvesting. Nequasset may be Abnaki for "pond."

**NESKEAG POINT** (Hancock) Neskeag is an Abnaki expression for "place at the end." This point was the scene of the Battle of Neskeag during the American Revolution in 1778, when a settler fired his gun into an English barge and killed one of the men.

**NEZINSCOT RIVER** (Oxford) The Nezinscot is about 11 miles long and flows into the Androscoggin River. Chief Sabattus and his tribe lived in the region and befriended an early settler they named Father Thomas, who became an arbitrator of their quarrels. First known as Twenty Mile River, the name was later changed to Nezinscot, and Abnaki word for "place of descent," or "going downriver by canoe."

**OGUNQUIT RIVER** (York) Ogunquit was derived from a Micmac word, pog-um-ik, meaning "lagoons formed at mouths of rivers by dune beaches driven by the wind," or from obumkegg, for "sand bar." Another interpretation was "place of waves," derived from antegwquit. It was also thought to be Natick for

"a beautiful place by the sea." John Elliot gave the Praying Indians the name Natick.

**OLAMON ISLAND** (Penobscot) Deposits of red hematite on this island were very popular with the Indians who used it for adornment and making pigments. Olamon may be derived from oolamon-oosuk (or oulamon-i-suk), an Abnaki word for "red paint," or "red paint his place."

**OSSIPEE RIVER/MOUNTAIN** (Oxford) Before settlement, the Sokokis Indians had their villages along this river, but they disappeared by the 1600s. An early settlement was Acton Corner, followed by other hamlets as new roads were constructed. The water power of the river brought the establishment of a prosperous mill industry. Ossipee is an Abnaki word for "water on the other side." Ossipee Mountain is home to the Mountain Fire Tower, originally built in 1918.

**PAMOLA PEAK** (Piscataquis) This peak is about 4,902 feet high. It was named for Pamola, an evil spirit the Abnaki Indians believed inhabited the mountain, which was created by the Council of Gods to serve as their special meeting place. Apparently, Pamola was not allowed into the Council, and as a result was outraged and withdrew to the peak. The Indians believed that anyone who ventured onto the mountain would run into Pamola and be seen no more.

**PASSADUMKEAG RIVER** (Penobscot) The Indians who roamed the region were called Red Paint People, as evidenced by artifacts found near Passadumkeag. Early inhabitants were Enoch and Joshua Ayers in 1813. The Passadumkeag River provided water power for the manufacture of shingles and staves, shipped out via the European & North American Railroad. When the village of Passadumkeag was founded, it took its name from the river, an Abnaki word for "above the gravel bar," "stream above falls," "falls running over gravelly bed," or "quick water."

**PASSAGASSAWAKEAG RIVER** (Waldo)  This river is at the head of Belfast Harbor and runs through the town of Belfast. Passagassawakeag is an Abnaki word meaning "a sturgeon's place," or "a place for spearing sturgeon by torchlight."

**PENNAMAQUAN RIVER** (Penobscot) The town Pembroke was founded near the river and originally called Pennamaquan until it was changed to Pembroke in 1832. The town used the water power of the river for factories that manufactured iron nails and ship fittings. Pennamaquan was derived from the Abnaki word meaning "extensive" or "opens out."

**PENOBSCOT RIVER** (Penobscot) The Penobscot is the longest river in the state, rising from numerous lakes in central Maine and flowing into Penobscot Bay. The river was first explored by an Englishman named Martin Pring in 1603, followed a year later by French explorer Samuel de Champlain. Penobscot may be a Maliseet or Micmac word meaning "the rocky place," or "the descending ledge place." Legend says that when the Indians noticed the river water getting lower every day, they sent one of their people to see if the river was being blocked, and discovered a giant frog. The Indian council called on Klose-kur-beh, the first man on this land. He took a giant pine tree and hit the frog with it, which burst and spewed water in a thousand directions and created Penobscot River. Folklore also says that great white swans brought the fair-skinned (white) people to this place.

**PISCATAQUIS RIVER** (Piscataquis) In 1603 Martin Pring explored this river (as he did the Penobscot) searching for sassafras. Transportation in early days were boats called gundalows, which operated for more than 200 years. During the timber era, logs were floated down the river to Portsmouth Harbor in New Hampshire for loading onto waiting ships. Piscataquis is an Abnaki word meaning "at the river branch." In 1771, a wooden lighthouse was established about a mile from the mouth of the Piscataqua River, the first light station at a military installation of the British colonies.

**QUAKISH LAKE** (Penobscot)  This lake bears an Abnaki word for "flooded place." It was also thought to be Micmac for "rough strewn." During the 1900s, the Great Northern Paper Company used the lake as a conduit for moving logs to its mill.

**SACO RIVER** (Oxford)  The Saco is about 105 miles long, originating in the White Mountains and emptying into the Atlantic Ocean. The town of Saco was established about 1623 and took its name from the river. The falls on the river were used to power the textile industry established along the stream. Saco is an Abnaki word for "outlet."

**SAGADAHOC BAY** (Sagadahoc) During 1607 the Plymouth Colony began its colonization of the United States on the bay. John Parker settled along the bay at a place called Parker's Island. It was changed to Georgetown in 1714. Sagadahoc is a Penobscot word for "mouth (or "entrance") into a river." It was also interpreted as an Abnaki phrase for "the outflowing of a swift stream as it meets the sea."

**SASANOA RIVER** (Lincoln)  The Sasanoa was an important transportation route for Indians who conducted fur trade with the whites. It later supported a ferry business established by John Carlton. The stream was named for Chief Sasano, an Abnaki sachem who met Samuel de Champlain in 1607. His name origin is unknown.

**SCHOODIC LAKE** (Piscataquis)   Considered one of the state's largest cold-water lakes, Schoodic is about 9 miles long. During the 1880s, the Merrick Thread Company was established near the lake, manufacturing about 69 million spools of thread each year. Schoodic is home to two of the state's largest blueberry growers, which draw water from the lake for their fruit. Schoodic may be a Micmac word meaning "the end."

**SEBASCODEGAN ISLAND** (Cumberland)   Sebascodegan became part of the Massachusetts Bay Colony in 1652. A century later the Indian War, supported by the French in Quebec, caused many of the settlers living on the island to be killed. Sebascodegan may be a Passamaquoddy word for "near through," descriptive of the island's shape with its many points and passages.

**SEBASTICOOK RIVER** (Kennebec)   Rising near the town of North Dexter, the river merges with the Kennebec River. It was a main transportation route for the Indians and French missionaries. John Houstin was the first settler along the river, and supported himself by trapping. By 1808, others had taken up residence and established the town of Newport. Sebasticook was interpreted as a Penobscot word for "passage river," or "almost through river."

**SEGUIN ISLAND** (Washington)   This 64-acre island is located at the mouth of the Kennebec River, and was used as a landfall for early ships. When Champlain sailed to the region in 1612, he made note that the island resembled a tortoise. In

1795, George Washington commissioned a lighthouse on the island (one of the oldest lighthouses in America). Seguin may be a Maliseet or Micmac word for "humped up," or "cluster," descriptive of a turtle.

**SOKOKIS LAKE** (York)   The Holland Woolen Mill was established on the shores of the lake, and in 1899 became known as the Limerick Mill in the hamlet of Limerick, which was also supported by grist mills and shingle mills. Sokokis was named for the Sokokis Indian tribe that resided in the region, but their origin is unknown.

**UMBAGOG LAKE** (Oxford/Coos, NH)   Umbagog Lake is about 10 miles long and borders the states of Maine and New Hampshire. It is an Abnaki word for "clear lake." The Umbagog contains one of the largest nesting concentrations of the common loon in the state of New Hampshire.

**UMBAZOOKSUS LAKE** (Piscataquis)   Umbazooksus was interpreted as an Abnaki expression for "clear, gravelly outlet." This lake was connected to the Penobscot River via Chesuncook Lake, and was an ideal waterway for driving logs, which were transported to the lake via the Eagle Lake and West Branch Railroad to await shipment.

**WASSOOKEAG, LAKE** (Penobscot)   Wassookeag is a 1,700 acre lake that is divided into Big and Little Wassookeag, separated by a bridge and causeway. Originally named Silver Lake, it was changed to Wassookeag, a Penobscot word meaning "shining lake."

**WEBHANNET RIVER** (York)   Webhannet may be Abnaki for "at the clear stream." The river is only 4 miles long, but with a fall of over 100 feet it was ideal as a millstream. In 1643 Edmund Littlefield built the first permanent mills along the river.

**WESKEAG RIVER** (Knox)    During the early 1700s, Thomas LaFebvre moved from Quebec and purchased land along this river, where he established a gristmill at the site where the village of Thomaston would later be founded. Weskeag is an Abnaki word describing a creek that runs dry with low tides.

# MARYLAND

**ANACOSTIA RIVER** (Prince Georges) The Anacostia is a branch of the Potomac River, where members of the Nanchotank (or Nacotchtank) Indians established their villages. Captain John Smith's visit to the region in 1608 opened it for settlement. Walter Shaw claimed part of the Anacostia River wetlands in 1880 and established an aquatic garden growing water lilies and other water plants. Later called the Shaw Aquatic Gardens, Shaw became one of America's largest exporter of cut water flowers. Anacostia may come from an Algonquian term meaning "at the trading town," or "stream, current."

**ANTIETAM CREEK** (Washington)    On September 17, 1862, Union General Joseph Hooker attacked the Confederate Army, and more than 23,000 Federal and Confederate troops were killed or wounded at what became the Battle of Antietam. The creek is a tributary of the Potomac River. Antietam is an Algonquian word meaning "flow," "current," or "swift water."

**ASSACORKIN ISLAND** (Worcester) This island is situated in Chincoteague Bay. Assacorkin is an Algonquian word derived from acaw, meaning "across" or asaw and quak, interpreted as "yellow earth."

**ASSATEAGUE ISLAND** (Worcester) Assateague is one of the barrier islands on the Eastern Shore. In 1945, the U.S. Government purchased part of the island that is situated in Virginia and created the Chincoteague National Wildlife Refuge. Assateague is an Algonquian word interpreted as "running stream between," or "stony river."

**ASSAWOMAN BAY** (Worcester)    This bay is a tidal lagoon. Assawoman is an Algonquian word meaning "stream or inlet in the middle," or "midway fishing stream."

**BROCKATONORTON BAY** (Worcester)    The bay is located at the mouth of Boxiron Creek, and bears an Algonquian name meaning "fire people" (or "nation"), derived from bocootawwonauke. During the 1670s, the bay was first called Pocketty Norton and later changed to Brockatonorton.

**CATOCTIN    RIVER/MOUNTAIN** (Frederick)    Immigrants found the river (a tributary of the Potomac) while looking for a new place in which to settle. The community of Catoctin grew around an iron furnace that was established in 1774, which later made cannon balls for the siege of Yorktown during the Revolutionary War. Catoctin was derived from the Algonquian word ketagi, meaning "spotted (or speckled)." It was also thought to mean "mountain," or "place of many deer." During the Depression, people were put to work transforming part of the mountain into a recreational area. Rock quarried from the mountain was used to build the columns in Statuary Hall at the U.S. Capitol.

**CHAPTICO BAY** (St. Marys)  Chaptico was derived from the friendly Choptico Indians, whose name means "big broad river that is." It was also interpreted as "deep water." This was the site where a Protestant rebellion was held in 1669 by soldiers who had just been mustered out of the army and organized the protest. One of Maryland's oldest hamlets established in 1689, Chaptico was located near the head of the bay, and served as a river port of entry for the county.

**CHESAPEAKE BAY**  The bay comprises about 3,237 square miles and separates the eastern shores of the state, extending into Virginia. The bay was explored by Captain John Smith in 1608, which later became important for commercial fishing of oysters and crabs. Chesapeake is an Algonquian word meaning "mother of waters" or "great salt bay." It may be a corruption of tschiswapeki or k'tschishwapeki, interpreted as "highly salted."

**CHICAMACOMICO RIVER** (Dorchester)  Chicamacomico was derived from the Algonquian expression ahkamikwi and kehtci-kami, translated as "dwelling place by the big water," or from tschikenumiki, meaning "place of turkeys." This river is a branch of the Transquaking River.

**CHICAMUXEN CREEK** (Charles)  The creek bears an Algonquian name that was interpreted as "there lies high ground," derived from chi and amehki. Located along the Chicamuxen was a Civil War encampment established by Union General Joseph Hooker.

**CHICONE CREEK** (Dorchester)  This tributary of the Nanticoke River bears a Powhatan word derived from coan and kehtei, meaning "big snow." The Nanticoke Indian Reservation was established in 1698 and the Chicone River served as one of its boundary lines.

**CHOPTANK RIVER** (Caroline)  The Choptank flows into Chesapeake Bay and also forms part of the boundary between Caroline, Talbot and Dorchester counties. The river supported tobacco farmers and also served as the main transportation route for schooners until the early 1930s. Choptank is an Algonquian expression, kehtei, api and ehtan, meaning "it flows back strongly." It is the longest river on the Eastern Shore.

**CUTMAPTICO CREEK** (Wicomico)  Cutmaptico is from the Algonquian expression kehtci, mehittuk and a-wi, translated as "big tree creek." The Cutmaptico is a tributary of the Wicomico River.

**GEANQUAKIN CREEK** (Somerset)  This creek is a tributary of the Manokin River. The village of Geanquakin was once situated nearby during the 1600s, supported a boat-building industry, but eventually the site was abandoned. Geanquakin is derived from the Algonquian word meaning "where it is high."

**HONGA RIVER** (Dorchester)  The Honga River is an arm of Chesapeake Bay, and bears an Algonquian word derived from kahunge, which means "goose." The river once supported local crab fisherman. Legend says a place called Golden Hill received its name when Spanish pirate boats sailed up the Honga River and buried their treasure there.

**MAGOTHY RIVER** (Anne Arundel) A tributary of Chesapeake Bay, the river was a place where the Indians came on their annual migration from the state of New York to get their stores of winter food. Some authorities believed Magothy was in reference to maggots. Others suggested it was a Lenape word meaning "without timber," or "open place in the forest." Another derivation was from magucke, meaning "a wide plain."

**MANOKIN RIVER** (Somerset) Manokin River is a tributary of Chesapeake Bay, and was once a main transportation route. Manokin is an Algonquian expression defined as "dig, dig away," or "people who dig the earth." Another derivation was from awak, meaning "earth is dug out." Settlement along the river occurred during the 1660s.

**MATAPONI CREEK** (Prince Georges) Records of 1635 show this name spelled as Mattapanian. The creek is a tributary of the Patuxent River. Mataponi may be derived from the Lenape expression that means "no bread at all," but others interpreted it as a corruption of the Natick word mattappuu, meaning "he sits down," or matta and apo, for "joined water."

**MATTAWOMAN CREEK** (Charles) The former village of Mattawoman was situated near the headwaters of Mattawoman Creek. Derived from mataughquamend, Mattawoman is a Piscataway word meaning "where one goes pleasantly." In the 1600s Captain John Smith met the Piscataway Indians at the stream during his explorations, which was the Indians' first contact with the whites. The Mattawoman Indians were part of the Piscataways, principal tribe of the Conoy Federation. Mat-

tawoman is a tributary of the Potomac River and one of the boundaries of the Naval Surface Warfare Center, Indian Head Division.

**MINGO BRANCH** (Baltimore) This stream is a tributary of Gunpowder Falls. It was named for the Mingo Indians of Pennsylvania, who came here to attack the Susquehannock Indians near the town of Hereford. Mingo was the Lenape Indians' word (mingwe) for their enemies, the Iroquois, meaning "stealthy," or "treacherous."

**MONIE CREEK** (Somerset) The Monie Indians who lived along the creek were visited by Reverend John Huett in 1682 who practiced his ministry to them. Monie was derived from the Natick words munnoh ("island") and moonoi ("it is deep"), or from the Powhaten expression onowmanient, meaning "it is beneath."

**NASSAWANGO CREEK** (Worcester) When bog iron was discovered along this creek during the 1780s, the Maryland Iron Company was established, as was the short-lived town of Nassawango. The company later became known as the Nassawango Furnace, the only bog ore furnace in the state. Because of financial difficulties, the furnace and town lasted only until about 1847. Nassawango may be a Natick word meaning "between land." "or ground between streams," indicative of a piece of land that has streams on either side. The Nassawango merges with the Pocomoke River, and it part of the Nassawango Creek Cypress Swamp Preserve.

**OKAHANIKAN COVE** (Dorchester) Situated on Bloodsworth Island, Okahanikan Cove was interpreted from an Algonquian word accohanoc, meaning "as far as the river," or "narrow, winding stream." It may also mean "place where there are many bends in the stream."

**PASSERDYKE CREEK** (Wicomico/ Somerset)   A dam was constructed at the head of the Passerdyke, which created a mill pond for the settlers' use. During the 19th century, the creek served a thriving commerce trade. Passerdyke may be derived from the Powhatan word, pasaugh-tacock, meaning "stream that scoops banks," or "split stream." The creek is a tributary of Wicomico Creek.

**PATAPSCO RIVER** (Carroll/Anne Arundel)   Attracted by the river's water power, numerous settlements were established and supported by flour and textile mills. In 1835, the Thomas Viaduct was built across the stream for the Baltimore & Ohio Railroad. The river originates at the harbor of Baltimore City which connects it with Chesapeake Bay. Patapsco was derived from the Lenape word petaps qui, meaning "backwater, tide river," or "jutting rock at."

**PATUXENT RIVER** (St. Marys)   Before European settlement, local Indian tribes used the river for fishing, mainly oysters, evident by the large oyster mounds found in the region. During the 1600s, the settlement of Coxtown was a chief tobacco port. The U.S. Naval Air Station built along the river was commissioned in 1943. Considered the longest river entirely within Maryland, the Patuxent rises at Parr's Ridge and flows about 100 miles into Chesapeake Bay. Patuxent is an Algonquian word meaning "at the little rapid in a stream."

**PICCOWAXEN CREEK** (Charles)   The Piccowaxen is a tributary of the Potomac River, and bears an Algonquian word which means "torn shoes," "broken shoe," or "break shoe." All are indicative of the brambles and crags that grew the region.

**PISCATAWAY CREEK** (Prince Georges)   The village of Piscataway was established in the 1700s, but was later deserted after the creek silted up and the port disappeared. The Piscataway Indians who lived here had a totem that signified a beaver, thus Piscataway could mean "big beaver." It was also interpreted from a Lenape expression meaning "high passable bank around a bend in the river," or "branch of a stream."

**POKATA CREEK** (Dorchester)   Pokata is a tributary of Island Creek. It may be derived from the Lenape word pokety, meaning for "open, clear," or "where it is opened or cleared."

**POMONKEY CREEK** (Charles)   This tributary of the Potomac River once had a thriving village by the same name, with a post office established about 1867. Pomonkey is an Algonquian word meaning "it is sloping," or "twisting in the land."

**QUANTICO CREEK** (Wicomico)   Before white settlement, The Nanticoke Indians had established a village at the creek called The Dancing Place. The name was changed in 1670 when Augustine Herman noted on his map the name Quantico. It is an Algonquian word meaning "long tidal stream" or "at the long inlet." The first tomato canning factory on the Eastern Shore was established there.

**QUIRAUK MOUNTAIN** (Washington)   Quirauk Mountain is about 2,145 feet high, and bears an Algonquian name for "gull." In 1926 Fort Ritchie was built at the bottom of the mountain, its purpose to train Maryland's National Guard. It operated until 1998.

**REWASTICO CREEK** (Wicomico)   Rewastico Creek is a tributary of the Nanticoke River, and may bear the Lenape name derived from liwasquall, meaning "weeds," or "weedy stream."

**ROCKAWALKING CREEK** (Wicomico) Rockawalking Creek is a tributary of the Wicomico River. It bears the Lenape word lehauwak, meaning "fork" or "place of the fork." Another interpretation was from lekau, awank and ink, meaning "at the sandy ground."

**SINEPUXENT BAY** (Worcester) The bay is home to Maryland's only coastal town located on a barrier island, Ocean City. The bay was used only by fishermen until the mid-1800s, when an Inn was built to accommodate them, which encouraged more people to settle in the region. The Baltimore Salt Company was established during the Revolutionary War, where it evaporated water to create salt. The Wicomico and Pocomoke Railroad built a trestle across the bay in 1876, connecting Ocean City to other towns. Sinepuxent is from the Lenape expression sotny and puxen, meaning "stones are lying broken up," or "stones lie shallow."

**TOMAKOKIN CREEK** (St. Marys) Tomakokin is a tributary of St. Clement Bay, and is a Lenape expression meaning "beaver place."

**TYASKIN CREEK** (Wicomico) Tyaskin was also the name of an old village, derived from the Algonquian word taiaskon, meaning "bridge people," or tyaskin for just "bridge." Another interpretation was taken from the Tawachquan Indians, referred to as "the Indians at the bridge."

**WETIPQUIN CREEK** (Wicomico) A planter named Samuel Jackson was granted 300 acres of land along the creek in 1668. About 15 years later, the hamlet of Wetipquin was ordered founded by an Act of Assembly for trading and shipping purposes. Wetipquin Creek flows into the Nanticoke River. It is an Algonquian word derived from wilipkwin, which means "skull place."

**WOOTENAUX CREEK** (Talbot) The Wootenaux is a tributary of Kings Creek. It was interpreted as an Algonquian word meaning "fine squirrel" "fisher," or "it rushes forth from the ground."

# MASSACHUSETTS

**ABERJONA RIVER** (Norfolk) Many lakes and streams flow into the river, which provided an abundance of power that spurred industrial growth, producing more than 100 tanning factories. A canal was also built which connected the village of Woburn with the port of Boston. During the late 1800s, the Merrimac Chemical Company was established and became the one of the largest chemical companies to manufacture arsenic and explosives during the World Wars. Aberjona is a Natick word for "junction," or "confluence." The river flows through the community of Woburn and empties into the Mystic Lakes.

**ASSABET RIVER** (Worcester)  This 30-mile-long stream flows into the Sudbury River. The Assabet was a busy transportation route from the Merrimack, Concord and Sudbury rivers. The town of Concord was founded at the confluence of the Sudbury and Assabet rivers. It shared the honors with Lexington as the birthplace of the American Revolution in the state. Thousands of Indian artifacts were discovered along the river at a site called Pine Hawk. These tools and arrowheads dated back as far as 7,000 years. Assabet is a Nipmuc word meaning "miry place."

**CHAPPAQUIDDICK ISLAND** (Dukes) Chappaquiddick was derived from tseppiaquidne-auke, a Wampanoag word for "at the separated island," descriptive of the island's separation from Martha's Vineyard by a narrow strait. In 1801, the Cape Poge Lighthouse was built on the northeast tip of the island. Chappaquiddick is probably best known for the night of July 18-19, 1969, when Mary Jo Kopechne died after the car Ted Kennedy was driving plunged over a bridge.

**CHICOPEE RIVER** (Hampden)  Indians who lived along the Chicopee River were the Nipmuc ("freshwater") Indians. This river joins the Connecticut River. The town of Chicopee is located along the river and established the region's first cotton mill in 1828. It became known for its textile mills and invention of farm implements. The name may be Nipmuc for "violent water," or "raging, rushing water."

**COCHITUATE LAKE** (Middlesex) Settlers moved here from Boston and purchased land that included the lake, which they initially called Long Pond. Cochituate is a Natick or Nipmuc expression for "place of swift water."

**CUTTYHUNK ISLAND** (Dukes)

Cuttyhunk is the outermost of the Elizabeth Islands. Bartholomew Gosnold made landfall in 1602 and settled there temporarily. In 1688, Peleg Sanford purchased the island, selling half of it to Ralph Earle, who became the first permanent resident. In 1924, the last squared-rigged whaler was lost at sea near Cuttyhunk. The name was derived from a Wampanoag word, poocutohhunkunnoh, thought to mean "point of departure," or open, cleared field."

**HOUSATONIC RIVER** (Berkshire) Rising in the Berkshires, the Housatonic flows about 150 miles into Long Island Sound. The Mohican Indians called the river usi-a-di-en-uk ("beyond the mountain place," or "at the place"), from where Housatonic is derived. The town of Housatonic grew around the establishment of numerous mills. The river's estuary was a large producer of seed oysters, and generated over one-third of all the oyster seeds available to the state. There are five hydroelectric facilities on the river today.

**KONKAPOT RIVER** (Berkshire)  This river flows into the Connecticut River. Early settlers to this region were Lieutenant Isaac Garfield, Thomas Slayton, and Captain Brewer, who built the first sawmill using the water power of the Konkapot. It was also a site where fur trading was conducted. The second mill built in the United States was established along the river, where paper was made from straw. Konkapot was the name of a Stockbridge chief named Konkapot, a Mahican word meaning "long spout."

**MEGANTIC LAKE** (Franklin)  In 1759, the English established an overland route from New England to the city of Quebec. Part of the trade route was along Megantic Lake, where the Abnaki Indians had their villages. Megantic was derived from namagwottik, Abnaki for "place of many fish," or "lake trout place."

**MERRIMACK RIVER** (Essex)   The Merrimack is about 100 miles long. It has its origins in the town of Franklin and flows into the Atlantic Ocean. The Pennacook Indians had their villages there until white settlers brought their diseases that wiped many of them out. Merrimack is from the Abnaki word monnomoke (or merrimake), meaning "sturgeon," or "at the deep place."

**MONOMOY ISLAND** (Barnstable) The first inhabitants on the island were merchants who built a tavern for sailors about 1711. The community of Whitewash Village was established in the 1800s, but was eventually abandoned because the harbor shoaled up. Monomoy Lighthouse was built in the 1820s and operated until 1923. It is listed on the National Register of Historic Places. Monomoy may be a Wampanoag word for "lookout," or "deep water."

**MUSKEGET ISLAND** (Nantucket) Once home to a life-saving station, the island bears a Wampanoag expression for "great green place," or "grassy place."

**NANTUCKET ISLAND** (Nantucket) The island is about 14 miles long and a little more than 3 miles wide at its widest point. Nantucket is a Wampanoag word meaning "the far away land." In 1621, the island was included in the royal grant to the Plymouth Colony. Colonists came here during the 1660s because of religious intolerance in other towns. When the soil would no longer produce crops, whalers were recruited to teach the local men how to whale. Nantucket was known as the "Whaling Capital of the World" until the industry declined when other petroleum products replaced whale oil, and tourism took over as its economy.

**NASHAWENA ISLAND** (Dukes)   In the early 1900s, the Massachusetts Board of Charity purchased land on the island, which is part of the Elizabeth Islands. When residents learned the board was considering establishing a leper colony there, they rose in protest. As a result, the board sold their property and were forced to look elsewhere. During World War II, military batteries were placed on the island for American defense, which consisted of 90-mm guns, generators, station and barracks. Nashawena is a Wampanoag expression meaning "lies between."

**NAUSHON ISLAND** (Dukes)   This privately owned island bears a Wampanoag name for "angular," "middle," or "big spring." A group of men, including the president of National Bell Telephone Company, purchased the island in 1843. It later became the Forbes Family Preserve.

**NEMASKET RIVER** (Plymouth)   The Nemasket joins the Winnetuxet River. Indians camped along the stream because of the fishing and hunting it afforded them. This is the site of a ford where the Indian trail from Plymouth to Middleborough crossed the river. Nemasket is a Wampanoag expression for "at the fishing place," or "grassy place."

**NISSITISSET RIVER** (Middlesex) During the 1760s, the town of Brookline was established and laid out so the river ran through the middle of it. Nissitisset is a Natick word for "near the two small rivers." It enters the Nashua River at the town of Pepperell.

**ONOTA LAKE** (Berkshire)   The lake comprises about 617 acres and situated next to the town of Pittsfield. Onota may be a Mahican word for "blue," "deep," or from oyatuck, meaning "he dwells at a water stream." Another interpretation was "lake of the white deer," because legend says a pure albino doe came here to drink. The Indians believed if she was killed, evil things would befall them. After a French officer heard about the doe, he laid in wait for the animal and then killed her. The officer was killed heading back to Canada, the Indians suffered dwindling crops, and a plague came upon them until they all disappeared.

**PAMET RIVER** (Barnstable)  Pilgrims who came over on the Mayflower temporarily settled at what today is the town of Truro. While exploring the region they accidentally found bushels of seed corn the Pamet Indians had put away for storage. Tradition says the corn saved the Pilgrims from starving until they moved to Plymouth. In 1797, a lighthouse was established on the river. The town of Truro, because of its proximity to the river's harbor, became an important whaling center. Pamet is a Wampanoag word for "wading place," or "at the shallow cover."

**PENTUCKET RIVER** (Essex)  This river supported an ironworks that was built in 1721. The Pentucket flows through the town of Haverhill and terminates at the Merrimack River. Pentucket is a Natick word for "at the twisting river," descriptive of the river's course.

**POCUMPTUCK MOUNTAIN** (Franklin)  Indian legend says this mountain is the petrified body of a huge beaver that was killed by a spirit named Hobomuck. The beaver's body turned to stone which became the mountain's peaks. Mount Sugar Loaf is the beaver's head, the north part of the mountain its shoulders, and Pocumtuck Rock the back and tail. Pocumtuck is an Algonquian word meaning "narrow swift river," or "clear, open stream."

**QUABOAG RIVER** (Worcester)  In 1720, the Quaboag Plantation was established, of which the town of Warren was once a part. The Quaboag River flows through the center of town and supported Warren's many textile mills. Only a few farms and mills remain. Quaboag is a Nipmuc word for "before the pond," or it may come from m'squ'boag, meaning "red pond."

**QUEQUECHAN RIVER**  (Bristol)  The site that would become Fall River was once home to the Wampanoag Indian Tribe until King Phillip's War in 1675. The town was established in 1803 next to the river and made use of its water power for textile mills. Quequechan is a Narragansett word meaning "swift water," or "torrent." In the Wampanoag language it means "falling water," because the river becomes a steep fall before joining the Taunton River. Legend says an old hag lived in a hut on the banks of this river, until she was driven out by neighbors who thought she was in league with the devil. After stoning her, they torched her hut. In the debris they found a letter from Captain Kidd that indicated she was one of his early mistresses.

**QUINSIGAMOND LAKE** (Worcester)  Quinsigamond is a Nipmuc expression for "pickerel fishing place," or "enclosed place at the long brook." The lake is about 9 miles long and was once known for its recreational facilities, social, and athletic clubs.

**SCARGO LAKE** (Barnstable)  Scargo may be a Wampanoag word meaning "it flows out." Eli Howes and his son discovered and developed a cranberry in the 1840 (later named the Howe cranberry). Indian legend says Princess Scargo and an Indian brave from another tribe fell in love. The brave gave Scargo four fish and told her he would return before the fish were grown. Time went by and the small pond eventually dried up, killing all the fish but one. Weeping over her lost love, Scargo's tears kept the one fish alive. When her father saw her distress he had his people create the lake for the one remaining fish. As he promised, the young brave returned before the fish was fully grown.

**SESUIT CREEK** (Barnstable) Sesuit Creek was once the site of the Shiverick Shipyard, where some of the best clipper ships in the world were built. Sesuit is a Wampanoag word for "cold water" or "cold creek."

**SIPPICAN RIVER** (Plymouth) The settlement of Sippican was founded along this river in 1680, and later incorporated as part of the town of Rochester. The first mill in the region was established by Aaron Barlow and Joseph Burge in 1863. Sippican is a Wampanoag expression for "long stream," or "gravelly stream," descriptive of the river's topography. It was also interpreted as "land of many waters." The Sippican empties into Sippican Harbor on Buzzards Bay.

**SKUNKAMAUG RIVER** (Barnstable) Before white settlement, the region was home to the Pequot and Mohegan Indians. The town of Tolland in the state of Connecticut was founded near the stream with anticipation of becoming a port of entry for steamers. Skunkamaug is a Wampanoag word for "green field."

**SQUAM RIVER** (Essex) This river joins the Pemigewasset River. The water power of the river brought in settlers who founded the town of Ashland and established hosiery mills, glove factories, lumber and paper mills. Squam was thought to be a Natick word meaning "at the end (or "top") of the rock."

**SQUANNACOOK RIVER** (Worcester)

The 1700s brought the establishment of the towns of Fitchburg, West Groton, Townsend and Pepperell that used the river for paper mills and other industries. The river is about 25 miles long, originates near the town of Fitchburg and joins the Nashua River. Squannacook may be a Natick expression meaning "green place."

**TUCKERNUCK ISLAND** (Nantucket) Located west of Nantucket Island, Tuckernuck is a Wampanoag word for "a round loaf of bread," because of the island's appearance. It may also be derived from togguwhonk, meaning "a mortar," or ketah tugooak, for "great waves." The island was purchased by the Mayhew brothers in the 1660s. Today, about 30 homes on the island are used seasonally. The island is also used for sheep grazing.

**WACHUSETT MOUNTAIN** (Worcester) The mountain is located near the city of Princeton and rises about 2,006 feet. It is an Algonquian word for "great hill." The first hotel on the mountain's summit was constructed in 1882, and the Civilian Conservation Corps cut the first trails into the mountain in 1932.

**WAQUOIT BAY** (Barnstable) Established near the bay were the villages of East Falmouth, Hatchville, and Waquoit. The land they occupy was purchased by the Proprietors of Falmouth from the Indians about 1865. Waquoit is a Wampanoag word meaning "at the end."

**WEWEANTIC RIVER** (Plymouth) In 1845, the Tremont Nail Works was established and used the power of the river for its operation. Weweantic may be a Wampanoag word meaning "crooked stream," or "stream that wanders about," which was descriptive of its course. Originating at the town of Carver, the river flows about 20 miles into Buzzards Bay.

**WICKASAUKE ISLAND** (Middlesex) Wickasauke has many interpretations. It may be a Natick or Penacook expression for "house at the end of the outlet." Another derivation is from woweaushin-woweau, which describes wandering, such as a river's course. It may have been taken from weweantet, meaning "at or near the place of."

# MICHIGAN

**BAY DE NOC** (Delta)   Consisting of Little Bay De Noc and Big Bay De Noc, separated by a peninsula, this feature was named for the Noquet Indians who were resident in the region and conducted fur trade on Grand Island. Their name was interpreted as "bear foot." In 1844 surveyor Douglass Houghton mapped the region. The bay was an important shipping point for iron or and timber products, and the first ore dock was built in 1864.

**COBMOOSA LAKE** (Oceana)   In 1855, the U.S. Government signed a treaty with the Ottawa and Chippewa Indians who ceded their territory in exchange for land near the lake. When Ottawa Chief Cobmoosa moved there, a house was built for him. The post office that was established in 1866 was given his name, which was interpreted as "the walker." He died at the lake in 1872.

**COCOOSH PRAIRIE** (Branch)   The first settler to this prairie area was a Quaker named Abram Aldrich, who built the Cacoosh Mill. Cacoosh is an Potawatomi word meaning "pork" or "hog," and may have been the name of a chief, but this is conjecture.

**ESCANABA RIVER** (Marquette)   The Escanaba is 40 miles long and empties into Little Bay de Noc. The region was home of the Chippewa Indians who had their villages along the stream's banks. The town of Escanaba was founded about 1830 and became one of the most important ore-shipping points in the Upper Peninsula. Escanaba means "flat rock," or may have been derived from eshkonabang, an Algonquin word which means "land of the red buck." Longfellow's *The Song of Hiawatha* tells about Hiawatha who went across the Escanaba and slew the Mudekeewis to avenge the death of his mother.

**GOGEBIC LAKE** (Gogebic, Ontonagon) The lake is situated in the Ottawa National Forest and is the largest inland lake in the Upper Peninsula. After Nat Moore found iron ore in the mountain ranges, prospectors rushed to the lake in search of the material. Gogebic may be a Chippewa expression for "body of water," or from agojebic, meaning "rock" or "rocky shore." Another interpretation was Chippewa for "he dives down."

**GOGUAC LAKE** (Calhoun)   The lake bears a Chippewa expression meaning "pleasant water." Settlement began there about 1836 near the town of Milton, which would later become Battle Creek. In 1879, a fire occurred at the lake which destroyed steamers, boat houses and some of the homes. At one time there was a sanatarium located along the lake shore.

**ISHKOTE LAKE** (Iron, Gogebic)    This lake bears the Ojibwa word for "fire." This may have been in reference to the mythical Ishkote (or Ashkote), who was a great shaper and transformer of the forests.

**KALAMAZOO RIVER** (Jackson)    The Kalamazoo River is about 138 miles long and flows into Lake Michigan. The name is derived from the Potawatomi word, kikalamazoo, meaning "boiling water," or "rapids at a river crossing." During the 1830s, a trading post was established along the river.

**KAMLOOPS ISLAND** (Keweenaw) Kamloops is a transfer name from British Columbia. The name is from the Shuswap-Salish Indians, which was interpreted as "meeting place," or "point between the rivers," and may refer to the confluence of the North and South Thompson rivers.

**KAWKAWLIN RIVER** (Bay)    Located at the mouth of the Kawkawlin River was a trading post where traders conducted business with the Chippewa Indians. The wealth of pine and hemlock trees drew Israel Catlin to move there in 1844 and build a sawmill. The river was called oganconning (or uguhkonning) by the Indians, and may be Chippewa for "the place of the pike."

**KEEGO HARBOR** (Oakland)    The harbor bears an Algonquian name that refers to a species of slender fish. In 1902, J.E. Sawyer converted what was known as Dollar Lake into a harbor and built cottages along its shores. He renamed the site Keego Harbor.

**KEWEENAW BAY** (Baraga)    The bay was visited by Jesuit missionary Father Menard during the winter of 1660. Father Baraga established a mission along the bay in 1843. During the 1800s fur trading was a major source of revenue; the logging industry later came into prominence. The Keweenaw Bay Chippewa Indian Community is comprised of the Lac Vieu and L'Anse, and Ontonogan Band of Indians. Keweenaw is a variation of Kewaunee, Chippewa for "prairie hen," or "wild duck."

**LEELANAU, LAKE** (Leelanau)    Separated by a narrow stretch of land, the lake has a north and south part. According to Schoolcraft, Leelaneau is Algonquian for "delight of life," but this interpretation was proven wrong. Schoolcraft had a penchant for making up Indian names. The closest translation for the name was the Algonquian word laleu, meaning "seashsore." The town of Leland is located along the lake and was settled in 1853 by Antoine Manseau. Its main industry was timber.

**MACATAWA LAKE** (Ottawa)    In 1847, Reverend A.C. Van Raalte was looking for a site to establish a Dutch settlement and selected land along the lake, which became known as the Holland Settlement. Sandbars and silt blocked what could have been a shipping channel to Lake Michigan. Van Raalte asked Congress for help in digging a channel, but was refused, so the Dutch did the job themselves and completed it in 1859. First known as Black Lake, the name was changed to Macatawa, an Ottawa word meaning "black."

**MACKINAC ISLAND** (Mackinac) Jean Nicolet was the first white man to the island while he was searching for a route to the Orient in 1634. Father Claude Dablon wintered on the island in 1670, his purpose to do missionary work with the Huron Indians. With a swelling beaver population, the American Fur Company was established in the early 1800s. Fishing took over when the fur trade declined. Mackinac may be an Chippewa word derived from michinnimakinong, interpreted as "land of the great fault," designating a large crevice on the island. Others have defined it as "great turtle." In 1895, the island was ceded to the state of Michigan for use as a park.

**MANISTIQUE RIVER** (Mackinac/ Luce)   The river has its origins at Manistique lake and empties into Lake Michigan. The Manistique Pulp and Paper Company was established in 1916, but needed a dam for powering the factory. Because of the size that was required, a dam large enough would have flooded the city. Engineers designed a concrete tank with artificial banks higher than the natural river banks. Manistique was derived from the Chippewa word, unamanitigong, meaning "red."

**MEAUWATAKA LAKE** (Wexford) Located in the Manistee National Forest, the village of Meauwataka was settled near the lake about 1867. Only a few houses remain today. Meauwataka is Ojibwa for "half way."

**MILLECOQUINS RIVER** (Mackinac) Millecoquins took its name from an Algonquian Indian named Mananakoking (or Minakoking), interpreted as "a place where the hardwood is plentiful." It was also thought to be a French word for "a thousand thieves." In 1849, a 62-foot sailing ship was discovered by a survey party, but nothing was done about it at the time. During 1990, a young boy found part of the ship sticking out of the sand near the mouth of the river near the town of Naubinway. Barrels of salt, Chinese, tobacco and other artifacts from England were discovered.

**MUNUSCONG BAY** (Chippewa)   The village of Munuscong was founded near the bay, and the post office established in 1884. Munuscong was interpreted from an Algonquian word meaning "bay of the rushes," although Vogal disagrees with that interpretation.

**NEEBISH ISLAND** (Chippewa)   The island also contains a settlement named Neebish, an Algonquian word that describes a type of plant on the island. It was also interpreted as "where the water boils." John Johnston and his family claimed land on the island in 1864. He was an interpreter for Indian agent, Henry Schoolcraft, who named many sites in the region. The island was later donated to the Neebish Pioneer Association for preservation purposes. Neebish is home to the Sault Ste. Marie Chippewa (Ojibwa) Indians.

**OCQUEOC RIVER** (Presque Isle)   In 1897, C.R. Miller founded the village of Millersburg along the river, which grew up as a small farming community. The river empties into Lake Huron. Ocqueoc is an Algonquian word meaning "crooked waters," because of the river's course. It was also thought to mean "sacred waters." Others disagree, and believe Ocqueoc was corrupted from Ocanauk, an Ojibwa signer of the Treaty of Saginaw in 1832. The name may be more closely derived from okwik, for "cross stick in a snowshoe," or okwanim, meaning "beaver dam."

**ONTONAGON RIVER** (Ontonagon) The Ontonagon was the main mode of transportation to the interior for the Chippewa Indians and French traders. Its name was derived from the Chippewa word nantonagun, meaning "my bowl is lost." Tradition says it received this name because an Indian girl dropped her bowl in the river. Another interpreation was "hunting river." Located along the river was the Ontonagon boulder, a 5-ton copper rock thought to have been used by the Chippewa as a place of sacrifice. They believed the huge copper rock was a go-between to the Great Spirit. When fur trader Alexander Henry found the rock in 1764, it began a rush by miners seeking more copper, and opened the area for mineral development.

**PABAMA LAKE** (Oceana)   The lake was named for an Indian named Joseph Pabama of the Grand River bands of Chippewa and Ottawa. He and his band came to the region after signing a treaty in 1855. He later converted to Catholicism and became a lay reader. At one time Pabama was treasurer of Elbridge Township, one of the few Indians ever elected to public office in Michigan. His name origin is undetermined, but some suggested it may come from babamisse, meaning "it is flying about," or from babamosse ("I walk about").

**POTAGANNISSING BAY** (Chippewa) In 1815, British troops occupied this region until it was taken back by the Americans in 1828. Lumbering and dolomite quarrying were the main industries along the bay. Potoganassing is a Chippewa word meaning "at the gaps," descriptive of the entrances to all the islands and bodies of water in the region.

**SEBEWA CREEK** (Ionia)   Early settlement of this region occurred in 1838 when Sebewa Township was formed by John Terrill, Charles Ingalls and John Brown. Sebewa is an Ojibwa word meaning "little river." Another derivation as from sibiwan, meaning "rivers" or "streams." The township of Sebewa was created about 1845 and took its name from the creek.

**SEBEWAING RIVER** (Huron)   Looking for a place for his followers to live, Lutheran minister John Auch found a site along the river in 1845 and conducted mis-

sionary work among the Indians for more than five years. Sebewaing is a Chippewa word for "where the river is." It was also interpreted as "winding (or "crooked") creek," descriptive of the river's course.

**SHIAWASSEE RIVER** (Oakland) About 85 miles long, the Shiawassee flows to form the Saginaw River. Early settler Henry Boleu established a trading post along the river in 1816, but it would be about 20 years before permanent settlement began. Until then, this region was the hunting and fishing ground of the Chippewa Indians. Located in the river was a rock called Chesaning by the Indians, who venerated the stone. But early settlers blasted it out of the water, indifferent to the Indians' beliefs, and burned the rock to extract limestone. Shiawasee means "river that twists about."

**SISKIWIT LAKE** (Keweenaw)   In 1845 the Siskiwit Mining Company was established and operated for about ten years. The town of Cornucopia was founded near the lake by Thomas J. Stevenson in 1902, which lived its life as a lumber town. Siskiwit was derived from the Ojibwa word penitewiskowet, meaning "that which has oily flesh," descriptive of a type of trout that inhabited the lake.

**TAHQUAMENON RIVER** (Luce)   The river is about 80 miles long and empties into Lake Superior at Whitefish Bay. This one-time logging river floated millions of feet of pine. It bears the Chippewa word meaning "dark waters," because it has a copper-speckled bed. It was also described as "this is a short route" (or "path"). In Longfellow's poem, Hiawatha's friend, Kwasind, was beaten in a fight with diabolic otters along the river.

**TITTABAWASSEE RIVER** (Ogemaw) The Tittabawassee is located in what was called the "Michigan Pine Belt." The river is about 75 miles long and was once a major transporter of logs, with more than a million logs floated down the stream in less than ten years, making it the largest rollway of pine logs in the world. In 1841, the township of Tittabawassee was formed, taking its name from the river, an Algonquian word meaning "following the shore river."

**TONQUISH CREEK** (Wayne)   During 1819, Potawatomi Chief Tonquish (origin unknown) and his band engaged in numerous conflicts with the white settlers because they were taking Indian land. After one of the white men was killed, angry settlers chased the chief and his men to this creek, where he was killed. Tonquish was buried along the creek. After his death, Indian uprisings ceased. The creek is located within the Holliday Forest and Wildlife Preserve.

**WAISKA BAY** (Chippewa)   This bay bears the name of Chippewa Chief Waishkai ("head man"). The town of Bay Mills was established along the bay, followed in the 1870s by the Hall and Munson Lumber Mill. During the 1880s a trestle was built across the bay which connected the villages of Bay Mills and Brimley.

# MINNESOTA

**AQUIPAGUETIN ISLAND** (Mille Lacs)   This island is only a mile wide and a half mile long, surrounded by Rum River, Third Lake and a swamp. It was once home to a Sioux village headed by Chief Aquipaquetin, who became friends with Father Hennepin during 1680, and also adopted Hennepin as his son (others say Hennepin was taken captive by Aquipaquetin). His name origin is unknown.

**BEMIDJI LAKE** (Beltrami)   French fur traders called the lake Lac Traverse. It was changed to St. Ann's Lake by Henry Schoolcraft in 1832, and later renamed Bemidji. It is a Chippewa word derived from bemidgegumaug, meaning "the lake where the current flows directly across the water," or "river flowing crosswise." An-

other interpretation was "cross lake." It was also thought to originate from Chippewa Chief Bemidji, although his real name was Shaynowishkung, Chippewa for "rattler" or "one who makes a jingling sound." A friend to the white man, he was born about 1833 and died in 1904.

**CHAMPEPADAN CREEK** (Murray)   Explorer Nicolet named the creek, derived from the Sioux expression tchan pepedan, meaning "thorny wood river," descriptive of the thorn bushes and trees along the river's banks.

**CHANKASKA CREEK** (LeSueur)   Chankaska is a Sioux word that means "forest enclosed." It is an outlet of Lake Washington.

**ESQUAGAMAH LAKE** (Aitkin) Esquagamah township took its name from the lake, which is an Chippewa word meaning "the last lake," in reference to its being the last and most western in a series of three lakes. The region was surrounded by forests of red and white pine trees, bringing in the timber companies who built logging roads around the lake. By 1898 most of the forest had been depleted. The lake comprises approximately 80 acres.

**HANSKA, LAKE** (Brown) Hanska is a Sioux word interpreted as "long" or "tall," descriptive of the lake that is long and narrow. The village of Hanska, established in 1899, took its name from the lake.

**KABETOGAMA LAKE** (St. Louis) Kabetogama Lake comprises about 25,000 acres and is located along the United States-Canadian border. It lies within Voyageurs National Park. Kabetogama is a Chippewa word, meaning "lying parallel lake," indicative of its relation to Rainy Lake.

**KANARANZI CREEK** (Rock) The town of Kanaranzi was founded in 1844 and took its name from the creek. Kanaranzi was interpreted as an Algonquian word for "crazy woman." When Nicollet mapped this region, he wrote Karanzi, thought to be for the Kansas (or Kaw) Indians who were killed here. If in fact the name is from the Kansas Indians, then the interpretation would be "south wind people."

**KANDIYOHI LAKE** (Kandiyohi) Kandiyohi township was established in 1868 and took its name from the lake, a Sioux word meaning "where the buffalo fish come." Artist Edwin Whitefield came here in 1856 for the purpose of developing and exploring the lake region.

**KASOTA LAKE** (Kandiyohi) Kasota is a Sioux word meaning "clear," or "cleared

off," and may be descriptive of a treeless ridge. In 1870, Andreas Broman and his family came from Sweden and settled along the river to farm the land.

**KAWISHIWI RIVER** (Lake) Bearing an Ojibwa expression meaning "river full of beaver houses," the Kawishiwi is about 60 miles long. It splits into two forks, one of which flows to Farm Lake, the other enters Birch Lake. The entire river is situated in the Superior National Forest.

**MANYASKA LAKE** (Martin) Manyaska is also the name of a township. It bears a Sioux word meaning "white bank" or "white bluff." It was also interpreted as "white iron" and "silver white."

**MINNEHAHA CREEK/FALLS** (Hennepin) This creek connects a chain of Minnesota lakes with the Mississippi River below Minnehaha Falls. It was at this point that the Sioux and Chippewa Indians worshiped their great spirit. The falls were first named Brown's Falls, then changed to Minnehaha, which is a Sioux expression taken from owah-menah, meaning "falling water." The name was officially spelled Minnehaha after Governor Ramsey and his party renamed the falls in 1852.

**MINNESOTA RIVER** (Big Stone) This 332-mile-long river originates in Big Stone Lake and enters the Mississippi River just south of Minneapolis. The river was first called Sans Pierre by French explorers. It was changed to St. Pierre, and then Minnesota, a Sioux word meaning "sky-clouded." The town of Mankato was established along the river in 1852.

**MINNETONKA LAKE** (Hennepin) The year 1822 was the first recorded exploration of the lake, when Joseph Brown and William Snelling came to the region. In 1852, Simon Stevens and Calvin Tuttle explored the lower part of the lake. This was the same year Minnetonka Township was settled, taking its name from the lake. First called Peninsula Lake, the name was changed by Governor Ramsey to Minnetonka, a Sioux word interpreted as "big water."

**MINNEWASKA LAKE** (Pope)   The lake bears the name of the township located along its shores. Early settlers named the lake Minnewaska, from the Sioux expression mine and washta, translated as "water good." It was also known as White Bear Lake and Lake Whipple until changed to Minnewaska in 1883.

**MISQUAH HILLS** (Cook)   These hills are the highest lands in the state at about 2,200 feet above sea level, located between Lake Superior and the Canadian Border. The exposed red granite rocks bear the Chippewa word that means "red."

**MISSISSIPPI RIVER** (Beltrami)   The great Mississippi rises at Lake Itaska as a small stream. Henry Schoolcraft discovered its origin in 1832 while exploring its course. One of the most important rivers in the country, the Mississippi was tantamount in the growth of this country, and has always been a major artery for all types of river craft, shipping supplies and passengers up and down its course. It has also been a blight for people living along the river where flooding has been prevalent throughout its history. Major campaigns were waged along the Mississippi during the Civil War. The name is common to many Indian languages, and was interpreted as "great river."

**MUSTINKA RIVER** (Otter Tail)   The Mustinka is about 80 miles long and enters the Bois de Sioux River. In 1923, the state of North Dakota sued the state of Minnesota because that state built ditches and straightened the river, causing the Mustinika to flow into Lake Traverse and the Bois De Sioux River, flooding North Dakota farmland. Mustinka is a Sioux word that means "rabbit."

**NAMAKAN LAKE** (St. Louis)   This lake borders on Canada, and is an Algonquian expression interpreted as "dark deep water." During World War II, a mica mine was in operation for the U.S. Army. Namakan may also be Chippewa for "sturgeon."

**NEBISH LAKE** (Beltrami)   Nebish Lake became a lumber camp when Arpin Lumber was built. The logs were collected here to await transport via the Red Lake Railroad. The settlement of Old Nebish was also a lumber camp, with a mill, saloon, depot and a rooming house. It ceased to exist after the railway was abandoned about 1912. Nebish is an Chippewa word for "tea colored."

**NEMADJI RIVER** (Douglas)   The river is known for its Nemadji pottery, which has been manufactured since 1923 using soil from the banks. First use of the product was making floors for local churches. Nemadji is a Chippewa word translated as "left hand." The name refers to its being on the left-hand side when one passes from Lake Superior into the St. Louis River. Another interpretation was the Chippewa expression nemadjitigweiag, defined as "a river falling perpendicularly from a considerable elevation."

**OGECHIE LAKE** (Mille Lacs)   Before white settlement, this region was home to the Sioux Indians, better known as the Mdewakanton ("water of the Great Spirit"). Ogechie is a Sioux word meaning "worm." An early visitor to this region was French explorer Daniel Greysolon about 1679. It was thought the Chippewa Indians drove the Sioux from the region, although archaeological finds show that the Sioux had already been migrating west before the Chippewa arrived.

**OKABENA CREEK** (Jackson)   The village of Okabena was established along the creek in 1879. One of its major industries in the early 1900s was the Okabena Clay Works, makers of brick and tile that operated until 1931. The creek is an outlet of West Okabena Lake, and bears a Sioux word for "nesting place of the heron."

**OKSHIDA CREEK** (Murray)   This creek rises from the Des Moines River. The township took its name from the creek, but spelled it Okcheeda. Okshida is a Sioux word that means "to mourn," derived from ocheya or akicheya, honoring two young Indian boys who were killed by their enemies.

**OWATONNA RIVER** (Steele)   The town of Owatonna was settled near this river in the 1850s. Originally the river was named Owatonna, but it was changed in 1870 to Straight River, and later renamed Owatonna, a Sioux word meaning "straight," jokingly named because the river is actually quite crooked.

**POKEGAMA LAKE** (Itasca)   Pokegama is a Chippewa word that means "the water which juts off from another water," perhaps describing the falls that drop 15 feet. It was also translated as "the lake with bays branching out," and "water that turns off to one side." The falls disappeared when a dam was built. With its wealth of forests, the region experienced the establishment of many lumber companies during the 1860s. The first logs from the lake were floated down the Mississippi River in the spring of 1868, and more than 15 lumber camps were in operation by 1872.

**PUPOSKY, LAKE** (Beltrami)   The town of Puposky was established in 1905 as a lumber town along the lake by the Minneapolis, Red Lake and Manitoba Railway. Eventually the timber played out and by 1939 the railroad ceased to exist. Today Puposky has only a few buildings. Puposky may be an Chippewa word for "end of shaking lands," descriptive of the marshes or bogs common in the region.

**SAGANAGA LAKE** (Cook)   During the 1700s this region consisted of a number of trading posts for French traders and the Indians, and was also a major fur trade route. Saganaga is a Chippewa word derived from ga-sasuganagag-saigiigun, meaning "lake surrounded by thick forests," or "many islands." Another interpretation was a Chippewa expression saging or saginang, meaning "at the mouth of the river."

**SHETEK, LAKE** (Murray)   Shetek township was organized in 1872 near the lake. The name was derived from sheetak, a Chippewa word meaning "little pelican." Another interpretation was from sagaigan, meaning "island lake." The Sioux call this group of lakes rabechy ("the place where the pelicans nest").

**SHINGOBEE CREEK** (Cass)   Shingobee is the name of a township that took its name from the creek. It bears a Chippewa word that describes the spruce trees common to the region.

**TOQUA LAKE** (Big Stone)   Taking its name from the lake, Toqua Township was established in 1877. The name may be derived from the Sioux expression ta and kahra, meaning "moose of the Kahra," or "wild rice." Kahra was a band of the Sioux Indians.

**WABEDO LAKE** (Cass)   Wabedo is also the name of a township that took its name from the lake. It may come from the

Chippewa expression wabuto sagiigun, which means "mushroom lake."

**WAPSIPINICON RIVER** (Mower) This river is about 225 miles long. It originates on the Minnesota state line and empties into the Mississippi River. Wapsipinicon is a Sioux word meaning "white potatoes," descriptive of the white artichokes that grew along the riverbanks. Indian Legend says Wapsi was the daughter of Sac Chief Good Heart and Pinicon was the son of Sioux Chief Black Feather. The two fell in love, but Fleet Foot, a warrior who was also in love with Wapsi, vowed that if he couldn't have her, then neither could Pinicon. On their wedding night they were out on a canoe when Fleet Foot shot Pinicon with an arrow into his heart, who fell into the water. Wapsi jumped in after him and the two were never seen again. If you listen, tradition says you can hear the two whispering to each other.

**WATAB RIVER** (Benton)    Watab is an Chippewa expression signifying the roots of the Jack Pine or Tamarack trees, used by the Indians for thread in making their birch-bark canoes. At one time the river was a boundary line between the Sioux and Chippewa Indians. Watab Township was created in 1858 and became an important commerce center until railroads were established.

**WATONWAN RIVER** (Watonwan) This river was a transportation route for the logging companies during the 1850s. The town of Watonwan was established near the river in 1857, but never amounted to much and by 1863 there was nothing left. Watonwan is a Sioux word meaning "fish bait," or "where fish bait abounds."

**WAYZATA BAY** (Hennepin)    The village of Wayzata was established along the bay in 1854. The Sioux Indians spent part of the their time here, and when a treaty was signed in 1851 they asked that some of the land be reserved for them, but it was denied. Wayzata was derived from the Sioux word, waziya, referring to the Indians' god of the north who blew cold air from his mouth. Another interpretation was "at the mouth."

**WINNIBIGOSHISH LAKE** (Cass) Winnibigoshish Lake is about 15 miles wide. It was derived from the Chippewa expression winnibiosh, meaning "wretched dirty water," descriptive of the lake's properties. The lake was so shallow that when storms came up the water would roil, dredging up mud from the bottom. Winnibigoshish Lake is within the Chippewa National Forest and borders the Leech Lake Indian Reservation.

**WITA LAKE** (Blue Earth)    This lake is located in Lime Township. Wita is a Sioux word that means "island lake," descriptive of two islands in the lake.

# MISSISSIPPI

**AMITE RIVER** (Amite)   The Amite is about 100 miles long and empties into Lake Maurepas in the state of Louisiana. Spanish and French hunters settled in the region about 1750, followed about 20 years later by the English who established trading posts to conduct business with the French and Spanish. The wealth of timber brought in lumber companies, and numerous sawmills were built along the river banks. Amite may be a Choctaw word meaning "red ant." Others have suggested it is a French word for "friendship" or derived from the Choctaw word, himmita (corrupted by the French), meaning "young."

**BOGUE CHITTO RIVER** (Lincoln) The river is about 105 miles long. It runs through the town of Bogue Chitto and empties into the Pearl River. Bogue Chitto is a Choctaw word for "big creek." The town of Holmesville, located along this stream, was the site of Mississippi's First Territorial General Assembly in 1815.

**CHEWALLA LAKE** (Marshall)   This lake is located in Holly Springs National Park. Chewalla is derived from the Choctaw expression, chihow-la, translated as "supreme being." It was also thought to mean "cedar." Indian burial or ceremonial mounds were found close to the lake.

**CHICKASAWHAY RIVER** (Clarke) The Chickasawhay rises at the confluence of the Okatibbee and Chunky creeks near the town of Enterprise. It is about 210 miles long and flows into the Pascagoula River. Enterprise used the river for shipping supplies on the river, which was also

a means of transportation for the numerous sawmills. The river was once home to the Choctaw Indians, and bears their name for "potato."

**CHUNKY RIVER** (Neshoba)   The community of Chunky is located along the river, and was originally a Choctaw village named Chanki Chitto, which means "big chunky." It referred to a ball game the Indians played near the river. Chief Tecumseh visited the village in 1811 in an attempt to unite all the tribes against the white men.

**COPIAH CREEK** (Copiah)   A road that crossed this creek was once a way station for travelers. Copiah is an Algonquian word meaning "calling panther."

**HATCHIE RIVER** (Union)   The Hatchie river bears the Cherokee word meaning "stream." The river is about 175 miles long and empties into the Mississippi River in Tennessee. The Hatchie was an important route for the Indians, who used it to transport their hunt downriver to their villages.

**HOMOCHITTO RIVER** (Copiah) The Homochitto is about 90 miles long and empties into the Mississippi River. Homochitto is an Algonquian word meaning "big red river." It was also defined as "shelter creek." The Homochitto National Forest was established in 1936, and was the first national forest in the state.

**NOXUBEE RIVER** (Choctaw)   Flowing into the Tombigbee River, the Noxubee is about 140 miles long. It is derived from a Choctaw word oka nakka shua (or okaonoxubba) meaning "strong smelling water," or "stinking water," descriptive of odors that emanate from the river during a freshet. The Choctaw and Creek Battle occurred in 1793 because of an argument over a beaver pond on the banks of this river. The dispute was settled by a ball game observed by about 5,000 Indians, but ended up with a Creek killing a Choctaw Indian and a free-for-all ensued, resulting in the death or more than 300 Indians. Folklore says the river received its name of stinking water because of all the bodies that rotted there over a period of several weeks.

**OKATUPPA CREEK** (Winston)   This creek flows into Alabama to join the Tombigbee River. Once home to the Choctaw Indians, the Okatuppa is located within the Choctaw National Wildlife Refuge. It is derived from oktapi meaning "water dammed," in reference to a dam built by the U.S. Army Corps of Engineers.

**PASCAGOULA RIVER** (Jackson)   The city of Pascagoula is the only natural seaport in the state. The Port of Pascagoula was created in the 1830s when the east branch of the Pascagoula River was dredged. Pascagoula was derived from the Choctaw expression, paska and okla, and means "bread people" (okla evolved to goula). The stream is called "The Singing River," because of the sound it makes, similar to a swarm of bees. The river originates at the confluence of the Leaf and Chickasawhay rivers. It is 90 miles long and flows to the port of Pascagoula on the Mississippi Sound.

**PELAHATCHIE CREEK** (Rankin) The town of Pelahatchie was named for the creek it borders, Choctaw for "hurricane creek," or "crooked creek," because the creek twists and turns. The early 1900s brought the lumber industry that flourished until the 1940s.

**SENEASHA CREEK** (Attala)   Seneasha is an Algonquian expression meaning "sycamore little." An Indian named Hoksa-ja owned about 80 acres of land along the creek.

**TALASHA CREEK** (Newton)   The region was home to the Choctaw Indians who established a village called Mokalusha, which became one of the most populous Indian towns at the headwaters of this creek. When smallpox hit the region in 1824, the Indians deserted the town. Talasha is a Choctaw word meaning "palmettos are there."

**TALLAHALA CREEK** (Jasper)   This river is about 95 miles long and joins Leaf River. In 1862, an organization called the Newt Night Company was organized, which fought many battles with the Confederates along the creek. Tallahala may be derived from the Choctaw expression talla and halalua, meaning "rock smooth."

**TALLAHATCHIE RIVER** (Quitman) The Battle of Tallahatchie Bridge occurred at the river during the Civil War as the Federal Army worked its way to Vicksburg. The Tallahatchie rises at the confluence of the Coldwater and Little Tallahatchie Rivers and joins the Yalobusha River. It is about 230 miles long. Tallahatchie is a Choctaw word interpreted as "river of rocks," or "rock stream," indicative of a type of boundary marker.

**TCHULA LAKE** (Holmes)   Tchula Lake was a shipping point for cotton and later was of commercial importance for its abundance of catfish. During the Civil War, the steamboat *Ben McCulloch* was pressed into service by the Confederates, transporting supplies on the lake. They burned the vessel in 1863 so the Union Army could not confiscate her. Once known as Little River, the name was changed to Tchula, which means "fox" or "marked."

**TEOC CREEK** (Carroll)   One of the oldest settlements in the county was the town of Teoc, which took its name from the stream. The creek was believed to have healthful minerals, and a tonic factory was established to process the water. Greenwood LeFlore was the last Choctaw chief (who was also a white man), and built his home (Malmaison) near the river. Senator John McCain's father owned a plantation along the Teoc and called it Waverly. Teoc is Choctaw for "pine tree."

**TOMBIGBEE RIVER** (Prentiss)   The 400-mile-long Tombigbee joins the Alabama River in the state of Alabama. During 1817, a trading post was established along the river, which eventually evolved into the town of Columbus. To improve transportation, locks and dams were built along the river. Tombigbee is derived from the Choctaw word itumbibikpi, meaning "coffin makers." It was a name given to the Indians who prepared their dead. In 1859 Ben Johnson discovered what would be called the Tombigbee Meteorite, discovered to be the most phosphorus-rich meteorite known to date.

**TUSCOLAMETA CREEK** (Coahoma) After Walnut Grove was founded along the creek, its growth was tied to the establishment of the Jackson and Eastern truck Line. Located on the bottom land of the creek, the fertile soil enabled residents to make a comfortable living. Tuscolameta is a Choctaw expression for "warrior young."

**YACONA RIVER** (Pontotoc)   This river flows 130 miles to the Tallahatchie

River. A man named Hodge purchased land near the river from the U.S. Government in 1839 which later became the community of Spring Hill. In 1837, John Taylor built the first mill in the county along the river. Yacona is derived from the Chickasaw expression yocona and petopha, which means "split land."

**YALOBUSHA RIVER** (Chickasaw) Choctaw Indians lived in the village of Chocchuma located along the river's banks. The Yalobusha was also the site of the U.S. Land Office in 1833, which forced removal of the Indians after they sold off their land. The hamlet of Grenada, founded in 1836, served as a commerce center shipping its cotton down the river via keel boats. Grenada saw prosperous years after it became headquarters for the building of the Mississippi Central, and the Mississippi and Tennessee Railroads in the 1850s. Yalobusha is a Choctaw word meaning "place of the tadpoles." The river, which is 165 miles long, enters the Tallahatchie River.

**YAZOO RIVER** (Leflore)   The Yazoo is about 189 miles long and rises at the confluence of the Tallahatchie and Yalobusha Rivers. It enters the Mississippi River at Vicksburg. As part of the Treaty of Doak's Stand, Chief Greenwood Leflore received a plot of land in 1826 and later sold it to developers. The town was named Manchester until 1839, when residents change it to Yazoo City. The name may have come from the Choctaw word, yazoo-ok-hin-nah, "Yazoo, river of ancient ruins." It has also been defined as "home of the people who are gone." Some historians believe Yazoo refers to blowing on an instrument.

# MISSOURI

**HUNKAH PRAIRIE** (Barton)   The prairie is remnant of a tallgrass prairie of the Osage Plains Natural Division and owned by the Prairie State Park, Department of Natural Resources. It comprises about 3,000 acres and is dedicated to the restoration of the tallgrass. Hunkah is an Osage word meaning "earth people."

**MERAMEC RIVER** (Phelps/Crawford) The Meramec was once a main transportation route for French and American trade. Rumors of a possible lead mine along the river reported by Father Gravier in 1700 brought settlement to the region. Originating in the Ozark Mountains, the Meramec flows 200 miles to merge with the Mississippi River. The name may be a corruption of a Chippewa word for "catfish."

**MINA SAUK FALLS** (Iron)   These falls drop almost 200 feet and bear the name of legend. Mina Sauk was the daughter of a Piankishaw chief. She married an Osage warrior whom the chief's advisors said bewitched the girl. In order to release her from the curse, the warrior had to die. He was thrown off Taum Sauk Mountain and Mina Sauk leaped after him. After she fell to the bottom of the mountain, a flash of lightning split the mountain and created the falls. Sauk is interchangeable with Sac, and means "outlet." *See also* Taum Sauk Mountain

**MONEGAW SPRINGS** (St. Clair) These waters have long been associated with their healing properties. The site was first inhabited by the Osage, Shawnee and Sac Indians who drank from what they thought was healing water. During the 1850s, one of the settlers took advantage of its purported properties by selling bottled water. With more than 100 springs, by the early 1900s the place became a health resort. Monegaw was an Osage chief who received his name after he helped an injured Spaniard, who told him of buried silver. Monegaw used it to purchase horses and food for his people. His name means "owner of much money."

**NIANGUA RIVER** (Webster)   When explorer Zebulon Pike came to this region in 1806, he recorded the river's name as Yungar. The Indians called it Nehembar, meaning "bear," because of the prevalence of the animals in the area. Niangua is an Osage word that means "many springs," for the springs that feed this river. It originates in the Ozarks and flows about 90 miles into Lake of the Ozarks.

**PEMISCOT BAYOU** (Pemiscot)   Settlers found the region's topography was mainly swamp land. The bayou bears a descriptive name, Fox for "liquid mud." It was also interpreted as "at the long place," or "runs next to." In 1811, a tremendous earthquake hit that would have registered more than 8 on the Richter scale, causing the river to change its course.

**PERCHE CREEK** (Boone)   Lewis and Clark crossed this creek in 1804 before making their way west. The first covered bridge in the state of Missouri was built there in 1851. The Perche flows into the Missouri River. It was originally named Split Rock Creek, and changed to Perche, from the Osage word paci, interpreted as "hilltop." In 1821, the community of Perchetown was established on both sides of the creek where settlers built a dam and erected a sawmill. Cancellation of the town's mail contract and washing away of mill spelled the demise of the community.

**TARKIO RIVER** (Montgomery)   This river is about 130 miles long and enters the Missouri River near the town of St. Joseph. Tarkio is a Sac or Fox word for "walnut" or "place where walnuts grow." The river no longer resembles its original course, since it has been dredged and channeled into different courses.

**TAUM SAUK MOUNTAIN** (Iron) The mountain was named, in part, for the Sauk Indian Tribe. Taum was interpreted from the Sac words tongo, for "big," and sauk meaning "outlet." Situated in the St. Francois Mountain Range, the mountain is about 1,772 feet above sea level. Danny Washbuckle was the first person to climb it in 1901. Tradition says Jesse James used the mountain as a hideout after robbing a train. An Osage brave was thrown off the mountain by his bride's people because they said she was bewitched by him. *See also* Mina Sauk Falls

**WAH KON TAH PRAIRIE** (St. Clair/Cedar)   This 2,858-acre prairie was named to honor the Osage Tribe, or may have been the name of an Osage family who once lived in the region. Wah Kon Tah is an Osage word meaning "great spirit" or "great mystery." The Nature Conservancy and Missouri Department of Conservation jointly own the land. The prairie is located about two miles from El Dorado Springs.

**WAH SHA SHE PRAIRIE** (Jasper) Situated in the Osage Plains Natural Division and owned by the Nature Conservancy, the prairie bears an Osage word meaning "water people." The prairie comprises about 160 acres with a 10-acre pond to attract migrating birds.

**WAPPAPELLO LAKE** (Wayne) Cherokee, Shawnee and other nomadic Indian tribes used the region as their hunting ground. Wappapello is the second largest lake in the state, comprising about 6,000 acres. The lake bears the name of a friendly Shawnee Chief called Wappepello (or Wapelillese), thought to mean "white bird."

# MONTANA

**KINTLA LAKE** (Flathead)   Located in Glacier National Park, Kintla is a little more than eight miles long. It is an Indian word meaning "bag" (tribal origin obscure). The Great Northern Railway laid its tracks in 1892, opening the region for settlement and tourism. Oil was discov-ered about 1901 around the lake and claims were filed, but a financial panic later caused them to be abandoned.

**KOOTENAI RIVER** (Canada)   This river rises in British Columbia and flows into the northwest corner of Montana, then back to British Columbia. Part of its course flows through a canyon so deep that travel down parts of its sides is impossible. It was named for the Kootenai Tribe of Indians, and may be a French corruption of Ksunka meaning "people of the standing arrow." Another interpretation was "deer robes," because of the Indians' prowess as deer hunters.

**MISSOURI RIVER** (Gallitan)   The "Big Muddy" flows 2,315 miles and is the longest tributary of the Mississippi River. The Missouri received its nickname because of the tremendous amount of silt it carries. The river rises at the confluence of the Jefferson, Madison, and Gallatin rivers in the Rocky Mountains and joins the Mississippi River near St. Louis, Missouri. In 1673 French explorers Jacques Marquette and Louis Joliet were the first Europeans to see the river. In the Sioux language, Missouri means "thick wooded river."

**SKALKAHO CREEK** (Ravalli))   Lewis and Clark stopped at the creek on September 8, 1805. The Salish Indians used the river for hunting and fishing. Skalkaho Creek bears a Salish word for "place of the beaver," for the animal that was abundant in the region. The town of Gransdale was settled near the headwaters of the creek, where the first flour mill was established by H.H. Grant.

# NEBRASKA

**MINATARE, LAKE** (Scotts Bluff)   The lake was built by the U.S. Bureau of Reclamation in 1915 for the purpose of irrigation. Once home to the Minnataree Indians who were a branch of the Sioux Tribe, the lake was named for them, which means "clear water." During the Depression, the Veterans Conservation Corps hired jobless people to build a simulated lighthouse on the lake, which was actually an observation tower. Lake Minatare was included as part of the North Platte Wildlife Refuge in 1916.

**MINNECHADUZA   CREEK/LAKE** (Cherry)   Minnechaduza Lake was created after George Ritterhush established a flour mill at Valentine and in 1892 built a dam on the creek to harness the water power. Valentine also depended on the creek for its water supply during the 1800s. Minnechaduza is a Sioux expression that means "murmuring water," or rapid stream.

**NEMAHA   RIVER** (Nemaha)   The town of Nehama was founded in 1854 and took its name from the river, which is Sioux for "miry ( or "swampy") waters," descriptive of the bottom land. It was also thought to be an Otoe expression meaning "water of cultivation." S.H. Long made the first record of the name and spelled it Nemahaw. In 1860, the Territorial Legislature granted John Foremand and D. Vanderslice permission to operate a ferry across the river. Tradition says gold was hidden somewhere along the river by miners in 1854, but it was never found.

**WAHOO   CREEK** (Saunders)   This

area was a favorite camping area of the Otoe Indians. Wahoo was thought to be an Otoe word meaning "burning bush," descriptive of a plant used for medicinal purposes by the local medicine man. Another theory was from Pawhoo, Pawnee for "round bluffs."

# NEVADA

**BIG WASHOE LAKE** (Washoe)   This lake is located at the southern part of the Washoe Valley. It is bears the Washoe word washiu, meaning "person."

**DESATOYA MOUNTAINS/CREEK** (Nye/Churchill/Lander)   Desatoya Creek rises at Mount Nagaha Wongops and enters Sheep Creek. The mountain is formed in Nye County and stretches as far as the New Pass Range. Desatoya may be a corruption of toyap, Shoshone for "mountain." Others have ascribed it to a Shoshone word meaning "grassy hill creek."

**GOSHUTE CREEK** (White Pine)   The creek originates in the Cherry Creek Mountains and terminates at the Steptoe Valley. The name is taken from the Gosiute Indians who lived in the region, and may be derived from kotsip-ro-gustip, meaning "ashes" or "parched earth."

**HIKO RANGE** (Lincoln)   This range was given a Shoshone name for "white man's city," or simply "white man," and referred to the first white men who came to the future site of the town of Hiko. Located east of the Pahranagat Valley, the mining camp of Hiko was established at the base of the range in 1866 and became county seat. Not much gold was found, causing Hiko to go into decline, and the county seat was moved to Pioche in 1871. Tradition says the lost mine of Hercules Proper is in the Hiko mountains. He was beaten and hanged by outlaws because he wouldn't tell them where his claim was located. His claim was never found.

**ILLIPAH CREEK** (White Pine)   Illipah may come from the Shoshone words illa and pah, meaning "rock water." The creek begins in the White Pine Range and terminates in Jakes Valley.

**JARBIDGE MOUNTAINS/RIVER/ CANYON** (Elko)   The mountains are located in the Humboldt National Forest, and divide the east and west forks of the Jarbidge River. In 1909, the village of Jarbidge was founded as a gold camp 2,000 feet down along the steep confines of Jarbidge Canyon. The name comes from the Shoshone word, jahabich, which means "devil." Indian legend says a man-eating giant called Tswhawbitts lived in a crater. He captured Indians, put them into a basket he had strapped on his back, took them home and ate them.

**KAMMA MOUNTAINS** (Pershing/ Humboldt)   These mountains are located near the Seven Troughs Range and extend into Humboldt county. Kamma is derived from the Northern Paiute word ka-mu, meaning "jackrabbit." The name was given to the mountains by the Fortieth Parallel Survey.

**KAWICH RANGE** (Nye)   Kawich honors a Shoshone Indian chief whose name means "mountain." The range stretches from the Hot Creek Range to Pahute Mesa. The town of Bellehelen was a short-lived gold camp established in a canyon in the Kawich Range about 1904, and its post office operated less than a year. This gold rush to this site was an outgrowth of the Tonopah/Goldfield boom.

**KOBEH VALLEY** (Eureka)   Kobeh was recorded by Captain James H. Simpson in 1859. While at his camp, the Digger Indians (band of the Shoshones) visited Simpson and told him they called the place ko-bah, which means "face valley," or simply "face." The valley is located between the Roberts and the Sulphur Springs Mountains.

**MOAPA PEAK** (Lincoln)   The peak took its name from the Moapa Indian Reservation. It is derived from a Southern Paiute word moapariats, meaning "mosquito creek people." The peak is located at the south end of Mormon Mountain.

**MOJAVE LAKE** (Clark)   This name is derived from the Mojave words hamok and avi, meaning "three mountains," descriptive of the mountains in California and Arizona. The lake was formed by Davis Dam along the Colorado River. It was built to meet requirements of the Mexican Water Treaty of 1944, which was to provide Mexico an annual 1.5 million acre-feet of water. It also delayed flash flood discharges from side washes below Hoover Dam. The lake is ituated in Nevada and part of Arizona on the Lake Mead Recreational Area.

**NARINO HONGUY HILL** (Elko)   Al-though Reservation Hill is the official name, it is still called by its Shoshone name which means "back of a saddle," descriptive of the topography. The hill is located on the north side of the Owyhee River on the Duck Valley Indian Reservation. In 1873, John Wesley Powell mentioned in his notes the name Nar'-ino-sti, meaning "saddle."

**NAYANTOVOY CREEK** (Elko)   The Nayantovoy flows through the Duck Valley Indian Reservation. It bears a Shoshone expression interpreted as "standing Indian."

**PAH RAH MOUNTAINS** (Washoe)   These mountains are located near Pyramid Lake. Pah Rah is a Shoshone word for "river." An early settler was Elias Olinghouse, a sheepman who had a camp at the base of this mountain. During the 1860s, gold was discovered in the mountains and Olinghouse himself discovered a gold claim and built a stamp mill. By 1903, more than $410,000 in gold and silver had been taken out.

**PAHRANAGAT   VALLEY/LAKES** (Lincoln)   The first people to see the Pahranagat Valley may have been miners of Death Valley fame. The valley was first settled about 1864 and was at one time used by horse thieves to graze their animals. In 1865, silver was discovered in the region and the Pahranagat Mining District was formed. There are two Pahranagat Lakes, Upper and Lower, situated in the Pahranagat National Wildlife Refuge. Together they comprise about 750 acres. Pahranagat is a Ute word derived from pah ran-agat, meaning "water melon" or "vine growing." It was also thought be mean "land of many waters" in the Paiute language.

**PANGUIPA CREEK** (Elko)   This stream rises on the Duck Valley Reservation and joins Indian Creek. It may be a

Shoshone word derived, in part, from dirdui panguipa honops, which means "little fishes creek."

**SAHWAVE RANGE** (Pershing)   The mountain range was given the Northern Paiute name by the Fortieth Parallel Survey, which means "sage." The Sahwave Range is bounded by Sage Hen Valley, Granite Spring and Copper Valley.

**SEDAYE MOUNTAINS** (Lander/ Churchill)   Captain James H. Simpson gave the mountains their name, which is a Shoshone expression meaning "lookout mountain." The Sedayes form part of the county boundaries.

**SHOSHONE MOUNTAINS** (Nye/Lander)   These mountains were named for the Shoshone Indians, whose name was interpreted from shawnt and shaw-nip, meaning "abundance of grass." The Indians selected camp sites where there was enough grass to feed their horses, hence the name. The Berlin Ichthyasaur State Park is located in the Toiyabe National Forest at the edge of the mountains. During the 1950s, Charles Camp, director of the Paleontologial Museum in Berkeley, gave the ichthyosaurs (prehistoric marine reptiles) the name Shonisaurus for the mountains.

**TECHATTICUP WASH** (Clark)   Techatticup may be a Southern Paiute word taken from tecahenga ("hungry") and tosoup ("flour"), which translated to "hunger, come and eat some flour." The wash empties into the Colorado River. Tradition says Spaniards worked a mine here at one time. Gold and silver were discovered by the whites in 1863 and one of the mines produced more than $3 million.

**TEMPIUTE RANGE** (Lincoln)   This range is approximately 13 miles long, and bears a Southern Paiute word derived from timpi, pa and ute, meaning "rock water people." In 1865, silver was discovered in the range and the Tempiute Mining District was organized. Because of the scarcity of water, mining was very difficult, and as a result not much was taken out of the mountains.

**TENABO PEAK** (Lander/Eureka)   New Mexicans were thought to have named this peak, which may have been named for an ancient pueblo near the town of Socorro. Others believe Tenabo is a Paiute word meaning "dark-colored water."

**TIPPIPAH SPRING** (Nye)   Tippipah is a Bannock word taken from tipi and ba, meaning "rock water," indicative of the spring which flows from the rocks. It was an early camp site of the Indians.

**TIVA CANYON** (Nye)   The canyon extends from the Shoshone Mountains to Topopah Spring. Tiva may be a Paiute word meaning "pine."

**TOANO MOUNTAINS** (Elko)   These mountains bear a Gosiute name, meaning "pipe camping place."

**TOHAKUM PEAK** (Washoe)   Tohakum Peak is located in the Lake Range, and bears a Northern Paiute expression to-ha-kum, meaning "large, white rabbit."

**TOIYABE MOUNTAIN** (Nye/Lander)   Silver brought an onslaught of miners to this mountain about 1862 after former Pony Express rider William Talcott found silver. This brought on the establishment of the town of Austin. Nevada Goldfields, Inc. operated one of the largest producers of gold, the Victorine Mine, which brought out more than 96,000 ounces of gold. Toiyabe is a Shoshone word that means "mountain."

**TOQUIMA RANGE** (Nye) Rising more than 7,000 feet above sea level, this range extends from Big Smoky Valley to Monitor Valley, and is situated about 25 miles from the town of Tonopah. There was once an ancient Indian village in the mountains known as Alta Toquima, which was not discovered until the 1970s. Toquima was derived from the name of a band of Mono Indians, which means "black backs."

**TOQUOP WASH** (Lincoln) This wash originates at Tule Flat and joins the Virgin River in Clark County. Toquop is from the Southern Paiute word to-kwop, meaning "black tobacco," and refers to a type of plant the Indians used for their tobacco.

**TUSCARORA MOUNTAINS** (Elko)

Tuscarora is a transfer name for the Tuscarora Indians, who lived in North Carolina. Their name means "hemp gatherers."

**TYBO CREEK** (Nye) Tybo Creek was home to the Western Shoshone Indians. It bears a Shoshone or Gosiute word meaning "white man," derived from tai-vu or tybbabo. During 1870 gold was discovered by the Indians, but it would be 1875 before the white man came to take up claims and form the gold camp of Tybo. Because of problems with ore reduction, the gold camp was short-lived.

**WAGUHYE PEAK** (Nye) This peak is located in the Grapevine Mountains. It was thought to be a Southern Paiute word for "summit."

# NEW HAMPSHIRE

**AMMONOOSUC RIVER** (Coos) This 50-mile-long river rises in the White Mountains and enters the Connecticut River. At one time gold was discovered along the river, which consisted of flakes called flower gold. This precipitated a small gold rush with miners who had come back home from the gold fields in California. Ammonoosuc may be an Abnaki word taken from o-mano-sec, meaning "the narrow fishing place," or derived from coosuck, interpreted as "at the place of the pines."

**ANDROSCOGGIN RIVER** (Coos) The Androscoggin flows for 175 miles. It originates at Umbagog Lake and terminates in Merrymeeting Bay. Its name was taken from the Abnaki expression nahmays and coggin, meaning "fish curing place." The Indians who lived in this region were members of the Anasigunticook tribe, a subgroup of the Abnaki.

**ASHUELOT RIVER** (Cheshire) Originating at a pond in the town of Washington, the river flows to merge with the Connecticut River. Ashuelot is derived from nashue (or nashueut), a Narragansett word meaning "in the midst," designating a point or angular piece of land lying between two branches of a stream. In 1819, Lewis Page was given the authority by the New Hampshire Legislature to deepen and straighten the river.

**ASQUAM LAKE** (Carroll/Grafton) First note of this lake was about 1724 when Captain John Lovewell and his men camped at what he called Casumpy Pond. Asquam is the second largest lake in the state. At one time an engineering camp of Harvard University was located along the lake. Asquam was derived from an Abnaki expression wonn-as-squam-auke, meaning "the beautiful surrounded by water place," or kees-ee-hunk-nip-ee, translated as "goose lake of the highlands." Other interpretations were "salmon place," "water," "at the summit," or "end of rock." It is also known as Squam Lake. The lake is about 7 miles long, and gained attention when it was the site of the movie, *On Golden Pond*.

**BABOOSIC LAKE** (Hillsboro) The town of Amherst was established at the lake when Lord Jeffrey Amherst was granted the land in 1728. He was Commander-in-Chief of the Colonials during the French and Indian War. Baboosic is an Abnaki or Penacook word meaning "sluggish current." It was also suggested the name came from babeskw ("a leach").

**CHOCORUA MOUNTAIN/ LAKE** (Carroll) The mountain and lake were named for Chief Chocorua, a member of the Pequawket Tribe. His name was translated as "frog," "fox," or "a sharp knife." A village established along the lake (in the town of Tamworth) was also named for the chief. Indian myth says the Indians considered the lake sacred. They believed if any human voice was heard on the lake, the person's canoe would disappear to the bottom.

**COCHECO RIVER** (Strafford) Mill towns were built along the river during the 1600s, followed by extensive shipbuilding in the 1700s. During the Civil War, the Cocheco Manufacturing Company was es-

tablished, which later developed into the shoe industry. The river flows to merge with the Piscataqua River. Cocheco is an Abnaki word for "rapid current place."

**CONNECTICUT RIVER** (Coos) The longest river in New England, the Connecticut flows more than 400 miles from the Canadian border along the Vermont-New Hampshire border through Massachusetts and Connecticut, and terminates at Long Island Sound. The first Europeans reached the river in 1614. During the 1630s, the river was the site of numerous fur trading posts, and by 1736 the Massachusetts Bay Colony had established at least six villages along its banks. Connecticut is an Abnaki word taken from kwini-teguh, meaning "the long river."

**CONTOOCOOK RIVER** (Cheshire) The water power of the river brought in settlers who established numerous mills along its bank. Contoocook may be a Penacook word meaning "nut trees river," or Natick for "small plantation at river," or "crow river." It was also thought to mean "place of the river near the pines." The Contoocook has its origins near the town of Jaffrey and joins the Merrimac River. In 1884, the Mediums' Camp Meeting of the Two Worlds was established on the lake shore. This enterprise was created specifically for training mediums and the dissemination of modern spiritualism and its doctrines.

**ESCUMBUIT ISLAND** (Rockingham) Escumbuit is a Micmac word meaning "at the watching place." It was the name of an Abnaki Indian Chief who took part in a retaliation raid against the Iroquois. He was later knighted by King Louis XIV for killing at least 150 English settlers.

**KANCAMAGUS MOUNTAIN** (Grafton) The mountain was named for Kancamagus (origin unknown), son of

Nanamocomuck, a sachem of the Penacook Indians. Kancamagus was against the English settlers because they were taking more and more of their hunting grounds. As a result, he united the Penacooks and other tribes to oppose the English in 1689.

**KEARSARGE MOUNTAIN** (Merrimack)  Early maps show this name as Carasarga. Kearsarge was derived from an Abnaki or Penacook word meaning "pointed mountain." It was also thought to be derived from kesaugh, interpreted as "born of the hill that first shakes hands with the morning light." The U.S. Navy named its famous war vessel for the mountain.

**MAGALLOWAY MOUNTAIN** (Coos)  Situated near the town of Pittsburg, the mountain is about 3,360 feet tall. In 1910, the New Hampshire Timberland Owners Association built a lookout station on the mountain, which was one of the first such structures built in the state. Magalloway is a Malecite word meaning "the shoveler," descriptive of the caribou which forage for their food by using their hooves to shovel the snow from side to side.

**MASCOMA, LAKE** (Grafton)  In 1782, a religious group called the Enfield Shakers moved from New York state to the lake and established their community, which lasted until about 1923. These people were part of the United Society of Believers in the Second Appearance of Christ. The lake later became a resort area. Mascoma may be a Natick word meaning "big beach," or "grassy swamp." It was also thought to come from an Abnaki expression meaning "salmon fishing." Dartmouth College skulling crews once used to practice rowing in this lake.

**MASSABESIC LAKE** (Hillsboro)  Massabesic Lake covers more than 25 square miles and was once a retreat for artists and writers. In an attempt to bring the Osprey there, an artificial nest was built at the lake in 1997 to attract the birds. The experiment was a success when in 1999 a pair of Osprey laid an egg in the nest. This was the first time the birds had ever nested in this region of the state. Massabesic may be an Abnaki word derived from massapeseag, meaning "great water," or "near the great brook."

**MASSASECUM LAKE** (Hillsboro)  The lake became a resort area after a country inn was established in 1760. It was named for a Penacook chief and sachem, whose name means "tall" or "slender."

**METALLAK ISLAND** (Coos)  The island was named for a Coosuck (or Cooashauke) Indian. In the Penacook language, his name means "the last man," because he was the last of the Coosucks. Metallak spent much of his life as a guide for the white men. He died about 1850 at the town of Stewartstown.

**MINNEWAWA RIVER** (Cheshire)  The Minnewawa Manufacturing Company was established at the town of Marlborough by Fred Hemenway and Ernest Blombach. They selected the name because the river ran past their property. Minnewawa is a Malacite word meaning "many waters."

**MONADNOCK MOUNTAINS** (Cheshire)  These mountains are about 3,165 above sea level, and were a source of spiritualism for the Indians. Monadnock is an Abnaki word meaning "at the mountain that sticks up like an island," or "island mountain place." Part of the mountain was used by the Indians as lookout stations. Plumbago was in abundance on the Monadnocks, and was once used in the manufacture of crucibles and pencils.

**MOOSILAUKE PEAK** (Grafton) Rising 4,802 feet, this peak is the highest in the Western White Mountains. Moosilauke is an Algonquian word thought to mean "bald place," which may be descriptive. In 1785, European Chase Whitcher was the first man to scale the peak.

**NARMARCUNGAWACK RIVER** (Coos) Also spelled Narmacungawak, the river bears an Abnaki expression meaning "a deep fishing place." It originates in the village of Success and merges with the Androscoggin River.

**PASSACONAWAY PEAK** (Grafton) Rising 4,060 feet, this peak is the second highest point in the Sandwich Range. It was named for a Penacook chief, whose name means "papoose bear," or "bear cub," from papisse-conwa. The Indians believed that Passaconaway rose to the heavens after he was taken away in a sled driven by wolves to a summit of Mount Washington.

**PEMIGEWASSET RIVER** (Belknap) One of the largest rivers in the state, the Pemigewasset is about 70 miles long. It rises at Profile Lake in the Franconia Notch State Park and enters the Winnipesaukee River. Logging and paper manufacturing were the biggest industries during the 1800s. The Plymouth Peg Mill was established near the river in 1898, and processed more than 2,500 of birch logs annually. Pemigewasset is an Abnaki word for "extensive rapids, " or "narrow and swift current."

**PISCASSIC RIVER** (Rockingham, Strafford) This small river rises at the town of Brentwood and flows into the Lamprey River. Piscassic is an Abnaki expression meaning "at the branch."

**PISCATAQUOG RIVER** (Hillsboro) The Piscataquog is about 30 miles long and originates from two streams near the town

of Goffstown, then joins the Merrimack River. It is an Abnaki word for "where the river divides." During the early 1800s, canals were built on the river to provide water power for industries. The first settlement along this river was the village of Grasmere, which was once a seat of government.

**PLAUSAWA MOUNTAIN** (Merrimack) Plausawa was an Abnaki warrior who was killed in the region about 1753. His name was interpreted as "wild pigeon," or "short yell."

**SOUGHEGAN RIVER** (Hillsboro) Settlement along the river began in the early 1700s when land grants were awarded the colonists. The town of Milford was established during the 1790s as a farming town, and later went into industry with textile mills after the river was dammed up. Soughegan is a Penacook word meaning "watching place," or "still water fishing."

**SUNCOOK RIVER** (Belknap) Land along the river was granted by the King of England to settlers who survived the Indian wars of 1725. The Suncook is about 35 miles long and enters the Merrimack River. About 1759, the town of Pembroke was established, and the river provided the water power for its mills built during the Industrial Revolution. Suncook is an Algonquian word meaning "at the rocks."

**UNCANOONUCKS MOUNTAIN** (Hillsboro) Because the peaks in these mountains are so symmetrical, it bears a Penacook word that was interpreted as "breasts."

**WANTASIQUET MOUNTAIN** (Cheshire) This mountain is 1,335 feet high and located in the Wantastiquet Mountain State Forest. It bears an Abnaki name derived from wanas-kwa-tekhu, interpreted as "the source of the river," or "the top place of the river." Stone quarried from the mountain was used to face buildings in the town of Brattleboro.

**WEETAMOO MOUNTAIN** (Grafton) The mountain bears the name of Weetamoo, a sunscksqua (female chief) of the Pocasset Indians, and daughter of Chief Passaconway. Her name origin is unknown. During King Philip's War, Weetamoo was against the English. While trying to escape Philip's army she drowned, and her head was later put on public display at the town of Taunton.

**WINNEPESAUKEE, LAKE** (Belknap/Carroll) Formed by glaciers, the lake comprises 72 square miles, and contains about 365 islands. It was discovered in 1652 by an expedition from the Massachusetts Bay Colony while they were seeking the headwaters of the Merrimack River. Winnepesauke is a Penacook expression for "land around the lakes," or "land at outlets around here." It was also interpreted as "good water with large pour out place." Indian legend says that Kona fell in love with Ellacaya, daughter of his enemy, Ahanton. Because Ahanton believed Kona really loved his daughter, he relented and gave her to Kona. He told his people that this would seal the peace between the tribes, and named the lake Winnepesaukke, which he said signified "the smile of the great spirit."

**WINNISQUAM LAKE** (Belknap) Settlement along the lake occurred in 1748 when the village of Winnisquam was founded. Today it is a resort area with numerous cottages along the shore line. The lake receives the waters from the Winnisquam River, which joins the Merrimack River. Winnisquam is Abnaki for "salmon fishing at lake outlet," or "pleasant water." The lake is about 9 miles long and 2 miles wide. The Ferry Point House was built at the lake by the Pillsbury family in 1800s for use as a summer retreat.

# NEW JERSEY

**ABSECON CREEK** (Atlantic) Absecon is a corruption of Absegami, the name of a sub-band of the Lenape Indians. It was interpreted as "plenty of swans," or "little [sea] water." The town of Absecon was founded in the 1700s and lived its early life as a port of call for sailing ships. Another staple industry was the harvesting of oysters and clams

**ALEXAUKEN CREEK** (Hunterdon) A Lenape settlement was located long the creek before the arrival of the white man. The stream was later used as a refuge for the Continental Army. The Alexauken rises at Mount Airy and enters the Delaware River. It bears a Lenape word that means "to separate," or "outlet." In 1707, Jacob Godown became one of the first settlers along the creek.

**ALLOWAY CREEK** (Salem) This creek originates at the town of Alloway and joins the Delaware River. It has borne the names Cotton, Monmouth and Roiters Run. Alloway is a Lenape word meaning "strong" or 'mighty," and was thought to be the name of Chief Alloes. The creek is surrounded by agricultural property, and is also important for commercial fishing.

**APSHAWA LAKE** (Passaic)    The lake is located near the town of Newfoundland. It is a Lenape expressing meaning "covered (or "wet") ground."

**ASSISCUNK CREEK** (Burlington) This stream was first called Wissahisk by Gabriel Thomas in 1698, then Barracks Creek by the British army in 1759 after they built a barracks along the creek. Before 1676, a trio of Dutchmen took up a settlement along the creek. Assiscunk is a Lenape word meaning "clay at," or "muddy creek."

**ASSUNPINK CREEK** (Mercer)    During the 1600s Quakers purchased land that was bounded by the creek. The Assunpink was the dividing line between George Washington and Cornwallis who engaged in what was called the Second Battle of Trenton in 1777. It ended with the withdrawal of the Continental Army. Assunkpink flows into the Delaware River. It is an Algonquian word thought to signify "at the stony place," or "stone in the water."

**BATSTO RIVER** (Burlington)    The Batsto is a tributary of the Mullica River, and bears an Algonquian name for "bathing." The river supposedly was a favorite place for the Indians to bathe. Other interpretations were "it sweats," and "I throw it down and burst it." Others believe it is not an Indian word, but stems from the Dutch language. At one time there was a village named Batsto. Its economy was tied to the manufacture of iron and cannonballs.

**CHEESEQUAKE RIVER** (Middlesex) Part of the Cheesequake State Park through

which it flows, the river terminates at Raritan Bay. The Lenape Indians inhabited this region for more than 6,000 years. Cheesequake is a Lenape word derived from chickhake, meaning "land that has been cleared." This river was known for its rum runners. During of low water, boats were able to fit under a bridge and meet ships offshore to offload illegal liquor, then hide the loot in hidden coves and docks.

**CHINAGORA CREEK** (Monmouth) This creek empties into Raritan Bay. During the 1700s Chinagora oysters were a delicacy, and as a result were cultivated along the creek. Chinagora may a Lenape expression chingo and rora, interpreted as "winding around many times." It was also thought to mean "where destroyed." This was in reference to freshets that destroyed the Indian corn stored underground near the river.

**CROSSWICKS CREEK** (Burlington) The Lenape Indians named the stream Crossweeksung, which means "separation." designating separation of boys from girls during certain periods. Others believed it referred to a separation of Crosswicks Creek. The creek runs through the center of the community of Crosswicks (settled by Quakers in 1677) and joins the Delaware River.

**CUSHETUNK MOUNTAINS** (Hunterdon)    The mountains may have been named for a Lenape chief, derived from gosh-gosch and unk, meaning "hog place," or "lowlands." Balthasar Pickel was a German immigrant who purchased the mountain and named it for himself. Other German settlers created a hog run in the mountain, and so "hog place," may be a more appropriate interpretation.

**KITTATINNY RANGE** (Warren/Sussex)    The mountain range was once home to the Minsi Indians. Kittatinny was translated as "endless hills," or "great hill." It may have been derived from the name of a Minsi village called Kituteney, meaning "great city," or "chief town." During the 1750s, a number of forts were built to protect settlers from occasional Indian raids. This range extends across northwest New Jersey into Pennsylvania. Today part of the mountain is a major resort and recreation area.

**LOCKATONG CREEK** (Hunterdon) Lockatong Creek rises from a spring in Franklin Township and joins the Delaware River. The village of Lockatong took its name from the creek, which is a Lenape word for "sand"(or "gravel"), or "hills place."

**MASHIPACONG ISLAND** (Sussex) This island is situated in the Delaware River. Although Europeans came through the area as early as 1609, settlement did not occur near the island until the early 1700s. The Indians who lived on the island and surrounding area were displaced by the white settlers. Mashipacong is a Lenape expression meaning "river place," or "at the bear hills."

**METEDECONK RIVER** (Ocean) The year 1750 brought the establishment of Brick Township. Its main industries were sawmills, and later charcoal and turpentine industries. Butcher's Forge was built in 1808, and used the water power when a pond was formed by damming part of the river, which was the largest mill pond in the state. Metedeconk was derived from the Algonquian words metu ("medicine man"), and saconk ("outlet of stream"). The river empties into Barnegat Bay.

**MINISINK ISLAND** (Sussex) A Lenape word meaning "where stones are gathered together," "at the place of small stones," or "people of the stony country,"

this small island is located in the Delaware River. It was home to the Munsee clan of the Lenape Indians, and was also the beginning of the Minisink Trail to the sea. Located near this island was the Minisink Valley Reformed Dutch Church built in the 1700s.

**MUSKONETCONG RIVER** (Sussex/Morris) Flowing 43 miles, the river originates at Lake Hopatcong and joins the Delaware River. During the 1700s, settlers built a water-powered forge, and during the American Revolution cannon balls were fabricated for George Washington. Iron-making later became a predominant industry. Muskonetcong is a Lenape word meaning "rapid running stream." Ancient Indian artifacts have been found along the river dating back more than 10,000 years.

**NACOTE CREEK** (Atlantic) The Nacote rises near the town of Pomona and joins the Mullica River. During the 1700s, Quakers moved to the river and influenced the future growth of the region. The Nacote later became a favorite creek for rum runners during Prohibition. The creek bears a Lenape word derived from niskeute, meaning "nasty" or "dirty."

**NESCOCHAGUE CREEK** (Burlington) In 1707 settlers formed the village of Nescochague and built the first church in the region. Jack Mullin moved here during the 1750s and built a sawmill along the creek. During the American Revolution, he dismantled his sawmill and donated the blades so broadswords could be fabricated for the war effort. Nescochague may be a Lenape expression meaning "wet grass" (or "meadow").

**NISHASAKAWICK CREEK** (Hunterdon) This creek is about 7 miles long, originates at the hamlet of Frenchtown and enters the Delaware River. Frenchtown was settled about 1794 when Paul Henri Mallet Prevost, along with a number of his colleagues, established a mill along the creek. Tradition says he came here after fleeing from the guillotine during the French Revolution. Nishasakawick is a Lenape expression derived from nisha, sacunk and wik, interpreted as "two outlets of a stream house," or "double outlet house."

**NUMMY LAKE** (Cape May)   King Namahomie (or Nummahauwan) was a chief of the Unalachtigo subtribe of the Lenape. The lake was named for him, which means "to be aware of someone."

**PEQUANNOCK RIVER** (Sussex)   Pequannock is a Lenape expression derived from paauau'unauke, meaning "land made clear for cultivation," or "cleared field opened." In 1766, Peter Hasenclever dammed up the river and established the Charlotteburg Furnace. The river flows through the town of Butler and joins the Pompton River. Numerous forges were built along the river, manufacturing what was called faggot iron, designed for shafts and boiler plates.

**PICATINNY, LAKE** (Morris)   The first land purchase of the lake area occurred in 1880. Landowner George Righter later sold the property to the U.S. Government. The Dover Powder Depot was established at the lake by the War Department in 1880. Shortly thereafter, it was renamed the Picatinny Powder Depot, then changed to Picatinny Arsenal, a Lenape expression interpreted as "body of water," or "body of still water." Another theory was "ragged cliff by water." The depot's original function was to produce munitions. It later expanded to research and development, and was also used to instruct officers in weaponry sciences.

**POCHUCK MOUNTAIN** (Sussex)   The mountain is situated near the town of

Sussex, and bears a Lenape name for "corner" or "recess." A hematite mine was located near the mountain, and about 1868 a spur road of the Sussex Railroad was built to the foot of the Pochuck range to the mine. A tunnel was built into the mountain to bring down the iron ore.

**RARITAN RIVER/BAY** (Morris)   Home to the Lenape Indians, this river rises in the Schooley Mountains and flows 85 miles into Raritan Bay at Perth Amboy. The bay was a natural harbor making it conducive to industry. The town of Perth Amboy was home to more than 100 factories, and was important during the American Revolution because of its tactical position. Raritan is Lenape for "stream overflows," or "a point on a tidal river."

**SANHICKAN CREEK** (Mercer)   A Lenape word for "stone implements," the creek runs near Trenton. The Sanhickan Indians were a band of the Lenapes, led by Chief Mosilian, and were resident in this region during the 1600s. They used stone implements, as evidenced by lance heads found near the stream.

**SHABAKUNK CREEK** (Mercer)   This creek flows through the city of Trenton. Shabakunk was derived from the Lenape word shabigaki, meaning "shore land." An important skirmish along the creek during the American Revolution commemorates the "holding" action against the British Army after the Second Battle of Trenton on New Year's Day, 1777.

**WATNONG MOUNTAIN** (Morris)   Located near the town of Parsippany, the mountain was used by soldiers of the American Revolution who lit fires to communicate with their troops to warn of any encroaching British troops. Watnong is a Lenape word derived from watschu and ong, meaning "hill place."

**WAWAYANDA, LAKE** (Sussex)    Once known as Double Pond, the name was changed to Wawayanda, a Lenape expression defined as "winding around many times." The lake encompasses 250,000 acres. During the 1840s, Oliver Ames operated an iron furnace which processed iron ore from the Wawayanda Mine located a few miles from the lake. In 1901, Charles C. Scott founded a boys camp called Camp Wawayanda along the lake.

**WAYCAKE CREEK** (Monmouth)    The Waycake flows between the communities of Union Beach and Keansburg. French privateers sailed up the creek and used it as a haven and for rendezvous. Waycake is taken from waackaack, a Lenape expression meaning "house land." It was also thought to come from wequa and quack, meaning "boundary," or "miry place."

**WESTECUNK CREEK** (Ocean)    The Westecunk flows through Stafford Forge and West Creek. An important commodity grown in the creek was oysters. Westecunk is derived from the Lenape expression wisu and onk, which means "fat meat place," in reference to the abundant game in the region.

**WICKECHEOKE CREEK** (Hunterdon) This 14-mile-long creek rises in Franklin and Raritan Townships, then flows into the Delaware River. It may be a Lenape expression, mechoak (or quachecoke) meaning "old (or "great") tree."

**WINBEAM MOUNTAIN** (Passaic) Winbeam Mountain is located near the town of West Milford. It bears a Lenape word meaning "lone tree mountain." The name was also interpreted as "heart of a tree."

# NEW MEXICO

**ABIQUIU CREEK** (Rio Arriba)    This creek originates near the former Tewa pueblo of Abiquiu and enters the Chama River. Abiquiu may be derived from the Tewa word, abay, which means "chokecherry." Or it may be a Spanish corruption of another Tewa word, pay shoo boo-oo, meaning "timber end town." Other interpretations were "a gapped upgrade," and "hooting of an owl," derived from abechiu. Dams were located in the creek, but they were torn out during the 1800s by miners panning for gold.

**APACHE CREEK** (Catron)/**CANYON** (Quay)    The creek rises near Apache Mountain and enters the Tularosa River. Apache leaders Mangas Coloradas, Victorio, Geronimo, Chato and Cochise attacked wagon trains in Apache Canyon when immigrants had to come through it in order to reach the valley. The warfare continued until Geronimo was captured in 1886. The Civil War extended even to this region, where the Union Army had its field headquarters in the canyon. In 1862, Union men fought Confederate troops at what was called the Gettysburg of the

West. The creek and canyon were named for the Apache Indians, whose name was translated from a Zuni word meaning "enemy," or a Yuman word meaning "fighting men."

**ASAAYI LAKE** (McKinley)   Asaayi is a man-made and located in the Chuska Mountains east of the village of Navajo. It bears a Navajo name meaning "in a bowl." The lake is used mainly by the Boy Scouts who have a large camp there.

**BISTI BADLANDS** (San Juan)   The badlands comprise about 4,000 acres, and once contained an ancient lake. The badlands bear a Navajo word meaning "badlands." It was also interpreted as "among the adobe formation." The badlands are composed of peculiar geological clay features, with a profusion of rock formations called hoodoos, which are ever-changing because they quickly erode. The Navajo Indians believed this was a place to walk around and get confused, so strange was its topography. Billy Hunter established the Bisti Trading Post in the badlands during the early 1900s.

**CHACO RIVER** (McKinley, Rio Arriba, San Juan/ CANYON (San Juan)   Originally called Agua de San Carlos in 1823 by Colonel Jose Viscarra, the river's name was changed to Chaco, which may be a shortened form of tseyan chalhalheel nline, Navajo for "flows along in darkness under rock." The river rises along the Continental Divide and joins the San Juan River. The canyon contains some of the greatest surface ruins in the United States. Archeologists have identified sites of the Basket Makers, built more than 1,500 years ago.

**CHACRA MESA** (McKinley)   Lt. James Simpson with the Corps of Topographical Engineers recorded the first reference to this name. Chacra is from the Navajo word tsegai, translated as "white rocks." Others

believe it is a Navajo word the Spaniards corrupted to "rock cut," or "white ring of rocks."

**CHAMA RIVER** (Rio Arriba)   The village of Chama is located in the Chama River Valley at the foot of Cumbres Pass. The river bears the Tewa name, tama, for "here they have wrestled," or "wrestling place." Another interpretation is a descriptive word for the color of the river, "red." The Monastery of Christ in the Desert was established by Fr. Aelred Wall along the Chama in 1946.

**CHICOMA MOUNTAIN** (Rio Arriba)   Located in the Jemez Mountains, Chicoma is about 11,561 feet high. It may be a Tewa word interpreted as "obsidian," or "flint." The Indians believe these mountains are the center of all creation, as evidenced by the remains of a shrine at the summit of Chicoma.

**CIBOLA CREEK** (De Baca)   Cibola may be a Spanish corruption of sibulada which the Isleta Indians called "buffalo." It was also thought to originate from the Plains Indian word for "buffalo plains." Julyan noted that it was unclear how Spanish explorers applied the name to the fabled Seven Cities of Cibola. The creek originates at Cibola Springs and flows into the Pecos River.

**COLLE CANYON** (Sandoval)   Located in the Jemez Mountains, the canyon bears a Tewa expression defined as "roof door canyon," and refers to the canyon's room-like (or box-like) topography. The abandoned mining camp of Albemarle was located in the canyon, and during 1899 was the first site in the state to use the cyanide process of ore reduction.

**CORRUMPA CREEK** (Union)   This creek begins as Corrumpa in New Mexico and changes to North Canadian River as it flows into the state of Oklahoma. Corrumpa is an Algonquian word meaning "wild" or "isolated." In 1828, two traders named McNees and Munro left their caravan and decided to rest at the creek. They were attacked by Indians and McNee was killed, which prompted many bloody conflicts. The site where the men stayed was named McNees Crossing. During the Civil War, the stream in Oklahoma was the headquarters of Confederate Col. Douglas Cooper while he was assembling his troops to drive out the Creek and Seminole Indians, who were Union sympathizers.

**DOWA YALANE MESA** (Cibola)   In 1540 Coronado attacked the Zuni Indians who fled to the mesa for refuge. During the Pueblo Revolt in 1680, they again used the mesa as a fortress. Dowa Yalane is about 1,000 feet high and associated with a Zuni myth that the mesa was a house of their god, who made rain, thunder and lightning. The name is from the Zuni expression taaiyalone, meaning "corn mountain." The Navajo words mean "rumbling inside the rock," or "rock house." Legend says that one day it began to rain and continued for many days, causing the rivers to flood, destroying the Indians and their villages. Those who survived took refuge on the mesa, taking their corn with them. The water kept rising to the mesa when Koloowisi, the water serpent, appeared. The people felt they had to present a human sacrifice to appease the serpent, and selected the youngest son and daughter of their priests. The girl was given a bowl of corn and they disappeared under the water. When the water receded, the children appeared, turned into pillars of stone. The mesa was first named Taaiyalone, but in 1983 the U.S. Board of Geographic Names changed it officially to Dowa Yalane.

**DZILDITLOI MOUNTAIN** (McKin-ley)   Dzilditloi is an extinct volcano, rising about 8,573 feet. It is derived from the Navajo word dzil ditloi, which means "stubby mountain." It is also known as Fuzzy Mountain because the pinyon and cedar trees situated around the cone give it a fuzzy appearance. In the Navajo Red Antway Myth, the mountain was attacked by supernatural people, but it was protected by Thunder and Bear.

**GILA RIVER** (Grant)   Once occupied by ancestors of the Pima and Papago Indians, the Gila River and its valley still hold the ruins of their homes in the Casa Grande Ruins and Gila Cliff Dwellings. Located in the Gila National Forest, the river originates in the Mogollon Mountains and flows through some of the most arid country in the U.S. It is 630 miles long and joins the Colorado River at Yuma, Arizona. Gila was thought to be a Spanish corruption of an Apache word meaning "mountain."

**HOSTA BUTTE** (McKinley)   This butte was named for Hosta, an Indian guide for William Jackson's Expedition into Chaco Canyon in 1877. Hosta was also civil governor of the Jemez Pueblo. His full name was from the Jemez waash-e-hoste, which means "the lightning." Others defined the name from ak'iih-nast'ani, for "mountain that sits on top of another mountain." The Navajo Indian consider the butte a sacred place that is home to Hadahoniye' Ashkie (mirage stone boy) and Hadahoniye' 'At'eed (mirage stone girl).

**JEMEZ MOUNTAIN/RIVER** (Los Alamos, Rio Arriba, Sandoval, Santa Fe) The settlement of San Toribio del Vallecito was settled in the mountains after a number of families were granted land there in 1768. The river has its origins in the Jemez Mountains and enters the Rio Grande. Once known as the San Diego River, it was changed to Jemez. The Tewa Indians called the mountains "western mountains," and to the Navajo they were "black mountains." Jemez may be a Tanoan word derived from hay-mish, interpreted as "people." Obsidian was found in the mountain during the 1800s, and penitentes used the stone to shape blades for making incisions. Penitentes were confraternity of the Catholic Church, called the Brotherhood, who believed in performing flagellation on themselves, depicting Christ's suffering

**KIM ME NI OLI VALLEY** (San Juan) This name is from the Navajo expression kin binaayoli, which means "house the wind blows around," or kin-bii'naayoli, for "house in which the wind whirls." The ancient Chaco Anasazi Indians built the Kin Bineola great house using sandstone from a mesa in the valley.

**PAJARITO PEAK/PLATEAU** (Sandoval) This peak is an important feature for the Navajo Indians' Windway Ceremony, where they use the white clay from the peak in their rituals. Pajarito is taken from the Navajo expression tl'iish jik'ahi, interpreted as "grinding snakes." The plateau is in the Los Alamos and Bandelier National Monument and was named by archaeologist Edgar Hewett.

**PICURIS CREEK** (Taos) This creek originates near the village of Picuris. It may be a Spanish corruption of pay kwee lay ta (or piwwe-tha), which means "at mountain gap" or "pass in the mountains." Another translation is from a Keresan word, pee-koo-ree-a, for "those who paint." The pueblo of Picuris is located near the creek and was a thriving community until the white man's disease almost annihilated the Indians.

**POJOAQUE RIVER** (Santa Fe) The Pojoaque flows into the Rio Grande River, and was named for the village of Pojoaque, derived from the Tewa word, po-suwae-geh (or posoong wa ghay), defined as "water drinking (or "gathering") place." It may be a corruption of povi age, meaning "place where the flowers grow along the stream." Settlement along the river occurred in 1700 when José Trujillo was given a land grant.

**SACATON CREEK** (Catron) Beginning in the Mogollon Mountains, this creek joins Duck Creek. Derived from a Pima word, its name could mean "tall, rank herbage, unfit for forage," or "broad, flat land." It has also been suggested that Sacaton is a misspelling of a Spanish word, zacoton, which was a type of fodder grass.

**TAIBAN CREEK** (De Baca) The creek is about 50 miles long and enters the Pecos River. A ranching community located nearby took its name from the stream. Taiban is a Navajo or Comanche word for "horsetail," possibly referring to all the tributaries on the Taiban Arroyo that come from the same direction. Another meaning is "three creeks."

**TESUQUE CREEK** (Santa Fe) Originating in the Sangre de Cristo Mountains, this tributary of Pojoaque Creek flows past the village of Tesuque, which was originally called Taytsoongay, but corrupted to Tesuque. The original spelling means "cottonwood tree place," or it may be a Tewa term, tat' unge' onwi, for "spotted dry place," referring to the way the river comes and goes under the sand.

**TUCUMCARI MOUNTAIN/LAKE** (Quay) Cattle drivers on the Goodnight Loving Trail used the lake as one of their watering places. Tucumcari is a Jemez word that means "place of buffalo hunt." Other translations were "squatty mountain," and "mother's breast." This was Comanche territory, and the word may have come from cuchtonaro and uah, translated as "two fires" or "burn, make a fire," in reference to signal fires for assembling Comanche war parties. Others believe it was derived from tukamukaru, meaning "to lie in wait for someone," descriptive of an Indian lookout on the mountain. Apache legend says Chief Wautonomah was dying and wondered who would take his place. Tonopah and Tocom were rivals who both loved the Chief's daughter Kari, but she loved Tocom. The two warriors engaged in a knife combat, and Tonopah killed Tocom. Kari took her knife intent on killing Tonopah, but her father grabbed the knife, and just before taking his own life, cried, "Tocom-Kari"!

**TUNSTA WASH** (San Juan)    Tunsta is derived from the Navajo word to ntsaa, interpreted as "much water." The wash originates in the Chuska Mountain and joins Captain Tom Wash. Colonel John Wash-ington and his men followed the wash in 1849 where they discovered a prehistoric ruin near Two Grey Hills. Major Oliver Shepherd was there in 1858 while looking for Cayetano's band of Navajo Indians. The U.S. Army operated a post near the wash in the 1860s.

**ZUNI MOUNTAINS/RIVER** (McKinley)    Zuni may be derived from the Tewa expression soonyee-ongwee, meaning "casting place pueblo," or "rock slide pueblo." Another interpretation was from naa t'ezh, meaning "enemies blackened with charcoal." The Zuni Indians called the mountain kwili yalone ("two mountains"). The Zuni name for themselves is A'shiwi, meaning "the flesh." In 1818, Alcalde Jose Ortiz and his men went into the mountains to fight the Navajo Indians. The river originates in the Zuni Mountains and joins the Little Colorado River in the state of Arizona.

# NEW YORK

**ADIRONDACK MOUNTAINS**
Adirondack is an Algonquian expression derived from doran and dak, interpreted as "a people who eat bark trees." The Adirondacks were virtually unknown until Joel Headley spent many summers in the mountains. Interest was generated in the region after he wrote his book *The Adirondacks, or Life in the Woods* in 1849. The mountains stretch from the St. Lawrence and Mohawk Valleys and are an extension of the Canadian Shield. The highest peaks rise more than 4,000 feet high.

**CANAJOHARIE CREEK** (Montgomery)    About 1730, the town of Canajoharie was settled along this creek by Dutch and German settlers who used its water power for their mills. The creek originates in the Shankley Mountain and flows through part of community. Mohawk Chief Brant defined Canajoharie as "the pot that washes itself," descriptive of a large pothole created by the constant action of water and pebbles on the limestone rocks in the gorge. It was also translated as "the boiling pot."

**CANISTEO RIVER** (Steuben)   After the Wyoming Massacre in Pennsylvania about 1788, survivors fled to the Canisteo. The river originates near the village of Arkport and enters the Chemung River. Its name was derived from te-car-nase-teo, an Iroquois word for "board on the water," referring to the village's location at the head of navigation. Arkport received its name because one of the settlers built four arks on which he shipped wheat and pork down the river.

**CANOPUS CREEK** (Westchester)   The Wappinger Indians lived along this creek, led by Chief Canopus, whose name was derived from Canopaug, meaning "long pond." During 1777, the Continental Village was established, which gained military importance during the American Revolution. Enough barracks were built to house 2,000 men. The site was under the leadership of Major Campbell.

**CATATONK CREEK** (Tioga)   Settled in 1794, the community of Candor was established near the creek. Catatonk is a tributary of Owego Creek, and bears an Algonquian word interpreted as "principal stream."

**CATTARAUGUS CREEK** (Wyoming) The town of Gowanda was founded near this creek, where in later years a hydroelectric generating facility was built. The stream flows 70 miles to Lake Erie. Cattaraugus is an Algonquian word meaning "fetid banks."

**CAYADUTTA   CREEK**   (Fulton) Cayadutta is an Algonquian word defined as "stone standing out of the water." The creek flows through the community of Mohawk. Gloversville was also founded near the Cayadutta, and became known as the "Glove Capital of the World," for the product it produced. The industry began

when Sir William Johnson brought a group of glovers from Perthshire, Scotland, in the 1760s.

**CAYUGA LAKE** (Cayuga)   Cayuga is an Algonquian expression derived from gweugweh, meaning "the mucky land," or "canoes pulled out of the water." It was also interpreted as "big lake." The lake is about 40 miles long and 2 miles wide, and is the longest of the Finger Lakes. It was once a main artery for transportation. The Indians believe these Finger Lakes were created by the Great Spirit as a benediction.

**CHAUTAUQUA LAKE** (Chautauqua) Chautauqua is a glacial lake that bears a Seneca expression for "the place where one is lost," "the place of easy death," "foggy place," and "a bag tied in the middle," descriptive of the lake's shape. It may be better translated from t'kantchata'kwan, meaning "one who has taken out fish there." The lake was important to French exploration of North America since it linked the navigation route between Canada and Louisiana. In 1827, Alvin Plumb built the first steamboat to travel on the lake. Tradition holds that a young Indian girl with a Seneca hunting party ate a root that made her thirsty. She went into the lake to quench her thirst and disappeared, never to appear again. Thus, Chautauqua was supposedly derived from jadaqueh, for "a body ascended."

**CHEMUNG RIVER** (Chemung)   In 1615, Stephen Brule, emissary and translator for Champlain, was sent to this region to get help from the Andaste Indians during the war between the French and Iroquois. His notes were the first record of this river. Settlement along the Chemung occurred about 1786, and the Chemung Canal was built to connect the river with Seneca Lake. The name was derived from an Iroquois or Lenape word meaning "big horn," or "horn-in-the-water." The "horn" was in reference to mammoth tusks discovered in the area.

**CHENANGO RIVER** (Oneida)    This river flows 90 miles to the Susquehanna River. The town of Chenango was established along the shore of the river, which bears an Onondaga word derived from o-che-nang, meaning "bull thistles."

**CHITTENANGO CREEK** (Madison) Chittenango is an Oneida word meaning "where the waters divide and run north," because the creek enters from the south, forming a western boundary on Oneida Lake, with Canasaraga Creek flowing in a northerly direction. It was also interpreted as "marshy place." Sir John Johnston conducted a raid on the Mohawk and Schoharie Valleys during the American Revolution, and instructed a detachment to stay at this creek to guard their supplies. Early settlers were here as early as 1790, attracted by the water power of the creek. The first gypsum in the state was found in the nearby hills and used in construction of the Erie Canal.

**CHOCONUT CREEK** (Broome)    A tribe known as the Chugnut had their villages along this creek until 1779, when they fled after part of General Sullivan's army came through on its mission to wipe out all the Indians. Choconut was derived from chokohton, meaning "blisters." However, other authorities believe it is an Onondaga expression for "place of tamaracks."

**CHUCTANUNDA CREEK** (Montgomery)    The town of Amsterdam (first known as Vedder's Mills) was established at the mouth of this creek in 1783, and the water power supplied many industries for the town, including carpet mills. Chuctanunda may be an Algonquian word meaning "stony," or "stone house."

**CONESUS LAKE** (Livingston)    This lake is about 8 miles long and is the westernmost of the Finger Lakes. Conesus was derived from the Algonquian word ganeasos, meaning "place of nannyberries," or "long string of berries," in reference to the abundant sheepberries that grew near the lake.

**CONHOCTON RIVER** (Steuben)    Ark navigation began on the river in 1800 with the first shipment of wheat sent by White's Mill. The ungainly craft were about 75 feet long and 16 feet wide. Transportation via these arks was precarious at best, but until other modes of transportation were initiated there was no choice in vessels. Conhocton is an Algonquian phrase meaning "trees in the water."

**COPAKE LAKE** (Columbia)    In the Algonquin language, Copake means "snake pond," taken from achkook-paug. Once the site of an Indian village, the horseshoe-shaped lake later had cottages dotting its shore for summer vacationers. At one time the community of Craryville was home to the Bordon's Milk plant which had a spur line built to the lake in order to harvest ice.

**ESOPUS CREEK** (Ulster)    Original settlers to this area were the Esopus Indians, followed by the white man in 1652, who located along the creek and named their settlement Esopus. It was later changed to Kingston. Residents fared well with the Indians until they began encroaching on Indian land, bringing rise to skirmishes between the two. General Stuyvesant sent troops here in 1657 to build a stockade and remove the Indians. Esopus means "river," from the Lenape word sopus.

**GAROGA    CREEK**    (Montgomery) This creek originates in the Mayfield Mountains near the town of Gloversville, a region once home to the Mohawk Indians. Garoga was derived from garogon, meaning "to make something of wood." It was also translated as "creek on this side," because there were no Mohawk villages located west of the creek. Another interpretation was from kaihogha, meaning "a creek."

**HACKENSACK RIVER** (Rockland) The Hackensack is about 45 miles long and flows into Newark Bay in the state of New Jersey. The town of Hackensack was settled by the Dutch in 1647 who started the first trading post, calling the site New Barbados. The name was changed to Hackensack in 1921, derived from the Lenape word, ahkinkeshaki, for "place of sharp ground."

**HOOSICK RIVER** (Rensselaer) Dutchman John Brimmer and his family made their home along the river about 1754. The Indians resented their intrusion and killed them, so the settlement remained abandoned for some time. During the 1770s the community of Que Quicke was formed, and the name was later changed to Hoosick Falls. Using the river's water power, small industries were established and a cotton factory was built. Hoosick may come from the Algonquian words hussun and ack, meaning "place of stones."

**ISCHUA CREEK** (Cattaraugus) Rising near the town of Machias, the river flows 30 miles to join the Allegheny River. The town of Ischua was founded in 1846 with the creek flowing through the center of it. One of the first settlers along the creek was Abram Farwell about 1812, who moved here from Massachusetts and built the first sawmill and gristmill. During 1845, what was called the first agrarian (land rights) strike in America occurred between settlers and the Holland Land Company. Ischua is an Iroquois word interpreted as "floating nettles."

**KASHONG CREEK** (Ontario) During skirmishes with the Seneca Indians, this site was the only place where a full-scale engagement occurred in the county with the U.S. Army. The creek was named for the Kashong Indians, translated as "creek of two branches." It was also thought to mean "the limb has fallen."

**KAYADEROSSERAS CREEK** (Montgomery) The Kayaderosseras Patent was granted to Daniel Campbell in 1800, who later leased his land to settlers along the creek banks. When the Mohawk Indians found out the whites had encroached on their hunting territory, they ordered the whites to leave. Kayaderosseras is a Mohawk expression for "lake country."

**KENJOCKETY CREEK** (Erie) Kenjockety is a Seneca word, a corruption of sga-dynh'-gwa-dih or sken-dyough-gwatti, meaning "beyond the multitude." Early settlers named the creek to honor an Indian family living on the creek.

**KEUKA LAKE** (Steuben) Part of the Finger Lakes, Keuka is Y-shaped and bears an Algonquian name meaning "canoe landing." Early settlers called it Crooked Creek. In 1908, famous aviator, Glenn Curtiss, built Drone No. 1 (known as the "Red Wing"), one of the first flying machines. It had a 24-hp, 8-cylinder motorcycle motor mounted between the wings. Casey Baldwin was the pilot who took off on runners on the lake's ice. Unfortunately the plane crashed, but he walked away unhurt.

**MANURSING ISLAND** (Westchester) The island saw its first settlers in 1660, but they eventually left and moved to the town of Rye. Manursing is an Algonquian word meaning "little island."

**MINISCONGA CREEK** (Rockland) This creek enters the Hudson River near

Stony Point. During the 17th century, settlers were attracted to the region because the creek had the water power to operate their textile mills. Minisconga may be an Algonquian word taken from minnis, con and ga, meaning "island object place."

**MINNEWASKA LAKE** (Ulster)   Minnewaska bears an Algonquian expression meaning "floating waters," in reference to its position atop the Shawangunk Mountains. The lake was formed during the Ice Age when the ice sheet, several thousand feet thick, slid over the mountain top and cut out blocks of sandstone.

**MOHAWK RIVER** (Herkimer)   This river originates near the town of Rome and flows into the Hudson River. It is about 140 miles long. Because of the river's speed and unpredictability, a series of locks were built. At one time, building of the Erie Canal on the Mohawk to reach the Lake Ontario outlet was considered, but the idea was scrapped. The river was named for the Mohawk Indians, taken from moho, whose name is thought to mean "to eat living things." The Mohawk people call themselves Ganiengehaka, meaning "the people of flint," or Onkweh-Onweh, for "real human beings."

**MOHONK LAKE** (Ulster)   Mohonk Lake was originally created in 1948 for use as a weather station. Albert and Alfred Smily purchased land along the lake, where they established a tavern, called Mohonk Mountain House. Mohonk is an Algonquian word derived from mohoan, interpreted as "to eat solid food," or from mohewoneck, meaning "a raccoon skin coat."

**NEVERSINK RIVER** (Orange)   The town of Fallsburg was founded at the river so it could take advantage of its water power to run their sawmills and gristmills.

Neversink is an Algonquian word meaning "point at," and may have been derived from Navesink.

**NOWADAGA CREEK** (Herkimer) This creek bears a Mohawk word meaning "place of mud turtles," a shortened form of canowedage. Mohawk Chief Joseph Brant built a home near the mouth of the creek. During the French and Indian War, stockades were built for the settlers' protection.

**OATKA CREEK** (Genesee)   Oatka is an Algonquian word meaning "an opening." The villages of Pavilion and Union Corners were established along the creek during the early 1800s, and the first mill was built by Bial Lathrop in 1816. Another village was Leroy, which has the distinction of being place where Jell-O was created. It was also the home of Nicholas Keeney who cross-fertilized string beans, and over the years marketed 'stringless' beans.

**ONEIDA LAKE** (Madison)   The lake was named for the Oneida Indians, whose name means "people of the living stone," and designated a large boulder the Indians venerated. It was also interpreted as "the people of the beacon stone." Indian legend says a particular stone followed the Indians wherever they traveled and took up residence atop one of their highest hills. It was used by the Indians for their beacon fires.

**ONISTAGRAW MOUNTAIN** (Schoharie)   Onistagraw is an Algonquian word meaning "corn mountain." It also bears the name Vrooman's Nose because it resembles a face with a bold profile of a nose.

**OSWEGATCHIE RIVER** (St. Lawrence) During 1749, French missionary Francis Piquet established a mission, which was the first permanent settlement in the state at the mouth of this river. The old settlement was later used to house cholera victims. The river was originally called River La Presentation, and later renamed Oswegatchie, an Iroquois word for "black water." Fort La Presentation was built as protection against the English and a place to serve French fur traders, but the Mohawk Indians burned it.

**OTSQUAGO CREEK** (Montgomery) This creek rises north of Summit Lake and flows to join the Mohawk River. Otsquago is a Mohawk word meaning "under a bridge," and may be indicative of a bridge consisting of felled trees the Indians put there. Others interpreted the name from osquage, meaning "place of hulled corn soup." Otsquago has been called The Gateway to Otsego Lake and Cooperstown (where baseball was born.)

**PASCACK CREEK** (Rockland) Pascack is an Algonquian expression derived from peasik, meaning "a small place" (or "thing"). An early settler in 1746 established a factory which manufactured wampum and other shell items for trade. The creek was first named Peasqua in 1697.

**PECONIC BAY** (Suffolk) The bay is located between the north and south forks of Long Island. Peconic Bay splits the eastern end of Long Island so it resembles the flukes of a whale. The Peconic was used by whalers, fisherman, and for shipping. It is an Algonquin word for "nut trees." Another interpretation was "little plantation," derived from pehikkonuk.

**PISECO LAKE** (Hamilton) Located along the shore was the village of Piseco which was settled about 1827. The region's industry consisted of sawmills with the wealth of timber nearby. Piseco is an Algonquian word meaning "a fish," or "miry place." It may have been for an Indian

named Pezeeko who lived along the lake. A surveyor may have named the lake for his friend.

**POCANTICO RIVER** (Westchester) Pocantico is an Algonquian word meaning "dark river," or "at the clear stream." A Dutchman purchased land here in 1861, and used the water power of the river to operated a gristmill.

**QUASSAIC CREEK** (Orange) This creek joins the Hudson River near the town of Newburgh. A group of Lutherans, led by their minister Joshua Kocherthal, settled along the banks in 1709 and established the Palatine Parish of Quassaick. They were forced to move when the English moved in because they could not get along. Quassaic is an Algonquian expression taken from qussuk-ick, meaning "stone place."

**RONKONKOMA, LAKE** (Suffolk) Ronkonkoma Lake was formed by a retreating glacier and served as a boundary between a number of Indian tribes. It later became a resort after discovery of the water's healing properties. Ronkonkoma is an Algonquian expression translated from ron, konk, and omack, meaning "boundary fishing place," or "wild goose resting place." It is Long Island's largest freshwater lake.

**SACANDAGA RIVER** (Saratoga) During the 1800s, Methodists came to the river to hold their camp meetings. After a railroad was established they were forced to leave and summer cottages replaced the camp. The river was also used as a log drive during the lumber era. In 1930, the region was inundated by a dam the state built to control flooding on the Hudson River. Sacandaga may be an Iroquois word meaning "swampy," or "drowned lands."

**SAUQUOIT CREEK** (Oneida) Sauquoit Creek rises near Paris Station and joins the Mohawk River 21 miles away. A 1736 patent spells the creek's name as Sadachqueda or Sahquate. It bears an Algonquian word meaning "smooth pebbles in a stream." The first sawmills and gristmills in the county were built along the Sauquoit after the American Revolution.

**SCHENEVUS CREEK** (Otsego) This unusual name is a Dutch corruption of an Iroquois expression for "hoeing of corn." It was also thought to be the name of a chief who hunted in the region. The creek joins the Susquehanna River. There is also a village within the town of Maryland named Schenevus which was settled in 1793 originally as Jacksonboro. Legend tells the story of Chief Schenevus' daughter, Manaho, who was in love with Manatee. While gazing into a pool they told each other that "where you are, there too, I shall always be." Another Indian named Ghangu also loved Manaho, and one day pushed Mantee into the pond near a gorge. Bereft, Manaho threw herself into the pond. Today, if you listen very carefully you can hear the two lovers whisper to each other, "where you are, there too, I shall always be."

**SCHROON LAKE** (Essex) Shroon Lake village lies at the head of the 9-mile-long lake. Its name has numerous interpretations. It may be derived from an Algonquian word ska-ne-tah-ro-wah-na, meaning "largest lake," or from sequinneau, for "it is left behind." Some think is was applied in honor of the Duchess of Skaron, favorite of Louis XIV. Local legend says a Mohawk brave fell in love with Scarona ("soft eyed fawn"). After returning home from battling the enemy, the brave was unable to sleep and went to the lake to play his flute. Scarona came out to listen to the music when the enemy at-tacked. The two lovers tried to escape by canoe, but the warrior was shot and Scarona dove into the lake rather than live without her lover. She never reappeared. Tradition says her name was corrupted to Schroon.

**SHAWANGUNK MOUNTAINS** (Orange) Huguenots settled in a valley near the mountains, and on early deeds the name was written skonemoghky. Shawangunk may be from the Lenape expression schawaneu and gammunk, translated as "south on the other side of the water." Others interpreted it from jewan, meaning "swift current," or "strong stream." The Mohegan expression shawan and gunk, means "white pile of rocks," in reference to a white rock precipice near the top of the mountain. Tradition says that Tom Quick, famous Indian killer, roamed these mountains in search of Indians and supposedly killed more than 100 of them.

**SUSQUEHANNA RIVER** (Otsego) The river is about 44 miles long. It originates at Otsego Lake, flows into Pennsylvania and empties into Chesapeake Bay. Once representing the western border of the frontier, the Indians conducted raids on the east side of the river. In 1690, William Penn considered building a settlement along the river in Pennsylvania. He wrote: "It is now my purpose to make another settlement, upon the River Susquehannagh, … There I design to lay out a plan for the building of another city in the most convenient place for communication with the former plantation on the east."[9] Susquehanna was interpreted from the Lenape words sisku and hanne, meaning "muddy river." Other derivations were "the long crooked river," or "river of the winding shore."

**TIOUGHNIOGA RIVER** (Cortland) Indians and explorers used this river as an early travel route. It was also a boundary line for the Onondaga Indians. The stream is about 70 miles long and enters the Chenango River. It is a long form of Tioga, an Iroquois expression meaning "forks of the river." It was also defined as "peaceful valley." In 1791, the village of Homer was established along the river and its economy was tied to the timber industry.

**UTOWANA LAKE** (Hamilton)   Land around the lake was purchased by settlers in 1904. The lake is little over 2 miles long. Utowana is an Onondaga expression meaning "big waves." The present owners donated land to the state in 1999 so that this part of the region would remain wild.

**UTSAYANTHA, MOUNT/LAKE** (Delaware) First known as Mount Prospect, Utsayantha rises about 3,365 feet and is the highest peak in the Catskill Mountains. It is an Algonquian word meaning "beautiful spring." Indian legend says that a maiden named Utsayantha is buried in the mountain. She was a Mo-hawk princess who fell in love with a Sioux warrior. Both tribes forbade them to marry each other. As a result, the princess drowned herself in Utsayantha lake. Her father recovered Utsayantha's body and had her buried at the top of the mountain. During the late 1930s, her grave was opened but nothing was in it.

**WAPPINGER CREEK** (Dutchess)   The creek was named for the Wappinger Indians, the majority who were killed in 1643-45 during the Wappinger War. Their name was derived from wabun and ahki, meaning "east land." It was also thought to come from the Lenape word waping, meaning "opossum." The creek supported many mills, its 75-foot falls providing a generous supply of water power.

**WILLOWEMOC CREEK** (Sullivan) The Willowemoc is about 26 miles long, runs through the town of Rockland, and flows into the Beaverkill. The name may be derived from the Algonquian word wu-lagamike, meaning "bottom land."

# NORTH CAROLINA

**CASHI RIVER** (Bertie)   The river is about 50 miles long and flows into Albemarle Sound. It was named for an Algonquian Indian chief (origin unknown). The community of Winberly was supposed to have been created here in 1752 on orders of the Colonial Assembly, but it never occurred. Warehouses were later established along the river and used to house tobacco that was cultivated to such a degree the product required storage.

**CATALOOCHEE VALLEY** (Haywood) Located in the Smoky Mountain National Park, this remote area was one of the last places to be settled before the Civil War. By the mid-1800s, more than 1,200 people were living at Cataloochee Village, but today not much is left of it. Elk were very prevalent in the region until they were overhunted. An experimental program was started in the 1990s with the introduction of 25 elk to see if they would stay in the valley and continue breeding. To date, three calves have been born. Cataloochee may be a Cherokee expression for "waves of mountains," or "trees standing in many rows," in reference to the rows of tree-covered ridges.

**CATAWBA RIVER** (McDowell)   The Catawba has its origins near Mount Mitchell and flows 220 miles into the state of South Carolina, where it becomes the Wateree River. It was named for the Catawba Indians who lived in the region until white settlement. They became master potters using clay from the river banks. The Indians called themselves Yap Ye Iswa, which means "people of the river." Their reservation is located on the banks of the river just below Rock Hill in South Carolina. Catawba may be a from the Choctaw word katapa, meaning "divided" or "separated."

**CHEOAH LAKE/RIVER** (Graham) The lake was created by the Aluminum Company of America (ALCOA) when it dammed the flow of the Cheoah River in order to supply electric power for the mining industry. The Tennessee Valley Authority supplemented the water supply during World War II. Cheoah is a Cherokee word for "otter place."

**CHOCOWINITY CREEK** (Beaufort) The community of Chocowinity took its name from the river, which flows into the Pamlico River. First called Worsley Creek, the name was changed to Chocowinity, a Tuscarora expression choca-wa-na-teth, meaning "fish from many waters." It may also mean "smoking stumps," from Chocowinekee. The name was originally spelled Chocawanateth Creek.

**CHOWAN RIVER** (Gates/Hertford) The river is formed close to the state line with the merging of Virginia's Blackwater and Nottoway rivers. The Wapeamok Indians lived on the west side of the river, and the Chowanokes on the east side. White settlers later used the stream as their main mode of transportation. During the American Revolution, the river allowed protection for American ships. It was also an important supply line for Washington's army. Chowan was named for the Chowanoc Indians, whose name was interpreted as "south country."

**CONTENTNEA CREEK** (Wilson) Rising at the confluence of Moccasin and Turkey creeks, the Contentnea merges with the Neuse River. The creek took its name from a Tuscarora village named Cotechney, interpreted as "thief," or "rogue." During the 1700s, conflict arose between the whites and Tuscarora Indians, led by King Hancock. He later captured John Lawson, early surveyor of the region. In 1711, the Indians finally surrendered and a peace treaty was signed, ending the Indian War. Starting out as a trading post along the creek, the town of Snow Hill was founded about 1828.

**COWEE       VALLEY/MOUNTAIN** (Macon)   Since 1895, the Cowee Valley has produced ruby and sapphire crystals, which let to the establishment of the American Prospecting and Mining Company. Cowee was once the name of one of the oldest and largest Cherokee villages, which was destroyed during the American Revolution. Cowee may be a Cherokee expression meaning "place of the Deer Clan." The Cowee Mountains are about 5,080 feet high. In 1861, a British expedition with more than 2,000 soldiers traveled over the mountains on its mission to destroy the Cherokee Indian villages.

**CULLASAJA RIVER** (Macon)   This region was home to the Cherokee Indians, and the river bears their word kaulsetsiyi, interpreted as "honey locust place." It may also be from kulsaygee, meaning "sugar," or "sweet." The river flows into the Little Tennessee River. In 1875, the town of Highlands was established, and prospered greatly during the 1920s when the Cullasaja River was dammed to provide hydroelectric power.

**CULLOWHEE CREEK** (Jackson) This creek joins the Tuckasegee River. Cullowhee was derived from the Cherokee words gualiya or callaugh-ee, defined as "place of the spring." Another interpretation was "place of the lilies." Originally established at Webster, the Cullowhee Baptist Church was moved to the creek in 1830 near what was once an old Cherokee village, and may be the county's oldest church. Part of Western Carolina University is situated near the Cullowhee.

**ELLIJAY CREEK** (Macon) In 1816, Major William Higdon moved to the region after the Civil War and established a general store and mill along the creek. The Ellijay flows into the Cullasaja River. It bears a Cherokee expression that means "verdant earth." Other interpretations were "many waters," "new ground," or from elatsay yi, meaning "earth green there," or "place of green things."

**ENO RIVER** (Orange) The Eno flows into Flat River. It name was derived from the Tuscarora word e-eno, meaning "a great way," or "far off." Located along the river was the Great Indian Trading Path, used by the Indians traveling back and forth between Virginia. Once a main route for colonial traders, mill dam sites were later established along the river's banks. It was there that the Constitutional Convention of 1788 was held.

**HATTERAS ISLAND** (Dare) Colonists spent time on Hatteras Island trading with the Hatteras Indians and collecting shells. The village of Hatteras is located on the southwest side of the island. Federal troops stormed the island during the Civil War and set up an encampment just outside the village. In 1878, a lifesaving station was built on the island, as was a weather station in 1880. Hatteras may be a corruption of an Algonquin word that described an area of sparse vegetation

**HAW RIVER** (Guilford) The Haw River was named for the Sissipahaw Indians (origin unknown). It originates near the town of Greensboro and flows about 100 miles to merge with Deep River. The arrival of Adam Trollinger in 1745 was the seed of what would become the village of Haw River. The stream held a great wealth of treasures that were hidden during the Civil War, although none of it was ever found.

**HYCO RIVER** (Person) Rising at the confluence of the North and South Hyco creeks, this stream flows into the state of Virginia and merges with Dan River. Hyco may be a shortened form of an Algonquian word, hicootomony, meaning "turkey buzzard river," indicative of the numerous birds that roosted in the trees growing along the river.

**JUNALUSKA LAKE** (Haywood) The lake comprises about 250 acres and is the summer recreational and education center of the Methodist Episcopal Church. It was first named for Cherokee Chief Gulkalaski, who was responsible for helping General Andrew Jackson at the Battle of Horseshoe Bend during the Creek War of 1812. When Jackson was directing the forced removal of the Cherokee from their native lands in the 1830s, Gulkalaski had an audience with Jackson, who told the Indian there was nothing he could do. Gulkalask said, "If I had known that Jackson would drive us from our homes, I would have killed him that day at the Horseshoe."[10] When he told his people what happened, Gulkalaski was given the name Tsunlahunski, which means "one who tries, but fails." The settlers were unable to pronounce his name, and so they spelled it Junaluska.

**KANUGA LAKE** (Henderson)   George Stephens, a banker and newspaper publisher, purchased more than 900 acres and created the lake by damming Mud Creek. In 1909, the Kanuga Lake Club was established in order to attract the wealthy. The Episcopal Church bought the lake and club in 1928, and today it is an Episcopal conference center and retreat. Kanuga is a Cherokee expression meaning "meeting place of many peoples." It was also thought to describe some type of scratching device used in a Cherokee stickball game.

**MATTAMUSKEET, LAKE** (Hyde)   On July 11, 1585, about 60 English explorers sailed across Pamlico sound to Wysocking Bay, then walked to the lake the Indians called Paquippe. It would be more than 100 years before the lake would be renamed Mattumuskeet, an Algonquian expression meaning "dry dust." In 1934, Mattumuskeet National Wildlife Refuge was created when the U.S. Government acquired the land.

**NANTAHALA MOUNTAINS/RIVER** (Macon)   Formerly called Ayoree Mountain, these mountains range from North Carolina and extend into Georgia. They rise about 5,000 feet high. The mountain and river bear the Cherokee word nantoh-eeyah-heh-lih, interpreted as "sun in the middle," descriptive of the time of day (noon). The name was first applied to a place where part of the mountain cliffs kept the sun from shining until noon. The

river originates in the Nantahala Mountains in the Nantahala National Forest and flows into Swain County.

**NEUSE RIVER** (Durham)   This is the site where the Colonials fought and beat the Tuscarora Indians in 1713. Quakers moved to the river in the 1750s to practice their religion, and had to hold their services in a member's home until the Neuse Meeting House was built in 1841. During the Civil War, Sherman's Army camped at the river on its march to Richmond. The Neuse River rises at the confluence of the Eno and Flat Rivers, then flows to Pamlico Sound. It was named by Arthur Barlowe in 1584 for the Neusiok Indians, who called the river Gowtano, meaning "pine in water." The Tuscarora Indians called it gow-ta-no, signifying "pine in water."

**NOLICHUCKY RIVER** (Mitchell/ Yancey)   The Nolichucky has its origins at the confluence of the Toe and Cane Rivers and flows 105 miles to the French Broad River in Tennessee. It is a Cherokee expression meaning "spruce tree place." They considered this river sacred, for it contained spirits who lived in its waters. Indian hunting parties steered clear because they believed the spirits would rise up and eat the men. Jacob Brown moved to the river in 1771 and built the Cherokee Meeting House for worship. John Sevier also lived along the river in the state of Tennessee. He was on trial for treason, but escaped, and later became the first governor of Tennessee.

**OCONALUFTEE RIVER** (Swain) This river runs through Smoky Mountain National Park and joins the Tuckasegee River near the town of Bryson City. It was once home to the Cherokee Indians until they were removed via the Trail of Tears to Oklahoma in 1838. Oconaluftee is a Cherokee word for "near river." William

Thomas lived along the river, and was the only white man to serve as a Cherokee chief.

**OCRACOKE ISLAND** (Hyde)    The lee side of Ocracoke served as the home port of Blackbeard before he was killed in 1718. Tales of his treasure have long been circulated, but it has never been found. The wind- and wave-swept island was also home to wild ponies, thought to be descended from the Barbary ponies. The name may be a corruption of an Algonquin word, waxihikami, designating an enclosed place or stockade

**PASQUOTANK RIVER** (Camden/ Pasquotank)    The Pasquotank River was at one time an inspection station for hemp, flax, pork, turpentine, and other products shipped to their various destination. It is about 50 miles long, and has its origins in Dismal Swamp, then empties into Albemarle Sound. The town of Camden was established along the river about 1650. Pasquotank is an Algonquian word derived from pasketanki, meaning "where the current divides."

**PERQUIMANS RIVER** (Perquimans) Rising in Dismal Swam, this river flows 30 miles to an estuary near the town of Hertford. It was named for the Perquiman Indian tribe (origin unknown). Settlement along the river occurred about 1650 with the arrival of English settlers.

**POTECASI CREEK** (Northampton) Potecasi is an Algonquian phrase meaning "parting of the waters." The creek flows into Meherrin River. During the Civil War in 1863, the schooner *G.H. Smoot* was captured by Lt. Edmond Calhoun of the U.S. Navy as the ship made its way upriver.

**PUNGO RIVER** (Beaufort)    The river is about 20 miles and rises at Dismal

Swamp. It empties into Pamlico Sound. Settlement in the region began about 1691. First known as Machapunga River, the name was changed to Pungo, a Machapunga Indian word meaning "bad dust."

**ROQUIST CREEK** (Bertie)    The Roquist flows into Cashi River. It bears a Tuscarora word that means "turtle." During the 1600s, the Tuscarora villages were decimated by the whites and many the Indians were removed to the Indian Woods Reservation about 1717. The reservation was comprised of about 58,000 acres, bounded by Roquist Creek, the Roanoke River and Deep Run Creek.

**SANTEETLAH LAKE/CREEK** (Graham)    This man-made lake was created when the Cheoah River was dammed up in 1928 by the ALCOA Company. It covers 2,800 acres. The creek flows into Santeetlah Lake. It may be a Cherokee word meaning "sandplace stream." In 1939, the U.S. Forest Service purchased the land around the lake and the village of Santeetlah was founded.

**SCUPPERNONG RIVER** (Tyrrell) Scuppernong is derived from askup'-onong, Algonquian for "at the place of the sweet bay tree." Tradition says scuppernong grapes were discovered by two brothers nearby in the 18th century. In 1819, Senator Nathaniel Macon sent two bottles of scuppernong wine to Thomas Jefferson at Monticello, describing it as the best in America. The river begins at Dismal Swamp and empties into Albemarle Sound.

**SKEENAH CREEK** (Macon)    Rising at its North and South Forks, the Skeenah flows to merge with the Little Tennessee River. It is an Algonquian word interpreted as "the abode of satan" (more likely "devil"). In 1839 Willis Woody built the Skeenah Creek Mill for grinding corn, which became a favorite meeting place for residents at Skeenah Gap. The dam that was built to power the mill was destroyed by a flood in 1969.

**STECOAH CREEK** (Graham) The river flows to unite with the Little Tennessee River. An old Cherokee town was located along the Stecoah, which is Cherokee for "lean," indicative of not having enough, such as game.

**SWANNANOA RIVER** (Buncombe/McDowell) Settlement along the river began during the mid-1700s. The Vanderbilts had an estate near the stream where an ancient Connestee Mound was discovered dating back to about 200 A.D. It was believed to be a ceremonial site. Swannanoa was named by the Cherokee Indians, and means "trail of the Suwali tribe." It was also defined as "to the south." The river rises near Swannanoa Gap and enters the French Broad River.

**TOE RIVER** (Mitchell/Yancey) This river's name may have been taken from Estatoe, an Indian princess who drowned herself in the river after her lover was slain by another Indian tribe (origin unknown). During the late 1800s, the Carolina, Clinchfield and Ohio Railroad was established along the banks of the river. Rising at the confluence of the North and South Toe, this stream joins the Cane River.

**TOXAWAY, LAKE** (Transylvania) Home to the Cherokee Indians until settlers pushed them out, Lake Toxaway was created when J.F. Hayes arrived in 1890 for his health and constructed a 540-acre lake and the Toxaway Hotel. He also built exquisite homes and advertised for millionaires to move there. The hotel opened in 1903 and boasted steam heating, elevators, and imported French chefs. In 1916, heavy rains resulted in a huge flood, bursting a dam, and destroying the lake. The hotel was closed in 1916. Toxaway was taken from a Cherokee chief whose name means "red bird."

**TUCKASEGEE RIVER** (Jackson) Western Carolina University is located along the river. During the Civil War military details were stationed along the Tuckasegee to manufacture salt petre for military powder. The Cherokee Indians once had their principal town of Kituhwa along the Tuckasegee, which is derived from their word tsiksitsi, interpreted as "crawling turtle," descriptive of the river's sluggishness. It is about 50 miles long and flows into Little Tennessee River.

**WACCAMAW LAKE** (Columbus)/**RIVER** (Bladen) Land in this region was granted to a Lord Proprietor during the 1700s by Charles the Second, who in turn made individual grants to settlers. Charles Beers moved to Waccamaw in 1869 and built a shingle mill along the lake. He joined forces with Henry Short and created the North Carolina Lumber Company. In 1890, the name was changed to Lake Waccamaw. It may be connected to Waccanaow, translated as "tobacco." The Waccamaw River flows about 140 miles and empties into Winyah Bay in South Carolina. Indian legend says the lake was once a field of flowers, but was flooded when the Indian gods flooded it as punishment.

**WATAUGA RIVER** (Watauga) This stream rises in the Blue Ridge Mountains and flows about 60 miles into the state of Tennessee. In 1761, a Cherokee village along the river was burned by General Griffith Rutherford. Watauga is a Cherokee word for "beautiful river."

**WAYAH BALD MOUNTAIN** (Macon) This feature rises about 5,385 feet. Wayah is a Cherokee word meaning "wolf," and was the name of a young Cherokee Indian. In 1776, the Indians waged their last stand in Wayah Gap against General Griffith Rutherford.

**WOCOCON ISLAND** (Hyde, Carteret) When Queen Elizabeth sent Sir Walter Raleigh to search for heathen lands in 1584, he sent two ships which landed on the island. During 1585 Sir Richard Greene ran his ship aground near the island, losing all the supplies that were destined for the colonists. Since the settlers had arrived too late to plant crops, they were on the verge of starving. An Indian chief invited the colonists to relocate to Roanoke where they would have plenty of food. Wococon is an Algonquian expression, derived from wahkahikani, meaning "enclosed place," or "stockade."

# NORTH DAKOTA

**KANDIOTTA LAKE** (Sargent)   This lake was first known as Fish Lake, so named by the Sibley Expedition which stopped there on its way to Camp Buell in 1862. It was renamed Buffalo Lake, and finally changed to Kandiotta, a Wahpeton Sioux word meaning "buffalo fish," which were abundant in the lake. The former village of Kandiotta was established nearby in 1883.

**METIGOSHE LAKE** (Bottineau) Metigoshe was derived from the Chippewa expression metigoshe washgum, meaning "clear water lake surrounded by oaks." The lake is located in the Turtle Mountains. During the 1930s, Lake Metigoshe State Park was built by the Works Programs Administration, which was established for the purpose of creating jobs for people who were out of work during the Depression.

**MINNEWAUKAN LAKE** (Benson) Minnewaukan is a Sioux expression meaning "heart of the enchanted water," or "spirit water." Settlers who were encroaching on Indian land in 1862 brought about conflict, and as a result General Sibley and his men were ordered to drive the Indians away from the lake area. The community of Minnewaukan was founded during the 1880s next to the lake, but the waters receded so much over the years, the town was eventually more than two miles away from it.

**PEMBINA RIVER/MOUNTAINS** (Pembina)   The river flows from the Pembina Mountains and joins the Red River. Pembina is a Chippewa word meaning "summer berry," derived from anepeminan. (There is also a Pembina River in Canada originating in Alberta that bears the Cree word derived from neepinmenan, also meaning "summer berry.") Pembina is the oldest settlement in North Dakota and was established at the confluence of the Pembina and Red Rivers. In 1797, Charles Chaboillez built the first trading post there. Once known as Hair Hills, the mountains were a favorite hunting place for the Chippewa Indians and white fur traders.

**SAKAKAWEA, LAKE** (Mercer, Dunn) Sakakawea is the largest man-made lake in the state. It is about 190 miles long, formed when Garrison Dam was built in 1956 by the Army Corps of Engineers. The little village of Scatter established in 1933 was inundated with the formation of the lake. First named Garrison Lake, it was changed to Sakakawea, a derivation of Sacajawea, famous Indian guide of the Lewis and Clark Expedition. Her name comes from the Shoshone expression saca, tzaw and mean, interpreted as something akin to "to pull a boat."

**TEWAUKON    LAKE**    (Sargent) Tewaukon Lake is located within the Tewaukon National Wildlife Refuge. The numerous lakes and marshlands made the region a favorite place for hunting. The lake may have been named for Te Wauk Kon, an ancient religious leader who had a temple built near the lake. Other authorities believe it is a Sioux word meaning "skunk," or "spirit." It was once called Pole Cat Lake and later Skunk Lake, probably due to rotting algae during the summers. This large body of water covers about 1,000 acres and is about 2 miles long.

**WAMDUSKA,    LAKE**    (Nelson) Wamduska is also known as Stump Lake. The town of Wamduska was established along the shore in 1882 when it was thought the Great Northern Railroad would be built around the lake, but the survey for the tracks was made more than 10 miles away. By 1916, it was a ghost town. Wamduska is a Sioux word translated as "when on the water, oh look."

# OHIO

**ASHTABULA RIVER** (Ashtabula) Thomas Hamilton was the first permanent resident along the river in 1801; the city of Ashtabula would be established about 1828. The name was interpreted from an Algonquin phrase meaning "beautiful river," "river of fish," and "many fish." Tradition says surveyor Moses Cleaveland wanted to change the name of the river to Mary Esther for his daughter. His party didn't go along with the proposal until he gave them liquor and they agreed to change the name. When the wine was gone, so was any thought to change the name and it remained Ashtabula. The river is about 40 miles long and empties into Lake Erie.

**CUYAHOGA RIVER** (Geauga)   Resident Indians used the river during their travels between Lake Erie and the Gulf of Mexico. The Cuyahoga is about 80 miles long and enters Lake Erie. It flows through the town of Cuyahoga Falls, which was established in 1812, and bears an Algonquian word meaning "crooked river."

**GREAT MIAMI RIVER** (Hamilton) This river rises at Indian Lake and flows about 160 miles into the Ohio River. About

1750 the British established their trading posts near the Miami village of Pickaw-illany. The French tried to bring the tribe back under its influence in 1752. An attack on the village in addition to smallpox wiped out many of the Indians. Those remaining left the area to get away from the conflicts. During the 1830s, the Miami and Erie Canal linked the river with Lake Erie, and the Great Miami became a main route of commerce. Miami was interpreted as a Chippewa word for "people who live on a point," and Choctaw for "it is so wide."

**HOCKING RIVER** (Fairfield)   George Washington was one of a number of men granted land near the stream for service to their country. While surveying his section, Washington wrote in his field notes that they came across a small river the Indians called Little Hockhocking, a Lenape word that means "bottle." The Hocking was narrow and straight, like the neck of a bottle that suddenly widened near the falls, which gave the appearance of a bottle. The river is about 100 miles long and joins the Ohio River near the town of Marietta.

**JELLOWAY CREEK, BIG** (Knox)   This creek was named for Tom Jelloway, a noted Indian chief, who may have been of the Mohican Tribe (origin unknown). He and his people had their camps along the creek. In 1832, an early settler built the first grist mill and saw mill along the Jelloway, and about 10 years later the town of Jelloway was established.

**KOKOSING RIVER** (Morrow)   This stream rises near Mount Gilead and flows about 50 miles into the Mohican River. The Kokosing was used by the Delaware, Shawnee and Huron Indians for hunting and fishing. During the 1800s settlement began along the river, and numerous sawmills and gristmills were established. In later years, the mills and factories were shut down after deforestation and soil erosion altered the hydrology of the river. Kokosing may be an Algonquian word meaning "owls at."

**MAHONING RIVER** (Mahoning)   The community of Youngstown was founded in 1797 along the banks of this river. During the 1800s coal was discovered and in 1826 the first coal mine began its operations. When iron ore was found near Lake Superior, the steel industry came into prominence, and Union Iron and Steel Company was established in 1892. Mahoning is derived from the Lenape word mahonink, meaning "there a lick," descriptive of the salt deposits on the river where wildlife would come to "lick" the salt.

**MISSISSINEWA RIVER** (Darke)   The Mississinewa flows into the state of Indiana, and then joins the Wabash River. It is about 100 miles long. Chief Tecumseh and his people traveled down the Mississinewa on their migration from Ohio about 1808. Lt. Colonel John Campbell and his army were under orders to drive out the Miami Indians (in Indiana) and destroy their villages that were along the river on December 17, 1812. The following day the Miami Indians retaliated and killed a number of Campbell's men. Mississinewa is a Miami word for "big rock river," although some believe it is a corruption of namahchiss-inwi, meaning "an ascent." On the banks of the river were situated 60-foot cliffs called the Seven Pillars of the Mississinewa. They were revered by the Miami Indians who believed they symbolized the Great Father.

**MUSKINGUM RIVER** (Coshocton) The river has its origins at the junction of the Walhonding and Tuscarawas rivers and flows about 112 miles to enter the Ohio River. While constructing dams on the river during the 1830s, workers found exposed pockets of coal; as a result, the community of Coal Run was established. Muskingum's definition is obscure, but it may be an Algonquian word meaning "elk's eye."

**OLENTANGY RIVER** (Crawford)   The Olentangy flows through the middle of Ohio State University. It originates near the community of Galion, is about 75 miles long and enters the Scioto River near the town of Columbus. In 1840, the former village of Olentangy was established near the river. The name may come from a Shawnee or Lenape expression meaning "red face paint," or "paint from there," in reference to red pigment located along the river which Indians applied to their faces.

**PYMATUNING CREEK** (Ashtabula)   Pymatuning is an Algonquian word derived from pimeu w'doon, which means "slanting mouth," "crooked mouth," or "the home of the man with a crooked nose," in reference to a person with a deformity. The creek flows to the state of Pennsylvania and joins the Shenango River.

**SANDUSKY RIVER** (Crawford)   Sandusky was derived from an Iroquois (Wyandot) expression, lacsandouske, for "lake of cold water," or from outsandouke, meaning "pure water here." It was also suggested the name was from sa-un-dustee," interpreted as "water within pools." The 120-mile-long river terminates in Sandusky Bay. In 1831, the Seneca Indians who occupied sites along the river signed a treaty in 1831 in exchange for land west of the Mississippi.

**SCIOTO RIVER** (Scioto)   The region was once the hunting ground of the Shawnee Indians. The river's origin was explored by surveyor Nathaniel Massie in 1793. Three years later he founded the town of Chillocothe. The Scioto flows 237

miles to join the Ohio River. It is a Shawnee word meaning "hairy," descriptive of the shedded hair from herds of deer that drank from the river. It was also interpreted as "deer."

**TAPPAN LAKE** (Harrison)   This lake was constructed by the Army Corps of Engineers in 1936 for flood control. There had been a town named Tappan, but it was either moved or torn down during dam construction. Tappan may be a transfer name from the state of New York, which is an Algonquian word interpreted as "cold stream," "it freezes," or "white frost."

**TONTOGANY CREEK** (Wood)   The town of Tontogany was founded in 1830 along this creek. It was named for Ottawa Chief Tondoganie, whose name means "the dog."

**TUSCARARAS RIVER** (Tuscarawas)   Serving as a boundary between the Indians during the 1650s, the river was also a boundary line between the United States and Indians by the Fort McIntosh Treaty of 1785. Tuscararas was the tribal name interpreted as "hemp gatherers." The river joins the Walhonding River. In 1817, German separatists founded a village after they purchased land along the river banks. It was abandoned when the Germans disbanded in 1898.

**WABASH RIVER** (Auglaize)   The Wabash originates at Grand Lake in Ohio and flows 529 miles to enter the Ohio River on the Illinois-Indiana border. It was once a major transportation artery for boats traveling from the state of Louisiana to Quebec, Canada. Many Indian tribes lived along the river, among them the Miami, Potawatomi, and Kickapoo. Fort Ouiatenon was built by the French in 1717, which was the site where Chief Pontiac signed a peace treaty with the British in

1765. Wabash is derived from the Miami expression wah-bah-shik-ki, interpreted as "white-shining," indicative of the white limestone river bed.

**WAKATOMIKA CREEK** (Muskingum) Early settlement along this creek began in the early 1800s and the town of Fallsbury was founded about 1815. There was once a trading post operating there in the late 1700s, as well as a mill and church. Wakatomika is a Shawnee word meaning "it is river bend land," and may have indicated the land itself, then the name was applied to the creek.

**WALHONDING RIVER** (Coshocton) First called White Woman's River, the Walhonding is 20 miles long and rises at the confluence of the Mohican and Kokosing rivers. In 1764, Colonel Henry Bouquet met with the Indians along the river and a treaty was signed. Walhonding may be a Lenape word meaning "ravine," or "ditch," and describes part of the river that flows through a ravine.

**WEGEE CREEK** (Belmont) Wegee is probably a corruption of an Algonquian word that means "crooked" or "winding," descriptive of the creek's course. David Burns became a member of the first grand jury to be impaneled in the state, and the first court met in 1795 at the mouth of Wegee Creek.

# OKLAHOMA

**CHILOCCO CREEK** (Kay) U.S. Inspector Major Haworth checked out the region to build an Indian Industrial School. He selected a piece of land along the creek because of its good farmland and natural spring. Colonel James Wade established a camp along the Chilocco in 1889 to instruct regiments on hypothetical military situations. After the training was completed, troops were sent to their assigned posts. Chilocco is derived from the Creek word cerakko, which means "horse," or "big deer."

**COWETA CREEK** (Muskogee) The Coweta Indians migrated to this region from Georgia. Coweta was the name of their head chief, whose name was interpreted as "falls" or "where there are falls." Nearby the Coweta Mission was established by Reverend Robert Loughridge, who preached to the Indians while his wife taught school. The mission operated until the buildings were burned down during the Civil War.

**OKMULGEE, LAKE** (Okmulgee) Okmulgee Lake comprises about 720 acres, and was the main water supply for the town of Okmulgee. The settlement was established by the Creek Indians who selected the site as its capital until the end of the 19th Century when Indian governments gave way to federal jurisdiction. The name comes from two Hitchiti words, oki and mulgi, for "water it is boiling."

**WICHITA MOUNTAINS** (Comanche) These mountains, which may be the oldest in the country, are located entirely within Comanche County and extend about 60 miles. Congress designated the mountains as a forest reserve in 1901 after the section of land near the mountain was opened for settlement. In 1905, they were made a game preserve, then in 1935 the Wichita Mountains Wildlife Refuge. The name comes from Wichita Indians, whose name was interpreted as "scattered lodges," "painted faces," or from wechate, meaning "red river people."

# OREGON

**ABIQUA CREEK** (Marion)   Rising in the Cascade Mountains, the Abiqua enters the Pudding River near the town of Silverton. During 1847, Mollala chief Crooked Finger visited the Klamath Indians in order to form an alliance to attack the whites. By 1851 the militia had forced the Indians to retreat. Abiqua may have designated a small tribe or camping place.

**ALSEA BAY/RIVER** (Benton/Lincoln) This river originates in the Coast Range and empties into Alsea Bay at the town of Waldport. The bay was surveyed in 1878 by order of Congress. Alsea Valley is located along the river and settled about 1852, supported by the timber industry. Logs were floated down the river to the bay, and from there shipped to San Francisco. Alsea may be derived from Alsi, the name of a Yakoan tribe of Indians who lived at the mouth of the river (origin unknown).

**CALAPOOYA RIVER/MOUNTAINS** (Douglas)   In 1832, the Hudson's Bay Company established a trading post along the river. The Calapooya Mountains are part of the Cascade Range. The name is derived from the Calapooya Indians (origin obscure) who were indigenous to the Willamette Valley when the first white settlers arrived. This waterway has its origins in the Calapooya Mountains and enters the Umpqua River. During the 1850s, Boston Mills (a water-powered flour mill) was established along the river.

**CALIMUS BUTTE** (Klamath)   Calimus Butte is situated near the Klamath Indian Reservation, and at one time contained one of the finest old-growth stands. An ancient conifer was also on the butte, said to have a 50-inch diameter breast height. It was destroyed in the Lone Pine Fire in August 1992. The Bureau of Indian Affairs built a fire lookout on the butte in 1920. Calimus may be a Klamath word meaning "flat butte."

**CATHLAMET BAY** (Clatsop)   The bay is located on the southern part of the Columbia River, and was home to the Cathlamet Indians. They moved across the river to Washington in 1852 after becoming panic-stricken when a series of epidemics occurred. Their name means "stone."

**CHASKI BAY** (Klamath)   Will G. Steel named the bay for one of the Klamath Indians' gods, Tchashkai, which means "weasel," which played an important part in Indian mythology. Chaski is located on the southern part of Crater Lake, between Phantom Ship and Eagle Point.

**CHEHULPUM CREEK** (Marion) Rising near the town of Jefferson, the Chehulpum flows into a branch of the Santiam River. It was first known as Doty Creek, until 1934 when residents petitioned to have it changed to Chehulpum, which was approved by Marion County Court and the Board of Oregon Geographic Names. Chehulpum is an Indian word (tribe unknown) meaning "beaver" or "land where beaver are plentiful."

**CHESNIMUS CREEK** (Wallowa) Early maps showed the spelling as Chesninimus. The creek joins Joseph Creek. The U.S. Board on Geographic Names changed the spelling to Chesnimus, an Algonquian expression meaning "thorn butte," descriptive of the thickets of thorns growing along its banks.

**CHETCO RIVER** (Curry) The Chetko Indians lived in this region and the river took their name (origin unknown). The stream originates in the Kalmiopsis Wilderness, which is part of the Siskiyou National Forest, and empties into the Pacific Ocean. Growing along this river is a rare species of the Myrtle tree.

**CHETLO LAKE** (Lane) Chetlo is a Chinook word interpreted as "oyster," descriptive of the lake's shape. It is located northwest of Waldo Lake.

**CLACKAMAS RIVER** (Marion) Bearing the name of the Clackamas Indians who once lived along its banks, the river is about 85 miles long. It rises at Olallie Lake and joins the Willamette River. In 1988, the river was designated Wild and Scenic. At one time a meteor fell near this river (the Willamette Meteor), which the Clackamas Indians called tomanowos ("vis-itor from the moon"). To them, the meteor represented union between the water, sky and earth, and they used the rainwater in the meteor's fissures to bless their arrows.

**COLLAWASH RIVER** (Clackamas/ Marion) A tributary of the Clackamas River, the Collawash was first known as Miners Fork because of gold mining in the region. It was changed to Collawash, an Algonquian expression for "a place where awl baskets were made."

**CULTUS CREEK** (Deschutes) Cultus Creek rises near Red Top Spring and joins Cavitt Creek near Shadow Falls. Its name is derived from the Chinook word kaltas, defined as "bad" or "wholly worthless," and may be descriptive of something lacking on the land, or bad-tasting water. It was given this descriptive name by a surveyor who had problems navigating the region.

**CUPIT MARY MOUNTAIN** (Lane) Cupit Mary was a daughter of Old Moses and the mountain bears her name, a Chinook word meaning "last," possibly because she was the chief's youngest daughter. The mountain is located near Waldo Lake and rises about 6,175 feet.

**ECOLA POINT** (Clatsop) The point took its name from the Ecola Creek. In 1806, Captain William Clark of the Lewis and Clark Expedition, was the first white man of record to visit the region. While camped here, the Indians reported to him that a whale had beached nearby. Clark went to investigate and found the Tillamook Indians cutting up the whale for its blubber. He purchased some of the oil and blubber for his men who were spending the winter at Fort Clatsop. Clark later named the creek Ecola, derived from ehkoli, a Chinook word for "whale." The stream's name was later changed to Elk Creek.

**EUCHRE CREEK** (Curry)   Euchre may come from the Tututni band of Yukichetunne Indians, whose name was interpreted as "people at the mouth of the river." Others believe it was a card game miners played in the 1850s. The Euchre is about 14 miles long and terminates at the Pacific Ocean.

**EWAUNA LAKE** (Klamath)   Part of the town of Klamath Falls is located along the banks of this lake, which has always been used as a log pond. In 1866, George Nurse (who named the Link River, later changed to Klamath) built his cabin at the confluence of the Klamath and the lake. Ewauna is a Klamath word translated as "elbow." The lake is a seasonal home to the white pelicans.

**HALO CREEK** (Lane)   In 1846, Lindsay Applegate claimed land at Yoncalla and built a grist mill along the creek. Halo was a chief of the Yoncalla Indians, and his name was Chinook for "none," indicating there was very little water in the creek. The Halo flows into Salmon Creek.

**HEHE BUTTE** (Wasco)   Located on the Warm Springs Indian Reservation, Hehe is a Chinook word for "laughter," because the butte was the place of good spirits. The Warm Springs Indians picked huckleberries and held their annual huckleberry feast on the butte.

**HIYU MOUNTAIN** (Clackamas/Hood River)   Hiyu is a Chinook word meaning "much" or "plenty," descriptive of the size of the mountain. It is located near Bull Run Lake.

**HOOSKANDEN CREEK** (Curry) This creek terminates at the Pacific Ocean

near the town of Carpenterville. Hooskanden is a corruption of the Wishtonatan Indians who lived along the creek's banks (origin unknown). Because settlers were unable to pronounce their name correctly, they spelled it Hooskanden.

**KLAMATH RIVER** (Klamath)   The river originates in the Upper Klamath and travels 250 miles into California, where it empties into the Pacific Ocean near the hamlet of Requa. Legend says a great spirit called Wahpecoomayow prepared to shape the world and told his lesser spirits they had a choice of what they wanted to be. One of them wanted to be a rock on the river. Wahpecoomayow granted his wish and said the rock should tell the fish when to leave the ocean and swim up the river each year. Today, the spirit guides the candlefish (smelt), so called because they are so oily they can be burnt as candles. Since 2001, the river has been a source of contention between farmers and the Klamath Indians. Because of the Endangered Species Act, the U.S. Government shut off water to farmers when thousands of Coho salmon were found dead. The Klamath Indians fought for more water to save the fish, and the farmers temporarily lost their irrigation water. First named Link River, Klamath may be derived from a Sahaptin (Nez Perce or Cayuse) word, kalamat, interpreted as "yellow water lily," a major food source for the Indians. Another interpretation was from the Klamath word maklaks, meaning "encamped."

**KOOSAH MOUNTAIN** (Deschutes) Koosah is a Chinook word for "sky," an appropriate description because the mountain is at the summit of the Cascade Range.

**METOLIUS RIVER** (Deschutes, Jefferson)   The Metolius originates in the Cascade Range and flows about 50 miles into the Deschutes River. It was considered the fastest river in the west. One of the largest spring-fed rivers in the country, the name was first mentioned in the Pacific Railroad surveys as Mpto-ly-as. Metolius is a Warm Springs Indian expression meaning "spawning salmon."

**MINAM RIVER** (Union/Wallowa)   This river is located entirely within the Eagle Cap Wilderness, and bears an Algonquian word derived from eminemah, meaning "valley" or "canyon." The lake is a boundary between the two counties. A bridge built across the river was the only decent wagon road leading into Wallowa County until railroads were built.

**MODOC POINT** (Klamath)   Situated on the shore of Upper Klamath Lake, this was the site where Captain Jack and his band of Modocs settled about 1869. The Klamath Indians continually harassed the Modocs in order to force them to move, who finally went to Lost River, but this conflict precipitated the Modoc War in 1872-73. Their name is derived form the Klamath words moa and takni, describing "Indians just to the south."

**MOLALLA RIVER** (Clackamas)   Molalla is derived from mo and alli, for "deer berries." It was the name of a tribe of Indians who inhabited much of the territory. In 1851 treaties were signed with the Molalla Indians and they were removed from this region. Unhappy living on a reservation, the Indians returned here only to find white settlers had taken up much of their land.

**MOOLACK   CREEK/MOUNTAIN** (Lincoln)   The creek flows near Agate Beach. The mountain was first named Elk Mountain, because of the abundance of the animal. The name was changed to Moolack, a Chinook word meaning "elk."

**MOOSMOOS   CREEK**   (Clatsop) Moosmoos is a Chinook word meaning "cattle." The creek joins Youngs River near Youngs River Falls.

**MOWICH CREEK** (Douglas)   This creek rises in Elephant Mountain and flows to the Clearwater River. Located in the Umpqua National Forest, the stream bears a Chinook word meaning "deer."

**MUDJEKEEWIS MOUNTAIN** (Klamath)   Mudjekeewis was an one of the Klamath Indians' deities, and is an expression meaning "spirit of the four winds," and probably designated the extremely windy weather on the mountain. Mudjekeewis Mountain is located in the Cascade Range near Crater National Park and rises about 6,615 feet.

**NEACOXIE CREEK** (Clatsop)   Lewis and Clark stopped here during their explorations in 1804-05. At one time the creek emptied into the Pacific Ocean, but shifting sands and rechanneling changed it course. Neacoxie may be derived from neercawenaca, a Clatsop word for "a place with small pine trees."

**NEAHKAHNIE MOUNTAIN** (Tillamook)   The Clatsop and Tillamook Indians were early residents in this region. Legend says the mountain is an Indian deity named Neakarny who turned to stone. Tradition also says that the Indians saw a winged canoe that sailed near the mountain, carrying men and their treasure which they buried near the mountain. In 1890, what were called treasure rocks were found with strange markings on them. Ever since then, people have been searching for the treasure. Beeswax in the form of 20-pound blocks was found on Nehalem Beach near the mountain, and may have come from a wrecked Spanish ship in 1769. Neahkahnie was derived from the

Clatsop word acarna, meaning "chief deity" (or "god"). It was also thought to designate a precipice.

**NECANICUM RIVER** (Clatsop) Necanicum, meaning "gap," is descriptive of a gap in the mountains, or it may been derived from Ne-hay-ne-hum, for an Indian lodge. This river, which provides water for the city of Seaside, terminates at the Pacific Ocean. The region was once home to the Clatsop Indians who had a village called Necotat near the mouth of the Necanicum. The river is one of coast's most productive salmon streams.

**NESKOWIN CREEK** (Tillamook) First known as Slab Creek, the community of Neskowin was settled near the creek in the 1880s. Mrs. Page was postmaster and one day saw an Indian pointing to the creek one day, saying, "Neskowin, Neskowin," Mrs. Page asked him what it meant. He said, "plenty fish, plenty fish."

**NESTUCCA RIVER** (Tillamook/ Yamhill) This river rises in the Coast Range Mountains and empties at the Pacific Ocean near Pacific City. The region was home to the Nestucca band of Tillamook Indians (origin unknown). In 1855, some of the land near the river was set aside as an Indian reservation until 1876 when the region opened for homesteading. During the mid-1800s, the first sawmill was built along the river. In 1845, a tremendous fire occurred, consuming everything in its path, forcing settlers and the Nestucca Indians to flee their homes.

**OCHOCO CREEK** (Wheeler/Crook) The first settler along this creek was Elish Barnes in 1866 who built his cabin near the stream. Ochoco may have been named for a Paiute Indian chief, whose name was interpreted as "willows."

**OLALLIE BUTTE** (Jefferson/Marion) Olallie Butte is located at the summit of the Cascade Range Mount Hood and Mount Jefferson. It bears a Chinook word that means "berries." Olallie Butte rises about 7,210 feet.

**PITSUA BUTTE** (Deschutes) Pitsua Butte is located near the town of Bend, and bears a Klamath word that describes something important. It was also thought to come from the Paiute word, wapata pistua, a name for the Columbia 5-toed kangaroo rat that is resident in the region.

**POLALLIE CREEK** (Hood River) Polallie is a Chinook word meaning "powdery" or "sandy." Before it was named Polallie, the creek bore a descriptive name, Sand Creek. The U.S. Forest Service changed the name to Polallie in the 1920s. This creek has its origins near Cooper Spur and is a tributary of the East Fork Hood River.

**QUOSATANA CREEK** (Curry) Indians who lived in this region were called Cosuttheutun ("people who eat mussels"). The creek is located about 15 miles from the Rogue River, and was derived from quosaten, meaning "beautiful stream."

**SANTIAM RIVER** (Linn) After the Upper Santiam Indians left the region, the river became known for its timber industry. The stream flows into the Willamette River and is about 10 miles long. In 1845 Milton Hale claimed land along the river, which later became the former town of Syracuse. Andrew Wiley and a party of men traveled along the river in 1859 while looking for a practicable route into Central Oregon. Santiam's name origin is unknown.

**SEEKSEEQUA CREEK** (Jefferson) This tributary of the Deschutes River drains the south part of the Warm Springs

Indian Reservation. The Oregon Board of Geographic Names adopted the word Seek-seekwa, but it was later change to Seeksee-qua, a Paiute word describing a type of rye grass that grew along the creek's banks.

**SILETZ RIVER** (Lincoln/Polk)    Siletz may be derived from a Rogue River word, silis, for "black bear." The native interpretation is "crooked rope (or water)," because the river is one of the snakiest rivers in the state. When an Indian agent asked the Indians their name, they said "Se-La-Gees." He could not pronounce the word, so called them Siletz. The river originates in the Coast Range Mountains and empties into Siletz Bay near the town of Lincoln.

**SISI BUTTE** (Clackamas)    This butte is located in the Cascade Range and rises about 5,614 feet. Sisi is derived from a Chinook word meaning "blanket" or "cloth." The butte is home to a fire lookout station.

**SITKUM CREEK** (Lane)    Sitkum is a Chinook word meaning "half." It refers to the fact that the stream carries little water. The Sitkum joins Salmon Creek near the town of Oakridge.

**SIUSLAW RIVER** (Lane)    Originating near the city of Eugene, the Siuslaw is about 110 miles long and empties into the Pacific Ocean at the town of Florence. Swisshome was another hamlet which was established along the river as an agricultural community. The Siuslaw Indians, who were part of the Yakonan tribe, had their villages near the river close to the Oregon Coast. Siuslaw has been defined as "far away river," and "gleaming river,"

**SKIPANON RIVER** (Clatsop)    This river is about 6 miles long and rises near Cullaby Lake, then joins the Columbia River. When Lewis and Clark stopped there, they called the river Skipanarwin,

which may be a corruption of the Clatsop word meaning "a point."

**SKOOKUM CREEK/LAKE** (Clackamas)    Comprising about 10 acres, the lake is located on the slope of Thunder Mountain. The creek flows through the Umpqua-Rogue River Wilderness. Skookum is taken from a Chinook word meaning "strong" "powerful," or "spooky." It probably described a place inhabited by an evil spirit.

**TALAPUS, MOUNT** (Multnomah)    Situated between headwaters of Tanner Creek and Bull Run River, this peak was once called Shellrock Mountain. It was changed by the U.S. Board of Geographic Names to Mount Talapus, an Algonquian word meaning "coyote," or "barking wolf."

**TENASILLAHE ISLAND** (Clatsop)    Tenasillahe is derived from the Chinook words, tenas and illahe, meaning "small land." Settlers farmed on the island for some time until it became part of the Lewis and Clark Wildlife Refuge.

**TILLICUM CREEK** (Lane)    Tillicum is a Chinook word meaning "friend." The creek joins Salmon Creek near the community of Orange.

**TIMPANOGOS LAKE** (Douglas)    Located in the Cascade Range, the lake was named by J.G. Staack, an engineer with the U.S. Geographic Survey. Timpanogos is a Ute word defined as "rock river," and is a transfer name from Utah.

**TIPSOO PEAK/CREEK** (Douglas, Klamath)    Situated in the summit of the Cascade Range, Tipsoo Peak is a Chinook word meaning "grass," or "hair." The creek rises just east of the peak and terminates at Miller Lake. Tipsoo is a basaltic cinder cone that erupted within the last 100,000 years. A cinder cone is a volcanic cone built mostly of loose volcanic fragments.

**TOKETEE LAKE** (Douglas)   This lake was formed when the North Umpqua River was dammed above Toketee Falls for hydroelectric power. Toketee is a Chinook word interpreted as "pretty" or "graceful."

**TOT MOUNTAIN** (Deschutes)   Tot is actually a butte located on the south slope of Bachelor Butte. It bears a Chinook word meaning "uncle."

**TUALATIN RIVER** (Clackamas/Washington)   During the 1800s, the river was a main highway for the transportation of logs and supplies. The Tualatin originates at Haines Falls and travels about 80 miles into Gales Creek. The name was derived from a Tualatin word meaning "lazy" or "sluggish," descriptive of the water flow. It was also interpreted as "land without trees," and "forks," in reference to the river's tributaries.

**TUMALO CREEK** (Deschutes)   The Klamath Indians visited the creek to cut the willows that grew along the river's banks for basket-making, and the trees' wood for smoking their meat. Tumalo may be a Klamath word meaning "wild plum," or "ground fog," or derived from tumallowa, which means "icy water."

**TUTUILLA CREEK** (Umatilla)   The interpretation for Tutuilla is controversial. Some believe it was named for a little girl whose nickname was Tootie, and she called the creek Tutailla. Indians who lived on the Umatilla Indian Reservation disagreed, positive that it meant "a thorn bush," indicative of the plant that grows along the creek's banks.

**TYEE MOUNTAIN** (Douglas)   Tyee may be a Chinook word meaning "chief,"

or "high chief," in reference to its prominence. The mountain is near the town of Sutherland.

**UMATILLA RIVER** (Umatilla)   The Umatilla has its origins in the Blue Mountains and flows about 85 miles into the Columbia River. In 1851, the Umatilla Agency was established along the banks of the river, but burned down a few years later at the onset of the Yakima War. The Indians signed a treaty in 1854 ceding their land, part of which included the Umatilla watershed. Umatilla Landing was founded about 1863 and became an important trade and shipping center during the gold rush. Its name was thought to mean "water rippling over sand."

**UMPQUA RIVER** (Douglas)   The river was once home to the Confederated tribes of the Lower Umpqua, Siuslaw and Coos Indians until 1856 when they were removed temporarily to Fort Umpqua. In 1832, the Hudson's Bay Company established a trading post along the river. The Umpqua rises near the city of Roseburg and flows about 111 miles to the Pacific Ocean at the town of Reedsport. Part of the river is located in the Wallowa-Whitman National Forest. Its name origin is unknown.

**WAHTUM LAKE** (Hood River)   Wahtum is a Sahaptin expression which means "pond" or "body of water." It was named in 1901 by H.D. Langille with the U.S. Geographic Survey.

**WALLA WALLA RIVER** (Wallowa/Umatilla)   Located on the boundaries of the two counties, the river is about 60 miles long. It originates in the Blue Mountains and enters the Columbia River. In 1818, Fort Walla Walla was established at the mouth of this river in the state of Washington, which operated until 1855.

Walla Walla was derived from the Nez Perce word walastu, meaning either "running water," or "small, rapid streams."

**WALLOWA RIVER/MOUNTAINS** (Wallowa, Union)   Wallowa is a Nez Perce expression designating a willow fish trap. The river rises at its east and west forks and empties into the Grande Ronde River. During 1877, the U.S. Government tried to take Nez Perce land in the Wallowa valley, which enraged Chief Joseph. He refused to be removed to Idaho on a reservation, and the Army was sent in to force him to leave. The mountains extend from the Deschutes Valley through the Blue Mountains and up into Washington. A large part of the Wallowas are within the boundaries of the Eagle Cap Wilderness.

**WALLULA LAKE** (Umatilla)   This lake was created when part of the Columbia River was impounded at McNary Dam near the town of Umatilla. The community of Wallula is located near the river. It is a Nez Perce word meaning "abundance of water," descriptive of the town's proximity to the confluence of the Columbia and Walla Walla Rivers.

**WANOGA BUTTE** (Deschutes)   The butte rises about 5,740 feet, and is located near Bachelor Butte. Wanoga is derived from the a Klamath word meaning "son" or "male child." The butte was named by the U.S. Forest Service.

**WAPATO LAKE** (Washington/Yamhill)   Wapato is derived from the Chinook word, wapatoo, meaning "potato, or "big potato," designating the Camas root the Indians dug up for their food. Wapato is an intermittent (or irregular) lake.

**WAWA CREEK** (Clatsop)   This creek is a tributary to Youngs River near Youngs River Falls. It bears a Chinook word mean-ing "talk," descriptive of the noise the water makes as it flows over part of its gravel bed.

**WILLAMETTE RIVER** (Multnomah)   Originating in the Cascade Range, the Willamette flows 240 miles to the Columbia River. It is the largest river situated entirely within the state of Oregon. The river was discovered by Broughton in 1792, who named it River Mannings. The Willamette River Valley was settled in the 1830s and became a major fruit-growing and dairy region, making it the chief source of food for the west coast. In 1938, dams and reservoirs were built to control the river's tributaries for flood control. Willamette may be derived from wallamet, interpreted as "spilled water," descriptive of the falls. Although all resources showed Willamette as an Indian word, none determined the origin of the tribe.

**WINCHUCK RIVER** (Curry)   The Chetco Indians were once resident along the Winchuck, which is a Chinook word meaning "windy water," or "woman." It flows into the Pacific Ocean near the Oregon and California border.

**WINOPEE LAKE** (Deschutes)   Situated near the summit of the Cascade Range, this lake bears a Chinook expression for "by and by," or "wait," indicative of some person who was in no hurry to leave the region.

**YAMSAY MOUNTAIN** (Klamath, Lake)   Rising more than 8,000 feet, the mountain bears a Klamath word derived from Yamash, meaning "the north wind." Indian legend says the mountain was home to the North Wind and the Klamath Indians' supreme being called Kmukamteh. At one time the Yahooskin band of Indians lived near the mountain.

# PENNSYLVANIA

**ALLEGHANY MOUNTAINS** Some of the highest peaks in the Alleghany Mountains are situated in Pennsylvania. They extend from Quebec, Canada and stretch all the way to Alabama. Of all the mountains in the East, the Alleghanys were the most difficult to traverse for settlers and those who built roads and railroads. Alleghany is an Algonquian word, but its name origin is in dispute. The most popular is a corruption of welhikhanna, interpreted as "the best," or "the fairest river." It may be derived from alligewi-hanna, meaning "stream of the Alligewi." Alleghany may be from the Lenape expression talligewi, meaning "people of the cave country."

**APOLACON CREEK** (Susquehanna) This creek flows into the state of New York. At one time there was a stagecoach station along the mouth of the Apolacon in New York, which tied the region to the towns of Binghamton and Montrose. Apolacon is an Algonquian word meaning "messenger," or "to send someone."

**AQUASHICOLA CREEK** (Carbon) Lenape Chief Teedyuscung and his people moved here in 1737 after the Walking Purchase was signed on August 26. Aquashicola is a Lenape word meaning "bush net."

**AUGHWICK CREEK** (Fulton) During the 1840s, an Indian trader named George Croghan was given a 1,000-acre land grant and established a trading post along the creek, which would later become the hamlet of Burnt Cabins. The village received its name because the settlers who took up the land had not purchased it from the Indians, and were told to move by the

colonial government. Ignoring the order, their cabins were burned down by the militia in May of 1750. The Aughwick Indians' name was interpreted as "overgrown with brush."

**CANADOHTA LAKE** (Crawford) This natural feature was called Washington Lake in 1798, then changed to Oil Creek Lake in 1860. It was renamed Canadohta in 1894 for Chief Canadaughta of the Cornplanter Tribe (origin unknown). The Union and Titusville Railroad was built along the lake about 1865, which became a popular resort with the building of summer rentals. Today the lake is home to more than 800 cottages, and is the largest natural lake in the state.

**CATASAUQUA CREEK** (Lehigh) The village of Catasauqua is located along this creek, which flows into the Lehigh River. Early settlement began about the 1750s with the arrival of the Irish, who built their mills along the creek. First called Mill Creek and then Caladaqua Creek, the name was changed to Catasauqua, a Lenape word derived from gattoshacki, defined as "thirsty earth," or "burnt ground." The last is in reference to the Indians' practice of burning undergrowth to better track their game.

**CATAWISSA CREEK** (Columbia) Catawissa is Lenape for "pure water." The name may also come from gatawisi, which means "growing fat." The Indians who lived in the area abandoned it when the French and Indian War began. The creek enters the Susquehanna River near Bloomsburg.

**CHICKIES CREEK** (Lancaster) Early settlers were Scotch-Irish immigrants in 1715 who were attracted to the fertile land and dense timber lands. Chickies is a Lenape expression derived from chikiswalungo, translated as "place of crabs," or "place of crayfish."

**CHILLISQUAQUE CREEK** (Northumberland) Chillisquaque is taken from the Shawnee word chillilisuagi, interpreted as "song of the wild goose," or "place of the snow birds." The Shawnee Indians had their villages near this creek until white settlement. Later, a blockhouse (fort) was built along the Chillisquaque for the settlers' protection against Indian raids.

**COCOOSING CREEK** (Berks) The Cocoosing bears a Lenape name derived from gokhosing, meaning "place of owls." German immigrants settled along the creek during the early 1700s, establishing paper factories and mills.

**CODORUS CREEK** (York) After a treaty of 1736, the region about Codorus Creek was settled by colonists from Ireland and Germany. William Bennet built the Codorus Forge and Furnace in 1765 to manufacture iron. It also made cannons and cannonballs during the Revolutionary War, which were provided to the Continental Army. Codorus is an Algonquian word for "rapid water."

**CONEMAUGH RIVER** (Cambria) Conemaugh is from the Algonquian word conunmoch, defined as "otter." The river originates in the Allegheny Mountains and flows 70 miles to join the Allegheny River.

**CONESTOGA CREEK** (Lancaster) Conestoga may be a Lenape expression for "crooked stream." It was also interpreted from kanastoge, meaning "at the place of the immersed people," and andastoegue, for "people of the cabin pole." The creek has its origins near Welsh Mountain and flows 35 miles to enter the Susquehanna River. The village of Conestoga was established at the river in the late 1700s, and became known for its manufacture of large, broad-wheeled covered wagons bearing the name Conestoga.

**CONEWAGO CREEK** (Warren) Once home to the Iroquois Indians, the land was sold to the William Penn family about 1684. The township of Conewago was named for the creek, which may be a Lenape or Iroquois word derived from conewaugha (or ganowungo), meaning "at the place of rapids."

**CONOCOCHEAGUE CREEK** (Franklin/Adams) The Conococheague flows 80 miles into Maryland and joins the Potomac River. During the 1830s, a forge and furnace were built after the establishment of an ore works in the region. The forge was burned by Confederate forces in 1863 just prior to their engagement at Gettysburg. Conococheague was derived from the Lenape word gunenkitschik meaning "it is a long way," or "dull sound," indicative of small boulders that would strike each other in the water.

**CONODOGWINET CREEK** (Franklin) The creek may bear a Shawnee name derived from gunnipduckhannet, meaning "for a long way nothing but bends." The Conodogwinet flows into the Susquehanna River. Scotch-Irish were early settlers to the region, followed later by Germans who established the community of Carlisle.

**CONOLLOWAY CREEK** (Fulton) Conolloway (also spelled Conolaways) may be an Iroquois word for "running through hemlocks." In 1755, the Lenape and Shawnee Indians conducted raids near the stream, with the result that almost 50 settlers were killed or captured.

## CONOQUENESSING CREEK (Butler)

This creek joins the Beaver River. Conoquenessing was derived from the Lenape word gunachquenesink, interpreted as "for a long way straight." Others believe it was for an Indian named Conoquieson. During 1804, Harmony Society members built the first communal town along the creek. They were followed by Quakers in 1812 who purchased land and made several attempts to build a dam on the creek to harness the water power for their gristmills. The creek eventually washed out the dam and the Quakers left the region.

## CONOY CREEK (Lancaster)

During the early 1700s the Conoy (Piscataway) Indians were forced to leave their home in Maryland because of attacks by the Susquehannock Indians. After signing a treaty with William Penn, they migrated to the Conoy and established their villages. In 1730, Thomas Harris purchased land in the region and opened a trading post. Conoy was interpreted as "cornshellers."

## CUSSEWAGO CREEK (Crawford)

The township of Cussewago was established in 1800 and took its name from the creek, a Seneca word meaning "big belly," derived from kasseqaugo. Local legend says the Indians named the stream after they found a black snake that looked like it had swallowed a large animal.

## HOKENDAUQUA CREEK (Northampton)

The town of Hokendauqua was founded about 1854 with the arrival of the Thomas Iron Company. Located near Hokendauqua Creek, the site was named Hockyondocquay in the 1700s. The spelling was changed to Hockendauqua, a Lenape expression (from hachiundochure or hackiundochwe), meaning "searching for land," and may have signified negotiations the colonists made for the site.

## JUNIATA RIVER (Dauphin)

The Juniata River is about 90 miles long and joins the Susquehanna River. It was thought to be an Iroquois expression, interpreted as "a stone," or "standing stone," Other authorities defined it as "projecting rock."

## KINZUA CREEK (McKean)

Early settlers lived along this creek where the town of Morrison was later established. In 1882, the Kinzua Viaduct was built across the creek, one of the highest and longest in the world. Kinzua is a Lenape word meaning "they gobble," indicative of the abundance of wild turkeys in the region.

## KISHACOQUILLAS CREEK (Mifflin)

This tributary to the Juniata River joins the Susquehanna River. The Susquehannock Indians were resident during the colonial period, and conducted business with the fur traders. The Shawnee Indians later occupied the land until the 1750s, followed by the Amish people in the 1790s, who engaged in farming. The creek was named for Shawnee Chief Kishacoquilla, which means "the snakes are already in their dens." He was a friendly chief who tried to keep the Shawnee tribe neutral just before the French and Indian War.

## KISKIMINETAS RIVER (Armstrong, Indiana, Westmoreland)

The river originates at the confluence of Conemaugh River and Loyalhanna Creek and flows about 25 miles to the Allegheny River. The community of Apollo was founded after coal was discovered in the region. Salt was also found and more than 20 salt works were in operation, making it the third largest producer of salt in the United States. Kiskiminetas was derived from a

Lenape word meaning "day spirit," or a corruption of gieschgumanito, interpreted as "make daylight." It was also thought to mean "plenty of walnuts."

**LACKAWANNA RIVER** (Susquehanna) Settlers who moved here from Connecticut and tried to claim the land caused conflict with the Indians, which eventually resulted in the Massacre of Wyoming in 1778. The town of Union Dale was established in the 1800s, and its growth was stimulated with the founding of numerous water-powered industries. Lackawanna is derived from the Lenape word lechauhanne, for "the forks of a stream," indicative of the junction of the Lackawanna and north branch of the Susquehanna River.

**LEHIGH RIVER** (Lackawanna/Wayne) Moravian pioneers took up the land along the river about 1754. Colonel Weiss and surveyor William Henry later platted the town of Lehighton. One of the early towns in the mountain region after the discovery of coal was Mauch Chunk (Lenape for "bear mountain") about 1815. Another industry to emerge was steel-manufacturing. The Lehigh flows about 103 miles to join the Delaware River. It was called lechauweking by the Lenape Indians, meaning "where there are forks." German immigrants shortened it to Lecha, and the English changed it to Lehigh.

**LOYALHANNA CREEK** (Westmoreland) The village of Saltsburg was established in 1813 after settlers found vast amounts of salt at the confluence of Loyalhanna Creek and the Conemaugh River. The town later became one of the largest producers of salt in the country. Loyalhanna may be a Lenape word lawlhanna, meaning "middle stream." The river flows about 50 miles to join the Conemaugh River.

**LOYALSOCK CREEK** (Wyoming) This creek flows about 60 miles to the Susquehanna River near the town of Montoursville, which was founded in 1768 when Andrew Montour received a land grant. Home to the Susquehannock Indians, this region was later occupied by the Lenape and Shawnee Indians. Loyalsock may a Lenape expression, derived from lawisaquick, interpreted as "middle creek" because it flows between Muncy Creek and Lycoming Creek.

**LYCOMING CREEK** (Tioga) This creek bears a Lenape expression meaning "sandy stream," derived from legauihanne. In 1778 Indians who were allies with the British massacred the white settlers who lived there. The village of Ralston was established during the 1850s, and its main industry was a charcoal and anthracite furnaces.

**MANADA CREEK** (Dauphin) After settlers moved to the region, forcing the Indians from their homes, the Indians formed an alliance with the French. Traveling between Blue Mountain and the Manada Gap they raided the settlers' farms, which resulted in the building of forts for protection. During the Civil War, Confederate prisoners of war were used to build the Manada Furnace. Manada was derived from the Lenape word menatey, meaning "an island."

**MANATAWNY CREEK** (Berks) Manatawny may be a corruption of the Lenape expression menhaltanink, defined as "drinking place at," or "here we drink." The last of the Indian villages disappeared sometime after 1845. An iron forge was built along the creek in 1717 after iron ore and charcoal were discovered.

**MEHOOPANY CREEK** (Wyoming) During the early 1800s, the Mehoopany

Baptist Church was established near the mouth of this creek at what would become the community of Forkston. During the 1890s, the timber companies were established and used the creek as a splash dam. Mehoopany was thought to be derived from the Lenape word hobbenisink, meaning "place of wild potatoes."

**MONOCKONOCK ISLAND** (Luzerne) When the Wyoming Massacre occurred in July of 1778, many of the residents fled to the island for refuge. Monockonock is situated in the waters of the Susquehanna River. It is a corruption of the Lenape expression menachhenonk, which means "at the island" or "island place."

**MOOSIC MOUNTAIN** (Wayne/Lackawanna)   Moosic is a corruption of the Algonquian words moos and ink, meaning "elk place." During building of the Delaware and Hudson Canal in the 1820s, major problems occurred transporting the equipment over the mountain. As a result, a special system of wenches and cables were devised to haul the coal wagons on gravity railroads.

**MOSHANNON CREEK** (Clearfield, Centre)   The Moshannon was one of the migration paths for the Lenape Indians in 1724 as they made their way to the state of Ohio. Moshannon Mills was founded about 1849, and lived its early life as a factory town using the water power of the creek for its many mills. It bears the Algonquian word mooshanne, meaning "elk stream."

**NIPPENOSE CREEK** (Lycoming)   Lt. Col. Henry Antes claimed land along the creek before the Revolutionary War where he built a mill. After the Indians burned it down, Antes constructed a fort for protection. Nippenose may from the Lenape word nipeno-wi, meaning "like the summer." Other theories were for an Indian

named Nippenucy who lived there, or "summer hunt," referring to a place where special hunts were held.

**NITTANY MOUNTAIN** (Centre) Separating the Penns and Nittany Valleys, the mountain overlooks Penn State University. Settlers named the mountain in the early 1700s, which is derived from the Algonquian word nekti and attin, meaning "single mountain." Mountain lions roamed the region until the late 1800s, and when Penn State selected the mountain lion as its symbol, Nittany as added, thus the Nittany Lions.

**OCTORARO CREEK** (Chester)   This creek was created when a reservoir was constructed near the town of Oxford. The Octoraro enters the Susquehanna River near Conowingo Dam. It bears an Iroquois expression interpreted as "where the water is shallow and swift." Because of the threat of Indians, the region was not settled until the early 1700s. Octoraro Canal was built in the late 1700s, originating in Pennsylvania and ending near Fort Deposit in Maryland.

**OHIO RIVER** (Potter)   Ohio is a Seneca expression for "beautiful river." The Ohio is 981 miles long and is formed by the confluence of the Allegheny and Monongahela rivers at Pittsburgh. Although LaSalle may have seen the river in 1669, there was not much interest in it until the 1750s when the British and French were trying to take control of the stream. The river was the main means of transportation until railroads were established in the 1800s.

**PAXTON CREEK** (Dauphin)   This creek was the site of many trading posts. John Harris was an early settler in 1733, and also the father of the founder of Harrisburg. Numerous mills were later established along the creek. The region became more industrialized after the Pennsylvania Canal was built in 1826. Paxton (also Paxtang) was derived from a Lenape word meaning "pool at," It was also thought to mean "where the waters stand," from peekstank.

**PERKIOMEN CREEK** (Berks)   Chief of the Lenape Indians, Maughhongsink, sold his land along the Perkiomen about 1684. The creek travels about 35 miles to join the Schuylkill River. The region was later settled by Welsh and German immigrants. Famous naturalist John Audubon lived along the banks of this creek. Perkiomen is a corruption of the Lenape word pakihmomink (or pahkehoma) meaning "where there are cranberries," or "water where cranberries grow."

**POCONO MOUNTAINS** (Monroe) The Delaware, Iroquois, Shawnee, Minisink, and Paupack Indians were early residents. During 1659, the region became home to the Dutch until 1664 when the British forced them to leave. English and Germans took over the land in the early 1700s. The Pocono Mountains later became a resort area. Pocono may come from the Lenape expression pocohanne, meaning "a stream between mountains," or pochkapochka, interpreted as "two mountains near each other with a stream between."

**POCOPSON CREEK** (Chester)   Settlement along this creek began with Francis Smith who purchased land at the mouth of the Pocopson. Nearby is a stone marker, taken from the bed of the creek, to honor Hannah Freeman (1730-1802), one of the last Lenape Indians in this county. Pocopson is a Lenape word meaning "roaring creek."

**POQUESSING CREEK** (Bucks)   This creek joins the Delaware River. At one time it was proposed that Penn's Philadelphia be established at the mouth of the Poquessing, and for some time the region was called Old Philadelphia. Poquessing is a Lenape word poquesink, interpreted as "place of many mice."

**QUAKAKE CREEK** (Carbon)   Quakake is derived from euwenkeek, a Lenape word meaning "pine lands," or "pine woods." First settled by George Klees and Daniel Heil in 1790 who built the first sawmill, the timber industry that was established later gave way to coal mining. The Beaver Meadows Company built a railroad track from the town of Hazleton along the creek to Parryville, and the first car of coal was loaded in 1836.

**SAUCON   CREEK**   (Northampton) This creek originates at the town of Milford and joins the Lehigh River. It was once the site of Lenape Indian villages until white settlement in 1742. Saucon Township was created along the stream a year later. Saucon is a Lenape word, taken from sakunk, meaning "the mouth of a stream."

**SHOHOLA CREEK** (Pike)   Shohola is Lenape word that means "place of peace," or "distressed." Settlement along this creek began with the arrival of Tom Quick who built a cabin in 1741.

**TOHICKON   CREEK** (Bucks)   Tohickon Creek rises at Nockamixon Dam and flows about 8 miles to the Delaware River. During the 1700s, a Lenape chief named Tedyuskung caused problems when he charged the Penn family with purchasing the land near the creek under fraudulent conditions. But the deeds were found to be legitimate in 1742 and the chief lost his land. Tohickon is a Lenape expression thought to mean "deer bone creek," or may be derived from tohickham (or tohick-hanne), meaning "driftwood stream."

**TUCQUAN CREEK** (Lancaster)  The creek has its beginnings at the hamlet of Rawlinsville and flows about 6 miles into the Susquehanna River. Basswood trees that grew along the banks were used by the Indians for making rope and ceremonial masks. Tucquan was derived from the Algonquian word p'duchanna, meaning "a winding stream," or p'tuckhanne, for "a bend in a stream." The Tucquan is designated Wild and Scenic.

**TULPEHOCKEN CREEK** (Bucks) Tulpehocken is derived from the Lenape word tulpewihacki, meaning "turtle land." Early settlers were Germans from the Palatinate during the 1720s, followed by the Swiss. Farming was predominant as were the mills using the water power of the creek. In 1828, the Union Canal was built along the Tulpehocken.

**TUNEUNGWANT CREEK** (Bradford) Tuneungwant may be a Lenape word derived from tuneungwan, meaning "an eddy, not strong," but its definition is disputed. In 1871, oil was discovered, bringing premium prices for the land. The creek is a tributary of the Allegheny River and flows into the state of New York.

**WALLENPAUPACK LAKE** (Wayne/ Pike)  The lake was created in 1926 by the Pennsylvania Power & Light Company when it dammed up what was once Wallenpaupack Creek for the purpose of hydroelectric power. The name may a Lenape expression meaning "stream of swift and slow water," or "deep, dead water."

**WAPPASENING CREEK** (Bradford) This river, which flows into the Susquehanna River, bears an Algonquian name for "place of white stones." The town of Nichols was settled about 1791 at the confluence of the streams.

**WAPWALLOPEN CREEK** (Luzerne) Conrad Wickeiser was the first recorded settler in 1798. Others who followed him established sawmills and tanneries along the creek. In 1855, Williams Silvers built an explosive powder factory called The Powder Hole. The product was used in the local coal mines, and operated until 1914. Wapwallopen may be a corruption of the Lenape expression woaphallackpink, for "white hemp place" or "white hemp at."

**WICONISCO CREEK** (Dauphin) Wiconisco Creek discharges at the town of Millerburg. The village of Wiconisco is situated along the stream from which it takes its name. Wiconisco may be derived from an Algonquian word wikenkniskeu, interpreted as "a wet and muddy camp,"

**WINOLA, LAKE** (Wyoming)  Formerly known as Breeches Pond, Winola is an Algonquian word meaning "water lily," the name of Chief Capoose's daughter. She was in love with a white captive, who eventually escaped. The girl was distraught and went to the lake where they used to meet. One day she saw a reflection of her father in his war paint holding the scalp of her lover and promptly threw herself into the water, where she died. The lake was once owned by the Northern Electric Railroad.

**WYSOX CREEK** (Bradford)  Wysox may derived form wissuhacki, meaning "rich (or fat) land." It was also thought to come from assiskuhacki, defined as "muddy country." Others believe it is from a Lenape expression for "grapes at," descriptive of the wild grapes that grow in the region. First settlers along the creek may have been the Vlakenburg and Stropes families about 1776.

# RHODE ISLAND

**ANNAQUATUCKET RIVER** (Washington) The town of Bellville was founded along the river and became a manufacturing center with sawmills, grist mills and a cotton factory. Annaquatucket is an Algonquian phrase meaning "at the end of the river" (or "tidal current").

**CHEPIWANOXET ISLAND** (Kent) A Mr. Arnold purchased the island in 1868, which he generously opened to the public free of charge. It is now home to the Gallaudet Aircraft Corporation. Chepiwanoxet is a Narragansett expression meaning "end of small separated place," referring to a narrow neck of land that is periodically covered at high water.

**CONANICUT ISLAND** (Newport) This island is connected with the mainland by the Jamestown-Saunderstown Bridge. Conanicut was a refuge for the Quakers in early days. The island was occupied by the British 1776-79, and today is largely a resort. Conanicut was the name of an Indian the colonists knew as Canonicus (origin unknown)

**MATTATUXET RIVER** (Washington) Shady Lea was founded along the river, and its main industries were textiles (jeans, flannel and wool). During the early wars, General Walter Chapin's company made blankets for the military. Mattatuxet is an Algonquian word translated as "narrow river."

**MOSHASSUCK RIVER** (Providence) This river rises in the town of Lincoln and empties into the upper Narragansett Bay. Moshassuck is an Algonquian word meaning "big meadow stream," or "great fish." In 1636, Roger Williams and his group settled along part of the river, which has historically powered numerous mills.

**PASCOAG RIVER** (Providence) The water power of the river was used for the saw and gristmills that were built before 1740. Pascoag was a village within the town of Burrillville and its economy was tied to the river. The stream flows about 6 miles to merge with the Chepachet River. It is an Algonquian word meaning "forking place." It was also thought to indicate "pass a snake," indicative of the ledges that lined the side of the stream.

**PAWCATUCK RIVER** (Washington) Originating at Worden Pond, the Pawcatuck flows about 30 miles into Little Narragansett Bay. Part of the stream's course was named Charles River at one time. Colonists exploited the protected waters and began shipbuilding in 1680, which lasted until the 1800s when the Industrial Revolution came into prominence. Pawcatuck is an Algonquian expression meaning "open divided stream."

**PONAGANSET RIVER** (Providence) Ponaganset is an Algonquian word meaning "oyster place," or "waiting place at the cove." The river originates in the town of Glocester and flows into the Barden Reservoir. It is about 10 miles long. The town of Scituate was founded near the river and was the site of the first grist mill in 1725.

**WOONASQUATUCKET RIVER** (Providence) The Woonasquatucket originates near the town of Woonsocket and flows about 18 miles to empty into the Moshassuck River. During the Industrial Revolution, numerous chemical factories were established along the river. The water power of this river was prominent in the establishment of the city of Providence. Woonasquatucket is a Narragansett expression meaning "at the head of the tidal river."

# SOUTH CAROLINA

**ASHEPOO RIVER** (Colleton)  The river flows into Saint Helena Sound. Ashepoo was the scene of a U.S. Army and Navy expedition during the Civil War, which came up the river in order to cut off the Charleston and Savannah Railroad. Ashepoo is from a Muskohegan word meaning "river home."

**CHAUGA RIVER** (Oconee)  The Chauga is a tributary to the Oconee River. Its name may be a corruption of the Creek word chahki, interpreted as "shoal." It was also thought to be a Cherokee expression for "high uplifted river," descriptive of the rapids' turbulent water. This river is one of South Carolina's few remaining streams to be preserved almost entirely in its natural state.

**COMBAHEE RIVER** (Colleton)  Once the site of numerous rice plantations, the Combahee originates at the confluence of the Salkehatchie and Little Salkehatchie rivers and flows about 40 miles to join the Coosaw River. Combahee may be a Muskohegan expression that describes something desired or something of wonder. Harriet Tubman led a group of volunteers on an abolitionist raid on the river in 1863, freeing more than 700 Gullahs from slavery. During the action, volunteers found Confederate mines in the river.

**CONGAREE RIVER** (Richland)  This river rises at the junction of the Broad and Saluda rivers, and flows about 52 miles to join the Santee River. It may be a Catawba word meaning "river deep." At one time the Congaree Indians lived in the region, but may have later joined with the Catawba Tribe.

**COOSAW ISLAND** (Beaufort)  Coosa may be a Coosaw word for "reed," or Choctaw meaning "cane." Settlers who lived on the island were attacked by the Coosaw Indians during an upristing in 1715. They carried off the wife of a captain who was never found.

**EDISTO ISLAND/RIVER** (Colleton)  The Edistow Indians met their first white man when explorer Robert Sandford stopped at the island in 1666. Paul Grimball and his family settled there when he received a land grant about 1674. After the Depression two millionaires purchased substantial land that was transformed into a hunting preserve. The name comes from the Edistow Indians, whose name means "water sprinkler," for a ceremony the warriors performed by taking water from the river and sprinkling it about, signifying blood showered upon their enemies. The Edisto River is about 90 miles long and empties into the Atlantic.

**SAMPIT RIVER** (Georgetown)    This river flows about 25 miles to Winyah Bay. Charles Town was settled in 1670 along its banks, and the first trading post was built by the English to conduct business with the Indians. Following the trading post days, Indigo became a mainstay, in addition to lumber mills and cotton. Sampit is an Algonquian expression meaning "short river."

**SANTEE RIVER** (Georgetown)    The Santee rises at the confluence of the Congaree and Wateree rivers, and flows 143 miles to the Atlantic Ocean. The river was named for the Santee tribe of Indians, whose name may be a corruption of iswan'ti, meaning "the river is there." The first Europeans to see the Indians were members of a Spanish expedition in the 1600s.

**STONO RIVER** (Charleston)    A community named Stono was established near the stream, and its name is taken from an Indian tribe (origin unknown). The river is a tidal channel that runs between Wadmalaw and Johns Islands. During 1715-16 the Tuscarora Indians went on the warpath. Fearing for their lives, the settlers were aided by Colonels John Barnwell and James Moore who stemmed the Indians' onslaught. The Indian villages were later destroyed. In September of 1739, a slave insurrection occurred along the river, led by a slave named Jemmey, who proceeded to steal weapons and began killing the whites. It took about six months to capture and hang them.

**WANDO RIVER** (Berkeley)    Wando is a tribal name, but its origin is not known, although some have interpreted it as "deer." The Indians made pottery with limestone and clay found only on this river. In 1770, the South Carolina colonial government ordered a powder magazine to be built along the river on land owned by Captain Clement Lempriere. A later industry was the cultivation of Wando River oysters, which were shipped out to a packing plant at Shelmore Point.

**WATEREE RIVER** (Richland)    Wateree river is Catawba word for "washed away banks." During the 1770s, the Wateree was a major highway for commerce route and fur-trading route. The town of Camden was established near the stream, and experienced untold devastation when General Sherman came through on his famous March to the Sea. All the buildings and the Wateree River Bridge were set on fire. The river flows 395 miles into North Carolina and joins the Congaree River.

**WAXHAW CREEK** (Lancaster)    Waxhaw was thought to mean "people of the cane," and was taken from the Waxhaw Indians, who were members of the Siouan language group. The creek is tributary to the Catawba river in North Carolina. President Andrew Jackson was born near the creek in 1767. During the American Revolution, the British defeated the Americans at the Waxhaw.

**WIMBEE CREEK** (Beaufort)    This creek was named for the Wimbe Tribe (origin unknown). During the 1840s, the creek was found to contain large amounts of phosphate. Because of demand for the product, by 1880 more than five factories were mining the creek.

# SOUTH DAKOTA

**AKASKA LAKE** (Walworth)   The lake was named for the town of Akaska by Glen Matteson, who was employed by the Federal Emergency Relief Administration. It was formed when the Minneapolis and St. Louis Railroad cut a channel and changed the course of Swan Creek, damming part of the creek. Akaska may be a corruption of a Sioux word meaning "a woman who lives with several mean," or "to eat up."

**ARICAREE CREEK** (Haakon)   This creek enters the Bad River. It was named for the Arikara Indians who lived in the region before being driven out by the Sioux Indians. Aricaree means "horn," descriptive of their hair style.

**BEDASHOSHA LAKE** (Buffalo)   Bedashosha Lake is located about 15 miles from the town of Chamberlain. It may be a Sioux word meaning "roily waters," taken from beda and shosha. The lake is sometimes called Crow Creek Dam.

**BIG SIOUX RIVER** (Roberts, Lincoln, Union)   The Big Sioux rises near the community of Waubay and flows about 390 miles to the Missouri River. It takes its name from the Sioux Indians, whose name was interpreted as a Choctaw expression for "enemy." The Sioux Indians called the stream "winding" or "crooked."

**CHEYENNE RIVER** (Fall River)   Rising near the Black Hills, the Cheyenne flows about 370 miles to the Missouri River. The stream takes the name of the Cheyenne Indians, interpreted as "southerners." The Sioux called it "good river."

**HUNK PAPA CREEK** (Corson)   This tributary of the Missouri River was named for the Hunkpapa tribe of the Sioux Nation (origin unknown). It was first called Pocasse or Hay Creek. Fort Manuel was built along the stream in 1812 for protection against the Indians.

**KAMPESKA LAKE** (Codington)   Kampeska is a natural lake that was named by the Sioux Indians, meaning "shining" or "shell-like," descriptive of the clear water. The lake is located near the town of Watertown. Others believe it was derived from mdegatanska, meaning "lake of the white pelican." or from mdemagaska for "lake of the white swan."

**KEYAPAHA RIVER** (Todd)   The majority of this river flows through the state of Nebraska and enters the Niobrara River. Keyapaha is a Sioux expression which means "turtle hill," and took its name from a butte.

**LAKOTA SPRINGS** (Fall River)   The springs are located in the town of Hot Springs. They were named for the Sioux Nation, who originally owned the territory. Lakota is a variant of Dakota, a Sioux word meaning "ally" or "friend."

**MINA LAKE** (Edmunds)   The lake was named for the town of Mina, although its official name is Shake Maza, a Sioux word meaning "horseshoe," descriptive of its shape. Constructed in the 1930s, it was one of the first man-made lakes in the state. It was later named Mina for a railroad president's daughter.

**MINNECHADUSA RIVER** (Todd)
Minnechadusa River was given a Sioux name, meaning "rapid stream," because of the rapid currents or murmuring water. It enters the Niobrara River in Nebraska.

**MINNEKAHTA VALLEY** (Fall River)
The valley is located between the town of Hot Springs and Minnekahta. It is a Sioux expression translated as "hot springs," a descriptive word.

**MINNEWASTA LAKE** (Day)   Minnewasta is a natural lake and is about 10 miles from the town of Webster. The clear water and gravel bed earned the lake its name, a Sioux word meaning "good water."

**MUSH CREEK** (Hughes)   This creek is a tributary of the Missouri River. It was originally called Mastincala by the Sioux Indians, which means "cottontail," but corrupted by the whites to Mush. It is also known as Dry Creek.

**OKOBOJO LAKE** (Sully)/**CREEK** (Potter)   Located near the town of Okobojo, the lake was built in the 1930s as an emergency water conservation project. Okobojo Creek flows through Sully County and enters the Missouri River. It bears a Sioux expression which means "planting in the spaces."

**ONAHPE LAKE** (Douglas)   First called Alcazar, the name of this lake was changed when a dam was rebuilt in 1937. Onahpe was named by the Armour Community Club, and may be a Sioux word meaning "place of recreation."

**PONCA CREEK** (Tripp)   This creek enters the Missouri River. Ponca comes from a Siouan dialect derived from pahonga, which means "head leader."

**SNAYAN WAKUWA LAKE** (Shannon)
Situated near the town of Oglala, this lake was named for an Indian, whose name was interpreted as "Rattling Chase." The lake comprises about one acre and was created by the Civilian Conservation Corps and Indian Department.

**TETONKAHA LAKE** (Brookings)
Tetonkaha is a Sioux expression interpreted as "the standing of the big lodging house." It refers to a group of Sioux Indians who were caught in a blizzard while hunting along the lake, and raised their tents together to form one big space. When they left, the poles were not taken. The lake is located about 5 miles from the village of Bruce.

**WAUBAY LAKES** (Day)   These natural lakes were given the Sioux expression meaning "where wild fowl build their nests." They are located near the town of Webster. Early settlement around the lake was by a French trader named Francis Rondell in 1868.

# TENNESSEE

**CHICKAMAUGA LAKE** (Hamilton) The lake comprises about 35,000 acres. Chickamauga is a corruption of tsikam-agi, a Cherokee word meaning "bloody run," or "bloody river," describing the malaria that caused the Indians' death. It was also translated as "good place," and "to become filled with snags" (or "roots"). In 1936, construction of the Chickamauga Dam was begun for flood control, and was the fifth major Tennessee Valley Authority's project. It was completed in 1940. Sherman Dam was the first proposed name, but the United Daughters of the Confederacy were offended, and Chickamauga was chosen instead.

**CULLEOKO SPRING** (Maury) The village of Culleoko was founded around this spring about 1857. Culleoko is an Algonquian word meaning "sweet water."

**SEQUATCHIE RIVER** (Cumberland) Historical Ketner's Mill was built along the banks of the river, and a water-powered grist mill operated from 1824 to 1992. The river flows 80 miles into the Tennessee River. Sequatchie is derived from the Cherokee word for "hog river." It was also the name of a Cherokee chief who lived along the river during the 1700s.

**UNAKA MOUNTAIN** (Unicoi) Rising about 5,180 feet high, this mountain was a haven to fugitives of the Civil War, those men who had no wish to join either side. Unaka may be derived from the Cherokee word u'nika, translated as "white" or "fog-draped." The mountains are located in the Cherokee National Forest.

**UNICOI MOUNTAINS** (Unicoi) Situated in the Cherokee and Nantahala National Forests, Unicoi is a Cherokee word signifying "white," derived from unega. The Unicoi Mountains are part of the Appalachians and rise from 1,700 to about 5,600 feet. Inhospitable to the white man's intrusion, the Cherokee Indians proved to be formidable in protecting their land. But the Scotch-Irish settlers demonstrated their mettle and organized the community of Coker Creek. This stream contained gold bringing in the miners who pushed the Indians from their land. The mineral was discovered long before the California gold rush.

# TEXAS

**ANADARKO CREEK** (Rusk)   This creek was named for the Anadarko Indians, a Caddoan group. It joins the East Fork of the Angelina River near the town of New Salem. The Nadarko Indians were a band of the Caddo Indians. Their name was interpreted as "eaters of bumblebee honey," and "brown water bug."

**AYISH BAYOU** (San Augustine)   The bayou empties into the Angelina River. The name may have been for the Ais (or Ayish) Indians, who were a group of the Hasinais Indians (origin unknown). Settlement began with the arrival of Edmund Quirk in 1820.

**MUSHAWAY MOUNTAIN** (Borden) This interesting name is a controversy. Some believe it is a Comanche word derived from Mucha Koogato meaning "buzzard excretion," while others define it as a Comanche word describing an act of sexual intercourse. Neither definition has been proven.

**NAVASOTA RIVER** (Hill)   This river has its origins near Mount Calm and joins the Brazos River. Cynthia Ann Parker's family built a fort along this river for protection. She was captured in 1836 by Comanche Chief Nocona and bore him a son named Quanah. Navasota was derived from the Comanche word nabototo, meaning "muddy waters."

**NECHES RIVER** (Van Zandt)   The Neches is 416 miles long and originates in the Sandy Hills. It empties into Sabine Lake. During the 1700s the Neche Indians lived along the river and called the stream "snow river" (or "river of snows"). When Spanish explorer Alonso DeLeon came through in 1680 he named the river for the Indians. It was later used by settlers to ship their cotton and produce via flat-boats.

**TAMPACUAS, LAKE** (Hidalgo)   Also known as Lake Campacuas or Carter's Lake, this feature is about two miles long. It may have been named for the Coahuiltecan Indians who lived here in the 1700s (origin unknown).

**TANTABOGUE CREEK** (Houston) The Tantagobue joins the White Rock Creek in Trinity County. It bears a name, of which only bogue can be defined, a Muskogean word meaning "creek."

**TOYAH LAKE** (Reeves)   Toyah Lake is located near Blue Goose Hill. It is about 5 miles long and 2 miles wide. Toyah is an Algonquian expression translated as "flowing water" or "much water." It was also thought to mean "valley of flowers."

**WASHITA RIVER** (Roberts)   The Washita flows about 450 miles into the Red River in Oklahoma. It may be a variant of Ouachita, from the Choctaw words owa and chito, interpreted as "big hunt," "good hunting grounds," or "hunting trip." It was also thought to mean "sparkling silver water." In 1868, General Custer and his men were engaged in the Battle of Washita, where Custer defeated the Cheyenne Indians in Oklahoma.

**WICHITA, LAKE** (Wichita)   This artificial lake is located near Wichita Falls and was formed in 1901. The lake is a source of water for the town of Wichita Falls. Its name was taken from the Wichita Indians, meaning "scattered lodges," "painted faces," or from wechate, meaning "red river people."

# UTAH

**ANASAZI CANYON** (San Juan) Anasazi is a Navajo expression for "ancient ones." The canyon is located on the northern slope of Navajo Mountain near Rainbow Bridge National Monument and drains into the Colorado River.

**AWAPA PLATEAU** (Wayne) Rising about 8,000 feet, the plateau is about 30 miles long and 20 miles wide. It was named by A.H. Thompson from a Ute expression meaning "many waters," or from a Paiute expression meaning "water hole among the cedars."

**CHA CANYON** (San Juan) The canyon is a tributary of the San Juan River arm of Lake Powell. It is about nine miles long and bears the Navajo word Chaa', which means "beaver."

**DESHA CREEK** (San Juan) This creek originates in the Navajo Mountains and is a tributary of the San Juan River. Desha is from the Navajo word deez'a, interpreted as "ridge."

**HOVENWEEP NATIONAL MONUMENT** (San Juan) Hovenweep is a Ute word for "deserted valley." Explorers Escalante and Dominguez came through in 1776, followed by the Hayden Survey in 1874, whose cartographer, William Jackson, first mapped the valley. The monument was established in 1923 by presidential proclamation. Hovenweep is comprised of four groups of prehistoric cliff dwellings, whose people lived here until about 1300 A.D.

**IBAPAH PEAK** (Juab) Located in the Deep Creek Range, Ibapah is one of the most rugged of Utah's mountain ranges, rising about 12,100 feet. Home to the Gosiute Indians, Ibapah is from the Gosiute word aibimpa, interpreted as "white clay water," descriptive of the clay particles in Ibapah stream. Legend says that the coyote named Isapai-ppeh who lived in the mountains was punished because of his trickery by a hawk named Kinniih-Pa, and while doing so he formed the Deep Creek Range in which the peak is situated.

**JUAB VALLEY** (Juab) Juab is derived from the Ute word yoab, meaning "flat" or "level," descriptive of the valley floor. Mormons settled near Salt Creek in 1851 and conducted agriculture. In 1869, gold and silver were discovered in the region and Tintic Mining District was formed. The district took out more than $35 million between 1870-1899.

**KAIPAROWITZ PLATEAU** (Garfield) Located in the Grand Canyon, the plateau was named by A.H. Thompson with the

Second Powell Expedition in 1871, Kaiparowitz has numerous Paiute meanings: "big mountain's little brother," "one arm," "home of our people," and "mountain home of these people." It may be Navajo for "rock descending jagged," derived from ndoolzhaw. Another theory was from kaivavic, meaning "a mountain lying down."

**KANAB CREEK** (Kane)   Kanab is a Paiute word for "willow." The creek rises from the south rim of the Great Basin and flows into the state of Arizona to join the Colorado River. During the 1860s, Mormons settled near the creek and attempted to farm, but were unable to irrigate their crops because of the creek's unpredictability.

**MAGOTSU CREEK** (Washington)   Located near part of the Spanish Trail, this creek has its origins in Mountain Meadows and joins the Santa Clara River near the town of Gunlock. Magotsu is derived from the Paiute word mahautsu, meaning "long slope."

**MARKAGUNT PLATEAU** (Iron/ Garfield)   Markagunt is a Paiute word translated as "highland of trees," and was named by A.H. Thompson, a member of the Powell Expedition. The plateau is 11,315 feet high. The Kaibab-Paiute Indian land was located on a portion of the plateau.

**MUSINIA PEAK** (Sanpete)   Rising about 10,986 feet, this peak is a headland of Wasatch Plateau and served as an early landmark. Musinia may be derived from the Ute word mooseneah, meaning "white mountain."

**NASJA MESA/CREEK** (San Juan)   The creek rises in the Navajo Mountains and flows into the San Juan River. The mesa is located between Nasja and Anasazi creeks. Owls are very prominent in Navajo cul-

ture, and so the mesa and creek were given the Navajo name noesja (or ne'eshjaa), meaning "the owls." The Indians used the mesa for their religious ceremonies.

**NIATCHE CREEK** (Sevier)   This tributary of Salina Creek has its origins near Mount Terrill. Niatche is derived from the Ute word no-oche or no-ochi, interpreted as "notch."

**OLJETO MESA** (San Juan)   The mesa is located near the community of Goulding. Oljeto is a Navajo word meaning "moonlight."

**ONAQUI MOUNTAIN** (Tooele)   The mountain bears the Gosiute word ona, meaning "salt." In 1896, gold was discovered in the region and a district was formed which included part of the mountain. This is the home to wild mustangs, descendants of horses who escaped from local ranches. About 1971, the Wild Free-Roaming Horse and Burro Act was established to protect the animals.

**OQUIRRH MOUNTAINS** (Salt Lake/ Tooele)   Traditionally used by the Gosiute Indians for religious ceremonies, the mountains were once roamed by nomadic Ute Indians in search of food. Oquirrh is a Gosiute expression derived from opio gari, interpreted as "wooded mountain." It was also interpreted as "brush mountain." Once heavily timbered, lumber companies came in and depleted the forest. At an outcrop in the Oquirrhs artifacts were found in caves, indicating that ancient cave people once lived there.

**OWEEP CREEK** (Duchesne)   Oweep may be a Ute word meaning "grass," descriptive of the stream's flow through a grassy meadow. Oweep Creek rises in the Uintah Mountains and joins the Lake Fork River.

**PANGUITCH LAKE** (Garfield)   The lake first became known to white men in 1852. Panguitch comes from a Paiute word pangwi or pangwitc, which means "big fish." The Paiute Indians held their potlatches at the lake during the summertime.

**PARIA** (also **PAHREAH**) **RIVER** (Garfield)   The Paria River has its origins in the Paunsaugunt Plateau and flows about 75 miles into the Colorado River. Paria is a Paiute word meaning "dirty water," or "elk water." The first white man to the region may have been Mormon John Lee who was ordered by his church to find a safe crossing across the Colorado River.

**PAUNSAUGUNT PLATEAU** (Garfield/Kane)   John Wesley Powell named this plateau which rises between 7,000-9,000 feet. It was the early 1900s when tourists began coming to visit and the first accommodations were established. Paunsaugunt is a Paiute word that means "home of the beaver."

**PAVANT** (or **PAHVANT**) **PLATEAU** (Millard/Sevier)   This plateau is the northernmost of three plateaus that comprise the High Plateau Range. Pavant bears the name of the Pah Vant Indians, a prominent Western Ute band, whose name means "water people."

**QUICHAPA CREEK/LAKE** (Iron)   Rising in the Harmony Mountains, Quichapa Creek flows into Cedar Valley. Its name is from a Paiute word quitchup (or quitchupah) meaning "laxative waters," "dung," or "bed ground, watering place." Located near Cedar City, the lake first bore the name Shirts Lake, for Peter Shirts. Part of the Spanish Trail passes nearby.

**SANPITCH RIVER** (Sanpete)   This name may be a corruption of the Sanpitch Indians, sampitches, meaning "home-lands." In 1852, Mormons living at Manti relocated to the Sanpitch River, but had to leave when they had problems with the Indians. They returned in 1859 to resettle. The town of Gunnison was founded abut 1862 along the river.

**SKUTUMPAH CREEK** (Kane)   Skutumpah was derived from skootumpa, defined as "creek where the squirrels live." It was also thought to come from skutempah, meaning "rabbit brush water," descriptive of the rabbit bush that grows along the stream. It may be a Ute word, although the Navajo and Paiute Indians also lived in the region. The creek has its origins at the confluence of Mill and Mineral creeks.

**TICABOO CREEK** (Garfield)   Ticaboo Creek was named during the late 1800s by Lewis Hite, who came to the region looking for gold or silver and filed a claim along the creek. He gave it a Paiute word meaning "friendly." The Ticaboo rises near Ticaboo Mesa and empties into Lake Powell.

**TIMPANOGOS, MOUNT** (Utah)   When Escalante and his men came through in 1776, he named the feature Sierra Blanca de los Timpanogos. The mountain is located in the Wasatch Range and rises about 11,750 feet. It overlooks the city of Provo. Paiute Indians called the mountain Paakaret Kaib, meaning "very high mountain." It was also defined as "woman lying down." Timpanogos may also be a Ute word meaning "rock river." Legend says Timpanac's father, a Nez Perce Indian, was quite ill and unable to climb the mountain to pay tribute to the Great Spirit. So Timpanac took his place and asked the gods to help feed the people. He then went to a Ute village to trade horses for food. When he saw the chief's daughter, Ucanogos, he fell in love with her. To win her hand, Timpanac and other braves had to scale the mountain. Halfway up,

Timpanic was attacked by others in the contest who threw him down the mountain. He landed in a lake and was discovered by Ucanogos, who laid herself down at the foot of the mountain and died. The tribes combined the two names to honor the young people, which became Timpanogos.

**TINTIC MOUNTAINS** (Juab) These mountains were the scene of a gold rush beginning about 1869, bringing hundreds of miners to the region, and the formation of the Tintic Mining District. The mining towns of Eureka and Mammoth were also established. The mountains are 8,214 feet high and named for Ute Chief Tintick (or Tintic), who deeply resented the white intrusion. His name was translated as "renegade chief."

**TUKUHNIKIVATZ, MOUNT** (San Juan) Tukuhnikivatz is part of the Sierra La Sal Range. When Spanish missionary Escalante and his expedition came through this region in 1776, he named the mountain range Sierra La Sal ("Salt Mountains"). Rising 12,489 feet, Tukuhnikivatz was thought to be a Ute word meaning "place where the sun sets last."

**UINTAH MOUNTAINS/RIVER** (Uintah/Duchesne) The Uintah Mountains were first crossed by General William Ashley and his expedition in 1825. Hundreds of glacial lakes are located in the Uintas. The river is about 50 miles long and has its origins near Kings Peak, flowing into the Duchesne River. Trading posts were established along the river for trade with the Navajo and Ute Indians. Uintah is derived from the Ute expression uintaugump, defined as "at the edge of the pine."

**WAH WAH MOUNTAINS** (Beaver) The mountains, which rise 9,400 feet high, may have received their name from the springs, a Paiute expression meaning "good clear water." Others have translated it as "salty," and "juniper." The mountains contained bixbite deposits, a type of beryl, which were mined by the Gemstone Mining Company. This is one of only three places in the world that contain the gemstone. The others are in the Thomas Range in Utah and Black Range in New Mexico.

**WAHWEAP CREEK** (Garfield/Kane) First called Sentinel Rock Creek for a lone pillar at the mouth of this creek, the name was changed to Wahweap, a Paiute word meaning "alkaline seeps," descriptive of the brackish water. The creek rises on the Kaiparowits Plateau at Canaan Peak and empties into Lake Powell. In 1776, the Escalante Expedition camped for a time at the creek.

**WANSHIP PEAK** (Summit) Located in Weber Valley, this peak is 9,308 feet high and was named for a Shoshone Indian named Wanship. His name was interpreted as "good man."

**WASATCH MOUNTAIN RANGE** (Sanpete/Emery) Located in the Manti-La Sal National Forest, this mountain range rises from 10,986 to 11,300 feet. Fathers Francisco Dominguez and Silvestre Escalante were the first white men to see the range in 1776, although some believe that an Indian fighter named Juan de Rivera led an expedition there about 1761. Since the region held a vast wealth of timber and water, the majority of the state's population settled along the mountain's western front. Wasatch is a Ute expression which refers to a low pass over a high mountain range.

# VERMONT

**ASCUTNEY MOUNTAIN** (Windsor) Ascutney is an old Abnaki name for the mountain, interpreted as "at the end of the river fork." Others ascribe the name to cascadnack, which means "bald or peaked with steep sides." It was also thought to mean "three brothers," because the mountain comprises three peaks and three valleys.

**BOMOSEEN LAKE** (Rutland) Bomoseen is the largest natural body of water in the state, about nine miles long and a mile wide. The waterfalls at the lake's outlet provided a generous supply of water power for the mills that were established. During the American Revolution the Battle of Hubbarton was fought near the lake. In 1881, an island in the lake was the site of a ceremonty sponsored by the Rutland Historical Society, when it was christened Neshobe (see Neshobe Island). Bomoseen is derived from the Abnaki expression mas-kee-koh-wo-gam, thought to mean "big pond with grassy banks." Another interpretation was from obum-sawin, meaning "keepers of the ceremonial fire."

**COATICOOK RIVER** (Canada) The Coaticook flows into Norton Pond. It is derived from the Abnaki word koak-tekauk, for "river at the place of pines," or "pine river." An early settlement was Drew's Mills, later renamed Dixville, which was supported by sawmills along the river.

**MAQUAM BAY** (Franklin) The bay was first named Bopquam, then changed to Maquam, possibly a corruption of Bopquam, a Wampanoag word meaning "a beaver."

**MEMPHREMAGOG LAKE** (Orleans) Most of the 40-mile-long lake lies in Canada, with only about one-third in Vermont. Roger's Rangers may have been the first whites to see the lake in 1759 while they were returning from a successful offensive against St. Francis Village in Canada. Memphremagog is an Abnaki word translated as "where there is a great expanse of water." Tradition says the Indians warned early settlers they should not swim in the lake because it contained a sea monster that slept in a nearby cave.

**METTAWEE RIVER** (Rutland) First called Pawlet, the Mettawee originates in the Taconic Mountains. It may be derived from a Narragansett word for "black earth" or taken from a Natick expression meaning "poplar trees."

**MISSISQUOI RIVER** (Franklin) This major stream originates near the town of Lowell and empties into Lake Champlain. It is about 75 miles long. Missisquoi is an Abnaki expression that has been interpreted as "big rattlesnake," "big woman," "much flint," "much water fowl," or "people of the great grassy meadows." The last definition is the most popular because the mouth of the river once contained grassy meadows where the Abnaki village of Missisiasuk was situated during the 1700s. At one time there was an iron industry in the region, but it was a short-lived because there were no profitable markets.

**MOOSALAMOO, MOUNT** (Addison) Located near the town of Salisbury, Moosalamoo is an Abnaki word meaning "he trails the moose," or "the moose departs."

Legend says a cave on this mountain is the place where the Green Mountain Boys held secret conclaves.

**NESHOBE ISLAND** (Rutland)   Situated in the center of Bomoseen Lake, the 10-acre island bears an Abnaki expression meaning "place very full of water." It was named by the Rutland Historical Society in 1881 for an Indian scout who assisted Ethan Allen and his Green Mountain Boys in their fight for freedom. Famed New York drama critic Alexander Woolcott owned the island and built a summer home in the 1920-1930s. He invited the likes of Harpo Mark, Noel Coward and Irving Berlin to his home.

**NULHEGAN RIVER** (Essex)   Originating at the town of Averil, the Nulhegan flows 15 miles to the Connecticut River at the town of Bloomfield. The community was created in the 1800s when the Nulhegan Lumber Company was established so it could use the water power of the river for its mills. Nulhegan is an Abnaki word meaning "my log trap," indicative of an Indian fish weir. The river was a route the Abnaki Indians used to travel from St. Francis, Quebec to the Connecticut River. In 1759 some of Roger's Rangers followed this river as an escape route after they attacked the Indians at St. Francis.

**OKEMO MOUNTAIN** (Windsor)   First called Ludlow Mountain for the town that is situated at its base, the name was changed after a ski area was developed. Okemo may be an Abnaki word meaning "a louse," or derived from a Chippewa expression that signifies "a chieftain."

**OMPOMPANOOSUC RIVER** (Orange)   Early settlement along this river occurred in 1779 by Eldad Post who built the first mill. It later became the village of Post Mills. Ompompanoosuc may be an Abnaki word for "at the place of the mushy (or quaky) land." The river flows 25 miles to the Connecticut River near the town of Norwich.

**OTTAUQUEECHEE RIVER** (Windsor)   Settlement along the river occurred during the 1760s, where numerous mills and farms were established. The river is about 38 miles long. It is a Natick expression for "swift mountain stream," or "at the place of the wild dashing stream." It was once known as Quechee, but only the village of Quechee retained the name. The town became famous for its woolen mills, the first built in 1883 by J.C. Parker. After the Francis K. Nichols & Co. was established, it introduced "shoddy" fabric (reworked rags and new wool) which revolutionized the industry.

**PASSUMPSIC RIVER** (Caledonia)   This river flows about 40 miles to the Connecticut River near the town of Barnet. Originally called Pesammes, the name was changed to Passumpsic, an Abnaki word for "over clear sandy bottom." During the French and Indian War, Roger's Rangers traveled along the Passumpsic and stopped at the mouth of the river waiting for food from General Jeffrey Amherst and his men. They never arrived and many of Roger's men died of starvation.

**SADAWGA LAKE** (Windham)   The village of Sadawga Springs was established along the lake during the mid-1800s and became a summer resort. It was later renamed Whitingham. Sadawga may have been the name of an old Indian who lived along the lake, or from a Mohawk word for "swiftly flowing water."

**SHATTERACK MOUNTAIN** (Windham)   Although Shatterack is designated a mountain, it is only 900 feet high. Located in the south central part of Rupert,

Shatterack may be a Potumtuck expression meaning "big mountain," or "between mountains."

**SKITCHEWAUG MOUNTAINS** (Windsor) When William Bettergneau moved to the mountain region for the purpose of trapping beaver, he met an Indian named Skitchewaug, for whom the mountain was named, Abnaki for "big mountain." An outcropping in the mountain was a haven for deserters during the Civil War, and was also thought to be the hideout of the local Kentfield Gang.

**WALLOOMSAC RIVER** (Bennington) This river has its origins near the town of Pownal and flows 30 miles to join the Hoosic River in the state of New York. It

is a Mahican word for "beautiful rocks" or "painted rocks," descriptive of the yellow ocher the Indians used for paint. During the American Revolution, the British were defeated along the river in New York during August of 1777 near the town of Bennington.

**WINOOSKI RIVER** (Chittendon/ Washington) The Winooski is about 90 mile long, and empties into Lake Champlain near the town of Winooski, which was founded in 1787 by Ira Allen and Remember Baker. The water power of the falls in the river lent to the establishment of a great many woolen mills. Winooski is an Abnaki word derived from winoskietew, which means "onion land river," or "the wild onion river."

# VIRGINIA

**APPOMATTOX RIVER** (Appomattox) This is the place where General Lee surrendered to General Grant and ended the Civil War. The river was named for the Appamattoc Indians, who may have been from the Powatan confederacy, and were extinct by the 1700s. Appomattox was interpreted as "tobacco plant country." The original Jamestown settlers planned to settle along its banks in 1607, but went to Jamestown instead. The river flows 137 miles to the James River.

**AQUIA CREEK** (Stafford) Aquia village was established near the creek as a Catholic community after the Indian Wars of 1767, and became the first English-

speaking colony in the state. During the Civil War, the Union Army had its quartermaster based here, which was used for the transfer of war supplies. Aquia may be Piscataway for "bush nut," or "seagull." Sandstone, also known as free stone, was cut from a quarry near the creek and used in construction of the Capitol building in the District of Columbia.

**CHAPAWAMSIC CREEK** (Stafford) Chapawamsic is an Algonquian word meaning "by the separation of the outlet." While the Confederacy was trying to block the Potomac River, it established batteries along numerous streams, among them the Chapawamsic.

**CHICKAHOMINY RIVER** (Hanover/
Henrico/Charles City/New Kent)   This
90 mile-long river originates near Jamestown and joins the James River near
Williamsburg. The stream was home to the
Chickahominy Indians who were forced to
leave the area when white settlement occurred. Their name was interpreted as as
"course pounded corn people," or "land of
much grain." It may have been derived
from checahaminend, meaning "land of
much rain," or tschikenemahoni, for "a
lick frequented by turkeys."

**CHINCOTEAGUE ISLAND** (Accomack)   The island was granted to Captain William Whitington in 1662 by a king
of the Gingoteague tribe. Chincoteague is
derived from gingoteague, which means
"beautiful island across the water." The island's early economy was primarily farming and livestock, and the post office was
established in 1856. The famous pony pen-
ning began about 1835 and today the tradition continues. The ponies are owned by
the Chincoteague Volunteer Fire Department, rounded up from Assateague each
year, and brought to Chincoteague to preserve the balance of nature.

**CHUCKATUCK CREEK** (Nansemond)
The village of Eclipse, home to about 70
families, is located along the creek, taking
its name from a lunar eclipse. In 1863, the
U.S.S. *Commodore Morris* seized a number
of ships that were smuggling contraband
down the creek. Chuckatuck is an Algonquian word, part of which means "tidal
stream." Note: the county of Nansemond
was abolished and the region became simply Suffolk City.

**COAN RIVER** (Northumberland)   The
village of Chicacoan was established about
1640 with its first settler, John Mottrom.
Other people moved there after they became disenchanted with Catholic Mary-

land. The Coan River was named for the
Chicacoan Indians (origin unknown).
During the War of 1812 British ships sailed
up the river in August to seize three
schooners and ended up burning the Indian village.

**CORROTOMAN RIVER** (Lancaster)
The river region was once home to the famous Lee family during the 1700s. It received its name from the Corotoman Indians who lived here until 1790 (name
unknown). The river still has in operation
a cable-drawn ferry.

**MATTAPONI RIVER** (Caroline)   The
Mattaponi flows 120 miles to join the York
River. The name is from the Mattaponi Indians (origin unknown, but some have
defined it as "bad bread"), who were ruled
by Powhatan. The tribe still lives along the
river by virtue of treaties signed in 1658
and 1677.

**MEHERRIN RIVER** (Lunenburg/Meck-
lenburg)   The Meherrin River and surrounding region was first explored in 1670.
It flows into the Chowan River in North
Carolina. White settlers forced the
Meherrin Indians to move into North Carolina. A reservation was set aside for them
in 1726 at the mouth of the river, but they
eventually disbanded and moved away. In
1975, a minister helped to reorganize
them, and in 1986 the state of North Carolina gave the Indian tribe formal recog-
nition. Meherrin means "people of the
muddy waters."

**METOMKIN BAY** (Accomack)   The
Metomkin Bay Plantation was built along
the bay after the Curtis family purchased
land from Col. Edmund Scarburgh and
Edward Ravell. Metomkin is an Algonquian word meaning "to enter into a
house."

**MOBJACK BAY** (Mathews/Gloucester) Mobjack Bay is an arm of the Chesapeake Bay. Hezekiah Philpotts (also known as Captain Thornton) purchased the site in 1871. By 1910, Mobjack was a bustling community and its economy was based on agricultural products shipped by steamboat, in addition to oystering and crabbing. Known as Mobjack in the Virginia General Assembly since 1652, the name may be a corruption of an Algonquin word for "bad land." During the 18th century the bay was known as Mock-Jack Bay.

**NANSEMOND RIVER** (Nansemond [now Suffolk City]) This 25-mile-long river originates at the town of Suffolk and enters the James River. It was once home to the Nansemond Indians. During 1690 they drove Captain John Smith from the area after he showed an interest in the oyster beds. The town of Suffolk was established along the river in 1742, and became a major peanut processing center after Amedeo Obici established the Planters Nut and Chocolate Company. Nansemond is from the Algonquian word neunschimend, meaning "whence we fled" or "were driven off."

**NOMINI CREEK** (Westmoreland) The Nomini Church (then spelled Nominy) was erected on the west side of Nomini Creek during the 1600s. The creek was named for the Nomini Indians (origin unknown). In 1730, Robert Carter built Nomina Hall, which was a place where people could come and discuss new Baptist doctrines.

**OCCANEECHEE ISLAND** (Mecklenburg) Now a stock farm, the island was once home to the Occaneechee Indians (origin unknown) who conducted trade with other tribes. While Nathanial Bacon was tracking the Susquehannock Indians who had fled to the island in 1676, he per-

suaded the Occaneechees to help him in his quest to drive out the Indians. Problems occurred shortly after this episode between the white settlers and Indians, with the Occaneechee village being destroyed.

**OCCOQUAN RIVER** (Fairfax) Rising near the site of Manassas, the Occoquan flows 20 miles to the confluence of Broad Run and Cedar Run creeks. The Dogue Indians were once resident there because of the abundance of fish at the stream's headwaters. Occoquan is an Algonquian word that means "end of the waters." The Occoquan Church was established near the river, but later relocated to Pohick Creek. John Ballendine founded the town of Occoquan in 1750. Industry began with the building of a grist mill (the first automated one in the United States), sawmills, and a forge that produced cannon balls during the American Revolution.

**PAMUNKEY RIVER** (King William, Hanover, New Kent) The Pamunkey flows about 90 miles to join the York River. It bears the name of the Pamunkey Indians, a remnant of the Powhaten Confederacy. Their name was derived from pihmunga, meaning "where he sweats," or from pamanki, for "sloping hill." A German named John Lederer may have been the first European to explore the river region. Serving as an early transportation route, much of the trade was halted in 1862 during the Civil War when boats conveying McClellan's supplies went up the river on their drive to Richmond. Today, the Pamunkey Indian Reservation is located near the river on land set aside for them by the U.S. Government.

**PIANKATANK RIVER** (Middlesex, Mathews, Gloucester) This river is about 20 miles long and empties into Chesapeake Bay. Folklore says that in the 1600s while Hugh Gwynn was exploring the region, he heard a girl crying for help. She had fallen out of her canoe and Gwynn jumped in the water to save her. When he asked her name, she told him Pocahontas. Her father was so grateful he gave an island to Gwynn that today bears his name. During the American Revolution, Lord Dunmore sailed up the Piankatank in a campaign against General Andrew Lewis. Chief Powhaten named the river in 1870, which may come from the word pianka, meaning in part "winding (or "crooked") water."

**POHICK CREEK** (Fairfax) About 1695 the Pohick Church relocated from the Occoquan River near this stream and renamed Pohick Church. During the War of 1812, tradition says the church was raided because George Washington attended services there. Pohick was derived from the Algonquian word pohickory, which means "American tree," or "water place."

**RAPPAHANNOCK RIVER** (Fauquier/ Rappahannock) The Rappahannock is a major waterway which originates in the Blue Ridge Mountains and flows 212 miles into the Chesapeake Bay. Part of the Powhatan Confederacy lived along the river during colonial times. People of wealth built their homes along the stream's banks during the 17th century. It was also home to George Washington (Ferry Farm) as a youngster. The river provided a wealth of oysters, which are still being harvested today. Rappahannock has been translated as "river of quick, rising water," "back and forth stream," and "rise and fall of water," indicative of the tidewater.

**ROANOKE RIVER** (Montgomery/ Roanoke/Floyd) The Roanoke is about 410 miles long and flows into the state of North Carolina into Albemarle Sound. It is derived from the Algonquin words, rawrenock or rawranoke, meaning "shell money." During both the American Rev-

olution and Civil War, part of the river saw intense fighting.

**SAPPONY CREEK** (Dinwiddie) A tribe of Indians called the Soponi lived in this region before the 1740s. Records show a settler received a land grant there in 1726. Sappony may be a corruption of monasic-capano (or monasukapanough), meaning "shallow water."

**SHENANDOAH RIVER** (Rocking-ham/Augusta) The Shenandoah rises from two forks in the counties and flows 150 miles to join the Potomac River. Shenandoah is an Algonquian word meaning "daughter of the stars." It was also thought part of the word meant "spruce stream." First named Euphrates by Governor Spotswood, a member of his party wrote in his diary, "The Governor buried a bottle with a paper inclosed, on which he writ that he took possession of this place in the name and for King George the First of England....We drank the Governor's health and fired a volley."[11]

**TOTOPOTOMOY CREEK** (Hanover) Land was granted to Thomas Tinsley about 1638, which comprised about 300 acres along the creek. It was named for Pamunkey Chief Tototomoi, an ally of the English in the 17th century. His name origin is unknown.

**YEOCOMICO RIVER** (Northumberland) In 1655, the Yeocomico Church was built and is thought to be one of the earliest churches in the United States. Some of its members were George Washington and Robert E. Lee. The village of Kinsale was founded along the river and grew up as a shipbuilding center. It is the oldest town on the Virginia side of the Potomac River. Yeocomico may derive from the Chicacoan Indian expression meaning "as "tossed to and fro by the waters."

# WASHINGTON

**AHTANUM CREEK** (Yakima)   During the Yakima War in the 1850s, Major Gabriel Rains marched into Yakima territory and burned a Catholic mission that had been established along the creek. The community of Ahtanum is located on the edge of the Yakima Indian Reservation. The name means "creek by the long mountain," an apt name since the site was near Ahtanum Ridge. It was also interpreted as "people of the water by the long hill," derived from ahtanumlema.

**ALPOWA CREEK** (Asotin)   During the 1880s the community of Silcott was established at the mouth of Alpowa Creek, where a band of Indians known as the Alpowaima once lived. When Lewis and Clark stopped there in October of 1805, Clark's journals noted the Indians but spelled their name Alpowa because it was easier to pronounce. Alpowa was interpreted as "a spring forming a creek," but its definition is in dispute.

**CHEHALIS RIVER** (Lewis)   At one time the Chehalis, Chinook, and Cowlitz Indians lived in the region. Chehalis means "shifting sands," referring to the sandy banks of the Chehalis River, and was the name of an Indian village located at the mouth of the river. The Chehalis is about 115 miles long and empties into Grays Harbor.

**CHELAN, LAKE** (Chelen)   Alexander Ross and David Thompson were the first explorers to pass this way about 1811 looking for a place to establish a trading post. They met friendly Indians who called the river Tsill-ane, from which Chelan is derived, interpreted from a Chinook word meaning "land of bubbling water," or "deep water." The lake is about 55 miles long. Indian legend tells of the monster that came to the land before there was a lake. He ate all the animals and left the Indians to starve. The Great Spirit killed the monster but it kept coming back to life. Great Spirit finally struck the earth so hard it created a huge depression. He threw the monster's body into the hole, then poured water into it, forming Lake Chelan. The Indians never took their canoes on the lake because the monster's tail was still alive, causing threatening waves on the water's surface.

**CHOPAKA MOUNTAINS** (Okanogan) The mountain region was the scene of a gold rush during the 1870s. Although some gold was found earlier, not much attention was given to it until Okanogan Smith and his prospecting friends found the first claims, and the rush was on with the establishment of a mining district. In 1873, Chief Moses told the whites they were on reservation land, and soldiers forced the miners to leave. Chopaka is an Indian word meaning "high mountain." Its tribal designation is unknown.

**CLALLAM BAY** (Clallam)   The town of Clallam Bay is along the Strait of Juan De Fuca, and was once home to the Klallam Indians. The name was derived from the Klallam's word for themselves, Nu'sklaim, which means "strong people."

**CLE ELUM LAKE** (Kittitas)   The lake region was a favorite place of the Yakama Indians to fish and gather huckleberries. The name Cle Elum was defined as "swift water." According to Indian legend, the lake was the home of a very large beaver named Wishpoosh who killed lesser creatures. He was challenged by Speelyia, the Coyote god. While they were fighting, Wishpoosh tore out the banks of the Keechelus, sending most of the water down a canyon which created a number of lakes, one of them which was Cle Elum. Wishpoosh was washed into the ocean, where he devoured whales and fish, until Speelyia transformed himself into a floating branch, drifted down the river and into Wishpoosh's mouth. Once inside, Speelyia resumed his former shape and size and with his knife-edged teeth he slew the belligerent beaver. He then divided the carcass and from it formed Indian tribes.

**COWEMAN RIVER** (Cowlitz) The Coweman River is a tributary of the Cowliltz River. It was first named Gobar's River for Anton Gobar who worked for the Hudson's Bay Company. The name was changed to Coweman, from the Cowlitz word koweena, interpreted as "short man," for a very short Indian who lived in the region.

**COWLITZ RIVER** (Cowlitz) The Cowlitz Indians lived in the region until white settlement. Their name was interpreted as "holder of the medicine spirit," or "capturing the medicine spirit." Young Indian braves used the river to communicate with their great spirit. The river has its origins in the Cascade range and flows about 130 miles to join the Columbia River near the town of Longview. Its banks were the site of many sawmills that produced cedar shingles.

**CULTUS BAY** (Island) Located on Whitby Island, the bay was home to the Snohomish Indians. Cultus is a Chinook word that means "bad" or "worthless." The name was probably taken from a lake lo-cated in British Columbia. Numerous drownings occurred there, and the bodies were impossible to retrieve because the lake was thought to be bottomless. It was later discovered an underground river flowed through the lake carrying everything with it. Researchers found evidence of tsunamis at the bay with the accumulation of marsh subsidence and tsunami deposits, which show earthquake activity along the Seattle fault.

**DOSEWALLIPS RIVER** (Jefferson) This river bears the name of a legendary man named Doswailopsh in the Twana mythology. Tradition says he was turned into a mountain which became the river's source. Located in the Olympic National Park, the river flows 35 miles to Hood Canal.

**DUCKABUSH RIVER** (Jefferson) The Duckabush originates in the Olympic National Park and flows 30 miles to the Hood Canal. Duckabush is derived from the Indian word do-hi-a-boos, interpreted as "reddish face," descriptive of the local mountain bluffs (tribal designation unknown).

**DUWAMISH RIVER** (King) Once home to the Duwamish people, early settlement began in the 1850s when coal was discovered along the river's banks. Hostilities with the Indians caused delays in its development until the Indians were removed to the Muckleshoot Reservation in 1856. The river flows 12 miles into Elliott Bay at Seattle. Duwamish was derived from dewampsh, defined as "the people living on the river."

**ELWHA RIVER** (Jefferson) Until dams destroyed the fish runs on this river, it was teeming with salmon that were unusually large, some at more than 100 pounds each. The river has its origin at Mount Olympus and flows 30 miles into the Strait of Juan de Fuca. The name comes from the Elwha Indians, whose name was interpreted as "elk."

**ENUMCLAW MOUNTAIN** (King) Named for the mountain, the town of Enumclaw was established in 1885. Definitions of the name vary: "place of the evil spirits," "thundering mountain," or "loud, rattling noise." A band of Duwamish Indians were camped at the base of the mountain when a terrific thunder storm came through. The Indians thought the sound came from spirits inside the mountain, and were so frightened they called it Enumclaw. A Nisqually Indian legend says Enumclaw and Kapoonis were hunters. A spirit gave Enumclaw the power to lift huge boulders across the mountains which he threw at hunters, and Kapoonis would send out flashes of lightning. The spirit saw the men were gaining too much power, so Enumclaw was changed into thunder, and Kapoonis became lightning.

**HAMMA HAMMA RIVER** (Mason) Logging was prevalent along this river during the early 1900s. Hab'hab was once a Twana village located at the mouth or the river. The name was corrupted to Hamma Hamma, and refers to a reed that grows along the swampy portions of the river.

**HOH RIVER** (Jefferson) Rising in Olympic National Park, this glacial river is 30 miles long and terminates at the Pacific Ocean on the Hoh Indian Reservation (established in 1893) Hoh is a Quillayute word that means "fast moving water." Legend says that two rocks on either side of the river were created after the Great Changer asked Raven and Crow if they would like to be changed into humans. When they said no, Great Changer said humans would come regardless and asked them what animals would they like to be-

come when the humans arrived. Since they were being stubborn and neither wanted to be animals, Great Changer turned them into rocks.

**HOQUIAM RIVER** (Grays Harbor) James Karr and his family made their home on the banks of the river in 1859. When the post office was established it was named Hoquiam. It may be derived from ho-qui-umpts, which means "hungry for wood," referring to the driftwood at the mouth of the river. Timber was a big industry until the lumber played itself out and bottomed out with the Depression.

**HUMPTULIPS RIVER** (Grays Harbor) The village of Humptulips was established near the river and began its life as a logging town. Its name was derived from ho-to-la-bixh, a Quinault word for "hard to pole," descriptive of the Indians who poled their canoes down the river. During logging days, the Humptulips Boom and Driving Company operated 27 splash dams and floated the logs to be sorted and rafted for delivery to the mills. The Humptulips empties into Grays Harbor.

**KLICKITAT RIVER** (Yakima/Klickitat) This river originates in the Cascade Range and joins the Columbia River near The Dalles and Yakima Indian Reservation. The Klickitats were a Shahaptian tribe originally from the Cowlitz River area. They joined with the Yakima Indians in the Treaty of 1855 when they ceded their land. Klickitat has several meanings: "beyond" and "robber." "Beyond" is the accepted version as it applies to the Indians' reference to the Cascade Mountains. On the banks of the river was the site of the Gas Ice Corporation, which manufactured dry ice from natural carbon dioxide wells at the springs. The company obtained 99.6% pure carbon dioxide and was the first use of natural carbon dioxide for dry-ice production.

**LATAH CREEK** (Spokane)   The town of Latah was formed in 1886 and took its name from the creek. The Nez Perce Indians called the river Lahtoo, meaning "the place of pine trees and pestle." It was also translated from la-koh for "white pine." Others defined Latah as "stream where little fish are caught, "camping ground" or "place well supplied with food." The town was first known as Hangman Creek after Yakama Chief Qualchan was hung by Colonel George Wright in 1858.

**LILLIWAUP BAY** (Mason)   Once the center of activity as an outfitting point for prospectors, Lilliwaup is located on Lilliwaup Bay, three miles north of Hoodsport. The name has been translated as "inlet," derived from a Twana word, lil-la-wop.

**LUMMI ISLAND** (Whatcom)   The ancient name for this island was Skallaham, so called by the Lummi Indians. It was charted by Spanish explorers in 1792 and named Isle de Pacheco. Lummi was interpreted as "the people who repelled," or "capable of being repelled"; that is, they did not mix with other people. In the mid-1800s, many of the Lummis died from diseases and Indian raiding parties. Captain Christian Tuttle, a gold miner and whaler, was the first permanent settler on the island in 1871. By the 1960s, Lummi Island had become more or less a retirement community.

**MEMALOOSE ISLAND** (Klickitat) One of the largest funeral islands in the Columbia River Gorge, Memaloose means "dead," or "place of the dead," and was used by the Klickitat Indians as their burial ground. The only white man to be buried on this island was Victor Trevitt. He had more Indian friends that he did the whites, and wanted to be buried on the island with his Indian friends. When the Bonneville Dam was built in 1937, the bod-ies were moved to a higher part of the island because the dam was going to submerge the lower section.

**NACHES RIVER** (Yakima)   Named for the Naches Indians, this river rises in the Cascade Range and flows 75 miles to join the Yakima River. The Indians called the site Natcheez, interpreted as "turbulent waters," referring to the swift moving river. It was also defined as "oh water!" and "one water." The name was also thought to be derived from nahchess, meaning "plenty of water."

**NASELLE RIVER** (Pacific)   This was home to a branch of the Chinook Indians who called themselves Na-sil. A smallpox epidemic hit the region in the early 1800s, almost decimating the tribe. There were about six families left who settled at what they called the Na-sil River. William Whealdon and two Indian guides stopped at Naselle to visit a family in 1862. He wrote of this visit, and since he was an expert in the pure Chinook language, it is believed his account of the name origin is accurate. When asked what Na-sil meant, he was told it was an old Chinook word that meant "protection" and "shelter."

**NESPELEM RIVER** (Okanogan)   Nespelem may be a Colville word meaning "a beautiful valley between the hills." During the 1800s, the U.S. Government built gristmills and sawmills for the Indians along the river. Gold that was discovered in the region during 1889 was shipped to the mouth of the river to be loaded on trains to a smelter in Tacoma. Among the most productive was the Nespelem Placer Mine. Chief Joseph lived along this river, and a young boy named Erskine Wood lived with him for a time and wrote " Our usual camp was on the Nespelem River, in the little valley of that name on the Colville Indian Reservation … a sub-agency was on the Nespelem, where the government maintained a small grist- and saw-mill and a store house from which rations were issued to the Indians...."[12]

**NOOKSACK RIVER** (Whatcom) The Nooksack Indians gave their name to the river, which means "fern-eating people," because they ate the roots of the ferns. The town of Nooksack was established near the stream and experienced growth after the Whatcom Trail was built in 1858.

**OHANAPECOSH RIVER** (Lewis) Archaeologists found remnants of a seasonal Indian village at the river, which may have been used by the Yakama Indians who fished for salmon. Situated in the middle of the river is a stand of 1,000-year-old trees known as the "Grove of the Patriarchs." Ohanapecosh is an Algonquian word meaning "oh, look," descriptive of something pretty.

**OSOYOOS LAKE** (Okanogan) The first permanent white settler in this part of the county was Hiram Smith who immigrated from New England. Chief Tonasket was born near the lake about 1820, and a town in this county was named for him. Osoyoos was derived from the Kalispel word soyoos, meaning "narrow," descriptive of the lake's shape, which is about 10 miles long. Tradition says an Irish settler added an "o" to the name, forming Osoyoos.

**PALIX RIVER** (Pacific) The first white settler along this river was Joel Brown, who planned to establish a town called Brownsville, but it never occurred. He was followed in 1863 by another settler who built the first sawmill in 1863, but it was short-lived because the venture failed. The Palix River, which flows into Willapa Bay, was derived from the Chehalis word copalux, meaning "slough covered with trees."

**PESHASHTIN CREEK** (Chelan) Peshashtin is pronounced as pish-pish-astin, which means "broad bottom canyon." During the 1860s, gold was discovered in the region, and the Chelen Mining Company built a 20-stamp mill along the Peshashtin. One of the miners found a large ledge of quartz, but when an earthquake triggered landslides, it buried the discovery which was never found again.

**PILCHUCK, MOUNT/RIVER** (Snohomish) Pilchuck is a Chinook word meaning "red water," descriptive of the river's color. Early sawmills used the water power of the Pilchuck. Mount Pilchuck was named in 1877 and took its name from the river. The mountain was first climbed in 1897.

**PUYALLUP RIVER** (Pierce) The Puyallup originates from Mount Rainier and flows 45 miles to Puget Sound. Its name may be a Salish word meaning "generous people," or "shadows," descriptive of the shade made by the forest. Because the river was always full of log jams and subject to flooding, a new channel was created to bypass a bend in the river.

**PYSHT RIVER** (Clallam) The community of Pysht began as a timber camp, where log rafts were made for shipment to Puget Sound ports. At one time a band of the Klallam Tribe lived at the mouth of this river, until a logging company bulldozed down their homes to make way for its logging operations. Pysht is a Chinook word that means "fish."

**QUILCENE RIVER** (Jefferson) Once home of the Twana Indians, the area was explored by the Wilkes Expedition in 1841, where they noted on their charts the name "Kwil-sid." The village Quilcene is located at the mouth of the River, and the name may signify "salt water people."

QUILLAYUTE RIVER (Clallam)   This river is about 6 miles long, rising at the confluence of Soleduck and Bogachiel rivers, then empties into the Pacific Ocean. It was named for the Quillayute Indians who live at the mouth of the river. Their name was interpreted as "river with no head."

SAMISH ISLAND (Skagit)   The island is home to the Samish Indian Tribe, whose name was interpreted from samens, meaning "hunter." More than 2,000 Indians lived on the island until the white man's disease decimated them in 1847, caused by hunters and trappers. When the Point Elliot Treaty was signed, there were only about 150 Indians left to witness the treaty signing. The island contains a very large rookery of the great blue heron.

SAMMAMISH RIVER (King)   First known as Squak Slough, the river region was settled in the 1870s. Logging was the predominant industry and the timber was transported down the river to the markets at Lake Washington. The name was later changed to Sammamish for the Indian tribe, derived from samenamish, meaning "hunter people."

SATSOP RIVER (Grays Harbor)   This river is formed by its West and East Forks, and flows 6 miles to join the Chehalis River. The Satsop was once home to the Lower Chehalis Indians. Its name may have been derived from sachap (or satsapish), interpreted as "on a stream."

SATUS CREEK (Yakima)   Satus is a Yakima word meaning "people of the rye grass valley," derived from setaslema. When Governor Stevens was arranging for a meeting in 1856 for treaty negotiations, a Yakama Indian was offered money to give to certain leaders, which for some reason the Indian considered an insult. The Yakamas then went into battle with Colonel Cornelius and his men, known as the Battle of the Satus.

SEMIAHMOO BAY (Whatcom)   The bay was one of the deciding boundaries between the United States and Canada. The community of Semiahmoo was located on a peninsula along the bay, and saw great prosperity during the British Columbia gold rush in 1858. The name is derived from the Semiamu Indians, whose name was interpreted as "half moon," but some authorities believe this translation is suspect. The tribe was a division of the Coast Salish Indians.

SEQUALITCHEW CREEK (Pierce)   In 1833, the Hudson's Bay Company established a trading post called Nisqually House at the mouth of this creek. It was considered the first permanent European settlement on Puget Sound. During a U.S. scientific expedition in 1841 a bluff at the mouth of the creek was used as an observatory. Sequalitchew is an Indian word that means "shallow," a descriptive word. The creek flows into Puget Sound

SIMILK BAY (Skagit)   The Swinomish Reservation, comprised of over 7,000 acres, is bordered by Similk Bay. The community is a confederation of Coast Salish Indian tribes, and bears their name, meaning "salmon."

SIMILKAMEEN RIVER (Canada)   The Similkameen rises in Manning Provincial Park in British Columbia, then flows into Washington and joins the Okanogan River. It is named for the Nicola-Similkameen Indians, interpreted as "the river," and "whitefish river," but these definitions are open to speculation. In 1871 gold was discovered near the town of Conconnully and placer operations were conducted along the river. Some platinum was also found, but there was not enough of the material to make mining worthwhile. Actually, the only place in the United States that contained substantial platinum was Platinum, Alaska, which was mined until 1990.

**SKAGIT RIVER** (Skagit)    The Skagit River originates in British Columbia and flows 163 miles to empty into Puget Sound. During the 1880s, miners flocked to the river when gold was discovered. In the 1960s the Seattle City Light built three dams on the river to take advantage of the water's energy. The river was named for the Skagit Indians, whose name means "lost." The Skagit supports one of the largest wintering bald eagle populations.

**SKOKOMISH RIVER** (Mason)    Rising in the Olympic Mountains, this river travels 10 miles to Hood Canal. It was named for the Skokomish Indians, interpreted as "fresh water people." The river at one time provided some of the largest salmon in the region. The Skokomish Indian Reservation comprises about 5,000 acres and is located on the river delta.

**SNOQUALMIE RIVER** (King)    The river rises near the town of Snoqualmie and runs 45 miles to join with the Snohomish River. Historically, the Snoqualmie Indians lived in the Puget Sound area, and made first contact with the white man about 1833 when Fort Nisqually was built. The tribe has been classified as part of the Coast Salish Indians. Snoqualmie may be derived from sdoh-kwahlb, which means "moon people," or just "moon." The Indians believed this is where their ancestors originated; the place where their life source came from. Indian legend tells the story about a beaver named Si'Beow, who climbed to the sky and brought the trees and fire to earth, made the sun for daylight, and created the Snoqualmie Indians.

**SOLEDUCK RIVER/HOT SPRINGS** (Clallam)    The Soleduck has its origin in Olympic National Park, and flows 70 miles to empty into the Pacific Ocean. Its name is from an Indian phrase meaning "sparkling water" (tribe unknown). The Indians believed the water in the river had medicinal properties. Roosevelt elk make their home near the river. In September of 1951, a fire started along the river and destroyed more than 30,000 acres of trees. The devastation occurred because there had been no rain for 108 days. The springs come from legend. Sol Duc and Elwha were two dragons engaged in bitter conflict. Since both were equal in their strength, they could not beat each other. As a result the dragons crept into their respective caves and wept from mortification, creating the Soleduck and Olympic Hot Springs.

**SQUAXIN ISLAND** (Mason)    The Treaty of Medicine Creek was negotiated on the island on December 25, 1854. It is about 4 miles long and a half-mile wide. Originally named Squawksin of Case Inlet, the name was changed to Squaxin Island, meaning "in between" or "piece of land to cross over to another bay" in the Lushootseed language. It refers to a village on the isthmus between Puget Sound and Hood Canal. Others have translated the name as "split apart," in reference to legend that tells the story of a water force that created the bay and inundated the land. During the Indian War of 1856-57, many of the local Indians were confined to the island.

**STILLAGUAMISH RIVER** (Snohomish)    This river is about 20 miles long and enters Port Susan Bay in Puget Sound. The stream was home to the Stillaguamish Tribe, and bears their name, which means "river people." In 1857, Reverend Eugene Chirouse established a mission along the Stillaguamish, and during the 1870s was the site of extensive logging.

**TATOOSH ISLAND** (Clallam) This bean-shaped island is situated off the extreme northwestern point of the state near the Makah Indian Reservation, and traditionally a summer fishing village for the Makahs. John Meares named the island in 1788 to commemorate a Nootka chief named Tatoochatticus, interpreted as "milk" or "breasts." A similar Nootkan word, tatootshe, means "thunder," "fire from thunder," or "thunder bird." Not much importance was given to the island until a lighthouse was built by the Federal Government in 1857. Today, the island is a meteorological station. A Makah legend tells the story about the creation of Tatoosh. Destruction Island and Tatoosh Island lived together and had children (big rocks and small rocks). The parents would often argue, and one day Tatoosh left her husband. She took her children and paddled up the coast until she reached Point of Arches. Thinking her children would grow up as nasty as their father, she threw them overboard, which created Tatoosh Island and the rocks surrounding Point of Arches.

**TOUCHET RIVER** (Columbia) In 1806, the Lewis and Clark Expedition reached this point and made their camp. While there, Clark named the river White Stallion after Chief Yelleppet gave him a white horse. It was later renamed Touchet, from the Nez Perce word tu-se, which means "roasting." Another translation was from tousa, for "curing salmon before a fire." The Touchet River originates in the Umatilla National Forest and flows 85 miles to join the Walla Walla River.

**TUCANNON RIVER** (Columbia) Tucannon may be from the Nez Perce word tukannon, which means "abundance of bread root," or "bread root creek." The river provided an important food source for the elk habitat. The Tucannon rises in the Umatilla National Forest and flows about 70 miles to enter the Snake River.

**TULALIP BAY** (Snohomish) Captain George Vancouver was credited with accidentally discovering this bay in 1794 when his ship ran aground. The U.S. Government established a reservation there for the Snohomish, Snoqualmie, Skykomish and other allied tribes signatory to the Treaty of Point Elliot. Tulalip is a Salish word interpreted as "small mouthed bay."

**WALLACUT RIVER** (Pacific) The Chinook Indians crossed this river to reach their winter villages, and in 1805 was another site where Lewis and Clark made their camp. Wallacut is from the Chinook word wallhut, which means "place of stones," descriptive of the smooth rocks at the mouth of the river. Others derived it from duhhlaylup, meaning "a bay almost land locked," or "having a small mouth."

**WASHOUGAL RIVER** (Clark) This tributary of the Columbia River was visited by Lewis and Clark in 1806, which they called Seal River because they noticed many seals and their pups. Washougal is a Chinook word meaning "land of plenty," or "pleasant." It was also thought to mean "rushing water." The town of Parkersville was established about 1844 when David Parker settled along the river.

**WISHKAH RIVER** (Grays Harbor) The Wishkah is about 40 miles long and has its origins in Olympic National Forest. It empties into Grays Harbor. Wishkah is a Chehalis word derived from hwish-kah, interpreted as "stinking waters." The river was used by timber companies in addition to canneries that processed millions of tons of fish.

**WYNOOCHEE RIVER** (Grays Harbor) The Wynoochee Indians, who were closely connected with the Chehalis Indians, were resident in this area until white settlement. Their name means "shifting," and may in-dicate the river's course. It rises in the Olympic National Forest and flows 60 miles to join the Chehalis River.

# WEST VIRGINIA

**BUCKHANNON RIVER** (Randolph) This river is about 45 miles long and joins the Tygart River. One of the first perma-nent settlements between Fort Pitt and the Gulf of Mexico, Buckhannon was estab-lished about 1806. Buckhannon's origins are in dispute. Some believe it was not an Indian name, but a Colonel named Buchanan. Others have attached its origin to a band of Delaware Indians with a chief named Buckongehanon. It was also defined as "brick river," and "breaker in pieces."

**CACAPON     MOUNTAIN/RIVER** (Hardy, Hampshire, Morgan)   The river originates as Lost River, then becomes Ca-capon River near the town of Wardens-ville. It is about 115 miles long and joins the Potomac River. The mountain was vis-ited by George Washington in 1769, who also surveyed the river. In 1756, the Battle of Great Cacapon River occurred during the French and Indian War, where Captain John Mercer and 15 of his men were killed during the conflict. Cacapon may be an Al-gonquian expression meaning "rising river," because of the fact that it flows un-derground for part of its course. It was also defined as "medicine water," derived from capecapepehon.

**GUYANDOT     RIVER**    (Wyoming, Raleigh)   Guyandot may be a French cor-ruption for the Wyandot (or Wyandotte) Indians, who sometimes called them the Guyandots. The river rises on the border of the counties and joins the Ohio River. During the 1800s, fur trappers collected their stored pelts near the stream, and car-ried them to the town of Huntington, where they were exported.

**KANAWHA RIVER** (Kanawha)   The Kanawha River is the largest inland water-way in the state, and was known for its abundance of coal. In 1742, John Peter Sal-ley and his group of explorers were on an expedition across the Allegheny Moun-tains and found an outcropping of coal along a tributary of the Kanawha River. Salley named this tributary the Coal River, and his report became the first reference to coal in the region that is today West Vir-ginia; however, not much mining took place in the state until the early 1800s. Charcoal was replaced by coal in 1817, used as fuel for the numerous Kanawha River salt furnaces when the salt industry came into prominence. The Kanawha rises at the confluence of the New and Gauley rivers and flows 97 miles to the Ohio River. Kanawha is a Lenape word derived from ken-in-she-ka, meaning "white stone river," or "river of evil spirits."

**MONONGAHELA RIVER** (Marion) The Monongahela is about 128 miles long. It originates at the confluence of the West

Fork and Tygart rivers, then flows into Pennsylvania to form the Ohio River. In 1754, Captain William Trent and his soldiers built a stockade called Fort Trent. A few months later, the French captured the fort and renamed it Fort Duquesne. General Edward Braddock later attempted to drive the French from the Monongahela, and the fort was finally captured in 1758 by General John Forbes and his army. The river, which was the first in the United States to be improved for navigation, became the chief highway for transporting iron, steel and coal. Monongahela is a Seneca word meaning "river of curling waters," or derived from menaungehilla, interpreted as "high banks or bluffs, breaking off and falling down at places."

**PINNICKINNICK MOUNTAIN** (Harrison)   Rising about 1,450 feet, this mountain may be a variation of Kinniconick (see Kentucky) and Kinnickinnic (see Wisconsin). They all refer to a mixture of leaves and bark the Indians smoked, most likely dogwood and sumac.

**POCATALICO   RIVER**   (Roane/Kanawha/Putnam)   In 1790 Phillip Null discovered coal near the mouth of the river. Settlers used the resource for their personal use until the Industrial Revolution in the 1850s, when the coal became a valuable commodity. Pocatalico is an Algonquian word defined as "plenty of fat doe," or "river of fat doe." The river flows 75 miles to join the Kanawha River near the community of Poca.

**POTOMAC RIVER** (Preston)   This 285 mile long river rises as a spring at Fairfax Stone and flows through Maryland to enter Chesapeake Bay. The origin of the stream was discovered by Colonel William Mayo in 1736. It forms part of the boundary between Maryland and West Virginia, and was nicknamed the "Nation's River" since it flows through the nation's capital. Rich coal seams were discovered in the region, but the coal mine drainage was so acidic it left the area devoid of vegetation. During its early days, the Potomac was a major trade route. Potomac is an Algonquin word meaning "where something is brought."

**SENECA ROCK** (Pendleton)   Consisting of white Medina sandstone, this feature rises 1,000 feet. Indian legend says that the daughter of a Seneca chief named Snowbird lived near the rocks and learned how to climb. When she reached marriageable age, seven braves tried to win her hand. She told them she would marry the man who could scale the rock. Only one of her potential suitors survived the climb. This feature was named for the Seneca Indians, interpreted as "stone."

**TUSCARORA CREEK** (Berkeley)   The Tuscarowa Indians lived here until white encroachment. Their name means "hemp gatherers," for the plant the Indians made use of. It was also interpreted to mean "open mouth."

**YOUGHIOGHENY RIVER** (Preston)   The Youghiogheny originates at Backbone Mountain, and flows about 135 miles through Maryland and Pennsylvania to join the Monongahela River near the town of McKeesport. George Washington followed the river's course in 1754 when he was seeking a water route to Pittsburgh (at that time called Fort Duquesne). Youghiogheny may be from the Lenape expression juhwiah hanne, interpreted as "stream flowing in a contrary direction." It was also defined as a Powhatan word for "four streams," or "three main prongs."

# WISCONSIN

**AMNICON RIVER** (Douglas) This river originates in Bear Lake and flows into Lake Superior. It was thought to be an Ojibwa word for "spawning ground." Settlement along the river began with the arrival of the Finnish people.

**ASHWAUBENON CREEK** (Brown) Ashwaubamie was a Menominee chief, whose name means "looking out place." Another interpretation was derived from ashiwabiwining, meaning "place where they watch," in reference to enemies of the Indians.

**CARCAJOU POINT** (Jefferson) The Oneota Indians lived on the point more than 1,000 years ago, as remnants of their settlement were found with houses built over shallow pits. Carcajou is an Algonquian word meaning "wolverine."

**CHEQUAMEGON BAY/NATIONAL FOREST** (Ashland) Chequamegon may be a French corruption of shaugauwaumekong, Ojibwa for "a long narrow strip of land running into a body of water," or "place of shallow water." The name may have come from the Indian legend about Nanabozho, an Ojibwa spirit who attempted to catch the Great Beaver and built a dam. Each fistful of mud he dug up was tossed into the bay. As they landed, the Apostle Islands were formed. Thus, the name was thought to signify "place of the soft beaver dam." The national forest comprises about 850,000 acres and is an important source of timber for the state's forest products industries.

**CHENEQUA LAKE** (Bayfield) Chenequa may be an Algonquian word meaning "woman," or "pine," indicative of the sparse pine trees located on an island in the lake. Others attributed the name to a Potawatomi word derived from gihchinahquak, meaning "big tree grove," or "village," from the Winnebago word chenukra.

**DECORAH PEAK** (Trempealeau) Chief Decorah was a Winnebago chief who was friendly to the whites and aided them during the Black Hawk War. Part of his name was thought to mean "rattlesnake." While at war with the Chippewa Indians, Decorah was wounded and fled to the mountains to hide in a cave.

**KEGONSA, LAKE** (Dane) The lake was initially called First Lake by early settlers because it was the first of four lakes they passed. It was later renamed Kegonsa, which may be derived from gigosensag, a Chippewa word meaning "lake of small fishes," or "small fishes."

**KINNICKINNIC RIVER** (St. Croix) The town of River Falls was established along the river and prospered with sawmills, flour mills and planing mills using the river's water power. In 1876, the town was burned down, and in 1894 the river flooded and broke the mill dam, which destroyed the mills. Kinnickinnic is a Potawatomi word referring to ceremonial tobacco made of toasted willow or sumac bark. The Indians mixed the willow/sumac with Hudson Bay plug tobacco.

This name is similar to the Kinniconick River in the state of Kentucky, which is a Shawnee word for the willow bark, also used in tobacco.

**KOSHKONONG, LAKE** (Jefferson) In 1840, the Koshkonong Prairie settlement was established along the lake, which is a Potawatomi expression for "place of the hog," or "what he kept for himself." In the Chippewa language, Koshkonong was interpreted as "shut in," or "where there is a heavy fog" (which hung over the lake). French trader Thiebeau claimed Koshkonong was from the Winnebago language meaning "the place where we shave," because after returning from their trading ventures he and his friends would come to the lake to shave.

**MANITOWISH RIVER** (Vilas)   Part of the river was once a fur-trade route. During the 1880s, timber companies moved in with their sawmills. The logs were floated down the Manitowish to their destinations. Manitowish is a Chippewa word meaning "evil spirit," because the Indians believed an evil being lived in the river. It flows 45 miles to enter the Flambeau River.

**MARINUKA LAKE** (Trempealeau) This lake was named for Chief Decorah's granddaughter, Marinuka Nounko (origin unknown). She died in 1884 and was buried at Arctic Springs along the lake's shore. The town of Galesville was established about 1869 along the lake with the arrival of circuit rider Reverend D.O. Van Slyke, who firmly believed this place was the biblical Garden of Eden.

**MENDOTA, LAKE** (Dane)   Before white settlement the lake was home to the Winnebago Indians. Fur traders later established their trading posts along the lake's shores to conduct trade with the Indians. Mendota may be from the Winnebago expression wonkshekhomikla, for "where the man lies." In the Potawatomi language it means "snake maker," derived from mantoka, and may have indicated the snakes in the region. Another authority believes the lake was named by surveyor Frank Hudson in 1849 who gave it a Sioux name for "the mouth of the river."

**MENOMONEE RIVER** (Washington) Menomonee was the name of an Indian tribe who lived in the area and were visited by Nicolet in 1634. The name means "wild rice people." This tribe was generally at peace with the white men, but they disappeared from history. The river is about 25 miles long and enters the Milwaukee River.

**MILWAUKEE RIVER** (Fond du Lac) The Milwaukee flows 75 miles into Lake Michigan. During the early 1600s, there was a Potawatomi Indian village located at the mouth of the river, which was also a council meeting place for other tribes. Father Hennepin thought the name came from Millecki (or Melchi) which meant "good land." Other interpretations were "there is a good point," or "great council place." In the Sioux language, it means "firewater."

**MUSKEGO LAKE** (Waukesha)   Norwegians were early settlers at the lake during the 1830s. A Milwaukee Indian named O'nautesah was chief of his tribe who lived along the lake's shores. Muskego is a Potawatomi word for "swamp," "cranberry bog," "fishing place," or "sunfish," which were plentiful in the lake. It may also be an Ottawa word for "swamp."

**NASHOTAH LAKES**   (Waukesha)

Nashotah is an Algonquian word meaning "twins" or "one of a pair," and was first applied to Upper and Lower Nashotah Lakes because of their shape and size. This region was first occupied by the Reverends Adams and Breck who opened the Nashotah Theological Seminary in 1842, which is the oldest Episcopal seminary in the Middle West. It was originally established to serve the Indians and settlers.

**NEBAGAMON LAKE** (Douglas) Nebagamon is a corruption of a Chippewa word meaning "watching for game at night from a boat," or "hunting of deer by canoes at night." The Chippewa Indians called the lake neebaygomowwin which means "place to still hunt deer by water." In 1899 the Hawthorne Nebagamon and Superior Railroad was established to transport logs; it operated until 1907. The railroad was owned by Lake Nebagamon Lumber Company.

**NEMAHBIN LAKE** (Waukesha) The lake was the site of the Cedarly Pastors Retreat. It is an Algonquian word meaning a type of fish (probably a trout).

**OCONOMOWOC RIVER** (Waukesha) The first white settler at the river was Charles B. Sheldon in 1837. Oconomowoc is an Algonquian word derived from coonomowauk, meaning "place where the river falls." Others believed it was derived from okonimawag, meaning "beaver dam."

**OCONTO RIVER** (Forest) The Oconto River flows more than 85 miles into Green Bay. Early missionaries named the river Lagaspardi and founded Mission St. Francis Xavier in 1669 at the mouth of the Oconto. In 1825, a fur trader named Farnsworth named it Cantone until it was changed to Oconto, a Menominee word meaning "pike place," or "place of the pickerels," derived from okontoe or oakatoe.

**OKAUCHEE LAKE** (Waukesha) The towns of Oconomowoc and Merton, and the Village of Okauchee are located along the lake. It bears a Winnebago or Potawatomi word meaning "chief is come," and designated Chief Blackhawk of the Sauk (or Sac) Indian Tribe. It was also defined as "pipe stem," and "something small."

**PECATONICA RIVER** (Iowa) The Pecatonica rises near the town of Cobb, and flows 120 miles into the state of Illinois where it joins the Rock River. The region was originally home to the Fox and Sac Indians. Some of the first settlers to arrive were Germans who came from Pennsylvania in 1827. Pecatonica may be derived from pekitanoi, meaning "muddy." It was also interpreted as "many canoes along the shore."

**PESHTIGO RIVER** (Forest) The river originates in the Nicolet National Forest and flows about 100 miles to Green Bay. Peshtigo may be a Menominee word for "snapping turtle," or "wild goose." In 1871, the great Peshtigo fire occurred with bigger casualties than the famous Chicago fire, claiming more than 1,200 lives. It was the most devastating fire in U.S. history that seared northeast Wisconsin. People fled their homes and took refuge at the Peshtigo River. Because this fire occurred at the same time as the Great Chicago Fire, it didn't receive much publicity.

**PEWAUKEE LAKE** (Waukesha) Once

the hunting ground for the Menomonee and Potawatomi Indians, the region was settled in 1843. Deacon Asa Clark purchased a quarter section of land about 1836 and established a sawmill, in addition to building a dam. George P. Peffer started a nursery and fruit farm, and went on to develop the Pewaukee Apple. Pewaukee is Algonquin for "swampy," or "lake of shells." Local folklore says a sea serpent was believed to be a frequent visitor to the lake during the 1890s.

**PUCKAWAY LAKE** (Green Lake)    The Indians were attracted to the lake because of the abundance of wild rice and fish. The lake is about 8 miles long, and bears an Algonquian name meaning "wild rice field." Another interpretation was "cat tail flag." Today, ducks still take advantage of the wild rice that grows at the lake.

**SHAWANO LAKE** (Shawano)    The Ojibwa Indians called the lake sha-wa-nah-pay-sa ("lake to the south"), from which Shawano was derived, and means "to the south." The lake served as a camp ground for the Indians where they gathered annually in the fall to harvest the wild rice. It was first named Head of the Lake.

**SHEBOYGAN RIVER** (Fond du Lac) This river is about 70 miles long. It was named for a Potawatomi Indian village called Shab-wa-wa-go-ning, which meant "rumbling waters," or "waters disappearing underground." It was also translated as "send through." The river supplied the power for operating woolen mills and sawmills.

**SISKOWIT LAKE** (Bayfield)    Timber brought settlers and logging companies in

1894, one of which was the Ashland Lumber Company. The Siskowit and Southern Railroad was built to the lake, in order to serve the timber companies. Siskowit is an Algonquian word meaning "fat lake trout."

**SUAMICO RIVER** (Brown)    The village of Little Suamico was founded during the 1870s along the river, but never grew because the Peshtigo fire destroyed all the timber residents depended on for their livelihood, and the sawmills were moved elsewhere. Suamico may be a Menominee or Potawatomi word meaning "place of the yellow beaver," or "at the beaver's tail." It was also interpreted as "yellow sand."

**WAUBESA LAKE** (Dane)    Waubesa was derived from wapishka, a Potawatomi word meaning "white foam." It also means "swan lake," from the Chippewa word wabisi. The lake was known for its ice harvesting industry until the 1920s. More than 8 million of tons of ice a year were taken from the lake and transported to meat packing plants and breweries.

**WAUPACA RIVER** (Waupaca)    This region was the camping ground for the Menominee and Chippewa Indians, until white settlement about 1849. Waupaca means "sparkling waters." Other interpreations were from waubuck-seba, meaning "clear water," or the name of Potawatomi Chief wapuke, whose name means "watching."

**WINGRA, LAKE** (Dane)    Wingra is a Winnebago word interpreted as "duck," because of the prevalence of the birds. It was also thought to mean "dead lake." The Indians called it dead lake because of the mass of water plants and rushes that grow around the swampy part of the lake. An old Indian legend says that when the last Indian left the lake, the waters would disappear. By 1832 (after the Black Hawk War) most of the Indians were gone, but the water was still here.

**WISSOTA LAKE** (Chippewa)   Located just east of Chippewa falls, this lake was formed from Chippewa River by backwater from a power dam. Wissota was de-rived from wita, which may be a Chippewa word meaning "island," since there are two large islands in the lake.

**YAHARA RIVER** (Dane)   Yahara is a Winnebago word meaning "catfish," descriptive of the abundance of that species. The river is about 45 miles long and enters the Rock River. It was first named Catfish River until the river's course was straightened in 1905.

# WYOMING

**ABSAROKA MOUNTAINS** (Fremont/ Park/Teton)   Known as the greatest slag pile on earth because of its topography, the mountains were inhabited by the Absaroka (Crow) Indians. Comprising almost 1 million acres, the mountains are part of the Absaroka-Beartooth Wilderness Area. First called Yellowstone Mountains, the name was changed to Sierra Shoshone in 1873 by Captain Jones. About 1893, the U.S. Geographic Survey renamed the feature and gave it an Absaroka word meaning "sharp people," derived from upsaraqu.

**CAMEAHWAIT LAKE**   (Fremont) The lake was named for a Shoshone Chief Cameahwait, which signifies someone not inclined to go. Clark (of Lewis and Clark) wrote that the name meant "one who never walks." When he asked the chief's name Clark was told he was chief of the tribe that "was not inclined to go." Cameahwait was the brother of Sacajawea.

**INYAN KARA MOUNTAIN** (Crook)   Located in the Black Hills region, the mountain was a landmark for explorers and settlers. The Sioux and other Indian tribes revered the mountain and left artifacts to appease their thunder gods. Inyan Kara may be a Sioux expression for "stone made." General Custer and his men went there to explore in 1874, and on July 23 Custer climbed to the top and carved his name in the rocks.

**MEETEETSE CREEK** (Park)   In 1884, a Frenchman named Victor Arland settled near the creek and founded the town of Arland. He became partners with John Corbett and together they established a trading post along the creek. When Arland began to decline in 1896, most of the people moved their buildings to Meeteetse, a Shoshone word that means "the meeting place," or "nearby place."

**NIOBRARA RIVER** (Niobrara)   The majority of the Niobrara flows through the state of Nebraska, but has its origins in the high plains of Wyoming and flows 430 miles to join the Missouri River. Niobrara is a Ponca or Omaha word meaning "spreading (or running) water," or "water that runs," in the Sioux language. The Ponca Indians ceded all their land in 1858 except for a portion along the river. But in a treaty of 1868, the U.S. Government gave that parcel to the Sioux in error, causing war between the tribes. As a result, the Ponca Tribe was removed to Oklahoma.

**PINGORA PEAK** (Fremont)   Located in the Wind River Mountain Range, Pingora bears a Shoshone expression meaning "high (or rocky) "peak." In 1940, O.H. Bonney, Frank Garnick and Notsie Garnick climbed the mountain and named it. Pingora Peak rises about 11,499 feet.

**POPO AGIE RIVER** (Fremont)   Between 1824-1840, the river was a rendezvous for trappers and traders. The Popo Agie has its origins in the Shoshone National Forest and flows 30 miles to enter the Wind River near the town of Riverton. It bears a Crow word meaning "head water." Another interpretation was "wild rye grass," for the plant the Indians used to build their wikieups.

**TAMINAH LAKE** (Teton)   Located near Jackson Hole, Taminah is a glacier lake, and bears a Shoshone word meaning "spring," indicative of the weather that is spring-like when it is summer or fall below the timberline.

**TEEWINOT MOUNTAIN** (Teton) Teewinot is a Shoshone word meaning "many pinnacles," and was once applied to the entire Teton Range. In 1929, F. Fryxell and Phil Smith climbed and named the mountain, which is about 12,325 feet high.

**TOGWOTEE PASS** (Teton)   In 1914, the Wyoming Tie and Timber Company cut railroad ties at the pass for use on the Chicago and Northwestern Railroad. Togwotee is a Shoshone expression meaning "goes (or "sees") from this place," or "shoots with a spear." It was also thought to be for Togwetee, a Sheepeater Indian and sub-chief, whose name meant "lance thrower," or "exactly there," descriptive of an Indian game. One warrior would throw his lance, and the others would see how close they could come to the first one.

**TOSI CREEK** (Sublette)   First named Little Gros Ventre Creek, the named was changed to Tosi, a Shoshone medicine man (origin unknown), who was a friend of writer Owen Wister. The Gros Ventre Lodge was opened in 1897 near the creek and was one of the first dude ranches in the state.

**WYOMING RANGE** (Lincoln)   This mountain range stretches about 80 miles. The highest elevation is Wyoming Peak at 11,363 feet, which was first climbed by John C. Fremont in 1842, although some believe it was first scaled by a member of the Hayden Survey in 1877. Wyoming is a transfer name from Pennsylvania, and is a Lenape expression for "large plains," or "large meadows," derived from maugh-wauwame.

# *Notes*

1. John Muir. *Travels in Alaska*. Penguin Books, 1993, p. 199.

2. *Off the Beaten Path*. Pleasantville: Reader's Digest, 2003. p. 44.

3. Erwin Gudde. *California Place Names*. University of California Press, 1962, p. 318.

4. Arps, Louisa W., and Elinor E. Kingery. *High County Names*. Denver: Colorado Mountain Club, 1966. p. 17.

5. Martin Stadius. *Dreamers: On the Trail of the Nez Perce*. Caldwell: Caxton Press, 1999, pp. 81, 85.

6. Aubrey L. Haines. *Historic Sites Along the Oregon Trail*. Patric Press, MO, 1981, p. 35

7. Thomas, Bill. *American Rivers: A Natural History*. New York: W.W. Norton, 1978, p. 210.

8. Federal Writers' Project. *Maine: A Guide "Down East."* Boston: Houghton Mifflin Co., 1937, p. 313.

9. Howry Esplanade. *Pennsylvania Place Names*. Pennsylvnia State College, 1925, p. 65.

10. Peattie, Roderick. *The Great Smokies and the Blue Ridge*. New York: Vanguard Press, 1943. p. 67.

11. Federal Writers' Project. *Virginia: A Guide to the Old Dominion*. New York: Oxford University Press, 1940, p. 501.

12. Erskine Wood. *Days with Chief Joseph: Diary and Recollections*. Portland: Oregon Historical Society. 1970, p. 1.

# Bibliography

## Alabama

Brewer, Rev. George E. "History of Coosa County, Alabama." *Alabama Historical Quarterly*. Vol. 4, Nos. 1 and 2. Spring/Summer, 1942.

Federal Writers' Project. *Alabama: A Guide to the Deep South*. New York: Richard R. Smith, Pub., 1941.

Foscue, Virginia O. *Place Names in Alabama*. Tuscaloosa: University of Alabama Press, 1989.

Jemison, Grace. *Historic Tales of Talledega*. Montgomery: Paragon Press, 1959.

McMillan, James B. (ed.). *Dictionary of Place Names in Talladega County, Alabama*. Tuscaloosa: James B. McMillan, 1985.

Read, William A. *Indian Place-Names in Alabama*. Tuscaloosa: University of Alabama Press, 1984.

## Alaska

Brown, Dale. *Wild Alaska*. New York: Time, Inc. 5th Printing, 1976.

Calasanctius, Sister Mary Joseph. *Voice of Alaska: A Missioner's Memories*. Quebec: Sisters of St. Ann Press, 1935.

Eppenbach, Sarah. *Alaska's Southeast*. Seattle: Pacific Search Press, 1983.

Federal Writers' Project. *Alaska: Last American Frontier*. New York: Macmillan Co., 1943.

Krause, Aurel. *The Tlingit Indians*. Seattle: University of Washington Press, 1956.

"Lake Clark-Iliamna Country." *Alaska Geographic Quarterly*. Vol. 8, No. 3. 1981: 136, 142.

Muir, John. *Travels in Alaska*. New York: Penguin Books, 1993.

Orth, Donald J. *Dictionary of Alaska Place Names*. Washington, D.C.: U.S. Government Printing Office, 1967.

Phillips, James W. *Alaska-Yukon Place Names*. Seattle: University of Washington Press, 1973.

Simmerman, Nancy L. *Wild Alaska*. Seattle: The Mountaineers, 1999.

*United States Coast Pilot: Alaska: Part I, Dixon Entrance to Yakutat Bay*. Washington, D.C.: U.S. Government Printing Office, 1932.

*United States Coast Pilot 8: Pacific Coast, Alaska*. Washington, D.C.: U.S. Government Printing Office, 1962.

Wayburn, Peggy. *Adventuring in Alaska*. San Francisco: Sierra Club Books, 1994.

## Arizona

Aleshire, Peter. "Adventure Backroad." *Arizona Highways*. April, 2003.

Barnes, Will C. *Arizona Place Names*. Introduction by Bernard L. Fontana. Tucson: University of Arizona Press, 1988.

Casey, Robert L. *Journey to the High Southwest.* Seattle: Pacific Search Press, 1983.

Cook, James E. *Arizona Landmarks.* Phoenix: Arizona Highways, 1985.

Dagget, Dan. *Arizona Rivers and Streams Guide.* Phoenix: Arizona State Parks, 1989.

Federal Writers' Project. *Arizona: A State Guide.* New York: Hastings House, 1940.

Fireman, Bert M. *Arizona: Historic Land.* New York: Alfred A. Knopf, 1982.

Fransworth, Janet W. "Ranch Life: Wannabes Saddle Up for Adventure in the Hassayampa River Canyon Wilderness." *Arizona Highways,* Sept., 2001.

Granger, Byrd H. *Arizona's Names (X Marks the Place).* Tucson: Falconer Pub., 1983.

Hegemann, Elizabeth C. *Navajo Trading Days.* Albuquerque: University of New Mexico Press, 1963.

Kaplan, Robert D. *An Empire Wilderness: Travels Into America's Future.* New York: Random House, 1998.

Kosik, Fran. *Native Roads.* Flagstaff: Creative Solutions Pub., 1996.

Mays, Buddy. *Indian Villages of the Southwest: A Practical Guide to the Pueblo Indian Villages of New Mexico and Arizona.* San Francisco: Chronicle Books, 1985.

Newton, Charles H. *Place Names in Arizona.* Phoenix: Primer Pub., 1954.

Sheridan, Thomas E. *Arizona: A History.* Tucson: University of Arizona Press, 1995.

Trimble, Marshall. *Roadside History of Arizona.* Missoula, MT: Mountain Press, 1986.

## Arkansas

*Biographical and Historical Memoirs of Southern Arkansas, Comprising a Condensed History of the State, Etc.* Chicago: Goodspeed Pub. Co., 1890.

Deane, Ernie. *Arkansas Place Names.* Branson, MO: Ozarks Mountaineer, 1986.

Federal Writers' Project. *Arkansas: A Guide to the State.* New York: Hastings House, 1941.

## California

Bahti, Tom. *Southwest Indian Tribes.* Flagstaff: KC Pub., 1973.

Blevins, Winfred. *Roadside History of Yellowstone Park.* Missoula: Mountain Press, 1989.

*California Pioneer Register and Index: 1542–1848.* Baltimore: Regional Pub., 1964.

Chittenden, Hiram M. *Yellowstone National Park: Historical and Descriptive.* Stanford: Stanford University Press, 1954.

*Encyclopedia of California.* New York: Somerset Pub. 2nd Edition, 1944.

Farquhar, Francis. *History of the Sierra Nevada.* Berkeley: University of California, 1966.

Federal Writers' Project. *California: A Guide to the Golden State.* New York: Hastings House. 4th Printing, 1945.

Fradkin, Phillip. *Seven States of California.* Berkeley: University of California, 1977.

Gudde, Erwin G. *California Gold Camps.* Berkeley: University of California Press, 1975.

_____, *1000 California Place Names.* Berkeley: University of California Press, 1959.

Hall-Patton, Mark P. *Memories of the Land: Placenames of San Luis Obispo County.* San Luis Obispo: EZ Nature Books, 1994.

Hanna, Phil T. *The Dictionary of California Land Names.* Los Angeles: Automobile Club of Southern California, 1946.

Heig, Adair. *History of Petaluma: A California River Town.* Petaluma: Scottwall Assoc., 1982

*History of Amador County, California.* Oakland: Thompson & West., 1881.

*History of Siskiyou County, California.* Oakland: D.J. Stewart & Co., 1881.

Holsinger, Rosemary. *Shasta Indian Tales.* Happy Camp, CA: Naturegraph Pub., 1982.

James, George Wharton. *California: Romantic and Beautiful.* Boston: Page Co., 1914.

Kroeber, Alfred L. *California Place Names of Indian Origin.* Berkeley: University of California Press, 1916.

Lang, Julian (ed.). *Ararapikva: Creation Stories of the People.* Berkeley: Heydey Books, 1994.

Mason, David. "Matilija Hot Springs Has

Colorful History." *The Ventura Free Press.* May, 1904.

Meschery, Joanne. *Truckee: An Illustrated History of the Town and Its Surroundings.* Truckee: Rocking Stone Press, 1978.

Muir, John. *The Mountains of California.* San Francisco: Sierra Club Books, 1988.

Orr, Elizabeth L., and William N. Orr. *Rivers of the West: A Guide to the Geology and History.* Eugene, OR: Eagle Web Press, 1985.

Parks, Annette W. *ghawala li, "Water Coming Down Place, A History of Gualala, Mendicino County, California.* Ukiah: Freshcut Press, 1980.

Pittman, Ruth. *Roadside History of California.* Missoula, MT: Mountain Press, 1995.

Sanchez, Nellie Van De Grift. *Spanish and Indian Place Names of California.* San Francisco: A. M. Robertson, 1930.


# Colorado

Arps, Louisa W., and Elinor E. Kingery. *High Country Names.* Boulder: Johnson Books, 1994.

Benson, Maxine. *1001 Colorado Place Names.* Lawrence: University Press of Kansas, 1994.

Blecha, Arvid D. *Blecha's Colorado Place Names.* Denver: Colorado Genealogical Society, 2001.

Bright, William. *Colorado Place Names.* Boulder: Johnson Books, 1993.

Dawson, Frank. *Place Names in Colorado.* Denver: J. Frank Dawson Pub., 1954.

Federal Writers' Project. *Colorado: A Guide to the Highest State.* New York: Hastings House. 4th Printing, 1946.

_____. *Ghost Towns of Colorado.* New York: Hastings House, 1947.

Marriott, Alice. *The Ten Grandmothers.* Norman: University of Oklahoma Press, 1945.

Matthews, Carl F. *Early Days Around the Divide.* St. Louis: Sign Book Co., 1969.

McTighe, James. *Roadside History of Colorado.* Boulder: Johnson Books, 1989.

Mooney, James. *Calender History of the Kiowa Indians.* Washington, D.C.: Smithsonian Institution Press, 1895–1896.

Pohlen, Jerome. *Oddball Colorado.* Chicago: Chicago Review Press, 2002.

Powell, J.W. *The Exploration of the Colorado River and Its Canyons.* New York: Dover Pub., 1961.

Ubbelohde, Carl, Maxine Benson, and Duane A. Smith. *A Colorado History.* Boulder: Pruett Pub., 1965.

Warren, Scott S. *Exploring Colorado's Wild Areas.* Seattle: The Mountaineers, 1992.


# Connecticut

Bayles, Richard M. *History of Windham County, Connecticut,* 1889.

Beardsley, Thomas R. *Willimantic Industry and Community: The Rise and Decline of a Connecticut Textile City.* Willimantic: Windham Textile & Historical Museum, 1993.

"A Brief History of Mystic." Mystic Celebration booklet, 1976.

Federal Writers' Project. *Connecticut: A Guide to Its Roads, Lore, and People.* Boston: Houghton Mifflin, 1938.

Frank, Judith. "The Mianus River." *Link Magazine.* Mid-Winter, 1962: 12.

Hughes, Arthur H., and Morse S. Allen. *Connecticut Place Names.* Hartford: Connecticut Historical Society, 1976.

*Nipmuc Place Names of New England.* Historical Series No. 3. 1st Edition. Thompson: Nipmuc Indian Association of Connecticut, 1995.

Trumbull, J. Hammond. *Indian Names of Places Etc. and on the Borders of Connecticut.* Hartford: Press of the Case, Lockwood & Brainard Co., 1881.


# Delaware

Dunlap, A.R., and C.A. Weslager. *Indian Place-Names in Delaware.* Wilmington: Archaeological Society of Delaware, 1950.

Federal Writers' Project. *Delaware: A Guide to the First State.* New York: Viking Press, 1938.

Heck, L.W., et al. *Delaware Place Names: Geological Survey Bulletin 1245.* Washington, D.C.: U.S. Government Printing Office, 1966.

Hoffecker, Carol E. *Delaware: A Bicentennial History.* New York: Norton Pub., 1977.

Neuenschwander, John A. *The Middle Colonies and the Coming of the American Revolution.* Port Washington, New York: Kennikat Press, 1977.

# Florida

Chapel, George L. "A Brief History of the Apalachicola Area." *Apalachicola Area Historical Society.* n.d.

Federal Writers' Project. *Florida: A Guide to the Southernmost State.* New York: Oxford University Press, 1939.

Gregware, Bill, and Carol Gregware. *Guide to Lake Okeechobee Area.* Sarasota: Pineapple Press, 1997.

*History of Lake County, Florida.* Tavares: Lake County Historical Society, 2002.

"History of Weeki Wachee." *Hernando Today.* March 28, 1997: 9.

Morris, Allen. *Florida Place Names.* Sarasota: Pineapple Press, 1995.

"Steinhatchee: Brimming with History, Brimming with Fish." *Progress '89.* Feb. 24, 1989: 19.

Valentine, Doris. *Looking Back, Sumter County: A Photographic Essay.* Sumterville: Sumter County Historical Society, 1981.

Waitley, Douglas. *Roadside History of Florida.* Missoula, MT: Mountain Press, 1997.

Will, Lawrence E. *Cracker History of Okeechobee.* Palm Beach: Glades Historical Society, 1977.

# Georgia

Federal Writers' Project. Georgia: *A Guide to Its Towns and Countryside.* Atlanta: Tupper & Love, 1954.

Flanigan, James C. *History of Gwinnett County, Georgia: 1818–1943.* Vol. I. Lawrenceville: Gwinnett Historical Society, 1943.

Godley, Margaret. *Historic Tybee Island.* Savannah Beach Chamber of Commerce, 1958.

Krakow, Kenneth K. *Georgia Place Names.* Macon: Winship Press, 1975.

Rogers, Norma K. *History of Chattahoochee County, Georgia.* Columbus: Columbus Office Supply Co., 1933.

*Tallapoosa Centennial: September 2, 3, 4, 1960.* Tallapoosa Centennial Committee, 1960.

Trogdon, Kathryn C. (ed.). *The History of Stephens County, Georgia.* Toccoa Woman's Club, 1973.

# Idaho

Alt, David, and Donald W. Hyndman. *Roadside Geology of Idaho.* Missoula, MT: Mountain Press, 1989.

Barber, Floyd R., and Dan W. Martin. *Idaho in the Pacific Northwest.* Caldwell: Caxton Printers, 1956.

Boone, Lalila. *Idaho Place Names.* Moscow: University of Idaho Press, 1988.

Conley, Cort. *Idaho for the Curious.* Riggins: Backeddy Books, 1982.

Derig, Betty. *Roadside History of Idaho.* Missoula: Mountain Press, 1996.

Elsensohn, Sister M., Alfreda. *Pioneer Days in Idaho County.* Vol. 1. Cottonwood: Idaho Corporation of Benedictine Sisters, 1978.

Federal Writers' Project. *Idaho: A Guide in Word and Pictures.* Caldwell: Caxton Printers, 1937.

_____. *The Idaho Encyclopedia.* Caldwell: Caxton Printers, 1983.

Friedman, Ralph. *Tracking Down Idaho.* Caldwell: Caxton Printers, 1978.

Morgan, Clay, and Steve Mitchell. *Idaho unBound.* Ketchum: West Bound Books, 1995.

# Illinois

Adams, James N. *Illinois Place Names.* Springfield: Illinois State Historical Society, 1989.

Batemen, Newton, and Paul Selby. *Historical Encyclopedia of Illinois and History of Livingston County.* Chicago: Munsell Pub., 1909.

Beckwith, H. W. *History of Iroquois County, Together with Historic Notes on the Northwest.* Chicago: H. H. Hill and Co., 1880.

*Encyclopedia of Illinois.* New York: Somerset Publishers, 1996–1997.

Federal Writers' Project. *Illinois: A Descriptive and Historical Guide.* Chicago: A.C. McClurg & Co., 1939.

*History of Livingston County, Illinois, Containing a History of the County, Its Cities, Towns, Etc.* Chicago: Wm. Le Baron, Jr. & Co., 1878.

*History of Peoria County, Illinois, Containing a History of the County, Its Cities, towns, Etc.* Chicago: Johnson & Company, 1880.

*Past and Present of Woodford County, Illinois.* Chicago: Wm. LeBaron, Jr. & Co., 1878.

Vogel, Virgil J. *Indian Place Names in Illinois.* Springfield: Illinois State Historical Society, 1963.


# Indiana

Baker, Ronald L. *From Needmore to Prosperity: Hoosier Place Names in Folklore History.* Bloomington: Indiana University Press, 1995.

_____, and Marvin Carmony. *Indiana Place Names.* Bloomington: Indiana University Press, 1975.

Bartholomew, Henry S. *Pioneer History of Elkhart County, Indiana, with Sketches and Stories.* Goshen: Goshen Printery, 1930.

Blanchard, Charles. *Counties of Howard and Tipton, Indiana, Historical and Biographical.* Chicago: F.A. Battey & Co., 1883.

*Counties of LaGrange and Noble Indiana: Historical and Biographical.* Chicago: F.A. Battey and Co., Pub., 1882.

*Counties of White and Pulaski, Indiana.* Chicago: F.A. Battey & Co., 1883.

Federal Writers' Project. *Indiana: A Guide to the Hoosier State.* New York: Hastings House, 1941.

Hanan, John W. *LaGrange County Centennial History, 1828–1928.* LaGrange: LaGrange Pub., 1929.

*History of Huntington County, Indiana, From the Earliest Time to the Present, with Biographical Sketches, Notes, Etc.* Chicago: Brant & Fuller, 1887.

"History of Lake Maxinkuckee." Culver-Union Township Public Library vertical files.

*Howard County, Indiana Family History: 1844–1994.* Oakford: Howard County Genealogical Society, 1994.

Morris, Harvey. "Washington County Giants." *Indiana Historical Society.* Vol. 7, No. 8, 1921.

Taylor, Robert M., Jr., et al. *Indiana: A New Historical Guide.* Bloomington: Indiana Historical Society, 1989.

Weesner, Clarkson. *History of Wabash County.* Chicago: Lewis Pub., 1914.


# Iowa

Dilts, Harold, Kathleen A. Dilts, and Linda J. Dilts. *From Ackley to Zwingle: A Collection of the Origins of Iowa Place Names.* Ames: Iowa State University Press, 1993.

*Encyclopedia of Iowa.* New York: Somerset Pubs., 1995.

Federal Writers' Project. *Iowa: A Guide to the Hawkeye State.* New York: Viking Press, 1938.

Hart, William H. *History of Sac County.* Indianapolis: B.F. Bowen & Co., 1914.

Hedge, Manoah. *Past and Present of Mahaska County, Iowa.* Chicago: S.J. Clarke Pub., 1906.

*History of Jones County, Iowa, Containing a History of the County, Its Cities, Towns, Etc.* Chicago: Western Historical Co., 1879.

*History of Kossuth County.* Lake Mills: Graphic Pub., 1976.

*History of Monona County, Iowa, Containing Full-Page Portraits and Biographical Sketches of Prominent and Representative Citizens, Etc.* Chicago: National Pub. Co., 1890.

*History of Muscatine County, Iowa, Containing a History of the County, Its Cities,*

*Towns, Etc.* Chicago: Western Historical Co., 1879.

"Maquoketa, No Other Town Like It." *Explore Jackson County.* 1996: 9.

McCulla, Thomas. *History of Cherokee County, Iowa.* Vol. I. Chicago: S.J. Clarke Pub., 1914.

Vogel, Virgil J. *Iowa Place Names of Indian Origin.* Iowa City: University of Iowa Press, 1983.

## Kansas

Blackmar, Frank. W. (ed.). *A Cyclopedia of State History, Embracing Events, Institutions, Industries, Counties, Cities, towns, Prominent Persons, Etc.* Chicago: Standard Pub., 1912.

Cutler, William. *History of Kansas.* Chicago: A.T. Andreas, 1883.

Federal Writers' Project. *Kansas: A Guide to the Sunflower State.* New York: Viking Press, 1939.

*History of Neosho and Wilson Counties, Kansas, Containing Sketches of Our Pioneers, Etc.* Fort Scott: L. Wallace Duncan, 1902.

Ingalls, Sheffield. *History of Atchison County.* Lawrence: Lawrence Standard Pub., 1916.

McCoy, Sandra V., and Jan Hults. *1001 Kansas Place Names.* Lawrence: University of Kansas, 1989.

Mooney, V.P. *History of Butler County, Kansas.* Lawrence: Lawrence Standard Pub., 1916.

Rydjord, John. *Kansas Place-Names.* Norman: University of Oklahoma Press, 1979.

Tennal, Ralph. *History of Nemaha County, Kansas.* Lawrence: Lawrence Standard Pub., 1916.

Tindle, Lela J. *Wilson County, Kansas: People of the South Wind.* Dallas: Curtis Media Corp., 1988.

## Kentucky

Federal Writers' Project. *Kentucky: A Guide to the Bluegrass State.* New York: Harcourt, Brace and Co., 1939.

Rennick, Robert M. *Kentucky Place Names.* Lexington: University Press of Kentucky, 1984.

Talley, Dr. William M. "Kinniconick Creek: A Natural and Historic Treasure of Lewis County: Part I." *Lewis County Herald.* May 12, 1998.

_____. "Kinniconick Creek: A Natural and Historic Treasure of Lewis County: Part II." *Lewis County Herald.* May 19, 1998.

## Louisiana

*Amite City: 1861–1961.* Amite City Centennial Celebration, 1961.

*Bogalusa Silver Jubilee Celebration, 1914–1939.* Official Souvenir Program. Bogalusa Silver Jubilee, Inc., 1939.

Ellis, Frederick S. *St. Tammany Parish: L'Autre Cote du Lac.* Gretna: Pelican Pub., 1981.

Federal Writers' Project. *Louisiana: A Guide to the State.* New York: Hastings House, 1941.

Hymal, Diane. "Natalbany: There's No Whistle Anymore." *Gumbo Magazine.* May 31, 1987.

Leeper, Clare D. *Louisiana Places: A Collection of the Columns from the Baton Rouge Sunday Advocate, 1960–1974.* Baton Rouge: Legacy Pub., 1976.

Read, William A. "Louisiana Place-Names of Indian Origin." *University Bulletin. Baton Rouge: Louisiana State University.* Vol. XIX. Feb., 1927, No. 2.

*Tangipahoa Parish: 1869–1969.* Official Souvenir Program, 1969.

## Maine

Albert, Julie D. *Madawaska: 1869–1969.* Town of Madawaska, 1969.

Attwood, Stanley B. *The Length and Breadth of Maine.* Augusta: Kennebec Journal Print Shop, 1946.

"Bits and Pieces of Allagash History." *Allagash Historical Society*, 1976.

Bourne, Edward E. *Ancient History of Kennebunk.* 1831.

Chadbourne, Ava H. *Maine Place Names and the Peopling of Its Towns: Cumberland and Sagadahoc Counties.* Freeport: Bond Wheelwright Co., 1957.

_____. *Maine Place Names and the Peopling of Its Towns: Franklin and Androscoggin Counties.* Freeport: Bond Wheelwright Co., 1957.

_____. *Maine Place Names and the Peopling of Its Towns: Kennebec and Somerset Counties.* Freeport: Bond Wheelwright Co., 1957.

_____. *Maine Place Names and the Peopling of Its Towns: Lincoln, Waldo and Knox Counties.* Freeport: Bond Wheelwright Co., 1957.

_____. *Maine Place Names and the Peopling of Its Towns: Penobscot County.* Freeport: Bond Wheelwright Co., 1957.

_____. *Maine Place Names and the Peopling of Its Towns: Piscataquis and Aroostook Counties.* Freeport: Bond Wheelwright Co., 1957.

_____. *Maine Place Names and the Peopling of Its Towns: Washington and Hancock Counties.* Freeport: Bond Wheelwright Co., 1957.

_____. *Maine Place Names and the Peopling of Its Towns: York and Oxford Counties.* Freeport: Bond Wheelwright Co., 1957.

Eckstrom, Fannie H. *Indian Place-Names of the Penobscot Valley and the Maine Coast.* Orono: University of Maine, 1978.

Federal Writers' Project. *Maine: A Guide to Down East. Boston*: Houghton Mifflin, 1937.

*History of Penobscot County, Maine, with Illustrations and Biographical Sketches, Etc.* Cleveland: Williams, Chase & Co., 1882.

*History of York County, Maine.* Philadelphia: Everts & Peck, 1880.

Lannon, Mary Minor. *Maine Forever.* Brunswick: Maine Chapter, The Nature Conservancy, 1984.

*Long Search of the Katahdin Area.* Penobscot Times, Inc., 1979.

*Penobscot Bicentennial: 1787–1987.* Penobscot Historical Society, 1987.

Perkins, Esselyn G. *History of Ogunquit Village.* Portland: Falmouth Pub., 1951.

Rich, Louise D. *State O' Maine.* New York: Harper & Row, 1964.

Rutherford, Phillip R. *The Dictionary of Maine Place-Names.* Freeport: Bond Wheelright Co., 1970.

"Saco History." Dyer Library vertical files.

Simpson, Dorothy. *The Maine Islands in Story and Legend.* Philadelphia: J.B. Lippincott Co., 1960.

Varney, George J. *A Gazetteer of the State of Maine.* Boston: B.B. Russell, 1886.

Williamson, William D. *The History of the State of Maine; From its First Discovery (1602) to the Separation (1820),* Vol. 2. Hallowell: Glazier, Masters & Co., 1832.

# Maryland

Arnett, Earl, et al. *A New Guide to the Old Line State.* Baltimore: Johns Hopkins University Press, 1999.

Federal Writers' Project. *Maryland: A Guide to the Old Line State.* New York: Oxford University Press, 1941.

Gannett, Henry. *Gazetteer of Maryland.* Washington, D.C.: U.S. Government Printing Office, 1904

Harris, Ann P. *The Potomac Adventure.* Potomac: Jantron, Inc., 1978.

Jacob, John E., Jr. *Salisbury and Wicomico County: A Pictorial History.* Norfolk, VA: Donning Co., 1981.

Johnson, Linck C. *Thoreau's Complex Weave: The Writing of a Week on the Concord and Merrimack Rivers, with the Text of the First Draft.* Charlottesville: University Press of Virginia, 1986.

Kaminkow, Marion J. *Maryland A to Z: A Topographical Dictionary.* Baltimore: Magna Carter Book Co., 1985.

Keatley, J. Kenneth. *Place Names of the Eastern Shore of Maryland.* Queenstown: Queen Anne Press, 1987.

Kenny, Hammil. *The Placenames of Maryland, Their Origin and Meaning.* Baltimore: Maryland Historical Society, 1984.

Rountree, Helen C., and Thomas E. Davidson. *Eastern Shore Indians of Virginia and Maryland.* Charlottesville: University Press of Virginia, 1997.

Truitt, Dr. Reginald V., and Dr. Millard G. Les Callette. *Worcester County, Maryland's Arcadia.* Snow Hill: Worcester County Historical Society, 1977.

## Massachusetts

Federal Writers' Project. *Massachusetts: A Guide to Its Places and People.* Boston: Houghton Mifflin Co., 1937.

_____. *The Origin of Massachusetts Place Names of the State, Counties, Cities, and Towns.* New York: Harian Pub., 1941.

Lossing, Benson J. *Pictorial Field Book of the Revolution.* Vol. I. New York, 1850.

Nason, Elias. *A Gazetteer of Massachusetts.* Boston: B. B. Russell, 1874.

Sheldon, G. *A History of Deerfield, Massachusetts* (facsimile of 1895-96 edition), Somersworth: New Hampshire Pub., 1972.

Todd, Charles B. *In Olde Massachusetts, Sketches of Old Times and Places During the Early Days of the Commonwealth.* New York: The Grafton Press, 1907.

## Michigan

*Encyclopedia of Michigan.* New York: Somerset Pubs., 1981.

Federal Writers' Project. *Michigan: A Guide to the Wolverine State.* New York: Oxford University Press, 1941.

*History of Manistee County, Michigan, with Illustrations and Biographical Sketches of Some of Its Prominent Men and Pioneers.* Chicago: H.R. Page & Co., 1882.

*History of the Upper Peninsula of Michigan.* Chicago: Western Historical Co., 1883.

Romig, Walter. *Michigan Place Names.* Detroit: Wayne State University, 1986.

*The Traverse Region, Historical and Descriptive, with Illustrations of Scenery.* Chicago: H.R. Page & Co., 1884.

## Minnesota

Blegen, Theodore C. *Minnesota: A History of the State.* Minneapolis: University of Minnesota Press, 1963.

Federal Writers' Project. *The WPA Guide to Minnesota.* St. Paul: Minnesota Historical Society Press, 1985.

Jones, Thelma. *Once Upon a Lake: A History of Lake Minnetonka and Its People.* Minneapolis: Ross and Haines, 1969.

Rose, Arthur P. *An Illustrated History of the Counties of Rock and Pipestone Counties.* Luverne: Northern Minnesota Pub. Co., 1911.

Rottsolk, James E. *Pines, Mines, and Lakes — The Story of Itasca County Minnesota.* Grand Rapids: Itasca County Historical Society, 1960.

Upham, Warren. *Minnesota Geographic Names.* St. Paul: Minnesota Historical Society, 1969.

## Mississippi

Brieger, James F. *Hometown Mississippi.* Jackson: Town Square Books, 1997.

Federal Writers' Project. *Mississippi: A Guide to the Magnolia State.* New York: Viking Press, 1938.

Haley, William. "History of Copiah: Recollection of an Old Citizen." Mississippi Democrat. August 12, 1876.

Higginbotham, Jay. *Pascagoula: Singing River City.* Mobile: Gill Press, 1967.

Walker, Durr., Jr. *Lincoln County, Mississippi: A Pictorial History.* Norfolk, VA: Donning Co. Pub., 1998.

Wayman, Norbury L. *Life on the River: A Pictorial History of the Mississippi, the Missouri, and the Western River System.* New York: Bonanza Books, 1962.

"Yazoo — What Does It Mean." Yazoo City Public Library vertical files.

## Missouri

Cramer, Rose. F. *Wayne County, Missouri.* Cape Girardeau: Ramfre Press, 1972.

Federal Writers' Project. *Missouri: A Guide to the "Show Me" State.* New York: Duell, Sloan and Pearce, 1941.

McMillen, Margot F. *A to Z Missouri: The Dictionary of Missouri Place Names.* Columbia: Pebble Pub., 1996.

Ramsey, Robert L. *Our Storehouse of Missouri Place Names.* Columbia: University of Missouri, 1952.

Watters, George F. *History of Webster County, 1855–1955.* Springfield: George F. Watters, 1955.

## Montana

Cheney, Roberta C. *Names on the Face of Montana: The Story of Montana's Place Names.* Missoula: University of Montana, 1971.

Johnson, Olga W. *Flathead and Kootenay: The Rivers, the Tribes and the Region's Traders.* Glendale, CA: Arthur H. Clark Co., 1969.

Merrill, Andrea, and Judy Jacobson. *Montana Almanac.* Helena: Falcon Press, 1997.

VanWest, Carroll. *A Traveler's Companion to Montana History.* Helena: Montana Historical Society, 1986.

Wright, John B. *Montana Places: Exploring Big Sky Country.* Mesilla: New Mexico Geographical Society, 2000.

## Nebraska

Butcher, Solomon. *Pioneer History of Custer County, Nebraska.* Denver, Colorado: Sage Books, 1965.

Federal Writers' Project. *Nebraska: A Guide to the Cornhusker State.* New York: Viking Press, 1939.

Fitzpatrick, Lilian L. *Nebraska Place-Names.* Lincoln: University of Nebraska Press, 1960.

Gaston, William. *History of Custer County, Nebraska.* Lincoln: Western Pub. & Engraving Co., 1919.

*History of the State of Nebraska.* Chicago: Western Historical Co., 1882.

Moulton, Candy. *Roadside History of Nebraska.* Missoula, MT: Mountain Press, 1997.

Perkey, Elton A. *Perkey's Nebraska Place-Names.* Lincoln: Nebraska State Historical Society, 1995.

## Nevada

Carlson, Helen S. *Nevada Place Names: A Geographical Dictionary.* Reno: University of Nevada Press, 1974.

Elliott, Russell R. *History of Nevada.* Reno: University of Nebraska Press, 1987.

Federal Writers' Project. *Nevada: A Guide to the Silver State.* Portland: Binfords & Mort, 1940.

_____. *Origin of Place Names: Nevada.* Reno: Nevada State Dept. of Highways and State Dept. of Education, 1941.

Hall, Shawn. *Romancing Nevada's Past.* Reno: University of Nevada, 1994.

Hulse, James W. *The Silver State.* Reno: University of Nevada, 1998.

Leigh, Rufus W. *Nevada Place Names: Their Origin and Significance.* Salt Lake City: Deseret Press, 1964.

Moreno, Richard. *Roadside History of Nevada.* Missoula, MT: Mountain Press, 2000.

Toll, David W. *The Complete Nevada Traveler: A Guide to the State.* Reno: University of Nevada Press, 1976.

## New Hampshire

Bartlett, John H. *The Story of Sunapee.* Washington. D.C.: Byron S. Adams, 1941.

"Chocorua and His Mountain." *Weirs Times.* Vol. 5, No. 52. Dec. 26, 1996.

Federal Writers' Project. *New Hampshire: A Guide to the Granite State.* Boston: Houghton Mifflin, 1938

Hayward, John. *A Gazetteer of New Hampshire.* Boston: John P. Jewett, 1849 (facsimile, Heritage Press, 1993).

Merrill, Eliphalet, and Phinehas Merril. *Gazetteer of the State of New Hampshire.* Exeter: C. Norris & Co., 1817.

Scales, John. *History of Strafford County, New*

*Hampshire, and Representative Citizens.* Chicago: Richmond-Arnold Pub., 1914.

## New Jersey

Becker, Donald W. *Indian Place-Names in New Jersey.* Cedar Grove: Phillips-Campbell Pub., 1964.

Bisbee, Henry H. *Sign Posts: Place Names and History of Burlington County, New Jersey.* Willingboro: Alexia Press, 1971.

Edwards, Carl I. *Pequannock Township: 1740–1956, A Town's Growth in Words and Pictures.* Pequannock Township: Carlton & Smith Print Co., 1956.

Federal Writers' Project. *New Jersey: A Guide to Its Present and Past.* New York: Hastings House, 1939.

Kraft, Herbert C. *The Lenape or Delaware Indians.* South Orange: Seton Hall University Museum, 1996.

"New Jersey Historic Sites Inventory." Prepared by Acroterion, Historic Preservation Consultants. Morris County Heritage Commission, 1987.

Orcutt, Samuel. *The History of the Old Town of Stratford and the City of Bridgeport, Connecticut.* New Haven: Press of Tuttle, Morehouse & Taylor, 1886.

## New Mexico

Casey, Robert L. *Journey to the High Southwest.* Seattle: Pacific Search Press, 1983.

Chronic, Halka. *Roadside Geology of New Mexico.* Missoula, MT: Mountain Press, 1987.

Clark, Mary Grooms. *A History of New Mexico: A Mark of Time.* Canyon, TX: Staked Plains Press, 1983.

Dutton, Bertha. *Indians of the American Southwest.* Englewood Cliffs: Prentice-Hall, Inc., 1975.

Federal Writers' Project. *New Mexico: A Guide to the Colorful State.* New York: Hastings House, 1940.

Fugate, Francis L., and Roberta B. Fugate. *Roadside History of New Mexico.* Missoula, MT: Mountain Press, 1989.

Gregg, Andrew. *New Mexico in the 19th Century.* Albuquerque: University of New Mexico, 1968.

Hinshaw, Gil. *Tucumcari: Gateway to the West.* Hobbs: Gil Hinshaw, 1997.

Julyan, Robert. *Place Names of New Mexico.* Albuquerque: University of New Mexico. 4th Printing, 1998.

Kosik, Fran. *Native Roads.* Flagstaff: Creative Solutions Pub., 1996.

Ludmer, Larry H. *New Mexico Guide: Be a Traveler, Not a Tourist.* Cold Spring Harbor, NY: Open Road Pub., 1999.

Mays, Buddy. *Indian Villages of the Southwest: A Practical Guide to the Pueblo Indian Villages of New Mexico and Arizona.* San Francisco: Chronicle Books, 1985.

Pearce, T. M. *New Mexico Place Names: A Geographical Dictionary.* Albuquerque: University of New Mexico Press, 1965.

Poling-Kempes, Lesley. *Valley of Shining Stone: The Story of Abiquiu.* Tucson: University of Arizona Press, 1997.

USDA Forest Service. General Technical Report, RMRS-GTR-5. 1998.

Whittington, Debra A. *In the Shadow of the Mountain: Living in Tucumcari,* Amarillo, Texas: Copperleaf Press, 1997.

## New York

Beauchamp, William M. *Aboriginal Place Names of New York.* Detroit: Grand River Books, 1971.

Child, Hamilton. *Gazetteer and Business Directory for Rensselaer County, N.Y.* New York: Journal Office, 1870.

Conover, George S., and Lewis C. Aldrich. *History of Ontario County, New York.* Syracuse: D. Mason & Co., 1893.

Federal Writers Project. *New York: A Guide to the Empire State.* New York: Oxford University Press, 1940.

French, J.H. *Gazetteer of the State of New York, Embracing a Comprehensive View of the Geography, Etc.* Syracuse: R.P. Smith, 1860.

Gordon, Thomas. *Gazetteer of the State of New York.* Philadelphia: T.K. & P.G. Collins Printers, 1836.

Greene, Nelson. *The Old Mohawk Turnpike Book*. Fort Plain: Press of Journal & Courier, 1924.

Herrick, Margaret. *Early Settlements in Dutchess County*, NY. Rhinebeck: Kinship, 1994.

*History of Montgomery and Fulton Counties, N.Y., with Illustrations Descriptive of Scenery, Private Residences, Public Buildings, Fine Blocks, Etc.* New York: F.W. Beers & Co. 1878.

Lossing, Benson. *Pictorial Field Book of the Revolution*. Vol. I, 1850.

Reid, Max. *The Mohawk Valley Its Legends and its History*: Harrison, New York, 1979.

Smith, Philip H. *General History of Duchess County: 1609–1876*. Pawling: Philip H. Smith, 1877.

Strong, John A. *The Algonquian Peoples of Long Island from Earliest Times to 1900*. Interlaken: Empire State Books, 1997.

Sullivan, Dr. James. *The History of New York State*. New York: Lewis Historical Pub., 1927.

Tooker, William W. *The Indian Place-Names on Long Island and Islands Adjacent, with Their Probable Significations*. New York: G.P. Putnam's Sons, 1911.

Wyld, Lionel D. *Canastota and Chittenango: Two Historic Canal Towns*. Charleston, South Carolina: Arcadia Pub., 1998.


# North Carolina

Federal Writers' Project. *North Carolina: A Guide to the Old North State*. Chapel Hill: University of North Carolina Press, 1939.

Payne, Roger L. *Place Names of the Outer Banks*. Washington: Thomas A. Williams, Pub., 1985.

Plemmons, Jan C. *Treasures of Toxaway*, Jacksonville, Florida: J.C. Plemmons, 1984.

Powell, William S. *The North Carolina Gazetteer: A Dictionary of Tar Heel Places*. Chapel Hill: University of North Carolina Press, 1968.

Preslar, Charles J., Jr. *A History of Catawba County*, Salisbury: Rowan Printing, 1954.

Sigalas, Mike. *North Carolina*. Emeryville, CA: Avalon Travel Pub., 2003.


# North Dakota

Federal Writers' Project. *North Dakota: A Guide to the Northern Prairie State*. New York: Oxford University Press, 1950.

Wick, Douglas A. *North Dakota Place Names*. Fargo: Prairie House, 1989.

Williams, Mary Ann B. *Origins of North Dakota Place Names*. Bismarck: Bismarck Tribune, 1966.


# Ohio

Federal Writer's Project. *The Ohio Guide*. New York: Oxford University Press, 1940.

Hill, Norman Newell, Jr. *History of Knox County, Ohio. Its Past And Present, Containing A Condensed, Comprehensive History, Etc.* Mt. Vernon, OH: A.A. Graham & Co., 1881.

Hurt, R. Douglas. *The Ohio Frontier: Crucible of the Old Northwest, 1720–1830*. Bloomington: Indiana University Press, 1996.

Large, Moina W. *History of Ashtabula County, Ohio*. Vol. I. Topeka: Historical Pub. Co., 1924.

Miller, Larry L. *Ohio Place Names*. Bloomington: Indiana University Press, 1996.

Peeke, Hewson. *A Standard History of Erie County, Ohio*. New York: Lewis Pub. Co., 1916.

Tontogany Times, *Story of Tontogany, Ohio: 1875–1975*. Tontogany History Committee, 1975.

Williams, William W. *History of Ashtabula County, Ohio*. Philadelphia: Williams Bros., 1878.


# Oklahoma

"Chilocco Indian School." *Arkansas City Traveler*. August 23, 1882.

Ellis, Doris E (comp.). *Choctaw, Oklahoma and Eastern Oklahoma County: A History, A Centennial Celebration of People,*

*Places, and Times: 1893–1993.* Harrah: Eagle Printing, 1993.

Federal Writers' Project. *The WPA Guide to 1930s Oklahoma.* Lawrence: University Press of Kansas, 1986.

Fugate, Francis L., and Roberta B. Fugate. *Roadside History of Oklahoma.* Missoula, MT: Mountain Press, 1991.

Gibson, Arrell M. *Oklahoma: A History of Five Centuries.* Norman: University of Oklahoma Press, 1965.

Gideon, D.C. *Indian Territory, Descriptive Biographical and Genealogical, Including the Landed Estates, County Seats, Etc.* New York: Lewis Pub., 1901.

Gould, Charles N. *Oklahoma Place Names.* Norman: University of Oklahoma Press, 1933.

Peck, Henry. *Proud Heritage of LeFlore County.* Muscogee: Hoffman Printing, 1967.

Shirk, George H. *Oklahoma Place Names.* Norman: University of Oklahoma, 1965.

# Oregon

Beckham, Stephen D. *Land of the Umpqua: A History of Douglas County, Oregon.* Roseburg: Douglas County Commissioners, 1986.

Catholic Encyclopedia. "Siletz Indians." Vol. 12. Robert Appleton Co., 1912. 791–792.

"Come to the Molalla River." Molalla Area Historical Society. n.d.

Federal Writers' Project. *Oregon: End of the Trail.* Portland: Binfords & Mort, 1940.

Gaston, Joseph. *Centennial History of Oregon.* Chicago: S.J. Clark. Pub., 1912.

Hays, Marjorie H. *The Land That Kept Its Promise: A History of South Lincoln County.* Newport: Lincoln County Historical Society, 1976.

LaLande, Jeff. *From Abbott Butte to Zimmerman Burn: A Place-Name History and Gazetteer of the Rogue River National Forest.* Medford: U.S. Forest Service, Pacific Northwest Region, 2001.

McArthur, Lewis L. *Oregon Geographic Names.* Portland: Binfords & Mort, 1944.

Rock, Alexandria. *Short History of the Little Nestucca River Valley.* Unpublished manuscript. Tillamook, 1949.

Wuerthner, George. *Oregon Mountain Ranges.* Helena: American Geographic Pub., 1987.

# Pennsylvania

Battle, J.A. *History of Bucks County, Pennsylvania, On Account of Its original Exploration.* Philadelphia: A Warner & Co., 1887.

Battle, J. H. *The History of Columbia and Montour Counties, Pennsylvania.* Chicago: A. Warner & Co., 1887.

Bradsby, H.C. *History of Bradford County, Pennsylvania, with Biographical Selections.* Chicago: S.B. Nelson & Co., 1891.

Brenckman, Frederick. *History of Carbon County, Pennsylvania, Also Containing a Separate Account of the Several Boroughs and Townships in the County.* Harrisburg: J.J. Nungessen, 1913.

Davis, W.W.H. *History of Bucks County, Pennsylvania, From the Discovery of the Delaware to the Present Time.* Doylestown: Democrat Book & Job Office Printing, 1876.

Donehoo. Dr. George P. *A History of the Indian Villages and Place Names in Pennsylvania.* Harrisburg: Telegraph Press, 1928.

Ellis, F. *History of Northampton County, Pennsylvania.* Philadelphia: P. Fritts, 1877.

Espenshade, Howry. *Pennsylvania Place Names.* State College: Pennsylvania State College, 1925.

Federal Writers' Project. *Pennsylvania: A Guide to the Keystone State.* New York: Oxford University Press. 3rd Printing, 1947.

*History of Lycoming County.* Philadelphia: J.B. Lippincott & Co., 1876

*History of Monroe County, Pennsylvania: 1725–1976.* Stroudsburg: Bicentennial Project of the Pocono Hospital Auxiliary, 1976.

Jones, Robert J. *Place Names of Monroe County, Pennsylvania.* Apollo: Closson Press, 1993.

*Juniata: A County for All Seasons: Sesquicentennial Year.* Mifflintown: Juniata County Historical Society, 1981.

Mathews, Alfred. *History of Wayne, Pike and Monroe Counties, Pennsylvania.* Philadelphia: R.T. Peck & Co., 1886.

Stewart, D.J. (ed.). *History of Lycoming County.* Philadelphia: J.B. Lippincott & Co., 1876.

## Rhode Island

Boucher, Susan M. *The History of Pawtucket: 1935–1986.* Pawtucket Public Library & Pawtucket Centennial Committee, 1986.

Cole, J.R. *History of Washington and Kent Counties.* New York: W.W. Preston & Co., 1889.

Douglas-Lithgow, R.A. *Native American Place Names of Rhode Island.* Bedford, MA: Applewood Books, 1909.

Federal Writers' Project. *Rhode Island: A Guide to the Smallest State.* Boston: Houghton Mifflin, 1937.

*History of Rhode Island: 1636–1878.* Philadelphia: Hoag. Wade & Co., 1878.

*History of the state of Rhode Island and Providence Plantations: Biographical.* NY: The American Historical Society, 1920

## South Carolina

Brown, Douglas S. *The Catawba Indians: The People of the River.* Columbia: University of South Carolina, 1966.

Federal Writers' Project. *Palmetto Place Names.* Columbia: Sloan Printing, 1941.

_____. *South Carolina: A Guide to the Palmetto State.* New York: Oxford University Press. 3rd Printing, 1946.

Neuffer, Claude H. (ed.). *Names in South Carolina. Vols. I–XII. 1954–1965.* Columbia: University of South Carolina, 1965.

Pluckette, Clara C., and Clara Childs Mackenzie. *Edisto: A Sea Island Principality.* Cleveland. Ohio: Seaforth Pub., 1978.

## South Dakota

Federal Writers' Project. *A South Dakota Guide.* Pierre: State Pub. Co., 1938.

_____. *South Dakota Place Names.* Vermillion: University of South Dakota, 1941.

Hasselstrom, Linda. *Roadside History of South Dakota.* Missoula, MT: Mountain Press, 1994.

Snever, Virginia Driving Hawk. *Dakota's Heritage: A Compilation of Indian Place Names in South Dakota.* Sioux Falls: Brevet Press, 1973.

Thompson, E. L. (ed.). *75 Years of Sully County History: 1883–1958.* Onida: Onida Watchman, 1958.

## Tennessee

Federal Writers' Project. *Tennessee: A Guide to the State.* New York: Hastings House, 1949.

Livingood, James W. *A History of Hamilton County, Tennessee.* Memphis: Memphis State University Press, 1981.

Miller, Larry L. *Tennessee Place Names.* Bloomington: Indiana University Press, 2001.

## Texas

Bradfield, Bill, and Clare Bradfield. *Muleshoe and More: The Remarkable Stories Behind the Naming of Texas Towns.* Houston: Gulf Pub., 1999.

Federal Writers' Project. *Texas: A Guide to the Lone Star State.* New York: Hastings House, 1940.

*Handbook of Texas.* Vol. II. Austin: Texas State Historical Association, 1952.

*Memorial and Biographical History of Navarro, Henderson, Anderson, Limestone, Freestone and Leon Counties, Texas.* Chicago: Lewis Pub., 1893.

Metz, Leon C. *Roadside History of Texas.* Missoula, MT: Mountain Press, 1994.

Tarpley, Fred. *1001 Texas Place Names.* Austin: University of Texas Press, 1980.

# Utah

Allred, Mildred M. *History of Tooele County*. Salt Lake City: Tooele Company, Daughters of Utah Pioneers, 1961.

Bancroft, Hubert H. *History of Utah*. San Francisco: The History Co., 1890.

Bennett, Cynthia L. *Roadside History of Utah*. Missoula, MT: Mountain Press, 1999.

Federal Writers' Project. *Utah: A Guide to the State*. New York: Hastings House, 1941.

*Kane County History*. Daughters of Utah Pioneers. Utah Printing Co., 1960.

Leigh, Rufus W. *Five Hundred Utah Place Names: Their Origin and Significance*. Salt Lake City: Deseret News Press, 1961.

Toya, Pia. *A Goshute Indian Legend. The Confederated Tribes of the Goshute*. Salt Lake City: University of Utah Press, 2000.

Uintah County Company, *Builders of Uintah: A Centennial History of Uintah County, 1872–1947*. Daughters of Utah Pioneers, Uintah County. Springville: Art City Pub. Co., 1947.

Van Cott, John W. *Utah Place Names*. Salt Lake City: University of Utah Press, 1990.


# Vermont

Federal Writers' Project. *Vermont: A Guide to the Green Mountain State*. Boston: Houghton Mifflin Co., 1937.

Huden, John C. *Indian Place Names in Vermont*. Burlington: John C. Huden, 1957.

Swift, Esther. M. *Vermont Place-Names: Footprints of History*. Brattleboro: S. Greene Press, 1977.


# Virginia

Federal Writers' Project. *Virginia: A Guide to the Old Dominion*. New York: Oxford University Press, 1940.

Hagemann, James A. *The Heritage of Virginia: The Story of Place Names in the Old Dominion*. Norfolk: Donning Co., 1986.

Hanson, Raus M. *Virginia Place Names*. Verona: McClure Press, 1969.

Reps, John W. *Tidewater Towns*. Williamsburg: Colonial Williamsburg Foundation, 1972.

Slaughter, James B. *Settlers, Southerners, Americans: The History of Essex County, Virginia. 1608–1984*. Salem, West Virginia: Don Mills. Inc., 1985.


# Washington

Alt, David D. *Roadside Geology of Washington*. Missoula: Mountain Press, 1984.

Capoeman, Pauline K. (ed.). *Land of the Quinault*. Seattle: Continental Printing, 1990.

*Chehalis Community Development Program*. Chehalis Community Development Program History Committee, 1954.

Edwards, Jonathan. *History of Spokane County*. San Francisco: W. H. Lever, Pub., 1900.

Elyea, Winifred. "The History of Tatoosh Island." *Washington Historical Quarterly*. Vol. 20, No. 3. July, 1929. 223–224.

"Enumclaw." *The Buckley News Banner*. May 20, 1998.

Federal Writers' Project. *Washington: A Guide to the Evergreen State*. Portland: Binfords & Mort, 1941.

Felt, Margaret. *Rivers to Reckon with*. Forks: Gockerell & Fletcher Pub., 1985.

"First Inhabitants of Naselle." *The Sou'wester. Pacific County Historical Society*. Vol. X, No. 1. Spring, 1975. 3.

Hiler, Mike. "Naches in a Nutshell." *Naches Basin Community History*, 1988.

Hitchman, Robert. *Place Names of Washington*. Tacoma: Washington State Historical Society, 1985.

Hull, Lindley. *A History of Central Washington*. Spokane: Shaw & Borden, 1929.

Kirk, Ruth, and Carmela Alexander. *Exploring Washington's Past*. Seattle: University Washington Press, 1990.

May, Pete (ed.). *History of Klickitat County*. Goldendale: Klickiat County Historical Society, 1982.

McNulty, Tim. *Washington's Wild Rivers: The Unfinished Work*. Seattle: The Mountaineers, 1990.

Meany, Edmond S. *Origin of Washington*

*Geographic Names.* Seattle: University Washington Press, 1923.

Phillips, James W. *Washington State Place Names.* Seattle: University Washington Press, 1971.

Reese, Gary F. *Origins of Pierce County Place Names.* Tacoma: R & M Press, 1989.

Steele, Richard F. *An Illustrated History of Stevens, Ferry, Okanogan and Chelen Counties, State of Washington.* Spokane: Western Heritage Pub., 1904.

Wilson, Bruce. *Late Frontier: A History of Okanogan County, Washington.* Okanogan: Okanogan County Historical Society, 1990.

With Pride in Heritage, *History of Jefferson County.* Port Townsend: Jefferson County Historical Society, 1966.

# West Virginia

Federal Writers' Project. *West Virginia: A Guide to the Mountain State.* New York: Oxford University Press, 1946.

Kenny, Hamill. *West Virginia Place Names.* Piedmont: The Place Name Press, 1945.

Koon, Thomas J. *Marion County, West Virginia: A Pictorial History.* Norfolk, VA: Donning Co., Pub. 1995

Ralston, R.H., Sr. "Who Put the K in Buckhannon." *Record Delta.* Dec. 5, 1986: 5.

# Wisconsin

Egar, Rev. John H. *The Story of Nashotah.* Milwaukee: Burdick & Armitage Printers, 1874.

Federal Writers' Project. *Wisconsin: A Guide to the Badger State.* New York: Duell, Sloan and Pearce, 1941.

Gard, Robert, and L.G. Sorden. *The Romance of Wisconsin Place Names.* New York: October House. Inc., 1968.

Hallock, Rev. Donald H.V. "The Story of Nashotah." *Historical Magazine of the Protestant Episcopal Church.* Vol. XI, No. 1. March, 1942.

*History of Fond du Lac County, Wisconsin , Containing an Account of Its Settlement,* *Growth, Development and Resources, Biographical Sketches, Etc.* Chicago: Western Historical Co., 1880.

*History of Jefferson County, Wisconsin.* Chicago: Western Historical Company, 1879.

*History of Washington and Ozaukee Counties, Wisconsin, Containing an Account of Its Settlement, Growth, Development and Resource, Etc.* Chicago: Western Historical Co., 1881.

*History of Waukesha County, Wisconsin, Containing an Account of Its Settlement, Growth, Development and Resources, Etc.* Chicago: Western Historical Co., 1880.

Stark, William. *Pine Lake.* Sheboygan: Zimmerman Press, 1971.

Vogel, Virgil. *Indian Names on Wisconsin's Map.* Madison: University of Wisconsin, 1991.

Ware, John M. *A Standard History of Waupaca County, Wisconsin.* Vol. I. New York: Lewis Pub., 1917.

# Wyoming

Barnhart, Bill. *The Northfork Trail: Guide and Pictorial History of Cody, Wyoming and Yellowstone Park.* Wapiti: Elkhorn Pub., 1982.

Federal Writers' Project. *Wyoming: A Guide to Its History. Highways and People.* New York: Oxford University Press, 1941.

"Meeteetse, Wyoming." Meeteetse Museum vertical files.

Moulton, Candy. *Roadside History of Wyoming.* Missoula, MT: Mountain Press, 1995.

Urbanek, Mae. *Wyoming Place Names.* Missoula, Montana: Mountain Press, 1988.

# General References

Allen, Hervey, and Carl Carmer. *Rivers of America: The Everglades, River of Grass.* New York: Rinehart & Co., 1947.

Allota, Robert I. *Signposts and Settlers: The History of Place Names in the Middle Atlantic States.* Chicago: Bonus Books, 1992.

Annerino, John. *Canyons of the Southwest.* San Francisco: Sierra Club Books, 1993.

Beckey, Fred. *Cascade Alpine Guide.* Seattle: The Mountaineers, 1973.

Beckham, Stephen D. *Lewis and Clark from the Rockies to the Pacific.* Portland: Graphic Arts Center Pub., 2002.

Bourne, Russel. *Rivers of America.* Golden: Fulcrum Pub., 1998.

Cantor, George. *Where the Old Roads Go.* New York: Harper & Row, 1990.

Chronic, Halka. *Pages of Stone: 3, The Desert Southwest.* Seattle: The Mountaineers, 1986.

_____. *Pages of Stone: 4, Grand Canyon and the Plateau Country.* Seattle: The Mountaineers, 1988.

_____. *Pages of Stone: 1, Rocky Mountains and Western Great Plains.* Seattle: The Mountaineers, 1984.

Clark, Ella E. *Indian Legends of the Pacific Northwest.* Berkeley: University of California Press, 1953.

Colombo, Marcella. *American Southwest: Places and History.* Vercelli, Italy: White Star, 1998.

Ekman, Leonard C. *Scenic Geology of the Pacific Northwest.* Portland: Binfords & Mort, 1962.

*Explore America Just off the Interstate.* Pleasantville, NY: Reader's Digest, 1996.

Farnsworth, Jack L., and Michael A. Ungersma (eds.). *Cascadia: The Geologic Evolution of the Pacific Northwest.* New York: McGraw-Hill, Inc., 1972.

Federal Writers' Project. *U.S. One: Maine to Florida.* New York: Modern Age Books, 1938.

Ferguson, Diana. *Native American Myths.* London: Collins & Brown, Ltd., 2002.

Ferguson, William M., and Arthur H. Rohn. *Anasazi Ruins of the Southwest in Color.* Albuquerque: University of New Mexico Press, 1987.

Fisher, Rong. *Blue Ridge Range: The Gentle Mountains.* Washington, D.C.: National Geographic Society, 1992.

*From Acadia to Yellowstone: The National Parks of the United States.* Toronto, Canada: Key Porter Books, Ltd., 1996.

Gannett, Henry. *The Origin of Certain Place Names in the United States.* Washington, D.C.: U.S. Government Printing Office, 1905.

Gutek, Gerald L. *Experiencing America's Past.* Hoboken, New Jersey: John Wiley & Sons, 1986.

Haines, Aubrey L. *Historic Sites Along the Oregon Trail.* Gerald, MO: Patrice Press, 1981.

Harder, Kelsie B. (ed.). *Illustrated Dictionary of Place Names: United States and Canada.* New York: Facts on File, 1976.

Hendrickson, Borg, and Linwood Laughy. *Clearwater Country.* Kooskia, ID: Mountain Meadow Press, 1989.

Holmer, Nils. M. *Indian Place Names in North America.* Cambridge: Harvard University Press, 1948.

Huden, John C. *Indian Place Names of New England.* New York: Museum of the American Indian Heye Foundation, 1962.

Jenkinson, Michael. *Wild Rivers of North America.* New York: E.P. Dutton & Co., 1973.

Johnson, Michael G. *The Native Tribes of North America: A Concise Encyclopedia.* New York: MacMillan Pub., 1994.

Judson, Katharine B. *Myths and Legends of the Pacific Northwest.* Chicago: A.C. McClurg & Co., 1910 (Facsimile, The Shorey Book Store, 1967).

Kingery, Hugh E. *High Country Names.* Boulder, Colorado: Johnson Books, 1994.

Linford, Laurance D. *Navajo Places: History, Legend, Landscape.* Salt Lake City: University of Utah Press, 2000.

*Magnificent Rockies: Crest of a Continent.* Palo Alto: American West Pub., 1973.

Nestor, Sandy. *Indian Placenames in America.* Vol. 1. Jefferson, NC: McFarland & Co., 2003.

_____. *Our Native American Legacy.* Caldwell, Idaho: Caxton Press, 2001.

*New England.* New York: DK Pub., 2001.

*Off the Beaten Path.* Pleasantville, NY: Reader's Digest, 2003.

Olmsted, Gerald W. *Fielding's Lewis and Clark Trail.* New York: William Morrow & Co. Inc., 1986.

Orchard, Vance. *Life on the Dry Side: A Nostalgic Journey Down the Backroads of the*

*Inland Northwest.* Walla Walla, WA: Pioneer Press, 1984.

Orr, Elizabeth L., and William N. Orr. *Rivers of the West: A Guide to the Geology and History.* Salem: Eagle Web Press, 1985.

*Our Native American Heritage.* Pleasantville, NY: Reader's Digest, 1996.

Quimby, Myron J. *Scratch Ankle, U.S.A.: American Place Names and Their Derivation.* New York: A.S. Barnes and Co., 1969.

Peattie, Roderick (ed.). *The Cascades.* New York: Vanguard Press, 1949.

_____. *The Great Smokies and the Blue Ridge.* New York: Vanguard Press, 1943.

Rand McNalley. *Encyclopedia of World Rivers.* London: Bison Books, 1980.

Rivers, K.E. *Standing Rocks and Sleeping Rainbows.* Ketchum, ID: Great Vacations, 1999.

*Rocky Mountain.* National Parks Division of World-Wide Research and Pub. Co., 1986.

Ruby, Robert, and John A. Brown. *Indians of the Pacific Northwest.* Norman: University of Oklahoma Press, 1981.

Salmonson, Jessica A. *Phantom Waters: Northwest Legends of Rivers, Lakes and Shores.* Seattle: Sasquatch Books, 1995.

Simpson, Dorothy. *The Maine Islands in Story and Legend.* New York: J.B. Lippincott, 1960.

Stadius, Martin. *Dreamers: On the Trail of the Nez Perce.* Caldwell, ID: Caxton Press, 1999.

Stewart, George R. *American Place Names.* New York: Oxford University Press, 1970.

_____. *Names on the Land.* New York: Random House, 1945.

Strong, John A. *The Algonquian Peoples of Long Island from Earliest Times to 1900.* Interlaken, New York: Empire State Books, 1997.

Swanton, John R. *Indian Tribes of the American Southwest.* Washington, D.C.: U.S. Government Printing Office, 1952 (Facsimile by Shorey Book Stores, 1974).

Tubbs, Stephenie A., and Clay S. Jenkinson. *The Lewis and Clark Companion.* New York: Henry Holt and Co., 2003.

Underhill, Ruth. *Indians of the Pacific Northwest.* Washington, D.C.: Bureau of Indian Affairs, 1944.

Walking Turtle, Eagle. *Indian America.* Santa Fe: John Muir Pubs. 4th Edition, 1995.

Wilson, Alan. *Navajo Place Names: An Observer's Guide.* Guilford, CT: Jeffrey Norton Pub., 1995.

Wood, Erskine. *Days with Chief Joseph: Diary, Recollections, and Photos.* Portland: Oregon Historical Society, 1970.

# Index

Abagadasset River, ME 72
Aberjona River, MA 84
Abiqua Creek, OR 137
Abiquiu Creek, NM 115
Abita Springs, LA 68
Absaroka Mountains, WY 183
Absecon Creek, NJ 111
Achonee Mountain, CO 39
Adak Island, AK 9
Adirondack Mountains, NY 119
Adugak Island, AK 10
Affonee Creek, AL 3
Agamenticus Mountain, ME 72
Agathla Peak, AZ 20
Aghiyuk Island, AK 10
Agulowak River, AK 10
Ahtanum Creek, WA 169
Aiktak Island, AK 10
Akaska Lake, SD 155
Akulik Creek, AK 10
Akun Island, AK 10
Akutan Bay/Island, AK 10
Alabama River, AL 3
Alagnak River, AK 10
Alaid Island, AK 10
Alamoosook Lake, ME 72
Alapah Creek/Mountain, AK 10
Alapaha River, GA 52
Alaqua Creek, FL 48
Alaska Range, AK 10
Alcovy River, GA 52
Alecks Creek, GA 52
Aleknagik, Lake, AK 11
Alexauken Creek, NJ 111
Allagash River, ME 72

Alleghany Mountains, PA 145
Alloway Creek, NJ 111
Alpowa Creek, WA 169
Alsea Bay/River, OR 137
Altamaha River, GA 52
Alyeska, Mount, AK 11
Amak Island, AK 11
Amaknak Island, AK 11
Amalik Bay, AK 11
Amatignak Island, AK 11
Amawk Creek/Mountain, AK 11
Ambajejus Lake, ME 72
Amicalola River/Mountain, GA 52
Amite River, MS 98
Ammonoosuc River, NH 107
Amnicon River, WI 179
Anacapa Island, CA 30
Anacostia River, MD 80
Anadarko Creek, TX 158
Anaktuvuk River, AK 11
Anasagunticook, Lake, ME 72
Anasazi Canyon, UT 159
Androscoggin River, NH 107
Aneewakee River, GA 53
Aniak River, AK 11
Aniakchak River, AK 11
Aniyuyaktuvik Creek, AK 12
Annaquatucket River, RI 152
Antero, Mount, CO 39
Antietam Creek, MD 80
Anvik River, AK 12
Apache Creek, NM 115
Apache Maid Mountain, AZ 20
Apalachee River, GA 53
Apalachicola River, GA 53

Apiatan Mountain, CO 40
Apishapa River, CO 40
Apolacon Creek, PA 145
Appomattox River, VA 165
Appoquinimink River, DE 47
Apshawa Lake, NJ 112
Aquashicola Creek, PA 145
Aquia Creek, VA 165
Aquipaguetin Island, MN 93
Aravaipa Creek/Canyon, AZ 20
Aricaree Creek, SD 155
Arikaree River, CO 40
Armuchee Creek, GA 53
Arolik Lake/River, AK 12
Aroostook River, ME 72
Arrigetch Creek/Peaks, AK 12
Asaayi Lake, NM 116
Ascutney Mountain, VT 163
Ashepoo River, SC 153
Ashtabula River, OH 133
Ashuelot River, NH 107
Ashwaubenon Creek, WI 179
Aspetuck River, CT 43
Asquam Lake, NH 108
Assabet River, MA 85
Assacorkin Island, MD 80
Assateague Island, MD 80
Assawoman Bay, MD 80
Assiscunk Creek, NJ 112
Assunpink Creek, NJ 112
Astatula Lake, FL 48
Atchafalaya River, LA 68
Aughwick Creek, PA 145
Auke Bay/Creek, AK 12
Autauga Creek, AL 3
Avawatz Mountains, CA 31
Awapa Plateau, UT 159

Ayish Bayou, TX  158
Azansosi Mesa, AZ  20

Babocomari River, AZ  21
Baboosic Lake, NH  108
Baboquivari Mountain, AZ  21
Bagaduce River, ME  73
Balukai Mesa, AZ  21
Bannock Creek, ID  58
Bantam Lake, CT  43
Bashi Creek, AL  3
Baskahegan River, ME  73
Bastineau, Lake, LA  68
Batamote Mountain, AZ  21
Batsto River, NJ  112
Baugo Creek, IN  62
Bay De Noc, MI  89
Bayou Goula, LA  69
Bayou Louis, LA  69
Bayou Manchac, LA  69
Bayou Plaquemine, LA  69
Bedashosha Lake, SD  155
Begashibito Canyon, AZ  21
Bekihatso Lake, AZ  21
Bemidji Lake, MN  93
Bidahochi Butte/Spring, AZ
   21
Big Jelloway Creek, OH  134
Big Sioux River, SD  155
Big Washoe Lake, NV  104
Bisti Badlands, NM  116
Bodaway Mesa, AZ  21
Bodkau Creek, AR  30
Bogue Chitto Creek, AL  3
Bogue Chitto River, MS  98
Bogue Falaya River, LA  69, 70
Bogueloosa Creek, AL  4
Bolam Creek/Glacier, CA  31
Bollibokka Mountains, CA  31
Bomoseen Lake, VT  163
Bonfouca Bayou, LA  69
Brockatonorton Bay, MD  80
Buckhannon River, WV  177
Bully Choop Peak, CA  31
Buttahatchee Creek, AL  4

Cacapon Mountain/River, WV
   177
Cahaba River, AL  4
Cahokia Creek, IL  60
Cahto Creek, CA  31
Calapooya River/Mountains,
   OR  137
Calcasieu River, LA  69
Calebee Creek, AL  4
Calimus Butte, OR  137
Calipeen River, ID  58
Caloosahatchee River, FL  48
Cameahwait Lake, WY  183
Canadohta Lake, PA  145

Canajoharie Creek, NY  119
Canisteo River, NY  120
Canoochee River, GA  53
Canopus Creek, NY  120
Canyon De Chelly, AZ  22
Capay Valley, CA  31
Carcajou Point, WI  179
Carrabassett River, ME  73
Casco Bay, ME  73
Cashi River, NC  126
Castine Bayou, LA  69, 70
Catahoula Lake, LA  70
Cataloochee Valley, NC  126
Catasauqua Creek, PA  145
Catatonk Creek, NY  120
Catawba River, NC  127
Catawissa Creek, PA  145
Cathance River, ME  73
Cathlamet Bay, OR  137
Catoctin River/Mountain, MD
   80
Cattaraugus Creek, NY  120
Caucomgomoc Lake, ME  73
Cayadutta Creek, NY  120
Cayuga Lake, NY  120
Cemochechobee Creek, GA  53
Cha Canyon, UT  159
Chaco River, NM  116
Chacra Mesa, NM  116
Chaistla Butte, AZ  22
Chama River, NM  116
Champepadan Creek, MN  93
Chankaska Creek, MN  93
Chaol Canyon, AZ22
Chapawamsic Creek, VA  165
Chappaquiddick Island, MA
   85
Chaptico Bay, MD  81
Chaski Bay, OR  137
Chassahowitzka River, FL  48
Chattahoochee River, GA  53
Chattooga River, GA  53
Chauga River, SC  153
Chautauqua Lake, NY  120
Cheaha Mountain, AL  4
Chebeague Island, ME  73
Chediski Mountain, AZ  22
Cheesequake River, NJ  112
Chehalis River, WA  169
Chehulpum Creek, OR  138
Chelan, Lake, WA  169
Chemehuevi Mountains, CA
   31
Chemung River, NY  120
Chenango River, NY  121
Chenequa Lake, WI  179
Cheoah Lake/River, NC  127
Chepiwanoxet Island, RI  152
Chequamegon Bay/National
   Forest, WV  179

Chesapeake Bay, MD  81
Chesnimus Creek, OR  138
Chestatee River, GA  53
Chesuncook Lake, ME  74
Chetco River, OR  138
Chetlo Lake, OR  138
Chewalla Lake, MS  98
Cheyenne Bottoms, KS  65
Cheyenne River, SD  155
Chicago River, IL  60
Chicamacomico River, MD  81
Chicamuxen Creek, MD  81
Chickahominy River, VA  166
Chickamauga Lake, TN  157
Chickasawhatchee Creek, GA
   54
Chickasawhay River, MS  98
Chickies Creek, PA  146
Chicoma Mountain, NM  116
Chicone Creek, MD  81
Chicopee River, MA  85
Chignik Bay/Island, AK  12
Chikapanagi Mesa, AZ  22
Chikasanoxee Creek, AL  4
Chikaskia River, KS  65
Chilatchee Creek, AL  4
Chilchinbito Spring, AZ  22
Chilkat Islands/River, AK  12
Chillisquaque Creek, PA  146
Chilocco Creek, OK  136
Chimon Island, CT  44
Chinagora Creek, NJ  112
Chinchuba Creek, LA  70
Chincoteague Island, VA  166
Chinde Mesa, AZ  22
Chingawassa Springs, KS  65
Chipola River, AL  4
Chippewanuck Creek, IN  62
Chiputneticook Lakes, ME  74
Chiricahua Mountains, AZ  22
Chisana River, AK  12
Chistochina River, AK  12
Chittenango Creek, NY  121
Choccolocco Creek, AL  4
Choconut Creek, NY  121
Chocorua Mountain/Lake,
   NH  108
Chocowinity Creek, NC  127
Choctawhatchee River, AL  4
Chokoloskee Island, FL  48
Chopaka Mountains, WA  169
Choptank River, MD  81
Choupique Bayou, LA  70
Chowan River, NC  127
Chowchilla River, CA  31
Chuckatuck Creek, VA  166
Chuctanunda Creek, NY  121
Chuginadak Island, AK  13
Chunky River, MS  98
Chuska Mountains, AZ  23

Cibeque Creek, AZ 23
Cibola Creek, NM 116
Clackamas River, OR 138
Clallam Bay, WA 169
Cle Elum Lake, WA 169
Clikapudi Creek, CA 31
Coan River, VA 166
Coaticook River, VT 163
Coatopa Creek, AL 5
Cobbosseecontee Lake, ME 74
Cobmoosa Lake, MI 89
Cobscook Bay, ME 74
Cocheco River, NH 108
Cochetopa Pass, CO 40
Cochituate Lake, MA 85
Cockenoe Island, CT 44
Coconino Plateau, AZ 23
Cocoosh Prairie, MI 89
Cocoosing Creek, PA 146
Codorus Creek, PA 146
Cohabadiah Creek, AL 5
Collawash River, OR 138
Colle Canyon, NM 116
Coma'a Spring, AZ 23
Combahee River, SC 153
Comobabi Mountain, AZ 23
Conanicut Island, RI 152
Conasauga River/Lake, GA 54
Concow Valley, CA 32
Conecuh River, AL 5
Conemaugh River, PA 146
Conestoga Creek, PA 146
Conesus Lake, NY 121
Conewago Creek, PA 146
Congaree River, SC 153
Conhocton River, NY 121
Connecticut River, NH 108
Conococheague Creek, PA 146
Conodoguinet Creek, PA 146
Conolloway Creek, PA 146
Conoquenessing Creek, PA 147
Conoy Creek, PA 147
Contentnea Creek, NC 127
Contoocook River, NH 108
Coosa River, GA 54
Coosaw Island, SC 153
Coosawattee River, GA 54
Copake Lake, NY 121
Copiah Creek, MS 98
Corrotoman River, VA 166
Corrumpa Creek, NM 116
Coso Hot Springs, CA 32
Cosumnes River, CA 32
Cotaco Creek, AL 5
Cotahaga Creek, AL 5
Cowee Valley/Mountain, NC
  127
Coweman River, WA 170
Coweta Creek, OK 136
Cowikee Creek, AL 5

Cowlitz River, WA 170
Crosswicks Creek, NJ 112
Cubahatchee Creek, AL 5
Cullasaja River, NC 127
Culleoko Spring, TN 157
Cullowhee Creek, NC 128
Cultus Bay, WA 170
Cultus Creek, OR 138
Cupit Mary Mountain, OR
  138
Curencanti Pass, CO 40
Currahee Mountain, GA 54
Cushetunk Mountains, NJ 112
Cussewago Creek, PA 147
Cutmaptico Creek, MD 81
Cuttyhunk Island, MA 85
Cuyahoga River, OH 133
Cuyama River/Valley, CA 32
Cuyamaca Peak, CA 32

Dahlonega River, ID 58
Decorah Peak, WI 179
Dekkas Creek, CA 32
Del Shay Creek, AZ 23
Desatoya Mountains/Creek,
  NV 104
Desha Creek, UT 159
Didallas Creek, CA 32
Dinnebito Wash, AZ 23
Distik, Mount, AK 13
Doolth Mountain, AK 13
Doonerak, Mount, AK 13
Dorcheat Bayou, AR 30
Dosewallips River, WA 170
Dowa Yalane Mesa, NM 117
Duckabush River, WA 170
Dulbi River, AK 13
Duwamish River, WA 170
Dzildtloi Mountain, NM 117

Eastonalee Creek, GA 54
Echeconnee Creek, GA 54
Ecofina River, FL 48
Ecola Point, OR 138
Econlockhatchee River, FL 48
Edisto Island/River, SC 153
Eek Lake/River/Mountains,
  AK 13
Eena Creek, ID 58
Egegik River, AK 13
Eklutna, Mount, AK 13
Ellijay Creek, NC 128
Elterpom Creek, CA 32
Elwha River, WA 170
Emuckfa Creek, AL 5
Enentah, Mount, CO 40
Enitachopco Creek, AL 5
Eno River, NC 128
Enumclaw Mountain, WA 171
Escambia Creek, AL 6

Escanaba River, MI 89
Escatawpa River, AL 6
Escumbuit Island, NH 108
Eshamy Bay/Creek/Lake, AK
  13
Esopus Creek, NY 121
Esquagamah Lake, MN 94
Etowah River, GA 54
Euchre Creek, OR 139
Ewauna Lake, OR 139

Fakahatchee River, FL 48
Fenholloway River, FL 49
Fordache Bayou, LA 70

Garoga Creek, NY 121
Geanquakin Creek, MD 81
Geuda Springs, KS 66
Gila River, NM 117
Gogebic Lake, MI 89
Goguac Lake, MI 89
Goshute Lake, NV 104
Grand Calumet River, IN 62
Great Miami River, OH 133
Gualala River, CA 32
Guatay Mountain, CA 32
Gulkana River, AK 14
Guyandot River, WV 177

Hackensack River, NY 122
Halawakee Creek, AL 6
Halo Creek, OR 139
Hamma Hamma River, WA
  171
Hammonasset River, CT 44
Hanska, Lake, MN 94
Harcuvar Mountain, AZ 23
Harqua Hala Mountain, AZ 24
Harraseeket River, ME 74
Hashbidito Creek, AZ 24
Hassayampa River, AZ 24
Hatchechubbee Creek, AL 6
Hatchie River, MS 98
Hatchineha, Lake, FL 49
Hattaras Island, NC 128
Haw River, NC 128
Haysop Creek, AL 6
Hehe Butte, OR 139
Hetch Hetchy Valley, CA 32
Hiamovi Mountain, CO 40
Hiko Range, NV 104
Hillabee Creek, AL 6
Hiyu Mountain, OR 139
Hockanum River, CT 44
Hocking River, OH 134
Hoh River, WA 171
Hoholitna River, AK 14
Hokendauqua Creek, PA 147
Holokuk Mountain/River, AK
  14

Homochitto River, MS 98
Homosassa River, FL 49
Honga River, MD 81
Hoosick River, NY 122
Hooskanden Creek, OR 139
Hopi Buttes, AZ 24
Hoquiam River, WA 171
Hoskininni Mesa, AZ 24
Hosta Butte, NM 117
Housatonic River, MA 85
Hovenweap National Monu-
    ment, UT 159
Huachuca Mountains, AZ 24
Hualpai Mountain, AZ 24
Huethawali Mountain, AZ 24
Humptulips River, WA 171
Hunk Papa Creek, SD 155
Hunkah Prairie, MO 101
Hyaak Creek, ID 58
Hyco River, NC 128
Hypoluxo Island, FL 49

Iaqua Buttes, CA 33
Ibapah Peak, UT 159
Ichabuckler Creek, GA 54
Ichawaynochaway Creek, GA
    55
Ichetucknee River, FL 49
Iditarod River, AK 14
Ifconjo Creek, GA 55
Igikpak, Mount, AK 14
Ihagee Creek, AL 6
Ikpikpuk River, AK 14
Iliamna, Lake, AK 14
Illinois River, IL 60
Illipah Creek, NV 104
Iluiliuk Bay, AK 14
Inmachuk River, AK 14
Inyan Kara Mountain, WY 183
Ipnek Creek/Mountains, AK
    14
Iroquois River, IN 62
Ischua Creek, NY 122
Ishkote Lake, MI 90
Istokpoga Lake, FL 49
Itkillik River, AK 15
Ivanpah Mountains, CA 33
Ivishak River, AK 15

Jadito Mesa/Spring/Wash, AZ
    25
Jarbidge Mountains/
    River/Canyon, NV 104
Jelloway Creek, Big, OH 134
Jemez Mountain/River, NM
    117
Jolon Creek, CA 33
Juab Valley, UT 159
Junaluska Lake, NC 128
Juniata River, PA 147

Kabetogama Lake, MN 94
Kachemak Bay, AK 15
Kagati Lake, AK 15
Kahiltna River, AK 15
Kahola Creek, KS 66
Kaibab Plateau, AZ 25
Kaibito Plateau, AZ 25
Kaiparowitz Plateau, UT 159
Kalamazoo River, MI 90
Kalispell Bay, ID 58
Kamiah Buttes, ID 58
Kamloops Island, MI 90
Kamma Mountains, NV 104
Kampeska Lake, SD 155
Kanab Creek, UT 160
Kanapaha Lake, FL 49
Kanaranzi Creek, MN 94
Kanawha River, WV 177
Kancamagus Mountain, NH
    108
Kandiotta Lake, ND 132
Kandiyohi Lake, MN 94
Kaniksu Mountain/National
    Forest, ID 58
Kankakee River, IN 62
Kannah Creek, CO 40
Kansas River, KS 66
Kanuga Lake, NC 129
Kasaan Island, AK 15
Kashong Creek, NY 122
Kaskaskia Island/River, IL 61
Kasota Lake, MN 94
Katahdin, Mount, ME 74
Katmai, Mount, AK 15
Kaweah River, CA 33
Kawich Range, NV 105
Kawishiwi River, MN 94
Kawkawlin River, MI 90
Kawuneechee Valley, CO 40
Kayaderosseras Creek, NY 122
Kayak Island, AK 15
Kearsarge Mountain, NH 109
Keego Harbor, MI 90
Keet Seel Canyon, AZ 25
Kegonsa, Lake, WI 179
Kekawaka Creek, CA 33
Kenduskeag River, ME 74
Kenjockety Creek, NY 122
Kennebec River, ME 74
Kennebunk River, ME 75
Kenosha Pass, CO 41
Kentucky Lake/River, KY 68
Keokuk Lake, IA 64
Keuka Lake, NY 122
Kewaunee River, WI 179
Keweenaw Bay, MI 90
Keyapaha River, SD 155
Khantaak Island, AK 15
Kibesillah Mountain, CA 33
Kickapoo Creek, IL 61

Kim Me Ni Oli Valley, NM 118
Kineo Mountains, ME 75
Kinnickinnic River, WI 179
Kinniconick River, KY 68
Kinterbish Creek, AL 6
Kintla Lake, MT 102
Kinzua Creek, PA 147
Kiokee Creek, GA 55
Kiowa Creek, CO 41
Kisatchie National Forest 70
Kishacoquillas Creek, PA 147
Kishwaukee River, IL 61
Kiska Island, AK 16
Kiskiminetas River, PA 147
Kissimmee River, FL 49
Kittatinny Range, NJ 112
Kiwa Creek, ID 59
Klamath River, OR 139
Klickitat River, WA 171
Klutina River/Lake, AK 16
Kobeh Valley, NV 105
Kobuk River, AK 16
Koip Peak, CA 33
Kokosing River, OH 134
Kokoweep Peak, CA 33
Kongakut River, AK 16
Konkapot River, MA 85
Konocti, Mount, CA 34
Ko-Op-Ke Mountain, AZ 25
Koosah Mountain, OR 139
Kootenai River, MT 102
Koshkonong, Lake, WI 180
Kowaligi Creek, AL 6
Kuna Peak, CA 34
Kuparuk River, AK 16
Kushtaka Lake, AK 16
Kuskokwim River/Mountain,
    AK 16

Lackawanna River, PA 148
Lake Aleknagik, AK 11
Lake Anasagunticook, ME 72
Lake Bastineau, LA 68
Lake Chelan, WA 169
Lake Hanska, MN 94
Lake Hatchineha, FL 49
Lake Iliamna, AK 14
Lake Kegonsa, WI 179
Lake Koshkonong, WI 180
Lake Leelanau, MI 90
Lake Mascoma, NH 109
Lake Mattamuskeet, NC 129
Lake Mendota, WI 180
Lake Minatare, NE 103
Lake Okeechobee, FL 50
Lake Okmulgee, OK 136
Lake Picatinny, NJ 114
Lake Puposky, MN 96
Lake Ronkonkoma, NY 124
Lake Sakakawea, ND 133

Lake Shetek, MN 96
Lake Tallac, CA 37
Lake Tampacuas, TX 158
Lake Tholocco, AL 8
Lake Toxaway, NC 131
Lake Tsala Apopka, FL 51
Lake Utsayantha, NY 126
Lake Wamduska, ND 133
Lake Wassookeag, ME 79
Lake Wawayanda, NJ 115
Lake Wichita, TX 158
Lake Wingra, WI 182
Lake Winnepesaukee, NH 111
Lake Winola, PA 151
Lakota Springs, SD 155
Lapwai Creek, ID 59
Latah Creek, WA 172
Leelanau, Lake, MI 90
Lehigh River, PA 148
Letohatchee Creek, AL 6
Lilliwaup Bay, WA 172
Lituya Bay/Mountain, AK 16
Lochloosa Lake, FL 49
Lochsa River, ID 59
Lockatong Creek, NJ 113
Lokasakal Spring, AZ 25
Lospe Mountain, CA 34
Loxahatchee River, FL 49
Loyalhanna Creek, PA 148
Loyalsock Creek, PA 148
Lubbub Creek, AL 6
Lukachukai Mountains, AZ 25
Lummi Island, WA 172
Luxapallila Creek, AL 7
Lycoming Creek, PA 148

Macatawa Lake, MI 90
Machias River, ME 75
Mackinac Island, MI 90
Macoupin Creek, IL 61
Madawaska Lake, ME 75
Magalloway Mountain, NH 109
Magothy River, MD 82
Magotsu Creek, UT 160
Mahoning River, OH 134
Manada Creek, PA 148
Manana Island, ME 75
Manatawny Creek, PA 148
Manistique River, MI 91
Manitook Lake, CT 44
Manitou Lake, IN 62
Manitowish River, WI 180
Manokin River, MD 82
Manursing Island, NY 122
Manyaska Lake, MN 94
Maquam Bay, VT 163
Maquoketa River, IA 64
Maranacook Lake, ME 75
Marinuka Lake, WI 180

Markagunt Plateau, UT 160
Mascoma, Lake, NH 109
Mashipacong Island, NJ 113
Massabesic Lake, NH 109
Massasecum Lake, NH 109
Mataponi Creek, MD 82
Matilija Creek/Springs, CA 34
Matinicus Island, ME 75
Mattamuskeet, Lake, NC 129
Mattaponi River, VA 166
Mattatuxet River, RI 152
Mattawamkeag River, ME 75
Mattawoman Creek, MD 82
Mattole River, CA 34
Maumee River, IN 62
Maxinkuckee Lake, IN 63
Mazatzal Mountains, AZ 25
Meauwataka Lake, MI 91
Medomak River, ME 76
Meeteetse Creek, WY 183
Megantic Lake, MA 85
Megunticook River, ME 76
Meherrin River, VA 166
Mehoopany Creek, PA 148
Memaloose Island, WA 172
Memphremagog Lake, VT 163
Mendota, Lake, WI 180
Menomonee River, WI 180
Meramec River, MO 101
Merrimack River, MA 86
Messalonskee Lake, ME 76
Metallak Island, NH 109
Metedeconk River, NJ 113
Metigoshe Lake, ND 132
Metinic Island, ME 76
Metolius River, OR 139
Metomkin Bay, VA 166
Mettah Creek, CA 34
Mettawee River, VT 163
Millecoquins River, MI 91
Milwaukee River, WI 180
Mina Lake, SD 155
Mina Sauk Falls, MO 101
Minam River, OR 140
Minatare, Lake, NE 103
Mingo Branch, MD 82
Minisconga Creek, NY 122
Minisink Island, NJ 113
Minnechadusa River, SD 156
Minnechaduza Creek/Lake, NE 103
Minnehaha Creek/Falls, MN 94
Minnekahta Valley, SD 156
Minnesota River, MN 94
Minnetonka Lake, MN 94
Minnewaska Lake, MN 95
Minnewaska Lake, NY 123
Minnewasta Lake, SD 156
Minnewaukan Lake, ND 132

Minnewawa River, NH 109
Mispillion River, DE 47
Misquah Hills, MN 95
Missisquoi River, VT 163
Mississinewa River, OH 134
Mississippi River, MN 95
Missouri River, MT 103
Moapa Peak, NV 105
Mobjack Bay, VA 167
Modoc Point, OR 140
Moenkopi Wash, AZ 25
Mohawk River, NY 123
Mohonk Lake, NY 123
Mojavae Lake, NV 105
Molalla River, OR 140
Monache Mountain, CA 34
Monadnock Mountains, NH 109
Monegaw Springs, MO 101
Mongoulois Lake, LA 70
Monhegan Island, ME 76
Monie Creek, MD 82
Mono Lake, CA 34
Monockonock Island, PA 149
Monomoy Island, MA 86
Monongahela River, WV 177
Moolack Creek/Mountain, OR 140
Moosalamoo, Mount, VT 163
Mooselookmeguntic Lake, ME 76
Moosic Mountain, PA 149
Moosilauke Peak, NH 110
Moosmoos Creek, OR 140
Moosup River, CT 44
Moshannon Creek, PA 149
Moshassuck River, RI 152
Mount Alyeska, AK 11
Mount Antero, CO 39
Mount Distik, AK 13
Mount Doonerak, AK 13
Mount Eklutna, AK 13
Mount Enentah, CO 40
Mount Igikpak, AK 14
Mount Katahdin, ME 74
Mount Katmai, AK 15
Mount Konocti, CA 34
Mount Moosalamoo, VT 163
Mount Neoto, CO 41
Mount Pilchuck, WA 173
Mount Shasta, CA 34
Mount Talapus, OR 142
Mount Tallac, CA 37
Mount Tamalpais, CA 37
Mount Timpanogos, UT 161
Mount Tinemaha, CA 37
Mount Tukuhnikivatz, UT 162
Mount Umunhum, CA 38
Mount Utsayantha, NY 126
Mousam River, ME 76

Mowich Creek, OR 140
Mudjekeewis Mountain, OR 140
Mugu, Point, CA 34
Munuscong Bay, MI 91
Muscatatuck River, IN 63
Muscatine Island, IA 64
Muscooten Bay, IL 61
Mush Creek, SD 156
Mushaway Mountain, TX 158
Musinia Peak, UT 160
Muskeget Island, MA 86
Muskego Lake, WI 180
Muskelonge Lake, IN 63
Muskingum River, OH 134
Muskonetcong River, NJ 113
Mustinka River, MN 95
Mystic River, CT 44

Naahtee Canyon, AZ 26
Naches River, WA 172
Nacoochee River, GA 55
Nacote Creek, NJ113
Naheola Bluff, AL 7
Nahneke Mountain, ID 59
Nahumkeag Island, ME 76
Nakai Peak, CO 41
Naknek River, AK 16
Namakan Lake, MN 95
Nanita Lake, CO 41
Nankoweap Canyon, AZ 26
Nanna Hubba Bluff, AL 7
Nansemond River, VA 167
Nantahala Mountains/River, NC 129
Nanticoke River, DE 47
Nantucket Island, MA 86
Napias Creek, ID 59
Narino Honguy Hill, NV 105
Narmarcungawack River, NH 110
Narraguagus River, ME 76
Narraguineep Canyon, CO 41
Naselle River, WA 172
Nashawena Island, MA 86
Nashotah Lakes, WI 180
Nasja Mesa/Creek, UT 160
Nassawango Creek, MD 82
Natalbany River, LA 70
Natchaug River, CT 44
Natoa Island, AK 17
Naugatuck River, CT 44
Naushon Island, MA 86
Navajo Mountain, AZ 26
Navasota River, TX 158
Nawtawaket Creek, CA 34
Nayantovoy Creek, NV 105
Nazlini Canyon/Creek, AZ 26
Neacoxie Creek, OR 140

Neahkahnie Mountain, OR 140
Nebagamon Lake, WI 181
Nebish Lake, MN 95
Necanicum River, OR 141
Neches River, TX 158
Neebish Island, MI 91
Negit Island, CA 35
Nemadji River, MN 95
Nemaha River, NE 103
Nemahbin Lake, WI 181
Nemasket River, MA 86
Nenana River, AK 17
Neosho River, KS 66
Neoto, Mount, CO 41
Nepaug River, CT 45
Nequasset Lake, ME 77
Nescochague Creek, NJ 113
Neshobe Island, VT 164
Neskeag Point, ME 77
Neskowin Creek, OR 141
Nespelem River, WA 172
Nestucca River, OR 141
Neuse River, NC 129
Neversink River, NY 123
Newhalen River, AK 17
Nezinscot River, ME 77
Niangua River, MO 101
Niatche Creek, UT 160
Nigu River, AK 17
Ninnescah River, KS 66
Niobrara River, WY 183
Nippenose Creek, PA 149
Nishasakawick Creek, NJ 113
Nishnabotna River, IA 64
Nissitisset River, MA 86
Nittany Mountain, PA 149
Nitzin Canyon, AZ 26
Nodaway River, IA 65
Nokai Canyon, AZ 26
Nokoni Lake, CO 41
Nolichucky River, NC 129
Nomini Creek, VA 167
Nonnewang River, CT 45
Nooksack River, WA 173
Nopa Range, CA 35
Nowadaga Creek, NY 123
Noxubee River, MS 98
Nuka Bay/Island, AK 17
Nulhegan River, VT 164
Nummy Lake, NJ 114
Nunivak Island, AK 17

Oakmulgee Creek, AL 7
Oatka Creek, NY 123
Occaneechee Island, VA 167
Occoquan River, VA 167
Ochlockonee River, GA 55
Ochoco Creek, OR 141
Ocklahawa River, FL 50

Ocmulgee River, GA 55
Oconaluftee River, NC 129
Oconee River, GA 55
Oconomowoc River, WI 181
Oconto River, WI 181
Ocqueoc River, MI 91
Ocracoke Island, NC 130
Octoraro Creek, PA 149
Ogechie Lake, MN 95
Ogeechee River, GA 55
Oglodak Island, AK 17
Ogotoruk Creek, AK 17
Ogunquit River, ME 77
Ohanapecosh River, WA 173
Ohio River, PA 149
Okabena Creek, MN 96
Okahanikan Cove, MD 82
Okahumpka Lake, Fl 50
Okatuppa Creek, MS 99
Okauchee Lake, WI 181
Okeechobee, Lake, FL 50
Okemo Mountain, VT 164
Okmulgee, Lake, OK 136
Okoboji Lake, IA 65
Okobojo Lake/Creek, SD 156
Okshida Creek, MN 96
Olallie Butte, OR 141
Olamon Island, ME 77
Olancha Peak/Pass, CA 35
Olentangy River, OH 135
Oljeto Mesa, UT 160
Olustee Creek, Fl 50
Ompompanoosuc River, VT 164
Omusee Creek, AL 7
Onahpe Lake, SD 156
Onahu Creek, CO 41
Onaqui Mountain, UT 160
Oneida Lake, NY 123
Onistagraw Mountain, NY 123
Onota Lake, MA 86
Ontonagon River, MI 91
Oostanaula River, GA 55
Oothkalooga Creek, GA 56
Opintlocco Creek, AL 7
Oquirrh Mountains, UT 160
Oraibi Wash, AZ 26
Osage River, KS 66
Osanippa Creek, AL 7
Oseligee Creek, AL 7
Osoyoos Lake, WA 173
Ossabaw Island, GA 56
Ossipee River/Mountain, ME 77
Oswegatchie River, NY 123
Otay Mountain, CA 35
Otsquago Creek, NY 124
Ottauquechee River, VT 164
Ouachita Mountains/River/Lake, AR 30

Owatonna River, MN  96
Oweep Creek, UT  160
O-Wi-Yu-Kuts Plateau, CO  41

Pabama Lake, MI  92
Pachitla Creek, GA  56
Pah Rah Mountains, NV  105
Pahlone Peak, CO  41
Pahranagat Valley/Lakes, NV  105
Pahreah River, UT  161
Pahsimeroi River, ID  59
Pahvant Plateau, UT  161
Pajarito PeakPlateau, NM  118
Pala Mountain, CA  35
Palatlakaha Creek, FL  50
Palix River, WA  173
Pamet River, MA  87
Pamola Peak, ME  77
Pamunkey River, VA  167
Panasoffkee Lake, FL  50
Panguipa Creek, NV  105
Panguitch Lake, UT  161
Paoha Island/Lake, CA  35
Papago Creek, AZ  27
Paria River, UT  161
Parissawampitts Canyon, AZ  27
Pascack Creek, NY  124
Pascagoula River, MS  99
Pascoag River, RI  152
Pasquotank River, NC  130
Passaconaway Peak, NH  110
Passadumkeag River, ME  77
Passagassawakeag River, ME  78
Passerdyke Creek, MD  83
Passumpsic River, VT  164
Patapsco River, MD  83
Patoka River, IN  63
Patsaliga River, AL  7
Pattymocus Mountain, CA  35
Patuxent River, MD  83
Paunsaugunt Plateau, UT  161
Pavant Plateau, UT  161
Pawcatuck River, RI  152
Pawnee River, KS  66
Paxton Creek, PA  149
Pecatonica River, WI  181
Peconic Bay, NY  124
Pelahatchie Creek, MS  99
Pembina River/Mountains, ND  132
Pemigewasset River, NH  110
Pemiscot Bayou, MO  101
Pennamaquan River, ME  78
Penobscot River, ME  78
Pentucket River, MA  87
Pequabuck River, CT  45
Pequannock River, NJ  114

Perche Creek, MO  101
Perkiomen Creek, PA  150
Perquimans River, NC  130
Peshashtin Creek, WA  173
Peshtigo River, WI  181
Petaluma Creek, CA  35
Pewaukee Lake, WI  181
Piankatank River, VA  167
Picatinny, Lake, NJ  114
Piccowaxen Creek, MD  83
Piceance Creek, CO  41
Picuris Creek, NM  118
Pilchuck, Mount/River, WA  173
Pinal Mountains/Creek, AZ  27
Pingora Peak, WY  184
Pinnickinnick Mountain, WV  178
Pintlala Creek, AL  7
Piru Creek, CA  35
Piscassic River, NH  110
Piscataquis River, ME  78
Piscataquog River, NH  110
Piscataway Creek, MD  83
Piseco Lake, NY  124
Pistakee Lake, IL  61
Pithlachascotee River, FL  50
Pitsua Butte, OR  141
Plausawa Mountain, NH  110
Pocantico River, NY  124
Pocatalico River, WV  178
Pochuck Mountain, NJ  114
Pocomoke River, DE  47
Pocono Mountains, PA  150
Pocopson Creek, PA  150
Pocotopaug Lake, CT  45
Pocumptuck Mountain, MA  87
Pohick Creek, VA  168
Point Mugu, CA  34
Pojoaque River, NM  118
Pokata Creek, MD  83
Pokegama Lake, MN  96
Pokywaket Creek, CA  35
Polallie Creek, OR  141
Pomeraug River, CT  45
Pomonkey Creek, MD  83
Ponaganset River, RI  152
Ponca Creek, SD  156
Poncha Springs, CO  41
Popo Agie River, WY  184
Poquessing Creek, PA  150
Potagannissing Bay, MI  92
Potecasi Creek, NC  130
Potlatch Creek, ID  59
Potomac River, WV  178
Pottawatomie River, KS  66
Puckaway Lake, WI  182
Pungo River, NC  130
Puposky, Lake, MN  96

Puss Cuss Creek, AL  8
Putah Creek, CA  35
Puyallup River, WA  173
Pymatuning Creek, OH  135
Pysht River, WA  173

Quaboag River, MA  87
Quakake Creek, PA  150
Quakish Lake, ME  78
Quantico Creek, MD  83
Quassaic Creek, NY  124
Quassapaug Lake, CT  45
Quequechan River, MA  87
Quichapa Creek/Lake, UT  161
Quilcene River, WA  173
Quillayute River, WA  174
Quinebaug River, CT  45
Quinnipiac River, CT  45
Quinsigamond Lake, MA  87
Quirauk Mountain, MD  83
Quosatana Creek, OR  141

Rappahannock River, VA  168
Raritan River/Bay, NJ  114
Rawah Peaks, CO  42
Rewastico Creek, MD  83
Roanoke River, VA  168
Rockawalking Creek, MD  84
Ronkonkoma, Lake, NY  124
Roquist Creek, NC  130

Sacandaga River, NY  124
Sacaton Creek, NM  118
Saco River, ME  78
Sadawga Lake, VT  164
Sadlerochit Mountains/River, AK  17
Sagadahoc Bay, ME  78
Saganaga Lake, MN  96
Sagavanirktok River, AK  18
Sahwave Range, NV  106
Sakakawea, Lake, ND  133
Salamonie River, IN  63
Samish Island, WA  174
Sammamish River, WA  174
Sampit River, SC  154
Sandusky River, OH  135
Sanel Mountain, CA  36
Sanenecheck Peak, AZ  27
Sangamon River, IL  61
Sanhickan Creek, NJ  114
Sanpitch River, UT  161
Santee River, SC  154
Santeetlah Lake/Creek, NC  130
Santiam River, OR  141
Sappa Creek, KS  67
Sappony Creek, VA  168
Sasanoa River, ME  78
Satsop River, WA  174
Satus Creek, WA  174

Saucon Creek, PA 150
Saugahatchee Creek, AL 8
Sauquoit Creek, NY 125
Sawatch Range, CO 42
Scantic River, CT 45
Scargo Lake, MA 87
Schenevus Creek, NY 125
Schonchin Butte, CA 36
Schoodic Lake, ME 79
Schroon Lake, NY 125
Scioto River, OH 135
Scuppernong River, NC 130
Sebascodegan Island, ME 79
Sebasticook River, ME 79
Sebewa Creek, MI 92
Sebewaing River, MI 92
Sedanka Island, AK 18
Sedaye Mountains, NV 106
Seekseequa Creek, OR 141
Segi Mesas, AZ 27
Seguin Island, ME 79
Seiad Creek, CA 36
Selway River, ID 59
Semiahmoo Bay, WA 174
Seneasha Creek, MS 99
Seneca Rock, WV 178
Sepulga River, AL 8
Sequalitchew Creek, WA 174
Sequatchie River, TN 157
Sespe Creek, CA 36
Sesuit Creek, MA 88
Sezhini Butte, AZ 27
Shabakunk Creek, NJ 114
Shakamak Lake, IN 63
Shasta, Mount, CA 36
Shato Plateau, AZ 27
Shatterack Mountain, VT 164
Shavano Mountain, CO 42
Shawangunk Mountains, NY 125
Shawano Lake, WI 182
Sheboygan River, WI 182
Sheenjek River, AK 18
Shenandoah River, VA 168
Shenipsit Lake, CT 45
Shepaug River, CT 46
Shetek, Lake, MN 96
Shetucket River, CT 46
Shiawassee River, MI 92
Shingobee Creek, MN 96
Shinumo Altar/Creek, AZ 27
Shipshewana Lake, IN 63
Shivwits Plateau, AZ 27
Shohola Creek, PA 150
Shoshone Mountains, NV 106
Shunganunga Creek, KS 67
Siletz River, OR 142
Similk Bay, WA 174
Similkameen River, WA 174
Sinepuxent Bay, MD 84

Sinuk River, AK 18
Sippican Creek, MA 88
Sipsey River, AL 8
Sisi Butte, OR 142
Siskiwit Lake, MI 92
Siskiyou Mountains, CA 36
Siskowit Lake, WI 182
Sisquoc River, CA 36
Sitkum Creek, OR 142
Siuslaw River, OR 142
Skagit River, WA 175
Skalkaho Creek, MT 103
Skeenah Creek, NC 130
Skipanon River, OR 142
Skitchewaug Mountains, VT 165
Skokomish River, WA 175
Skookum Creek/Lake, OR 142
Skunkamaug River, MA 88
Skutumpah Creek, UT 161
Snayan Wakuwa Lake, SD 156
Snoqualmie River, WA 175
Sokokis Lake, ME79
Soleduck River/Hot Springs, WA 175
Somonauk Creek, IL 61
Sonoita Creek, AZ 27
Sonsela Butte, AZ 28
Sopchoppy River, FL 51
Soughegan River, NH 110
Spokane River, ID 60
Squam River, MA 88
Squannacook River, MA 88
Squaxin Island, WA 175
Stecoah Creek, NC 131
Steinhatchee River, FL 51
Stikine River, AK 18
Stillaguamish River, WA 175
Stono River, SC 154
Suamico River, WI 182
Sukakpak Mountain, AK 18
Suncook River, NH 110
Susitna River, AK 18
Susquehanna River, NY 125
Swannanoa River, NC 131

Tabeguache Mountain/Creek, CO 42
Tahoe Lake, CA 36
Tahosa Valley, CO 42
Tahquamenon River, MI 92
Tahquitz Peak, CA 36
Taiban Creek, NM 118
Tajiguas Creek, CA 37
Taku River, AK 18
Talapus, Mount, OR 142
Talasha Creek, MS 99
Tallac, Mount/Lake, CA 37
Talladega Creek, AL 8
Tallahala Creek, MS 99

Tallahatchie River, MS 99
Tallahatta Creek, AL 8
Tallapoosa River, GA 56
Tallaseehatchee Creek, AL 8
Tallawampa Creek, AL 8
Tally Mountain, GA 56
Tamalpais, Mount, CA 37
Taminah Lake, WY 184
Tampacuas, Lake, TX 158
Tanima Peak, CO 42
Tantabogue Creek, TX 158
Tappan Lake, OH 135
Tarkio River, MO 102
Tatoosh Island, WA 176
Tattilaba Creek, AL 8
Taum Sauk Mountain, MO 102
Tchefuncta River, LA 70
Tchula Lake, MS 99
Techatticup Wash, NV 106
Teche Bayou, LA 71
Tectah Creek, CA 37
Tecuya Creek, CA37
Teewinot Mountain, WY 184
Tehachapi Mountains/Pass, CA 37
Tehipite Valley, CA 37
Tempiute Range, NV 106
Tenabo Peak, NV 106
Tenasillahe Island, OR 142
Tenaya Lake, CA 37
Teoc Creek, MS 100
Tesuque Creek, NM 118
Tetonkaha Lake, SD 156
Tewaukon Lake, ND 133
Tholocco, Lake, AL 8
Thonotosassa Lake, FL 51
Ticaboo Creek, UT 161
Tickfaw River, LA 71
Tillicum Creek, OR 142
Timpanogos Lake, OR 142
Timpanogos, Mount, UT 161
Timpas Creek, CO 42
Tinayguk River, AK 18
Tinemaha, Mount/Creek, CA 37
Tintic Mountains, UT 162
Tioughnioga River, NY 125
Tippecanoe River/Lake, IN 63
Tippipah Spring, NV 106
Tipsoo Peak/Creek, OR 142
Tish-Tang-A-Tang Creek, CA 38
Titicus Mountain/River, CT 46
Tittabawassee River, MI 92
Tiva Canyon, NV 106
Toano Mountains, NV 106
Tobesofkee Creek, GA 56
Tockwogh River, DE 47
Todokozh Spring, AZ 28

Toe River, NC 131
Togwotee Pass, WY 184
Tohakum Peak, NV 106
Tohickon Creek, PA 150
Tohopekaliga Lake, FL 51
Toiyabe Mountain, NV 106
Toketee Lake, OR 143
Tolani Lakes, AZ 28
Tolo Lake, ID 60
Tomakokin Creek, MD 84
Tombigbee River, MS 100
Tomichi Creek, CO 42
Tomoka River, FL 51
Tonahutu Creek, CO 42
Tongass Island, AK 18
Tonquish Creek, MI 93
Tontogany Creek, OH 135
Topa Topa Mountains, CA 38
Toqua Lake, MN 96
Toquima Range, NV 107
Toquop Wash, NV 107
Tosi Creek, WY 184
Tot Mountain, OR 143
Totem Bay, AK 19
Totoket Mountain, CT 46
Totopotomoy Creek, VA 168
Totosahatchee Creek, FL 51
Touchet River, WA 176
Towaliga River, GA 56
Toxaway, Lake, NC 131
Toyah Lake, TX 158
Tranquillon Mountain, CA 38
Truckee River, CA 38
Tsaile Creek/Butte, AZ 28
Tsala Apopka, Lake, FL 51
Tsedaa Hwiidezohi Peak, AZ 28
Tsin Lane Creek, AZ 28
Tualatin River, OR 143
Tucannon River, WA 176
Tuckabum Creek, AL 8
Tuckasegee River, NC 131
Tuckernuck Island, MA 88
Tucki Mountain, CA 38
Tucquan Creek, PA 151
Tucumcari Mountain/Lake, NM 118
Tugaloo River, GA 56
Tujunga Creek, CA 38
Tukuhnikivats, Mount, UT 162
Tukuto Creek, AK 19
Tulalip Bay, WA 176
Tulpehocken Creek, PA 151
Tumalo Creek, OR 143
Tumkeehatchee Creek, AL 9
Tune Creek, CA 38
Tuneungwant Creek, PA 151
Tunica Bayou, LA 71
Tunicha Mountains, AZ 28

Tunsta Wash, NM 119
Tunxis Island, CT 46
Tuolumne River, CA 38
Tuscararas River, OH 135
Tuscarora Creek, WV 178
Tuscarora Mountains, NV 107
Tuscolameta Creek, MS 100
Tussahaw Creek, GA 56
Tutuilla Creek, OR 143
Tuzigoot National Monument, AZ 28
Tyaskin Creek, MD 84
Tybee Island, GA 57
Tybo Creek, NV 107
Tyee Mountain, OR 143
Tyende Creek, AZ 28

Uchee Creek, AL 9
Uchee Creek, GA 57
Ugak Bay, AK 19
Ugamak Island, AK 19
Uinkarets Plateau, AZ 29
Uintah Mountains/River, UT 162
Umatilla River, OR 143
Umbagog Lake, ME 79
Umbazooksus Lake, ME 79
Umnak Island, AK 19
Umpqua River, OR 143
Umunhum, Mount, CA 38
Unaka Mountain, TN 157
Unalakleet River, AK 19
Unaweep Canyon, CO 43
Uncanoonucks Mountain, NH 110
Uncompahgre Peak/River, CO 43
Uncoway River, CT 46
Unga Island, AK 19
Unicoi Mountains, TN 157
Unimak Island, AK 19
Upatoi Creek, GA 57
Uphapee Creek, AL 9
Ute Mountains, CO 43
Utowana Lake, NY 126
Utsayantha, Mount/Lake, NY 126
Utukok River, AK19

Vekol Mountain, AZ 29

Wabash River, OH 135
Wabedo Lake, MN 96
Waccamaw Lake/River, NC 131
Wachusett Mountain, MA 88
Waconda Springs, KS 67
Waguhye Peak, NV 107
Wahatchee Creek, GA 57
Wah Kon Tah Prairie, MO 102
Wahoo Creek, NE 103

Wah Sha She Prairie, MO 102
Wahtum Lake, OR 143
Wah Wah Mountains, UT 162
Wahweap Creek, UT 162
Waiska Bay, MI 93
Wakarusa River, KS 67
Wakatomika Creek, OH 136
Walakpa Bay, AK 20
Walhonding River, OH 136
Walla Walla River, OR 143
Wallacut River, WA 176
Wallenpaupack Lake, PA 151
Walloomsac River, VT 165
Wallowa River/Mountains, OR 144
Wallula Lake, OR 144
Wamduska, Lake, ND 133
Wando River, SC 154
Wanoga Butte, OR 144
Wanship Peak, UT 162
Wantasiquet Mountain, NH 110
Wapato Lake, OR 144
Wappapelo Lake, MO 102
Wappasening Creek, PA 151
Wappinger Creek, NY 126
Wapsipinicon River, MN 97
Wapwallopen Creek, PA 151
Waquoit Bay, MA 88
Wasatch Mountain Range, UT 162
Washita River, TX 158
Washougal River, WA 176
Wassaw Island, GA 57
Wassookeag, Lake, ME 79
Watab River, MN 97
Watauga River, NC 131
Wateree River, SC 154
Watnong Mountain, NJ 114
Watonwan River, MN 97
Waubay Lakes, SD 156
Waubesa Lake, WI 182
Waucoba Mountain, CA 38
Waupaca River, WI 182
Wawa Creek, OR 144
Wawasee Lake, IN 64
Wawayanda, Lake, NJ 115
Waxhaw Creek, SC 154
Wayah Bald Mountain, NC 131
Waycake Creek, NJ 115
Wayzata Bay, MN 97
Wea Creek, KS 67
Weasel Creek, IN 64
Webhannet River, ME 79
Wedhadkee Creek, AL 9
Weekiwachee River, FL 51
Weetamoo Mountain, NH 111
Wegee Creek, OH 136
Weichpec Spring, CA 38

Wekiva River, FL 52
Weogufka Mountain/Creek, AL 9
Weoka Creek, Al 9
Wepawaug River, CT 46
Wepo Springs/Wash, AZ 29
Weskeag River, ME 80
Westecunk Creek, NJ 115
Wetappo Creek, FL 52
Wetipquin Creek, MD 84
Weweantic River, MA 88
Whiskey Chitto Creek, LA 71
Wichita Lake, TX 158
Wichita Mountains, OK 136
Wickasauke Island, MA 89
Wickecheoke Creek, NJ 115
Wiconisco Creek, PA 151
Willamette River, OR 144
Willimantic River, CT 46
Willowemoc Creek, NY 126
Wimbee Creek, SC 154
Winbeam Mountain, NJ 115
Winchuck River, OR 144
Wingra, Lake, WI 182

Winnepesaukee, Lake, NH 111
Winnibigoshish Lake, MN 97
Winnisquam Lake, NH 111
Winola, Lake, PA 151
Winooski River, VT 165
Winopee Lake, OR 144
Wishkah River, WA 176
Wissota Lake, WI 183
Wita Lake, MN 97
Withlacoochee River, FL 52
Wittawaket Creek, CA 39
Wococon Island, NC 132
Wononskopomuc Lake, CT 46
Woonasquatucket River, RI 152
Wootenaux Creek, MD 84
Wupatki National Monument, AZ 29
Wyaconda River, IA 65
Wyassup Lake, CT 46
Wynoochee River, WA 176
Wyoming Range, WY 184
Wysox Creek, PA 151

Yacona River, MS 100
Yahara River, WI 183
Yahula Creek, GA 57
Yalobusha River, MS 100
Yampa River, CO 43
Yamsay Mountain, OR 144
Yantic River, CT 47
Yantley Creek, AL 9
Yazoo River, MS 100
Ycatapom Peak, CA 39
Yeocomico River, VA 168
Yolla Bolly Mountains, CA 39
Yon Dot Mountains, AZ 29
Yonah Mountain, GA 57
Yosemite Valley/National Park, CA 39
Youghiogheny River, WV 178
Yukon River, AK 20

Zaca Lake, CA 39
Zayante Creek, CA 39
Zuni Mountains/River, NM 119